NT Server 4 in the Enterprise

The Cram Sheet

This Cram Sheet contains the distilled, key facts about NT Server 4 in the Enterprise. Review this information last thing before you enter the test room, paying special attention to those areas where you feel you need the most review. You can transfer any of these facts onto a blank sheet of paper before beginning the exam.

DISK MANAGEMENT

1. Review Disk Administrator menus and options.
2. Only primary partitions can be active: Select Mark Active from the Partition menu in Disk Administrator.
3. When working with Disk Administrator, one important command is the Commit Changes Now option in the Partition menu. This command instructs Windows NT to make your requested changes to the affected storage devices.
4. To be active, a partition must be a primary partition. A primary partition can be made active by using the Mark Active command on the Disk Administrator's Partition menu.

FAULT TOLERANCE

5. Windows NT Backup features and functions:
   - Do not back up temp files.
   - Back up the Registry on PDC and all BDCs.
   - Windows NT Backup cannot back up the Registry across the network.
6. About disk striping with parity:

   All partitions in set are equal sizes (or close). Partitions must be on different physical disks. Can be implemented with NTFS or FAT; 3 drives minimum; 32 drives maximum. Slower than striping without parity, faster than mirroring.
7. If one drive in a set fails, missing data can be rebuilt from remaining devices and parity info.
8. If you lose a member of a volume set or stripe set without parity, everything is lost!
9. Neither boot nor system partitions can reside on a volume set or disk stripe set, even with parity.
10. RAID levels, speeds, and details:
    - RAID 0; not fault tolerant; fastest; includes disk striping without parity, volume sets
    - RAID 1; fault tolerant; slowest; includes disk mirroring (slower), disk duplexing (faster)
    - RAID 5; fault tolerant; intermediate; includes disk striping with parity
11. When dealing with Directory Replication, all data placed in a subdirectory of an export server's export directory will be duplicated to all import servers' import directories. Files stored in the export directory itself will not be replicated. By default, the directory for the export server is:\Winnt\System32\Repl\Export\. Also, Directory Replication will not work if any application is accessing or viewing the export or import directories. The Application log of the Event Viewer displays error messages from the replication service.
12. Boot floppies should contain the following files: BOOT.INI, NTLDR, NTDETECT.COM, NTBOOTTDD.SYS (only if you are using a SCSI controller with BIOS translation disabled or

missing), and BOOTSECT.DOS (only if you need to boot into MS-DOS or another operating system present on your system).

USERS AND GROUPS

13. Access tokens are created when a user logs on and are not changed until the user logs off and logs on again. Therefore, any changes to a user or a group to which that user belongs will not affect those currently logged on. The changes will only affect him the next time he logs on.

14. There are two types of groups: local and global. Local groups are only available on local machines; global groups are available throughout a domain. Local groups can contain users and global groups; global groups contain users only. You can't place groups within global groups, nor can you place local groups within other local groups.

15. For group permissions, the least restrictive right takes precedence, except No Access always wins! When combining NTFS and share permissions, the least restrictive wins for each kind (except No Access); when combining resulting NTFS and share permissions, the most restrictive wins.

16. You can perform the following in User Manager For Domains:

- Produce, change, duplicate, and remove user and group accounts
- Enable account policies (assign defaults for passwords, account lockouts, disconnect status, and so on)
- Create user rights and audit policies
- Establish trust relationships

BOOT FACTS

17. Boot and system partitions can reside on the primary disk in a disk mirror or duplex set. If the primary fails, you must hand-edit the BOOT.INI file on the boot drive to point to the ARC name for the remaining mirror or duplex drive instead.

18. Boot files—NTLDR, BOOT.INI, NTDETECT. COM, and so forth—reside on the system partition; Windows NT OS files—including NTOSKRNL.EXE—reside on the boot partition. BACKWARDS!

19. Most important Windows NT boot process components:

- **BOOT.INI** Boot initialization file: Describes Windows NT boot defaults, plus OS location, settings, menu selections. It resides in root directory of system partition. (Required for Windows NT boot floppy.)
- **BOOTSECT.DOS** MS-DOS boot sector file: Used if NTLDR permits boot to some other Microsoft OS, like DOS or Windows 95. It resides in root directory of system partition. (Not required.)
- **NTDETECT.COM** PC hardware detection: Reads device and config info before Windows NT boots. It resides in root directory of system partition. (Required for Windows NT boot floppy.)
- **NTLDR** OS loader program: Loads Windows NT or other designated OS. Relinquishes control once loading completes. Resides in root directory of system partition. (Required for Windows NT boot floppy.)
- **NTOSKRNL.EXE** Executable file for Windows NT OS: Includes all basic capabilities and items necessary to establish runtime environment. Resides in \Winnt\System32 on boot partition.
- **OSLOADER.EXE** RISC OS loader: Provides services and info equal to NTDETECT. COM, BOOTSECT.DOS, and NTLDR on PCs. Resides in RISC boot PROM area.
- **NTBOOTDD.SYS** Used when system or boot SCSI drive has BIOS disabled. Replaces BIOS functions with software driver. Resides in root directory of system partition.

20. ARC name information:

- **scsi(*) or multi(*)** Most ARC names begin with multi(*); scsi(*) appears only when SCSI has BIOS disabled. Multi(*) applies to IDE, EIDE, ESDI, and SCSI (where BIOS enabled). (*) indicates address of hardware adapter. Numbers start at zero, with controller seated closest to slot 0 in PC.
- **disk(*)** Applies only when scsi(*) keyword appears. Then, value of (*) indicates SCSI bus ID, starting with zero, for drive where files reside. If multi(*) appears, disk(*) is always disk(0).
- **rdisk(*)** Applies only when multi(*) keyword appears, indicates SCSI logical unit number

MCSE NT Server 4 in the Enterprise

Third Edition

Ed Tittel
Kurt Hudson
James Michael Stewart

MCSE NT Server 4 in the Enterprise Exam Cram, Third Edition

Limits of Liability and Disclaimer of Warranty

The author and publisher of this book have used their best efforts in preparing the book and the programs contained in it. These efforts include the development, research, and testing of the theories and programs to determine their effectiveness. The author and publisher make no warranty of any kind, expressed or implied, with regard to these programs or the documentation contained in this book.

The author and publisher shall not be liable in the event of incidental or consequential damages in connection with, or arising out of, the furnishing, performance, or use of the programs, associated instructions, and/or claims of productivity gains.

Trademarks

Trademarked names appear throughout this book. Rather than list the names and entities that own the trademarks or insert a trademark symbol with each mention of the trademarked name, the publisher states that it is using the names for editorial purposes only and to the benefit of the trademark owner, with no intention of infringing upon that trademark.

The Coriolis Group, LLC
14455 N. Hayden Road, Suite 220
Scottsdale, Arizona 85260

480/483-0192
FAX 480/483-0193
http://www.coriolis.com

Library of Congress Cataloging-in-Publication Data
Tittel, Ed.
MCSE NT Server 4 in the enterprise exam cram/by Ed Tittel, Kurt Hudson, and James Michael Stewart. -- 3rd ed.
p. cm.
Includes index.
ISBN 1-57610-619-5
1. Electronic data processing personnel--Certification. 2. Microsoft software--Examinations--Study guides. 3. NT server 4. I. Hudson, Kurt. II. Stewart, James Michael. III. Title.
QA76.3.T5754 2000
005.4'4769--dc21 99-058380
CIP

Printed in the United States of America
10 9 8 7 6 5 4 3 2

President, CEO
Keith Weiskamp

Publisher
Steve Sayre

Acquisitions Editor
Shari Jo Hehr

Marketing Specialist
Cynthia Caldwell

Project Editor
Meredith Brittain

Technical Reviewer
Bob Flynn

Production Coordinator
Wendy Littley

Cover Design
Jesse Dunn

Layout Design
April Nielsen

14455 North Hayden Road • Suite 220 • Scottsdale, Arizona 85260

Coriolis: The Training And Certification Destination™

Thank you for purchasing one of our innovative certification study guides, just one of the many members of the Coriolis family of certification products.

Certification Insider Press™ has long believed that achieving your IT certification is more of a road trip than anything else. This is why most of our readers consider us their *Training And Certification Destination*. By providing a one-stop shop for the most innovative and unique training materials, our readers know we are the first place to look when it comes to achieving their certification. As one reader put it, "I plan on using your books for all of the exams I take."

To help you reach your goals, we've listened to others like you, and we've designed our entire product line around you and the way you like to study, learn, and master challenging subjects. Our approach is *The Smartest Way To Get Certified ™*.

In addition to our highly popular *Exam Cram* and *Exam Prep* guides, we have a number of new products. We recently launched *Exam Cram Audio Reviews*, which are audiotapes based on *Exam Cram* material. We've also developed *Practice Tests Exam Crams* and *Exam Cram Flash Cards*, which are designed to make your studying fun as well as productive.

Our commitment to being the *Training And Certification Destination* does not stop there. We just introduced *Exam Cram Insider*, a biweekly newsletter containing the latest in certification news, study tips, and announcements from Certification Insider Press. (To subscribe, send an email to **eci@coriolis.com** and type "subscribe insider" in the body of the email.) We also recently announced the launch of the Certified Crammer Society and the Coriolis Help Center—two new additions to the Certification Insider Press family.

We'd like to hear from you. Help us continue to provide the very best certification study materials possible. Write us or email us at **cipq@coriolis.com** and let us know how our books have helped you study, or tell us about new features that you'd like us to add. If you send us a story about how we've helped you, and we use it in one of our books, we'll send you an official Coriolis shirt for your efforts.

Good luck with your certification exam and your career. Thank you for allowing us to help you achieve your goals.

Keith Weiskamp

Keith Weiskamp
President and CEO

Look For These Other Books From The Coriolis Group:

MCSE Networking Essentials Exam Cram, Third Edition
Ed Tittel, Kurt Hudson, James Michael Stewart

MCSE NT Server 4 Exam Cram, Third Edition
Ed Tittel, Kurt Hudson, James Michael Stewart

MCSE NT Workstation 4 Exam Cram, Third Edition
Ed Tittel, Kurt Hudson, James Michael Stewart

About The Authors

Ed Tittel is a 20-year veteran in the computing business who owes his high-tech career to an ongoing affection for beautiful Austin, Texas. Ed covers numerous Windows subjects, with more than 30 Windows-related titles to his credit. He also teaches for NetWorld + Interop and The Internet Security Conference (TISC) on Windows security and performance tuning. Prior to starting a company in 1994, Ed worked at Novell for six years, where he started out as a field engineer and left as Director of Technical Marketing. Ed has contributed to more than 105 computer books, including many *Exam Preps* and *Exam Crams*, for which he is series editor. Ed has also written articles for *Certification Magazine*, *InfoWorld*, *Windows NT Magazine*, and *PC Magazine*.

In his spare time, Ed likes cooking homemade stock and the many good things that it makes possible. He also walks the company Lab, Blackie, at least five times a day. You can reach Ed via email at **etittel@lanw.com**.

Kurt Hudson, president of HudLogic, Inc., has earned MCSE, MCSE + Internet, MCT, and A+ Certified Technician ratings. He began his technical career with the U.S. Air Force, earning medals for systems efficiency, training excellence, and national security. He has worked for Unisys, where he helped launch two Windows 95 support operations for Microsoft and Compaq, and for Productivity Point International, where he trained hundreds of computer support engineers and system administrators. Today, he writes commercial technical publications, trains computer professionals, and troubleshoots networking problems. He has authored or co-authored several publications, which are listed at **www.hudlogic.com**. You can reach Kurt via email at **kurt@hudlogic.com**.

James Michael Stewart is a full-time writer focusing on Windows NT and Internet topics. Most recently, he has worked on several titles in the *Exam Cram* and *Exam Prep* series. Michael has been developing Windows NT 4 MCSE-level courseware and training materials for several years, including both print and online publications, as well as classroom presentation of NT training materials. He has been an MCSE since 1997, with a focus on Windows NT 4. You can reach Michael by email at **michael@lanw.com**, or through his Web page at **www.lanw.com/jmsbio.htm**.

Acknowledgments

Thanks to the team at Haights-Cross, particularly Kevin McAlily, and to the whole crew at Coriolis, particularly Keith Weiskamp, Shari Jo Hehr, and Paula Kmetz, for making *Exam Cram* build upon its successes. Once again, we are glad for the opportunity to refresh and replenish these titles, and to add more information and value for our readers.

Many thanks are due to the people who make these books happen. On the LANWrights side, I want to thank Dawn Rader, project manager, and Mary Burmeister, project editor, for superhuman efforts to meet an insane sequence of entirely necessary deadlines. I'd also like to thank James Michael Stewart for his herculean efforts to update the content on this book and to create a battery of scenario questions and online resources. And finally, oodles of thanks to Chelsea Valentine, who has helped us organize and manage our reading feedback and online updates to these books better than ever before.

On the Coriolis side, special thanks to all the people involved in this project, especially Meredith Brittain, who shepherded this third edition through the process, plus Wendy Littley, our production coordinator for this title. We'd also like to thank Cynthia Caldwell, Neil Gudovitz, and Gary Hull, among many others, for their efforts to make these books show up in as many places around the world as possible.

Finally, thanks to my friends and family for their support. To Robert Wiggins: Thanks for showing me that no matter how bad things get, they could always be worse! To Quge and the gang: Hang in there, relief is nigh! To Mom and Dad: Thanks for listening to me kvetch when nobody else would. And finally, to Blackie: Thanks for making me get up and walk around occasionally. It's helped me to stay (relatively) sane.

—*Ed Tittel*

I would like to thank the following people for their professional contributions to this book: Julie A. Hudson, Doug Dexter, and Lori Marcinkiewicz.

—*Kurt Hudson*

Acknowledgments

Thanks to my boss and co-author, Ed Tittel, for including me in this book series. Thanks to Dawn Rader; without you, this book would never have been complete. A warm howdy to Mary Burmeister (our other work slave). To my parents, Dave and Sue: Thanks for always being there and making it clear how much you care. To Dave and Laura: Buy the $20,000 home theater and I'll camp on your couch and cook your meals! To Mark: The cult of the Pocketgods will come back to haunt you—it is already noted in your permanent record. To HERbert: Please stop digging your claws into the back of my neck while I'm asleep. And finally, as always, to Elvis—I've been looking high and low for a glittery white jumpsuit of my own, but it seems that Wal-Mart is always sold out!

—James Michael Stewart

Contents At A Glance

Table Of Contents

Introduction

Welcome to *MCSE NT Server 4 in the Enterprise Exam Cram, Third Edition*! This book aims to help you get ready to take—and pass—the Microsoft certification Exam 70-068, titled "Implementing and Supporting Microsoft Windows NT Server 4.0 in the Enterprise." This introduction explains Microsoft's certification programs in general and talks about how the *Exam Cram* series can help you prepare for Microsoft's certification exams.

Exam Cram books help you understand and appreciate the subjects and materials you need to pass Microsoft certification exams. *Exam Cram* books are aimed strictly at test preparation and review. They do not teach you everything you need to know about a topic (such as the ins and outs of installing Windows NT Server 4.0, or all the nitty-gritty details involved in using Performance Monitor). Instead, we (the authors) present and dissect the questions and problems we've found that you're likely to encounter on a test. We've worked from Microsoft's own training materials, preparation guides, and tests, and from a battery of third-party test preparation tools and practice exams. Our aim is to bring together as much information as possible about Microsoft certification exams.

Nevertheless, to completely prepare yourself for any Microsoft test, we recommend that you begin by taking the Self-Assessment included in this book immediately following this introduction. This tool will help you evaluate your knowledge base against the requirements for an MCSE under both ideal and real circumstances.

Based on what you learn from that exercise, you might decide to begin your studies with some classroom training or some background reading. On the other hand, you might decide to pick up and read one of the many study guides available from Microsoft or third-party vendors on certain topics, including The Coriolis Group's *Exam Prep* series (for which a title on Windows NT Server 4.0 in the Enterprise is also available).

We also strongly recommend that you install, configure, and fool around with the software that you'll be tested on, because nothing beats hands-on experience and familiarity when it comes to understanding the questions you're likely to encounter on a certification test. Book learning is essential, but hands-on experience is the best teacher of all!

The Microsoft Certified Professional (MCP) Program

The MCP Program currently includes the following separate tracks, each of which boasts its own special acronym (as a would-be certificant, you need to have a high tolerance for alphabet soup of all kinds):

- **MCP (Microsoft Certified Professional)** This is the least prestigious of all the certification tracks from Microsoft. Passing any of the major Microsoft exams (except the Networking Essentials exam) qualifies an individual for the MCP credential. Individuals can demonstrate proficiency with additional Microsoft products by passing additional certification exams.
- **MCP+SB (Microsoft Certified Professional + Site Building)** This certification program is designed for individuals who are planning, building, managing, and maintaining Web sites. Individuals with the MCP+SB credential will have demonstrated the ability to develop Web sites that include multimedia and searchable content and Web sites that connect to and communicate with a back-end database. It requires one MCP exam, plus two of these three exams: "Designing and Implementing Commerce Solutions with Microsoft Site Server, 3.0, Commerce Edition," "Designing and Implementing Web Sites with Microsoft FrontPage 98," and "Designing and Implementing Web Solutions with Microsoft Visual InterDev 6.0."
- **MCSE (Microsoft Certified Systems Engineer)** Anyone who has a current MCSE is warranted to possess a high level of expertise with Windows NT (version 3.51 or 4.0) and other Microsoft operating systems and products. This credential is designed to prepare individuals to plan, implement, maintain, and support information systems and networks built around Microsoft Windows NT and its BackOffice family of products.

  To obtain an MCSE, an individual must pass four core operating system exams, plus two elective exams. The operating system exams require individuals to prove their competence with desktop and server operating systems and networking components.

  You must pass at least two Windows NT-related exams to obtain an MCSE: "Implementing and Supporting Microsoft Windows NT Server" (version 3.51 or 4.0) and "Implementing and Supporting Microsoft Windows NT Server in the Enterprise" (version 3.51 or 4.0). These tests demonstrate an individual's knowledge of Windows NT in smaller, simpler networks and in larger, more complex, and heterogeneous networks, respectively.

Note: The Windows NT 3.51 version will be retired by Microsoft on June 30, 2000.

You must pass two additional tests as well. These tests are related to networking and desktop operating systems. At present, the networking requirement can be satisfied only by passing the Networking Essentials test. The desktop operating system test can be satisfied by passing a Windows 95, Windows NT Workstation (the version must match the NT version for the core tests), or Windows 98 test.

The two remaining exams are electives. An elective exam may fall in any number of subject or product areas, primarily BackOffice components. However, it is also possible to test out on electives by taking advanced networking topics like "Internetworking with Microsoft TCP/IP on Microsoft Windows NT 4.0" (but the version of Windows NT must match the version for the core requirements). If you are on your way to becoming an MCSE and have already taken some exams, visit **www.microsoft.com/mcp/certstep/mcse.htm** for information about how to complete your MCSE certification.

In September 1999, Microsoft announced its Windows 2000 track for MCSE, and also announced retirement of Windows NT 4.0 MCSE core exams on 12/31/2000. Individuals who wish to remain certified MCSEs after 12/31/2001 must "upgrade" their certifications on or before 12/31/2001. The details are too complex to discuss here; to obtain those details, visit **www.microsoft.com/mcp/certstep/mcse.htm**.

Whatever mix of tests is completed toward MCSE certification, individuals must pass six tests to meet the MCSE requirements. It's not uncommon for the entire process to take a year or so, and many individuals find that they must take a test more than once to pass. Our primary goal with the *Exam Cram* series is to make it possible, given proper study and preparation, to pass any related Microsoft certification test on the first try. Table 1 shows the required and elective exams for the MCSE certification.

- **MCSD (Microsoft Certified Solution Developer)** The MCSD credential reflects the skills required to create multitier, distributed, and COM-based solutions, in addition to desktop and Internet applications, using new technologies. To obtain an MCSD, an individual must demonstrate the ability to analyze and interpret user requirements; select and integrate products, platforms, tools, and technologies; design and implement code and customize applications; and perform necessary software tests and quality assurance operations.

Table 1 MCSE Requirements*

Core

All 3 of these are required	
Exam 70-067	Implementing and Supporting Microsoft Windows NT Server 4.0
Exam 70-068	Implementing and Supporting Microsoft Windows NT Server 4.0 in the Enterprise
Exam 70-058	Networking Essentials
Choose 1 from this group	
Exam 70-064	Implementing and Supporting Microsoft Windows 95
Exam 70-073	Implementing and Supporting Microsoft Windows NT Workstation 4.0
Exam 70-098	Implementing and Supporting Microsoft Windows 98

Elective

Choose 2 from this group	
Exam 70-088	Implementing and Supporting Microsoft Proxy Server 2.0
Exam 70-079	Implementing and Supporting Microsoft Internet Explorer 4.0 by Using the Internet Explorer Administration Kit
Exam 70-087	Implementing and Supporting Microsoft Internet Information Server 4.0
Exam 70-081	Implementing and Supporting Microsoft Exchange Server 5.5
Exam 70-059	Internetworking with Microsoft TCP/IP on Microsoft Windows NT 4.0
Exam 70-028	Administering Microsoft SQL Server 7.0
Exam 70-029	Designing and Implementing Databases on Microsoft SQL Server 7.0
Exam 70-056	Implementing and Supporting Web Sites Using Microsoft Site Server 3.0
Exam 70-086	Implementing and Supporting Microsoft Systems Management Server 2.0
Exam 70-085	Implementing and Supporting Microsoft SNA Server 4.0

* This is not a complete listing—you can still be tested on some earlier versions of these products. However, we have included mainly the most recent versions so that you may test on these versions and thus be certified longer. We have not included any tests that are scheduled to be retired.

To become an MCSD, you must pass a total of four exams: three core exams and one elective exam. Each candidate must choose one of these three desktop application exams—"70-016: Designing and Implementing Desktop Applications with Microsoft Visual C++ 6.0," "70-156: Designing and Implementing Desktop Applications with Visual FoxPro 6.0," or "70-176: Designing and Implementing Desktop Applications with Visual Basic 6.0"—*plus* one of these three distributed application exams—"70-015: Designing and Implementing Distributed Applications with Microsoft Visual C++ 6.0," "70-155: Designing and Implementing Distributed Applications with Visual FoxPro 6.0," or "70-175: Designing and Implementing Distributed Applications with Visual Basic 6.0." The third core exam is "70-100: Analyzing Requirements and Defining Solution Architectures."

Elective exams cover specific Microsoft applications and languages, including Visual Basic, C++, the Microsoft Foundation Classes, Access, SQL Server, Excel, and more.

- **MCDBA (Microsoft Certified Database Administrator)** The MCDBA credential reflects the skills required to implement and administer Microsoft SQL Server databases. To obtain an MCDBA, an individual must demonstrate the ability to derive physical database designs, develop logical data models, create physical databases, create data services by using Transact-SQL, manage and maintain databases, configure and manage security, monitor and optimize databases, and install and configure Microsoft SQL Server.

  To become an MCDBA, you must pass a total of five exams: four core exams and one elective exam. The required core exams are "Administering Microsoft SQL Server 7.0," "Designing and Implementing Databases with Microsoft SQL Server 7.0," "Implementing and Supporting Microsoft Windows NT Server 4.0," and "Implementing and Supporting Microsoft Windows NT Server 4.0 in the Enterprise."

  The elective exams that you can choose from cover specific uses of SQL Server and include "Designing and Implementing Distributed Applications with Visual Basic 6.0," "Designing and Implementing Distributed Applications with Visual C++ 6.0," "Designing and Implementing Data Warehouses with Microsoft SQL Server 7.0 and Microsoft Decision Support Services 1.0," and two exams that relate to NT: "Internetworking with Microsoft TCP/IP on Microsoft Windows NT 4.0" and "Implementing and Supporting Microsoft Internet Information Server 4.0."

  Note that the exam covered by this book is a required core exam for the MCDBA certification. Table 2 shows the requirements for the MCDBA certification.

- **MCT (Microsoft Certified Trainer)** Microsoft Certified Trainers are deemed able to deliver elements of the official Microsoft curriculum, based on technical knowledge and instructional ability. Thus, it is necessary for an individual seeking MCT credentials (which are granted on a course-by-course basis) to pass the related certification exam for a course and complete the official Microsoft training in the subject area, and to demonstrate an ability to teach. MCT candidates must also possess a current MCSE.

  The teaching skill criterion may be satisfied by proving that one has already attained training certification from Novell, Banyan, Lotus, the Santa Cruz Operation, or Cisco, or by taking a Microsoft-sanctioned

Table 2 MCDBA Requirements

Core

All 4 of these are required	
Exam 70-028	Administering Microsoft SQL Server 7.0
Exam 70-029	Designing and Implementing Databases with Microsoft SQL Server 7.0
Exam 70-067	Implementing and Supporting Microsoft Windows NT Server 4.0
Exam 70-068	Implementing and Supporting Microsoft Windows NT Server 4.0 in the Enterprise

Elective

Choose 1 from this group	
Exam 70-015	Designing and Implementing Distributed Applications with Microsoft Visual C++ 6.0
Exam 70-019	Designing and Implementing Data Warehouses with Microsoft SQL Server 7.0 and Microsoft Decision Support Services 1.0
Exam 70-059	Internetworking with Microsoft TCP/IP on Microsoft Windows NT 4.0
Exam 70-087	Implementing and Supporting Microsoft Internet Information Server 4.0
Exam 70-175	Designing and Implementing Distributed Applications with Microsoft Visual Basic 6.0

workshop on instruction. Microsoft makes it clear that MCTs are important cogs in the Microsoft training channels. Instructors must be MCTs before Microsoft will allow them to teach in any of its official training channels, including Microsoft's affiliated Certified Technical Education Centers (CTECs) and its online training partner network.

Microsoft has announced that the MCP+I and MCSE+I credentials will not be continued when the MCSE exams for Windows 2000 are in full swing because the skill set for the Internet portion of the program has been included in the new MCSE program. Therefore, details on these tracks are not provided here; go to **www.microsoft.com/train_cert/** if you need more information.

Once a Microsoft product becomes obsolete, MCPs typically have 12 to 18 months in which to recertify on current versions. (If individuals do not recertify within the specified time period, their certifications become invalid.) Because technology keeps changing and new products continually supplant old ones, this should come as no surprise. This explains why Microsoft has announced that MCSEs have 12 months past the scheduled retirement date for the Windows NT 4.0 exams to recertify on Windows 2000 topics. (Note that this means taking at least two exams, if not more.)

The best place to keep tabs on the MCP Program and related certifications is on the Web. The URL for the MCP program is **www.microsoft.com/mcp/certstep/mcps.htm**. But Microsoft's Web site changes often, so if this URL doesn't work, try using the Search tool on Microsoft's site with either "MCP" or the quoted phrase "Microsoft Certified Professional Program" as a search string. You will then find the latest, most accurate information about Microsoft's certification programs.

Taking A Certification Exam

Alas, testing is not free. Each computer-based MCP exam costs $100, and if you don't pass, you may retest for an additional $100 for each additional try. In the United States and Canada, tests are administered by Sylvan Prometric and by Virtual University Enterprises (VUE). Here's how you can contact them:

- **Sylvan Prometric** Sign up for a test through the company's Web site at **www.slspro.com**. Or, register by phone at 800-755-3926 (within the United States or Canada) or at 410-843-8000 (outside the United States and Canada).
- **Virtual University Enterprises** Sign up for a test or get the phone numbers for local testing centers through the Web page at **www.microsoft.com/train_cert/mcp/vue_info.htm**.

To sign up for a test, you need a valid credit card, or contact either company for mailing instructions to send them a check (in the U.S.). Only when payment is verified, or a check has cleared, can you actually register for a test.

To schedule an exam, call the number or visit either of the Web pages at least one day in advance. To cancel or reschedule an exam, you must call before 7 P.M. pacific standard time the day before the scheduled test time (or you may be charged, even if you don't appear to take the test). When you want to schedule a test, have the following information ready:

- Your name, organization, and mailing address.
- Your Microsoft Test ID. (Inside the United States, this means your Social Security number; citizens of other nations should call ahead to find out what type of identification number is required to register for a test.)
- The name and number of the exam you wish to take.
- A method of payment. (As we've already mentioned, a credit card is the most convenient method, but alternate means can be arranged in advance, if necessary.)

Once you sign up for a test, you'll be informed as to when and where the test is scheduled. Try to arrive at least 15 minutes early. You must supply two forms of identification—one of which must be a photo ID—to be admitted into the testing room.

All exams are completely closed-book. In fact, you will not be permitted to take anything with you into the testing area, but you will be furnished with a blank sheet of paper and a pen or, in some cases, an erasable plastic sheet and an erasable pen. We suggest that you immediately write down on that sheet of paper all the information you've memorized for the test. In *Exam Cram* books, this information appears on a tear-out sheet inside the front cover of each book. You will have some time to compose yourself, to record this information, and take a sample orientation exam before you begin the real thing. We suggest you take the orientation test before taking your first exam, but because they're all more or less identical in layout, behavior, and controls, you probably won't need to do this more than once.

When you complete a Microsoft certification exam, the software will tell you whether you've passed or failed. Results are broken into several topic areas. Even if you fail, we suggest you ask for—and keep—the detailed report that the test administrator should print for you. You can use this report to help you prepare for another go-round, if needed.

If you need to retake an exam, you'll have to schedule a new test with Sylvan Prometric or VUE and pay another $100.

The first time you fail a test, you can retake the test the next day. However, if you fail a second time, you must wait 14 days before retaking that test. The 14-day waiting period remains in effect for all retakes after the first failure.

Tracking MCP Status

As soon as you pass any Microsoft exam other than Networking Essentials, you'll attain Microsoft Certified Professional (MCP) status. Microsoft also generates transcripts that indicate which exams you have passed and your corresponding test scores. You can order a transcript by email at any time by sending an email to **mcp@msprograms.com**. You can also obtain a copy of your transcript by downloading the latest version of the MCT Guide from the Web site and consulting the section titled "Key Contacts" for a list of telephone numbers and related contacts.

Once you pass the necessary set of exams (one for MCP or six for MCSE), you'll be certified. Official certification normally takes anywhere from four to six weeks, so don't expect to get your credentials overnight. When the package for a qualified certification arrives, it includes a Welcome Kit that contains a number of elements:

- An MCP or MCSE certificate, suitable for framing, along with a Professional Program Membership card.

- A license to use the MCP logo, which permits you to use that logo in advertisements, promotions, and documents, and on letterhead, business cards, and so on. Along with the license comes an MCP logo sheet, which includes camera-ready artwork. (Note: Before using any artwork, individuals must sign and return a licensing agreement that indicates they'll abide by its terms and conditions.)
- A subscription to *Microsoft Certified Professional Magazine*, which provides ongoing data about testing and certification activities, requirements, and changes to the program.
- A one-year subscription to the Microsoft Beta Evaluation program. This subscription will get you all beta products from Microsoft for the next year. (This does not include developer products. You must join the MSDN program or become an MCSD to qualify for developer beta products.)

Many people believe that the benefits of MCP certification go well beyond the perks that Microsoft provides to newly anointed members of this elite group. We're starting to see more job listings that request or require applicants to have an MCP, MCSE, and so on, and many individuals who complete the program can qualify for increases in pay and/or responsibility. As an official recognition of hard work and broad knowledge, one of the MCP credentials is a badge of honor in many IT organizations.

How To Prepare For An Exam

Preparing for any Windows NT Server-related test (including Windows NT Server 4.0 in the Enterprise) requires that you obtain and study materials designed to provide comprehensive information about the product and its capabilities that will appear on the specific exam for which you are preparing. The following list of materials will help you study and prepare:

- The Windows NT Server 4.0 product CD includes comprehensive online documentation and related materials; it should be a primary resource when you are preparing for the test.
- Microsoft offers a Resource Kit for Windows NT Server 4.0. It comes in two forms: a book/CD combination product from Microsoft Press, or an electronic version that's included with the TechNet CDs. It's a "must-have" resource when preparing for this exam. We provide more details on the ResKit, as it's affectionately known, later in this book.
- The exam prep materials, practice tests, and self-assessment exams on the Microsoft Training And Certification Download page (**www.microsoft.com/train_cert/download/downld.htm**). Find the materials, download them, and use them!

In addition, you'll probably find any or all of the following materials useful in your quest for Windows NT Server 4.0 expertise:

- **Microsoft Training Kits** Microsoft Press includes coverage of Windows NT Server 4.0 in several training kits. For more information, visit: **http://mspress.microsoft.com/prod/books/1046.htm** and **http://mspress.microsoft.com/prod/books/1047.htm**. These training kits contain information that you will find useful in preparing for the test.
- **Microsoft TechNet CD** This monthly CD-based publication delivers numerous electronic titles on Windows NT Server on the Technical Information (TechNet) CD. Its offerings include product facts, technical notes, tools and utilities, and information on how to access the Seminars Online training materials for Windows NT Server. A subscription to TechNet costs $299 per year, but it is well worth it. Visit **www.microsoft.com/technet/** and check out the information under the "TechNet Subscription" menu entry for more details.
- **Study Guides** Several publishers—including Certification Insider Press—offer Windows NT Server 4.0 in the Enterprise titles. The Certification Insider Press series includes:
  - **The *Exam Cram* series** These books give you information about the material you need to know to pass the tests.
  - **The *Exam Prep* series** These books provide a greater level of detail than the *Exam Cram* books and are designed to teach you everything you need to know from an exam perspective. *MCSE Windows NT Server 4 in the Enterprise Exam Prep* is the perfect learning companion to prepare you for Exam 70-068, "Implementing and Supporting Microsoft Windows NT Server 4.0 in the Enterprise." Look for this book in your favorite bookstores.

  Together, the two series make a perfect pair.
- **Multimedia** These Coriolis Group materials are designed to support learners of all types—whether you learn best by listening, reading, or doing:
  - ***Practice Tests Exam Cram* series** Provides the most valuable test preparation material: practice exams. Each exam is followed by a complete set of answers, as well as explanations of why the right answers are right and the wrong answers are wrong. Each book comes with a CD that contains one or more interactive practice exams.
  - ***Exam Cram Flash Card* series** Offers practice questions on handy cards you can use anywhere. The question and its possible answers appear on the front of the card, and the answer, explanation, and a

valuable reference appear on the back of the card. The set also includes a CD with an electronic practice exam to give you the feel of the actual test—and more practice!

➤ *Exam Cram Audio Review* **series** Offers a concise review of key topics covered on the exam, as well as practice questions.

- **Classroom Training** CTECs, online partners, and unlicensed training companies (like Wave Technologies, American Research Group, Learning Tree, Data-Tech, and others) all offer classroom training on Windows NT Server 4.0 in the Enterprise. These companies aim to help you prepare to pass the Windows NT Server 4.0 in the Enterprise test. Although such training runs upwards of $350 per day in class, most of the individuals lucky enough to partake (including your humble authors, who've even taught such courses) find them to be quite worthwhile.
- **Other Publications** You'll find direct references to other publications and resources in this book, but there's no shortage of materials available about Windows NT Server 4.0 in the Enterprise. To help you sift through some of the publications out there, we end each chapter with a "Need To Know More?" section that provides pointers to more complete and exhaustive resources covering the chapter's information. This should give you an idea of where we think you should look for further discussion.

By far, this set of required and recommended materials represents a nonpareil collection of sources and resources for Windows NT Server 4.0 in the Enterprise and related topics. We anticipate that you'll find that this book belongs in this company. In the section that follows, we explain how this book works, and we give you some good reasons why this book counts as a member of the required and recommended materials list.

About This Book

Each topical *Exam Cram* chapter follows a regular structure, along with graphical cues about important or useful information. Here's the structure of a typical chapter:

- **Opening Hotlists** Each chapter begins with a list of the terms, tools, and techniques that you must learn and understand before you can be fully conversant with that chapter's subject matter. We follow the hotlists with one or two introductory paragraphs to set the stage for the rest of the chapter.
- **Topical Coverage** After the opening hotlists, each chapter covers a series of topics related to the chapter's subject title. Throughout this section, we highlight topics or concepts likely to appear on a test using a special Exam Alert layout, like this:

This is what an Exam Alert looks like. Normally, an Exam Alert stresses concepts, terms, software, or activities that are likely to relate to one or more certification test questions. For that reason, we think any information found offset in Exam Alert format is worthy of unusual attentiveness on your part. Indeed, most of the information that appears on The Cram Sheet appears as Exam Alerts within the text.

Pay close attention to material flagged as an Exam Alert; although all the information in this book pertains to what you need to know to pass the exam, we flag certain items that are really important. You'll find what appears in the meat of each chapter to be worth knowing, too, when preparing for the test. Because this book's material is very condensed, we recommend that you use this book along with other resources to achieve the maximum benefit.

In addition to the Exam Alerts, we have provided tips that will help you build a better foundation for Windows NT Server knowledge. Although the information may not be on the exam, it is certainly related and will help you become a better test-taker.

This is how tips are formatted. Keep your eyes open for these, and you'll become a Windows NT Server in the Enterprise guru in no time!

- **Practice Questions** Although we talk about test questions and topics throughout each chapter, this section presents a series of mock test questions and explanations of both correct and incorrect answers. We also try to point out especially tricky questions by using a special icon, like this:

Ordinarily, this icon flags the presence of a particularly devious inquiry, if not an outright trick question. Trick questions are calculated to be answered incorrectly if not read more than once, and carefully, at that. Although they're not ubiquitous, such questions make regular appearances on the Microsoft exams. That's why we say exam questions are as much about reading comprehension as they are about knowing your material inside out and backwards.

- **Details And Resources** Every chapter ends with a section titled "Need To Know More?". This section provides direct pointers to Microsoft and third-party resources offering more details on the chapter's subject. In addition, this section tries to rank or at least rate the quality and thoroughness of the topic's coverage by each resource. If you find a resource you like in this collection, use it, but don't feel compelled to use all the resources. On the other hand, we recommend only resources we use on a regular basis, so none of our recommendations will be a waste of your time or money (but purchasing them all at once probably represents an expense that many network administrators and would-be MCPs and MCSEs might find hard to justify).
- Your authors have also prepared adaptive exams for Windows NT Server in the Enterprise that are available online. To take these practice exams, which should help you prepare even better for the real thing, visit **www.coriolis.com/cip/core4rev/**, follow the instructions from there, and pick the Windows NT Server 4 in the Enterprise book.

The bulk of the book follows this chapter structure slavishly, but there are a few other elements that we'd like to point out. Chapters 16 and 18 each include a sample test that provides a good review of the material presented throughout the book to ensure you're ready for the exam. Chapter 17 is an answer key to the sample test that appears in Chapter 16; likewise, Chapter 19 is the answer key to the sample test in Chapter 18. We suggest you take the first sample test when you think you're ready, and take the second one after studying some more if you don't get at least 70 percent of the questions correct.

Following the sample tests is the Scenarios section, which gives you extra practice answering real-world questions of the type frequently found on Microsoft exams. And after that, the Online Resources section points you to some useful certification Web sites.

Additionally, you'll find the Glossary, which explains terms, and an index that you can use to track down terms as they appear in the text.

Finally, the tear-out Cram Sheet attached next to the inside front cover of this *Exam Cram* book represents a condensed and compiled collection of facts and tips that we think you should memorize before taking the test. Because you can dump this information out of your head onto a piece of paper before taking the exam, you can master this information by brute force—you need to remember it only long enough to write it down when you walk into the test room. You might even want to look at it in the car or in the lobby of the testing center just before you walk in to take the test.

How To Use This Book

If you're prepping for a first-time test, we've structured the topics in this book to build on one another. Therefore, some topics in later chapters make more sense after you've read earlier chapters. That's why we suggest you read this book from front to back for your initial test preparation. If you need to brush up on a topic or you have to bone up for a second try, use the index or table of contents to go straight to the topics and questions that you need to study. Beyond helping you prepare for the test, we think you'll find this book useful as a tightly focused reference to some of the most important aspects of Windows NT Server 4.0 in the Enterprise.

Given all the book's elements and its specialized focus, we've tried to create a tool that will help you prepare for—and pass—Microsoft Exam 70-068, "Implementing and Supporting Microsoft Windows NT Server 4.0 in the Enterprise." Please share your feedback on the book with us, especially if you have ideas about how we can improve it for future test-takers. We'll consider everything you say carefully, and we'll respond to all suggestions.

Send your questions or comments to us at **cipq@coriolis.com**. Our series editor, Ed Tittel, coordinates our efforts and ensures that all questions get answered. Please remember to include the title of the book in your message; otherwise, we'll be forced to guess which book you're writing about. And we don't like to guess—we want to *know*! Also, be sure to check out the Web pages at **www.certificationinsider.com**, where you'll find information updates, commentary, and certification information.

Thanks, and enjoy the book!

Self-Assessment

Based on recent statistics from Microsoft, as many as 400,000 individuals are at some stage of the certification process but haven't yet received an MCP or other Microsoft certification. We also know that three or four times that number may be considering whether or not to obtain a Microsoft certification of some kind. That's a huge audience!

The reason we included a Self-Assessment in this *Exam Cram* book is to help you evaluate your readiness to tackle MCSE certification. It should also help you understand what you need to know to master the topic of this book—namely, Exam 70-068, "Implementing and Supporting Microsoft Windows NT Server 4.0 in the Enterprise." But before you tackle this Self-Assessment, let's talk about concerns you may face when pursuing an MCSE, and what an ideal MCSE candidate might look like.

MCSEs In The Real World

In the next section, we describe an ideal MCSE candidate, knowing full well that only a few real candidates will meet this ideal. In fact, our description of that ideal candidate might seem downright scary. But take heart: Although the requirements to obtain an MCSE may seem formidable, they are by no means impossible to meet. However, be keenly aware that it does take time, involves some expense, and requires real effort to get through the process.

More than 200,000 MCSEs are already certified, so it's obviously an attainable goal. You can get all the real-world motivation you need from knowing that many others have gone before, so you will be able to follow in their footsteps. If you're willing to tackle the process seriously and do what it takes to obtain the necessary experience and knowledge, you can take—and pass—all the certification tests involved in obtaining an MCSE. In fact, we've designed these *Exam Crams*, and the companion *Exam Preps*, to make it as easy on you as possible to prepare for these exams. But prepare you must!

The same, of course, is true for other Microsoft certifications, including:

- MCSD, which is aimed at software developers and requires one specific exam, two more exams on client and distributed topics, plus a fourth elective exam drawn from a different, but limited, pool of options.

- Other Microsoft certifications, whose requirements range from one test (MCP) to several tests (MCP+SB, MCDBA).

The Ideal MCSE Candidate

Just to give you some idea of what an ideal MCSE candidate is like, here are some relevant statistics about the background and experience such an individual might have. Don't worry if you don't meet these qualifications, or don't come that close—this is a far from ideal world, and where you fall short is simply where you'll have more work to do.

- Academic or professional training in network theory, concepts, and operations. This includes everything from networking media and transmission techniques through network operating systems, services, and applications.
- Three-plus years of professional networking experience, including experience with Ethernet, token ring, modems, and other networking media. This must include installation, configuration, upgrade, and troubleshooting experience.
- Two-plus years in a networked environment that includes hands-on experience with Windows NT Server, Windows NT Workstation, and Windows 95 or Windows 98. A solid understanding of each system's architecture, installation, configuration, maintenance, and troubleshooting is also essential.
- A thorough understanding of key networking protocols, addressing, and name resolution, including TCP/IP, IPX/SPX, and NetBEUI.
- A thorough understanding of NetBIOS naming, browsing, and file and print services.
- Familiarity with key Windows NT-based TCP/IP-based services, including HTTP (Web servers), DHCP, WINS, DNS, plus familiarity with one or more of the following: Internet Information Server (IIS), Index Server, and Proxy Server.
- Working knowledge of NetWare 3.x and 4.x, including IPX/SPX frame formats, NetWare file, print, and directory services, and both Novell and Microsoft client software. Working knowledge of Microsoft's Client Service For NetWare (CSNW), Gateway Service For NetWare (GSNW), the NetWare Migration Tool (NWCONV), and the NetWare Client For Windows (NT, 95, and 98) is essential.

Fundamentally, this boils down to a bachelor's degree in computer science, plus three years' experience working in a position involving network design, installation, configuration, and maintenance. We believe that well under half of all certification candidates meet these requirements, and that, in fact, most aspiring candidates meet less than half of these requirements—at least, when they begin the certification process. But because all 200,000 people who already have been certified have survived this ordeal, you can survive it too—especially if you heed what our Self-Assessment can tell you about what you already know and what you need to learn.

Put Yourself To The Test

The following series of questions and observations is designed to help you figure out how much work you must do to pursue Microsoft certification and what kinds of resources you may consult on your quest. Be absolutely honest in your answers, or you'll end up wasting money on exams you're not yet ready to take. There are no right or wrong answers, only steps along the path to certification. Only you can decide where you really belong in the broad spectrum of aspiring candidates.

Two things should be clear from the outset, however:

- Even a modest background in computer science will be helpful.
- Hands-on experience with Microsoft products and technologies is an essential ingredient to certification success.

Educational Background

1. Have you ever taken any computer-related classes? [Yes or No]

   If Yes, proceed to question 2; if No, proceed to question 4.

2. Have you taken any classes on computer operating systems? [Yes or No]

   If Yes, you will probably be able to handle Microsoft's architecture and system component discussions. If you're rusty, brush up on basic operating system concepts, especially virtual memory, multitasking regimes, user mode versus kernel mode operation, and general computer security topics.

   If No, consider some basic reading in this area. We strongly recommend a good general operating systems book, such as *Operating System Concepts*, by Abraham Silberschatz and Peter Baer Galvin (Addison-Wesley, 1997, ISBN 0-201-59113-8). If this title doesn't appeal to you, check out reviews for other, similar titles at your favorite online bookstore.

3. Have you taken any networking concepts or technologies classes? [Yes or No]

   If Yes, you will probably be able to handle Microsoft's networking terminology, concepts, and technologies (brace yourself for frequent departures from normal usage). If you're rusty, brush up on basic networking concepts and terminology, especially networking media, transmission types, the OSI Reference model, and networking technologies such as Ethernet, token ring, FDDI, and WAN links.

   If No, you might want to read one or two books in this topic area. The two best books that we know of are *Computer Networks, 3rd Edition*, by Andrew S. Tanenbaum (Prentice-Hall, 1996, ISBN 0-13-349945-6) and *Computer Networks and Internets*, by Douglas E. Comer (Prentice-Hall, 1997, ISBN 0-13-239070-1).

   Skip to the next section, "Hands-On Experience."

4. Have you done any reading on operating systems or networks? [Yes or No]

   If Yes, review the requirements stated in the first paragraphs after questions 2 and 3. If you meet those requirements, move on to the next section. If No, consult the recommended reading for both topics. A strong background will help you prepare for the Microsoft exams better than just about anything else.

Hands-On Experience

The most important key to success on all of the Microsoft tests is hands-on experience, especially with Windows NT Server and Workstation, plus the many add-on services and BackOffice components around which so many of the Microsoft certification exams revolve. If we leave you with only one realization after taking this Self-Assessment, it should be that there's no substitute for time spent installing, configuring, and using the various Microsoft products upon which you'll be tested repeatedly and in depth.

5. Have you installed, configured, and worked with:

   - Windows NT Server? [Yes or No]

     If Yes, make sure you understand basic concepts as covered in Exam 70-067 and advanced concepts as covered in Exam 70-068. You should also study the TCP/IP interfaces, utilities, and services for Exam 70-059, plus Internet Information Server capabilities for Exam 70-087.

You can download objectives, practice exams, and other data about Microsoft exams from the Training and Certification page at **www.microsoft.com/train_cert/**. Use the "Find an Exam" link to obtain specific exam info.

If you haven't worked with Windows NT Server, TCP/IP, and IIS (or whatever product you choose for your final elective), you must obtain one or two machines and a copy of Windows NT Server. Then learn the operating system, and do the same for TCP/IP and whatever other software components on which you'll also be tested.

In fact, we recommend that you obtain two computers, each with a network interface, and set up a two-node network on which to practice. With decent Windows NT-capable computers selling for about $500 to $600 apiece these days, this shouldn't be too much of a financial hardship. You may have to scrounge to come up with the necessary software, but if you scour the Microsoft Web site you can usually find low-cost options to obtain evaluation copies of most of the software that you'll need.

- Windows NT Workstation? [Yes or No]

If Yes, make sure you understand the concepts covered in Exam 70-073.

If No, you will want to obtain a copy of Windows NT Workstation and learn how to install, configure, and maintain it. You can use *MCSE NT Workstation 4 Exam Cram* to guide your activities and studies, or work straight from Microsoft's test objectives if you prefer.

For any and all of these Microsoft exams, the Resource Kits for the topics involved are a good study resource. You can purchase softcover Resource Kits from Microsoft Press (search for them at **http://mspress.microsoft.com/**), but they also appear on the TechNet CDs (**www.microsoft.com/technet**). We believe that Resource Kits are among the best preparation tools available, along with the *Exam Crams* and *Exam Preps*, that you can use to get ready for Microsoft exams.

You have the option of taking the Window 95 (70-064) exam or the Windows 98 (70-098) exam, instead of Exam 70-073, to fulfill your desktop operating system requirement for the MCSE. Although we don't recommend these others (because studying for Workstation helps you prepare for the Server exams), we do recommend that you obtain Resource Kits and other tools to help you prepare for those exams if you decide to take one or both of them for your own reasons.

6. For any specific Microsoft product that is not itself an operating system (for example, FrontPage 98, SQL Server, and so on), have you installed, configured, used, and upgraded this software? [Yes or No]

   If the answer is Yes, skip to the next section. If it's No, you must get some experience. Read on for suggestions on how to do this.

   Experience is a must with any Microsoft product exam, be it something as simple as FrontPage 98 or as challenging as Exchange Server 5.5 or SQL Server 7.0. For trial copies of other software, search Microsoft's Web site using the name of the product as your search term. Also, search for bundles like "BackOffice" or "Small Business Server."

If you have the funds, or your employer will pay your way, consider taking a class at a Certified Training and Education Center (CTEC) or at an Authorized Academic Training Partner (AATP). In addition to classroom exposure to the topic of your choice, you get a copy of the software that is the focus of your course, along with a trial version of whatever operating system it needs (usually, NT Server), with the training materials for that class.

   Before you even think about taking any Microsoft exam, make sure you've spent enough time with the related software to understand how it may be installed and configured, how to maintain such an installation, and how to troubleshoot that software when things go wrong. This will help you in the exam, and in real life!

Testing Your Exam-Readiness

Whether you attend a formal class on a specific topic to get ready for an exam or use written materials to study on your own, some preparation for the Microsoft certification exams is essential. At $100 a try, pass or fail, you want to do everything you can to pass on your first try. That's where studying comes in.

We have included two practice exams in this book, so if you don't score that well on the first test, you can study more and then tackle the second test. We also have built adaptive exams that you can take online through the Coriolis Web site at **www.coriolis.com/cip/core4rev/** . If you still don't hit a score of at least 70 percent after these tests, you'll want to investigate the other practice test resources we mention in this section.

For any given subject, consider taking a class if you've tackled self-study materials, taken the test, and failed anyway. The opportunity to interact with an instructor and fellow students can make all the difference in the world, if you can afford that privilege. For information about Microsoft classes, visit the Training and Certification page at **www.microsoft.com/train_cert/** (use the "Find a Course" button).

If you can't afford to take a class, visit the Training and Certification page anyway, because it also includes pointers to free practice exams. And even if you can't afford to spend much at all, you should still invest in some low-cost practice exams from commercial vendors, because they can help you assess your readiness to pass a test better than any other tool. All of the following Web sites offer practice exams online for less than $100 apiece (some for significantly less than that):

- Beachfront Quizzer at **www.bfq.com/**
- Hardcore MCSE at **www.hardcoremcse.com/**
- LANWrights at **www.lanw.com/books/examcram/order.htm**
- MeasureUp at **www.measureup.com/**

7. Have you taken a practice exam on your chosen test subject? [Yes or No]

   If Yes, and you scored 70 percent or better, you're probably ready to tackle the real thing. If your score isn't above that threshold, keep at it until you break that barrier.

   If No, obtain all the free and low-budget practice tests you can find (see the list above) and get to work. Keep at it until you can break the passing threshold comfortably.

When it comes to assessing your test readiness, there is no better way than to take a good-quality practice exam and pass with a score of 70 percent or better. When we're preparing ourselves, we shoot for 80-plus percent, just to leave room for the "weirdness factor" that sometimes shows up on Microsoft exams.

Assessing Readiness For Exam 70-068

In addition to the general exam-readiness information in the previous section, there are several things you can do to prepare for "Implementing and Supporting Microsoft Windows NT 4.0 in the Enterprise." As you're getting ready for

Exam 70-068, visit the MCSE mailing list. Sign up at **www.sunbelt-software.com** (look for the "Subscribe to..." button). This is a great place to ask questions and get good answers, or simply to watch the questions that others ask (along with the answers, of course).

You should also cruise the Web looking for "braindumps" (recollections of test topics and experiences recorded by others) to help you anticipate topics you're likely to encounter on the test. The MCSE mailing list is a good place to ask where the good braindumps are, or you can check Shawn Gamble's list at **www.commandcentral.com** (he's also got some peachy—and free—practice tests on this subject) or Herb Martin's Braindump Heaven at **http://209.207.167.177/**.

You can't be sure that a braindump's author can provide correct answers. Thus, use the questions to guide your studies, but don't rely on the answers in a braindump to lead you to the truth. Double-check everything you find in any braindump.

Microsoft exam mavens also recommend checking the Microsoft Knowledge Base (available on its own CD as part of the TechNet collection, or on the Microsoft Web site at **http://support.microsoft.com/support/**) for "meaningful technical support issues" that relate to Windows NT Server. Although we're not sure exactly what the quoted phrase means, we have also noticed some overlap between technical support questions on particular products and troubleshooting questions on the exams for those products.

As you review the material for Exam 70-068, you'll realize that hands-on experience with Windows NT Server 4.0 is not only invaluable, it's absolutely essential. You must be familiar with installing this operating system, configuring protocols, working with users, groups, and trust relationships, and so forth. In short, the more time you spend with the product, the better you'll do when you take the test!

Onward, Through The Fog!

Once you've assessed your readiness, undertaken the right background studies, obtained the hands-on experience that will help you understand the products and technologies at work, and reviewed the many sources of information to help you prepare for a test, you'll be ready to take a round of practice tests. When your scores come back positive enough to get you through the exam, you're ready to go after the real thing. If you follow our assessment regime, you'll not only know what you need to study, but when you're ready to make a test date at Sylvan or VUE. Good luck!

1

Microsoft Certification Exams

Terms you'll need to understand:

- ✓ Radio button
- ✓ Checkbox
- ✓ Exhibit
- ✓ Multiple-choice question formats
- ✓ Careful reading
- ✓ Process of elimination
- ✓ Fixed-length tests
- ✓ Adaptive tests
- ✓ Short-form tests
- ✓ Combination tests
- ✓ Simulations

Techniques you'll need to master:

- ✓ Assessing your exam-readiness
- ✓ Preparing to take a certification exam
- ✓ Practicing (to make perfect)
- ✓ Making the best use of the testing software
- ✓ Budgeting your time
- ✓ Guessing (as a last resort)

Exam taking is not something that most people anticipate eagerly, no matter how well prepared they may be. In most cases, familiarity helps offset test anxiety. In plain English, this means you probably won't be as nervous when you take your fourth or fifth Microsoft certification exam as you'll be when you take your first one.

Whether it's your first exam or your tenth, understanding the details of exam taking (how much time to spend on questions, the environment you'll be in, and so on) and the exam software will help you concentrate on the material rather than on the setting. Likewise, mastering a few basic exam-taking skills should help you recognize—and perhaps even outfox—some of the tricks and snares you're bound to find in some exam questions.

This chapter, besides explaining the exam environment and software, describes some proven exam-taking strategies that you should be able to use to your advantage.

Assessing Exam-Readiness

Before you take any more Microsoft exams, we strongly recommend that you read through and take the Self-Assessment included with this book (it appears just before this chapter, in fact). This will help you compare your knowledge base to the requirements for obtaining an MCSE, and it will also help you identify parts of your background or experience that may be in need of improvement, enhancement, or further learning. If you get the right set of basics under your belt, obtaining Microsoft certification will be that much easier.

Once you've gone through the Self-Assessment, you can remedy those topical areas where your background or experience may not measure up to an ideal certification candidate. But you can also tackle subject matter for individual tests at the same time, so you can continue making progress while you're catching up in some areas.

Once you've worked through an *Exam Cram*, have read the supplementary materials, and have taken the practice tests, you'll have a pretty clear idea of when you should be ready to take the real exam. Although we strongly recommend that you keep practicing until your scores top the 70 percent mark, 75 percent would be a good goal to give yourself some margin for error in a real exam situation (where stress will play more of a role than when you practice). Once you hit that point, you should be ready to go. But if you get through both practice exams in this book and the sample adaptive online exam (discussed in the Self-Assessment, the Introduction, and later in this chapter) without attaining that score, you should keep taking practice tests and studying the materials until you get there. You'll find more information about other practice test vendors in the Self-Assessment, along with even more pointers on how to study and prepare. But now, on to the exam itself!

The Exam Situation

When you arrive at the testing center where you scheduled your exam, you'll need to sign in with an exam coordinator. He or she will ask you to show two forms of identification, one of which must be a photo ID. After you've signed in and your time slot arrives, you'll be asked to deposit any books, bags, or other items you brought with you. Then, you'll be escorted into a closed room. Typically, the room will be furnished with anywhere from one to half a dozen computers, and each workstation will be separated from the others by dividers designed to keep you from seeing what's happening on someone else's computer.

You'll be furnished with a pen or pencil and a blank sheet of paper, or, in some cases, an erasable plastic sheet and an erasable pen. You're allowed to write down anything you want on both sides of this sheet. Before the exam, you should memorize as much of the material that appears on The Cram Sheet (in the front of this book) as you can, so you can write that information on the blank sheet as soon as you are seated in front of the computer. You can refer to your rendition of The Cram Sheet anytime you like during the test, but you'll have to surrender the sheet when you leave the room.

Most test rooms feature a wall with a large picture window. This permits the exam coordinator to monitor the room, to prevent exam-takers from talking to one another, and to observe anything out of the ordinary that might go on. The exam coordinator will have preloaded the appropriate

Microsoft certification exam—for this book, that's Exam 70-068—and you'll be permitted to start as soon as you're seated in front of the computer.

All Microsoft certification exams allow a certain maximum amount of time in which to complete your work (this time is indicated on the exam by an on-screen counter/clock, so you can check the time remaining whenever you like). All Microsoft certification exams are computer generated and most use a multiple-choice format. Although this may sound quite simple, the questions are constructed not only to check your mastery of basic facts and figures about Windows NT Server 4.0, but they also require you to evaluate one or more sets of circumstances or requirements. Often, you'll be asked to give more than one answer to a question. Likewise, you might be asked to select the best or most effective solution to a problem from a range of choices, all of which technically are correct. Taking the exam is quite an adventure, and it involves real thinking. This book shows you what to expect and how to deal with the potential problems, puzzles, and predicaments.

In the next section, you'll learn more about how Microsoft test questions look and how they must be answered.

Exam Layout And Design

Some exam questions require you to select a single answer, whereas others ask you to select one or more correct answers. The following multiple-choice question requires you to select a single correct answer. Following the question is a brief summary of each potential answer and why it is either right or wrong.

Question 1

Which Performance Monitor view should you use to create a baseline?

❍ a. Chart

❍ b. Alert

❍ c. Log

❍ d. Report

The correct answer to this question is c. Creating a baseline means watching network and server performance statistics over time; the only Performance Monitor view that records information over time is the Log view, so it's essential to log data at regular intervals to create a baseline. Answers a, b, and d are incorrect because they all track data in realtime, do not record samples over time, and do not work to create a baseline.

This sample question format corresponds closely to the Microsoft certification exam format—the only difference on the exam is that questions are not followed by answer keys. To select an answer, you would position the cursor over the radio button next to the answer. Then, click the mouse button to select the answer.

Let's examine a question where one or more answers are possible. This type of question provides checkboxes rather than radio buttons for marking all appropriate selections.

Question 2

Which of the following techniques represents a valid way to back up all or part of the Windows NT Registry? [Check all correct answers]

- ❑ a. Creating an ERD using the **RDISK /s** command.
- ❑ b. Using Windows NT Backup on the machine where the target Registry resides.
- ❑ c. Copying the contents of the \Winnt\System32\Config directory.
- ❑ d. Using the Disk Administrator utility.
- ❑ e. Using REGEDT32.

The correct answers are a, b, c, d, and e. All of these methods can capture either a partial or a complete copy of a Windows NT Registry. Creating an ERD with the **RDISK /s** command captures the keys that ERD needs to repair boot- and device-related information; therefore, answer a is correct. Using Windows NT Backup locally permits you to select an option to capture the Registry in its entirety; therefore, answer b is correct. If you copy the contents of the aforementioned directory, you will get a snapshot of the Registry as of the most recent reboot or execution of **RDISK /s** (if anything's changed in the Registry since your last login, you might want to reboot before backing up for that reason). This makes answer c correct. The Disk Administrator utility can also make a partial backup of the Registry (to capture boot and partition information). Therefore, answer d is also correct. Finally, REGEDT32 can capture most of the Registry by default (and all of it if you use the AT command to launch this application with System-level privileges). This makes answer e correct as well..

For this particular question, five answers are required. As far as the authors can tell (and Microsoft won't comment), such questions are scored as wrong unless all the required selections are chosen. In other words, a partially correct answer does not result in partial credit when the test is scored. For Question 2, you have to check the boxes next to items a, b, c, d, and e to obtain credit for a correct answer.

Although these two basic types of questions can appear in many forms, they constitute the foundation on which all the Microsoft certification exam questions rest. More complex questions include exhibits, which are usually screenshots of some aspect of the Windows NT Server interface or related utilities.

For some of these questions, you'll be asked to make a selection by clicking on a checkbox or radio button on the screenshot itself. For others, you'll be expected to use the information displayed therein to guide your answer to the question. Familiarity with the underlying utility is your key to choosing the correct answer(s).

Other questions involving exhibits use charts or network diagrams to help document a workplace scenario that you'll be asked to troubleshoot or configure. Careful attention to such exhibits is the key to success. Be prepared to toggle frequently between the exhibit and the question as you work.

Microsoft's Testing Formats

Currently, Microsoft uses four different testing formats:

- Fixed-length
- Adaptive

- Short-form
- Combination

Some Microsoft exams employ more advanced testing capabilities than might immediately meet the eye. Although the questions that appear are still multiple choice, the logic that drives them is more complex than older Microsoft tests, which use a fixed sequence of questions, called a *fixed-length test*. Other exams employ a sophisticated user interface, which Microsoft calls a *simulation*, to test your knowledge of the software and systems under consideration in a more or less "live" environment that behaves just like the original.

For some exams, Microsoft has turned to a well-known technique, called *adaptive testing*, to establish a test-taker's level of knowledge and product competence. Adaptive exams look the same as fixed-length exams, but they discover the level of difficulty at which an individual test-taker can correctly answer questions. At the same time, Microsoft is in the process of converting some of its fixed-length exams into adaptive exams as well. Test-takers with differing levels of knowledge or ability therefore see different sets of questions; individuals with high levels of knowledge or ability are presented with a smaller set of more difficult questions, whereas individuals with lower levels of knowledge are presented with a larger set of easier questions. Two individuals may answer the same percentage of questions correctly, but the test-taker with a higher knowledge or ability level will score higher because his or her questions are worth more.

Also, the lower-level test-taker will probably answer more questions than his or her more-knowledgeable colleague. This explains why adaptive tests use ranges of values to define the number of questions and the amount of time it takes to complete the test.

Adaptive tests work by evaluating the test-taker's most recent answer. A correct answer leads to a more difficult question (and the test software's estimate of the test-taker's knowledge and ability level is raised). An incorrect answer leads to a less difficult question (and the test software's estimate of the test-taker's knowledge and ability level is lowered). This process continues until the test targets the test-taker's true ability level. The exam ends when the test-taker's level of accuracy meets a statistically acceptable value (in other words, when his or her performance demonstrates an acceptable level of knowledge and ability) or when the maximum number of items has been presented (in which case, the test-taker is almost certain to fail).

Microsoft has also introduced a short-form test for its most popular tests (as of this writing, all of the Core Four exams, plus TCP/IP, can appear in this format). This test delivers 30 questions to its takers, giving them exactly 60 minutes to complete the exam. This type of exam is similar to a fixed-length test, in that it allows readers to jump ahead or return to earlier questions, and to cycle through the questions until the test is done. Microsoft does not use adaptive logic in this test, but claims that statistical analysis of the question pool is such that the 30 questions delivered during a short-form exam conclusively measure a test-taker's knowledge of the subject matter in much the same way as an adaptive test. You can think of the short-form test as a kind of "greatest hits exam" (that is, the most important questions are covered) version of an adaptive exam on the same topic.

A fourth kind of test you might encounter is what we've dubbed the combination exam. Several test-takers have reported that some of the Microsoft exams, including Windows NT Server (70-067), Windows NT Server in the Enterprise (70-068), and Windows NT Workstation (70-073), can appear as combination exams. Such exams begin with a set of 15 to 25 adaptive questions, followed by 10 fixed-length questions. In fact, many test-takers have reported that although some combination tests claim that they will present both adaptive and fixed-length portions, when the test-taker finishes the adaptive portion (usually in exactly 15 questions), the test ends there. Because such users have all attained passing scores, it may be that a high enough passing score on the adaptive portion of a combination test obviates the fixed-length portion, but we're not completely sure about this, and Microsoft won't comment. Most combination exams allow a maximum of 60 minutes for the testing period.

Microsoft tests can come in any one of these forms. Whatever you encounter, you must take the test in whichever form it appears; you can't choose one form over another. Currently, the Windows NT Server in the Enterprise exam may be adaptive (especially if you're taking it in a language other than English), in which case you'll have 90 minutes to answer between 15 and 30 questions (on average), or combination, in which case you'll get a maximum of 60 minutes. If anything, it pays more to prepare thoroughly for an adaptive or combination exam than for a fixed-length or a short-form exam: The penalties for answering incorrectly are built into the test itself on an adaptive exam or the first part of a combination exam, whereas the layout remains the same for a fixed-length or short-form test, no matter how many questions you answer incorrectly.

The biggest difference between an adaptive test and a fixed-length or short-form test is that on a fixed-length or short-form test, you can revisit questions after you've read them over one or more times. On an adaptive test, you must answer the question when it's presented and will have no opportunities to revisit that question thereafter.

Strategies For Different Testing Formats

Before you choose a test-taking strategy, you must know if your test is fixed-length, short-form, adaptive, or combination. When you begin your exam, the software will tell you the that test is adaptive, if in fact the version you're taking is an adaptive test. If your introductory materials fail to mention this, you're probably taking a fixed-length test. If the total number of questions involved is exactly 30, you're taking a short-form test. Combination tests announce themselves by indicating that they will start with a set of adaptive questions, followed by fixed-length questions, but don't actually call themselves "combination tests" or "combination exams"—we've adopted this term purely for descriptive purposes.

You'll be able to tell for sure if you are taking an adaptive, fixed-length, short-form, or combination test by the first question. If it includes a checkbox that lets you mark the question for later review, you're taking a fixed-length or short-form test. If the total number of questions is 30, it's a short-form test; if more than 30, it's a fixed-length test. Adaptive test questions (and the first set of questions on a combination test) can be visited (and answered) only once, and they include no such checkbox.

The Fixed-Length And Short-Form Exam Strategy

A well-known principle when taking fixed-length or short-form exams is to first read over the entire exam from start to finish while answering only those questions you feel absolutely sure of. On subsequent passes, you can dive into more complex questions more deeply, knowing how many such questions you have left.

Fortunately, the Microsoft exam software for fixed-length and short-form tests makes the multiple-visit approach easy to implement. At the top-left corner of each question is a checkbox that permits you to mark that question for a later visit.

> *Note: Marking questions makes review easier, but you can return to any question by clicking the Forward or Back button repeatedly.*

As you read each question, if you answer only those you're sure of and mark for review those that you're not sure of, you can keep working through a decreasing list of questions as you answer the trickier ones in order.

There's at least one potential benefit to reading the exam over completely before answering the trickier questions: Sometimes, information supplied in later questions sheds more light on earlier questions. At other times, information you read in later questions might jog your memory about Windows NT Server facts, figures, or behavior that also helps you answer earlier questions. Either way, you'll come out ahead if you defer those questions about which you're not absolutely sure.

Here are some question-handling strategies that apply to fixed-length and short-form tests. Use them if you have the chance:

- When returning to a question after your initial read-through, read every word again—otherwise, your mind can fall quickly into a rut. Sometimes, revisiting a question after turning your attention elsewhere lets you see something you missed, but the strong tendency is to see what you've seen before. Try to avoid that tendency at all costs.

- If you return to a question more than twice, try to articulate to yourself what you don't understand about the question, why answers don't appear to make sense, or what appears to be missing. If you chew on the subject awhile, your subconscious might provide the details you lack or you might notice a "trick" that points to the right answer.

As you work your way through the exam, another counter that Microsoft provides will come in handy—the number of questions completed and questions outstanding. For fixed-length and short-form tests, it's wise to budget your time by making sure that you've completed one-quarter of the questions one-quarter of the way through the exam period. For a short-form test, this means you must complete one-quarter of the questions one-quarter of the way through (the first 8 questions in the first 15 minutes) and three-quarters of the questions three-quarters of the way through (24 questions in 45 minutes).

If you're not finished when only five minutes remain, use that time to guess your way through any remaining questions. Remember, guessing is potentially more valuable than not answering, because blank answers are always wrong, but a guess may turn out to be right. If you don't have a clue about any of the remaining questions, pick answers at random, or choose all a's, b's, and so on. The important thing is to submit an exam for scoring that has an answer for every question.

At the very end of your exam period, you're better off guessing than leaving questions unanswered.

The Adaptive Exam Strategy

If there's one principle that applies to taking an adaptive test, it could be summed up as "Get it right the first time." You cannot elect to skip a question and move on to the next one when taking an adaptive test, because the testing software uses your answer to the current question to select whatever question it plans to present next. Nor can you return to a question once you've moved on, because the software gives you only one chance to answer the question. You can, however, take notes, because sometimes information supplied in earlier questions will shed more light on later questions.

Also, when you answer a question correctly, you are presented with a more difficult question next, to help the software gauge your level of skill and ability. When you answer a question incorrectly, you are presented with a less difficult question, and the software lowers its current estimate of your skill and ability. This continues until the program settles into a reasonably accurate estimate of what you know and can do, and takes you on average through somewhere between 15 and 30 questions as you complete the test.

The good news is that if you know your stuff, you'll probably finish most adaptive tests in 30 minutes or so. The bad news is that you must really, really know your stuff to do your best on an adaptive test. That's because some questions are so convoluted, complex, or hard to follow that you're bound to miss one or two, at a minimum, even if you do know your stuff. So the more you know, the better you'll do on an adaptive test, even accounting for the occasionally weird or unfathomable questions that appear on these exams.

Because you can't tell in advance if a test is fixed-length, short-form, adaptive, or combination, you will be best served by preparing for the exam as if it were adaptive. That way, you should be prepared to pass no matter what kind of test you take. But if you do take a fixed-length or short-form test, remember our tips from the preceding section. They should help you improve on what you could do on an adaptive test.

If you encounter a question on an adaptive test that you can't answer, you must guess an answer immediately. Because of how the software works, you may suffer for your guess on the next question if you guess right, because you'll get a more difficult question next!

The Combination Exam Strategy

When it comes to studying for a combination test, your best bet is to approach it as a slightly longer adaptive exam, and to study as if the exam were adaptive only. Because the adaptive approach doesn't rely on rereading questions, and suggests that you take notes while reading useful information on test questions, it's hard to go wrong with this strategy when taking any kind of Microsoft certification test.

Exam-Taking Basics

The most important advice about taking any exam is this: Read each question carefully. Some questions are deliberately ambiguous, some use double negatives, and others use terminology in incredibly precise ways. The authors have taken numerous exams—both practice and live—and in nearly every one have missed at least one question because they didn't read it closely or carefully enough.

Here are some suggestions on how to deal with the tendency to jump to an answer too quickly:

- Make sure you read every word in the question. If you find yourself jumping ahead impatiently, go back and start over.
- As you read, try to restate the question in your own terms. If you can do this, you should be able to pick the correct answer(s) much more easily.

Above all, try to deal with each question by thinking through what you know about Windows NT Server protocols, administrative utilities, installation, configuration, and management—the characteristics, behaviors, facts, and figures involved. By reviewing what you know (and what you've written down on your information sheet), you'll often recall or understand things sufficiently to determine the answer to the question.

Question-Handling Strategies

Based on exams we have taken, some interesting trends have become apparent. For those questions that take only a single answer, usually two or three of the answers will be obviously incorrect, and two of the answers will be plausible—of course, only one can be correct. Unless the answer leaps out at you (if it does, reread the question to look for a trick; sometimes those are the ones you're most likely to get wrong), begin the process of answering by eliminating those answers that are most obviously wrong.

Things to look for in obviously wrong answers include spurious menu choices or utility names, nonexistent software options, and terminology you've never seen. If you've done your homework for an exam, no valid information should be completely new to you. In that case, unfamiliar or bizarre terminology probably indicates a totally bogus answer.

Numerous questions assume that the default behavior of a particular utility is in effect. If you know the defaults and understand what they mean, this knowledge will help you cut through many Gordian knots.

Mastering The Inner Game

In the final analysis, knowledge breeds confidence, and confidence breeds success. If you study the materials in this book carefully and review all the practice questions at the end of each chapter, you should become aware of those areas where additional learning and study are required.

Next, follow up by reading some or all of the materials recommended in the "Need To Know More?" section at the end of each chapter. The idea is to become familiar enough with the concepts and situations you find in the sample questions that you can reason your way through similar situations on a real exam. If you know the material, you have every right to be confident that you can pass the exam.

After you've worked your way through the book, take the practice exams in Chapters 16 and 18. You'll also want to check out the Scenarios part of this book (immediately following the two sample tests), which includes our newly added scenario questions. The sample tests and scenarios provide a reality check and help you identify areas to study further. Make sure you follow up and review materials related to the questions you miss while practicing before scheduling a real exam. Only when you've covered that ground and feel comfortable with the whole scope of the practice questions should you take the online exam. Only if you score 75 percent or better should you proceed to the real thing (otherwise, obtain some additional practice tests and keep trying until you hit this magic number).

If you take a practice exam and don't score at least 75 percent correct, you'll want to practice further. Microsoft provides free Personal Exam Prep (PEP) exams and also offers self-assessment exams from the Microsoft Certified Professional Web site's download page (**www.microsoft.com/train_cert/download/downld.htm**). If you're more ambitious or better funded, you might want to purchase a practice exam from a third-party vendor. Check the Online Resources part of this book (right before the Glossary) for pointers.

As a special bonus to readers of this book, your authors have created adaptive practice exams on Windows NT Server 4 in the Enterprise. Coriolis offers these practice exams on its Web site at **www.coriolis.com/cip/core4rev**.

Armed with the information in this book and with the determination to augment your knowledge, you should be able to pass the certification exam. However, you need to work at it, or you'll spend the exam fee more than once before you finally pass. If you prepare seriously, you should do well. Good luck!

Additional Resources

A good source of information about Microsoft certification exams comes from Microsoft itself. Because its products and technologies—and the exams that go with them—change frequently, the best place to go for exam-related information is online.

If you haven't already visited the Microsoft Certified Professional site, do so right now. The MCP home page resides at **www.microsoft.com/mcp/certstep/mcps.htm**.

> *Note: This page might not be there by the time you read this, or may be replaced by something new and different, because things change regularly on the Microsoft site.*

Domain Models

Terms you'll need to understand:

- √ Domain model
- √ Primary Domain Controller (PDC)
- √ Backup Domain Controller (BDC)
- √ Trust relationships
- √ Single domain model
- √ Master domain model
- √ Multiple master domain model
- √ Complete trust domain model
- √ User authentication

Techniques you'll need to master:

- √ Understanding the domain model concept
- √ Familiarization with each domain model
- √ Knowing how to decide what domain model is best for what situation
- √ Using domains to distribute user authentication loads

Microsoft uses domain models to describe and define organizational schemes for networks. In theory, the domain model can scale up to handle any size network. However, in reality, the domain model fails to offer an adequate solution for networks with over 10,000 users. But setting reality aside, you need to have a clear understanding and functional grasp of the domain models as used by Microsoft. Other issues that you should be aware of include user accounts, groups, trust relationships, and domain controllers—these topics will be mentioned briefly in this chapter but will be discussed in more detail in Chapters 3 through 5.

The Domain Concept

The domain concept is a schema developed by Microsoft to organize and manage large groups of users and resources. Basically, a domain is a collection of computers that operate as a logical network for the purpose of sharing resources with a group of users. The size of a domain is usually limited by the geographic layout of the network as well as the level of hardware supporting the domain controllers.

The domain controllers—you know them as PDCs and BDCs—require significant computing power to support large, growing domains. As the number of users and resources increases, the number of relationships and security issues increases geometrically. Therefore, as the number of users grows, the demands on the domain controllers increase even faster. By monitoring simultaneous logon requests, quantity of network traffic, and performance of the domain browsers and controllers, network administrators will usually know when domain limitations have been reached. Additional domains should be created when the domain or network performance is substantially degraded.

As an afterthought, Microsoft generally recommends a maximum of 15,000 users per domain. On the other hand, there is documentation from Microsoft that states that up to 25,000 users have been supported in different configurations. Experts outside Microsoft agree that 10,000 or fewer accounts per domain is significantly more practical.

There are four separate models for domain administration according to Microsoft:

- Single domain model
- Master domain model
- Multiple master domain model
- Complete trust domain model

Each model is designed differently so each can accommodate organizations of various sizes and structures. It is necessary to consider the number of users, computers, and regions that are part of the network when you're choosing a domain model for your network. It is also wise to consider your growth potential when planning the organizational structure. The following sections briefly examine each domain model and the situations in which each should be used.

Single Domain Model

The single domain model should be considered for an organization with small networks in a single location, because it is easier to administer and maintain than the other domain models. Figure 2.1 illustrates the single domain model.

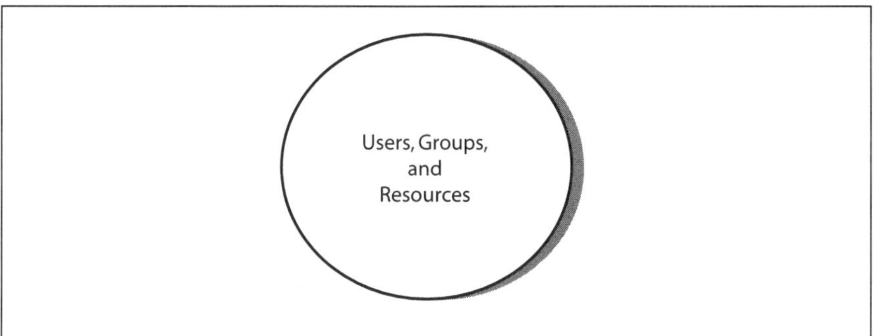

Figure 2.1 The single domain model.

The single domain model is characterized by its lack of trust relationships. No other domains are involved, so trust relationships are not necessary. The domain is regarded as a single administrative unit, in which most administrative tasks can be accomplished from a single server. There is one Primary Domain Controller (PDC) and one or more Backup Domain Controllers (BDCs) that control the security activity within the domain.

If a network experiences a significant amount of growth, the single domain model can scale into other domain models. In some cases, it may have to be split; therefore, if significant network growth is expected, you should consider using another domain model from the outset.

The advantages of the single domain model include:

- Works best for limited numbers of users and resources
- Centralized management of users and resources
- No trusts involved

The disadvantages of the single domain model include:

- Performance degradation as the domain grows
- Users and resources are not grouped by department
- Resource browsing is slowed as the number of servers increases

Master Domain Model

For growing companies or companies that already have a large user base, the master domain model is a good choice. This domain model is also useful for companies that wish to arrange the network into multiple resource domains and yet still have the benefits of centralized administration. Figure 2.2 displays the master domain model configuration.

Another name for the master domain is the accounts domain, because the user accounts for the entire domain structure reside within it. The resource domains (all other domains) trust the master domain. In other words, all users reside in the top, or master, domain, and all resources are located in the lower, or subordinate, domains. Using this model, resources

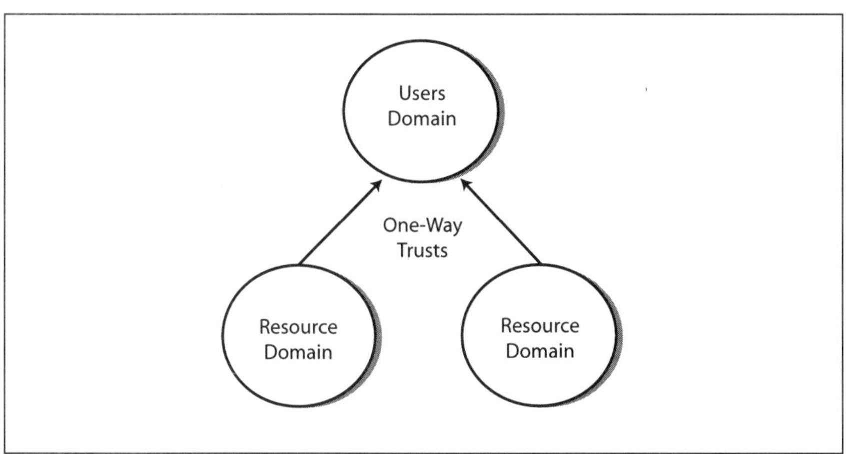

Figure 2.2 The master domain model.

can be grouped by department, geographic location, or any other organizational scheme.

The master domain model still offers centralized management, but it is split into two categories. User and group administration is performed in the top or master domain, and resource management is performed within the domain that hosts the particular resource. This gives each department control over its resources without compromising the overall security structure of the network.

The advantages of the master domain model include:

- A solid solution for moderately sized networks
- Departmental control of resources based on subordinate domains
- Centralized user account management
- Global groups are defined only once

The disadvantages of the master domain model include:

- Local groups must be defined within each resource domain
- Resource domains must rely on the master domain for current and secure group management
- Trust management is involved

Multiple Master Domain Model

The multiple master domain model can be used for companies that have a large and growing user base or that extend across multiple geographic regions. Figure 2.3 illustrates the multiple master domain model.

The master domain model and the multiple master domain model are closely related. In fact, the multiple master domain model is an extension of the master domain model. The difference is that the multiple master domain model has two or more master domains, all of which must trust each other using two-way trust relationships.

As with the master domain model, this model provides centralized administration of user accounts. The other master domains you may use for this model are typically used to hold user accounts by region. For example, if a company has branches located in Asia, South America, and Europe, it may want a master domain for each location.

Implementing this domain model requires administrators to maintain multiple trust relationships. As the number of master and resource domains increases, the number of trust relationships grows as well. The following formula helps you calculate the number of trust relationships required for a multiple master domain

```
T = M ( M - 1 ) + R M
```

where:

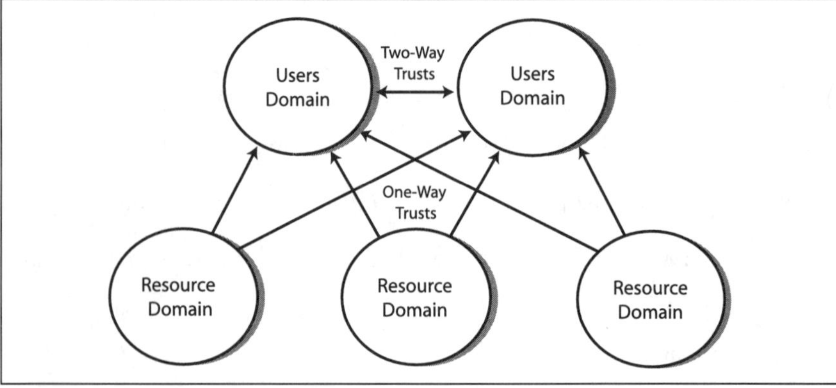

Figure 2.3 The multiple master domain model.

- **M** is the number of master domains in the organization.
- **R** is the number of resource domains in the organization.
- **T** is the number of trust relationships required.

The advantages of the multiple master domain model include:

- Good solution for very large and growing organizations
- Scaleable to accommodate any number of users
- Resources are locally and logically grouped
- Departmental-focused management of resources
- Any master domain can administer all user accounts

The disadvantages of the multiple master domain model include:

- Local and global groups must be defined for each master domain
- Large number of trust relationships to manage
- User accounts are spread across multiple domains

Complete Trust Domain Model

The complete trust domain model can be implemented by organizations of any size. It provides universal access to resources, while decentralizing administration of user accounts. The complete trust domain model should be considered for organizations that are spread over multiple geographic regions and do not require centralized administration. Figure 2.4 displays the complete trust domain model.

Using the complete trust domain model, users and resources can be grouped by department. Using two-way trusts, all users and all resources can be managed from any point in the network.

This model is also called a mesh. In a mesh network, every node is connected to every other node via a direct connection. As the number of nodes increases, the number of connections increases rapidly. Using Windows NT Server to establish a mesh, you must use two-way trust relationships.

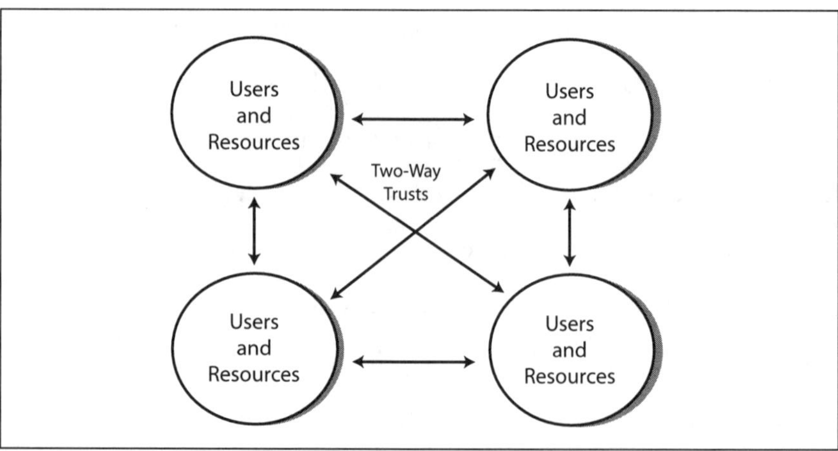

Figure 2.4 The complete trust domain model.

As you will learn in Chapter 3, a two-way trust is actually two one-way trusts created between the same two nodes. To compute the total number of trusts to create a mesh, use the following formula

```
T = N ( N - 1 )
```

where:

- N is the number of domains in the organization.
- T is the number of trust relationships required.

The advantages of the complete trust model include:

- Useful for organizations with no MIS department
- Scaleable for any number of users
- Each department has Full Control over its users and resources
- Users and resources are located within the same domain

The disadvantages of the complete trust model include:

- No centralized management
- Many trust relationships to manage
- All administrators must trust each other to properly manage users, groups, and resources

Practice Questions

Question 1

Which of the following statements are true about the multiple master domain model? [Check all correct answers]

- ❑ a. Two-way trust relationships are used.
- ❑ b. One-way trust relationships are used.
- ❑ c. There is only one user domain.
- ❑ d. User management is centralized.
- ❑ e. Resource management is centralized.

Answers a, b, and d are correct. Two-way trust relationships are used among all user domains in the multiple master domain model. Therefore, answer a is correct. One-way trust relationships are used between the resource and user domains in the multiple master domain model. Therefore, answer b is also correct. User management is centralized with the multiple master domain. Therefore, answer d is correct. There must be more than one user domain in any multiple master domain model. Therefore, answer c is incorrect. Resource management is not centralized in the multiple master domain model. Each domain must control its own resources. Therefore, answer e is incorrect.

Question 2

A small company with a few departments wants to deploy a domain model network. It requires the ability to access all servers and resources from each department and centralized management of user accounts. Which of the following domain models is best suited for this purpose?

- ❍ a. Single domain model
- ❍ b. Master domain model
- ❍ c. Multiple master domain model
- ❍ d. Complete trust domain model

Answer a is correct. The single domain model is the best solution for this situation. It offers centralized management, access to all resources, and supports small networks. The master domain model has separate domains for resources and users. This design is too much work for a small network. Therefore, answer b is incorrect. The multiple master domain model is too complicated for this size of a network. Therefore, answer c is incorrect. The complete trust domain model is also an unnecessarily complex design for this situation. Therefore, answer d is incorrect.

Question 3

A company has five branch offices scattered across the globe. They are located in New York, Moscow, Paris, Mexico City, and Hong Kong. Each office has about 750 users. Your corporate office is located in San Francisco. All of the branch offices are linked to your office via ISDN WAN links. It is your job to implement a domain model for this company.

Required results:

- All San Francisco users must be able to access resources in Hong Kong and Moscow.
- Users in New York, Paris, and Mexico City must be able to access resources in San Francisco.
- Security and logon validation traffic must be minimized over the WAN links.

Optional desired results:

- Centralized management of all user accounts.
- Each branch office is able to manage local resources.

Proposed solution:

- Use a complete trust model.
- Place all users in the San Francisco domain.
- All branch office domains to be used as resource domains.

Which results does the proposed solution produce?

❍ a. The required results and both of the optional results.

❍ b. The required results and only one of the optional results.

❍ c. The required results but none of the optional results.

❍ d. The required results are not all met.

Answer d is correct. The complete trust model can be used as a modified master domain model with good success. However, this solution does not reduce validation traffic over the WAN links. By placing all users in the San Francisco domain, each time a branch office user logs on, he or she will connect to the corporate domain. Thus, heavy loads on the WAN links will result from this security traffic. To make this solution work, a San Francisco domain BDC should be physically placed in each of the branch offices. Each branch user would access his or her branch PDC for authentication, thereby minimizing WAN usage for that purpose.

Question 4

A company has five branch offices scattered across the globe. They are located in New York, Moscow, Paris, Mexico City, and Hong Kong. Each office has about 750 users. Your headquarters is located in San Francisco. All of the branch offices are linked to headquarters via ISDN WAN links. It is your job to implement a domain model for this company.

Required results:

- All San Francisco users must be able to access resources in Hong Kong and Moscow.
- Users in New York, Paris, and Mexico City must be able to access resources in San Francisco.
- Security and logon validation traffic must be minimized over the WAN links.

Optional desired results:

- Centralized management of all user accounts.
- Each branch office is able to manage local resources.

Proposed solution:

- Use a single domain model.
- Place the PDC and all BDCs in San Francisco.

Which results does the proposed solution produce?

❍ a. The required results and both of the optional results.

❍ b. The required results and only one of the optional results.

❍ c. The required results but none of the optional results.

❍ d. The required results are not all met.

Answer d is correct. The single domain model can support a large number of users and offers centralized management of user accounts, but it does not reduce the WAN link overhead for user authentication. By placing a BDC in each of the branch offices, the logon traffic can be reduced.

Question 5

Your company is spread over multiple geographic locations within the same city. Users at each location need to access servers and resources at each of the other locations. Each office wants control over its locally hosted resources. You are solely responsible for maintaining the network at all of the locations and security is not an issue. What is the best domain model for this situation?

- ❍ a. Single domain model
- ❍ b. Master domain model
- ❍ c. Multiple master domain model
- ❍ d. Complete trust domain model

Answer d is correct. The complete trust model offers the ability for each office to manage resources, and you can administer the network from any server. The single domain model does not offer departmentalized management of resources. Therefore, answer a is incorrect. The single master domain model requires that one domain be reserved for users to better promote tight security and centralized control. These are not stipulations of the situation. Therefore, answer b is incorrect. The multiple master domain model is also not appropriate for this situation because it requires multiple user domains to support security. Therefore, answer c is incorrect.

Question 6

Your company has 40,000 users and numerous branch offices. You want central administration of users but decentralized control of resources. Security is important. Which domain model is best suited for this situation?

- ❍ a. Single domain model
- ❍ b. Master domain model
- ❍ c. Multiple master domain model
- ❍ d. Complete trust domain model

Answer c is correct. The multiple master domain model can support 40,000 with its multiple user domains, and each branch office can manage its own local resources. The single domain model cannot support 40,000 users. Therefore, answer a is incorrect. The master domain model cannot support 40,000 users in its single user domain. Therefore, answer b is incorrect. The complete trust domain model does not offer centralized management of user accounts and does not adequately support security. Therefore, answer d is incorrect.

Question 7

What are some advantages of using a master domain model instead of a single domain model? [Check all correct answers]

- ❑ a. Separation of user and resource management
- ❑ b. Uses trust relationships
- ❑ c. Departmentalized resource administration
- ❑ d. Support for a much larger number of users
- ❑ e. Single definition of local groups

Answers a and c are correct. Separation of user and resource management is an advantage of the master domain model. Therefore, answer a is correct. Departmentalized resource administration is a benefit of the master domain model. Therefore, answer c is also correct. The use of trust relationships is not an advantage but a liability. Therefore, answer b is incorrect. Both of these domain models are able to support roughly the same number of users (give or take a modest difference), because only one user domain is present in each. Because the difference in numbers of users supported between a single domain model and the master domain model is relatively modest, the master domain model does not offer support for a significantly larger number of users. Therefore, answer d is incorrect. Local groups must be defined for each of the resource domains in the master domain model. This is a disadvantage. Therefore, answer e is incorrect.

Question 8

A multiple master domain model consists of at least two user domains and one or more resource domains. What is true of the trust relationships of this domain model?

❍ a. All trust relationships are two-way.

❍ b. A two-way trust is used to connect each user domain to every other user domain; one-way trusts are created from each resource domain to connect it with each user domain.

❍ c. Only one-way trusts are used.

❍ d. All user domains are connected to resource domains by a one-way trust; all resource domains are connected to all other resource domains with two-way trusts.

Answer b is correct. The user or master domains are connected to each other with two-way trusts, and each of the resource domains is connected with each of the user domains with a one-way trust. Answer a is incorrect because it describes the trust pattern of the complete trust or mesh model. Answer c is incorrect becuse it does not describe any of the domain models. Answer d is incorrect because it does not describe any of the domain models.

Need To Know More?

Heywood, Drew: *Inside Windows NT Server, 2nd Edition*. New Riders, Indianapolis, IN, 1998. ISBN 1-56205-860-6. Chapters 4 and 5 discuss basic domain construction and how trust relationships are used.

Siyan, Karanjit S.: *Windows NT Server 4 Professional Reference, 2nd Edition*. New Riders, Indianapolis, IN, 1997. ISBN 1-56205-805-3. Chapters 5, 6, and 7 provide extensive coverage of the Windows NT domain models.

The Windows NT Server 4 manuals cover planning, configuration, and installation issues quite well. The *Concepts And Planning Manual* contains useful domain model issue discussions in Chapter 1.

The *Windows NT Server Resource Kit* contains lots of useful information about Windows NT's domain structure and domain models. The TechNetCD (or its online version through **www.microsoft.com**) can be searched using keywords like "domain model," "domains," and "centralized administration." In the *Networking Guide* volume, Chapter 2, "Network Security And Domain Planning," is an excellent resource for fully understanding and deploying Windows NT domains.

3

Trust Relationships

Terms you'll need to understand:

- √ Trust relationships
- √ Trusting domain
- √ Trusted domain

Techniques you'll need to master:

- √ Establishing and configuring trust relationships
- √ Breaking off a trust relationship
- √ Setting up trusts based on domain models
- √ Instituting permissions across trust relationships
- √ Knowing how to manage multiple trusts

As you learned in Chapter 2, Windows NT supports domains to enable the definition of distinct collections of machines, resources, users, and groups that can be administered and secured separately and independently. But because Windows NT permits networks to include multiple domains—and indeed requires multiple domains for larger networks—managing the relationship among individual domains is important whenever multiple domains coexist.

Terms And Conditions Of The Trust Relationship

As is so often the case with Windows NT, a special mindset is required to appreciate and understand the terminology used to describe the trust relationships that can exist between any two domains at a time. Figure 3.1 captures most of the terminology and important nuances, which are also explained in the following series of ground rules:

- When Domain A trusts Domain B, A is called the trusting domain, and B is called the trusted domain.

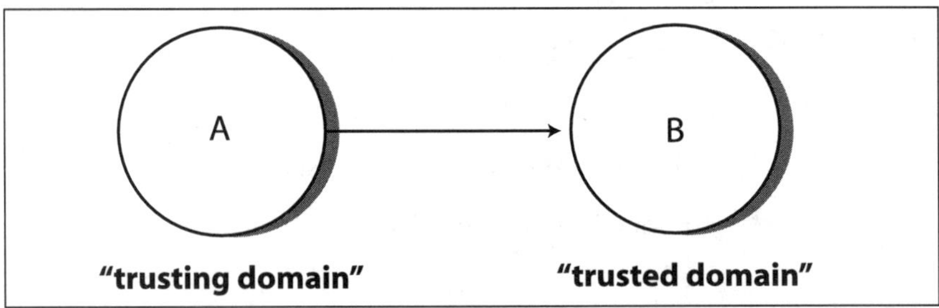

Figure 3.1 Domain A "trusts" Domain B, as indicated by the arrow that points from A to B.

- Although the relationship arrow points from Domain A to Domain B, it means that A may make resources available to B, not vice versa. It's essential to understand that this means only that users in B may be permitted to access resources in A. That's why it's so important to understand how trust relationships work, and how they behave, in Windows NT.
- All trust relationships are defined between pairs of domains. For each such relationship, there is only one trusting domain, and only one trusted domain.
- All trust relationships are one-way. If A trusts B, this says nothing about B's trust for A. For a two-way trust relationship to exist, it's necessary to create two separate one-way trusts, where A trusts B in one relationship, and B trusts A in the other. Even so, Microsoft uses a single two-headed arrow in its documentation and help files to indicate that two such relationships exist between a pair of domains.
- There is no transitivity in trust relationships, either. If A trusts B and B trusts C, this does not imply that A also trusts C. For such a relationship to exist, a third trust between A and C must be created explicitly.
- Creating a trust relationship simply makes it possible for an administrator in the trusting domain (A, in our example) to provide explicit access to resources for users or global groups in Domain B. By default, when a trust between two domains is created, this confers no automatic permissions for users or global groups in the trusted domain. Unless an administrator references some global group or user from Domain A in the permissions for a resource, all users and groups in B can only access resources available to the default global Domain Guests group in A.

Understanding (And Calculating) Trust Requirements

Despite these intricacies and special considerations, trust relationships are essential in large networks because they provide the foundation on which cross-domain resource access rests. In the single master domain model discussed in Chapter 2, for instance, it's necessary for all resource domains to trust the master domain. This is what makes it possible for administrators to reference global groups that belong to the master domain in local groups in any of the resource domains, thereby providing access for users from the master domain to local resources wherever they're needed. This manifold trust relationship is depicted in Figure 3.2.

Where multiple master domains exist, two-way trusts between each pair of masters are necessary to permit administrators to manage all the masters as a single logical, coherent entity. Because there are multiple master domains, it's also necessary for each resource domain to establish a trust with each individual master domain. This many-faceted trust relationship is depicted in Figure 2.3. The number of trusts involved may be calculated according

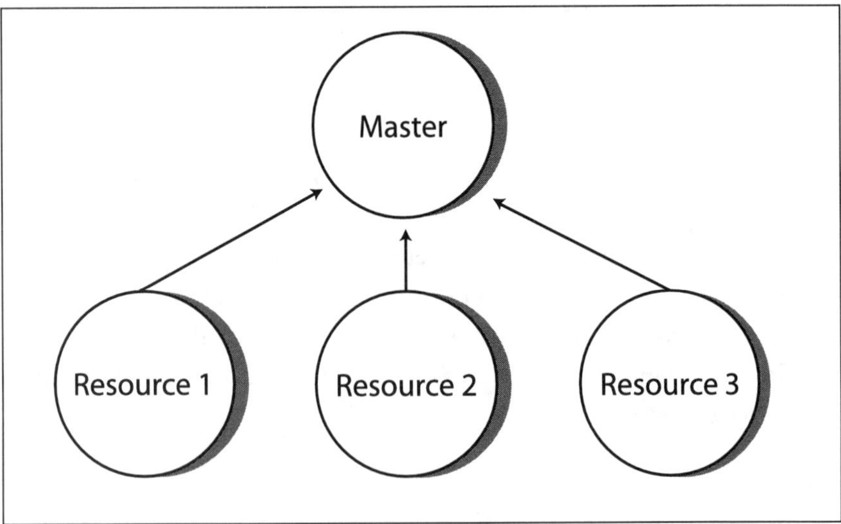

Figure 3.2 All three resource domains trust the master domain, thereby enabling global user groups from the master domain to be referenced in any resource domain.

to the following formula (where **m** is the number of master domains, and **n** is the number of resource domains):

```
trusts = m×(m-1) + m×n
```

In English, we can restate this as: The total number of trusts is equal to the number of trusts required among all master domains plus the number of trusts between all resource domains and every master domain. For master domains, this equals twice the number of edges in a complete mesh. (A mesh is a graph where every vertex is connected directly to all other vertices. We double this because two-way trusts are required.) This may be more simply calculated by multiplying **m** by **(m-1)**. In addition, we must also define one trust from each resource domain to each master domain (expressed mathematically as **m×n**). Because the number of master trusts grows geometrically, **m** should be kept as small as possible. For example, for 3 master domains and 10 resource domains, the value of this formula is **(3×2)+(3×10)**, or **6+30**, or 36 trust relationships.

The most complex multidomain trust model that Microsoft describes is the complete trust model. In this model, every domain maintains a two-way trust with every other domain in the network. Based on the preceding formula, this means the number of trusts is **d(d-1)**, where **d** is the number of domains. For the preceding example, with a total of **13** domains, complete trust means **13×12**, or 156 trust relationships. Microsoft no longer recommends creating complete trust among domains, even if the number of trust relationships remains small.

These calculations should help you understand why a single domain model is so attractive and why simple multidomain models should always be considered before using more complex models. Only organizations with large user populations should consider multiple masters. We cannot recommend the complete trust model except where nothing else works (this usually involves political considerations, not technical issues). To help you understand when multiple master domains may become necessary, please consult the section in Chapter 5 titled "Domain Database Info."

A good cutoff point is in the neighborhood of 25,000 to 26,000 users. Any less than that and a single master domain will probably suffice. Any more than 26,000 users and multiple masters become necessary.

Now that we have examined what a trust relationship is, let's move on to explore how to put these relationships to use in Windows NT.

Establishing And Configuring Trust Relationships

Creating a trust between one domain and another is like opening a door from the trusting domain to the trusted domain. The relationship makes it possible to insert users or global groups from the trusted domain into local groups in the trusting domain. The administrative tool wherein trust relationships may be defined is the same one where you use existing trust relationships to add users or global groups from a trusted domain within a trusting one—namely, the User Manager For Domains utility.

Establish A Trust

To establish a trust, it's necessary to perform operations in both of the domains involved—that is, in both the trusted and the trusting domains. In both cases, the same menu selection in User Manager For Domains must be invoked (from Start|Programs|Administrative Tools (Common)). Beneath the Policies menu, you'll find an entry named Trust Relationships. Selecting this entry produces the Trust Relationships dialog box shown in Figure 3.3.

In some ways, creating a trust is like a handshake (in the computing sense, rather than the human sense). That is, an administrator in Domain B must acknowledge the possibility of a trust, and an administrator in Domain A must do likewise. Both will use the User Manager For Domains utility, but A's window will show DOMAINA as the primary domain, and B's will show DOMAINB as the primary domain.

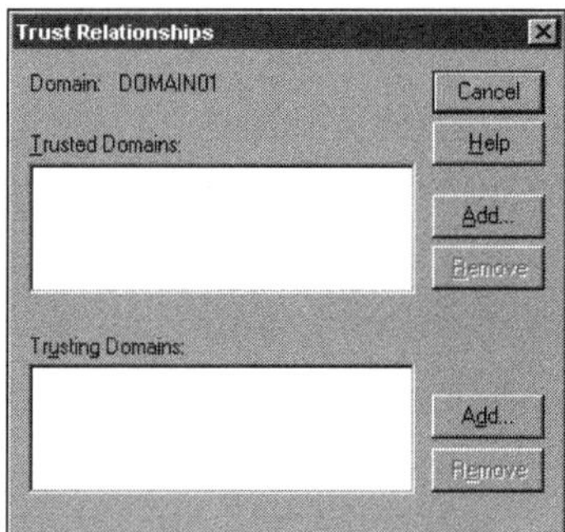

Figure 3.3 The Trust Relationships dialog shows trusts from the viewpoint of the domain in which it's opened (in this case, from DOMAIN01's perspective).

Here's the recipe for performing the handshake properly, according to Microsoft:

1. In the trusted domain (Domain B, in this example), open the Trust Relationships window in User Manager For Domains. Click the Add button next to the display area labeled Trusting Domains. Type the name of the trusting domain (DOMAINA) as seen in the pop-up list.
2. Specify a password for creating the trust relationship in the dialog box supplied for that purpose (this prevents the trust from unauthorized "hijack").
3. In the trusting domain (DOMAINA), open the Trust Relationship window in User Manager For Domains. This time, click the Add button next to the display area labeled Trusted Domains. Select the name of the trusted domain (DOMAINB) from the pop-up list, and supply the agreed-upon password in the ensuing dialog box.

Remember that both trusted and trusting domains must acknowledge trust relationships. Only when Step 3 is completed successfully may a trust relationship be used.

Using Trust Relationships

Once a trust relationship has been established, a domain administrator in the trusting domain will be able to view—and add—users and global groups from the trusted domain to global (users only) and local groups (users and global groups) in that administrator's domain (the trusting domain). To continue our ongoing saga of Domains A and B, this means that a Domain A administrator will be able to access users and global groups from Domain B when assigning permissions for resources hosted by Domain A. In other words, this means that the Domain A administrator can add users and global groups from Domain B into the groups controlling access to Domain A resources.

This display takes the form of *<domain name>**<group name>* or *<domain name>**<user name>*. For our hypothetical example, this means that you would be able to access groups like DOMAINB\Domain Users or DOMAINB\Domain Administrators when controlling membership in local groups as an administrator for Domain A.

Remember, only users may belong to global groups, and only global groups and users may belong to local groups. You'll see many apparently correct answers to trust-related questions that assume it's okay to insert a global group from Domain B into a global group from Domain A, or even a local group from Domain B into a global group in Domain B. Don't fall for this underhanded trickery. Read the questions twice, and consider carefully the assumptions about what kinds of elements can be placed into local and global groups before answering any such questions.

Now that you know how to set up trust relationships among domains, let's explore how to assign cross-domain permissions to users.

Permissions Across Trust Relationships

Permissions across trust relationships work the same way they work within a single domain environment. Don't let the existence of multiple domains throw you off course when evaluating permissions for access to Windows NT-based objects. You may, however, assume that when a user accesses resources across two domains, this access is remote (across the network) and not local (on the machine where the resource resides).

Given this simplifying assumption, here's how to determine permissions for an object under NTFS control (a file, folder, or application):

1. Compare all rights associated with the share, as determined by the user's group memberships and individual account status. Pick the most inclusive or permissive of all such rights.
2. Compare all NTFS permissions associated with the requested object, as determined by the user's group memberships and individual account status. Again, pick the most inclusive or permissive of such rights.
3. Compare the two results, and pick the less permissive of the two. This will be the user's effective permissions to the object.

Note: *If the object is in a FAT (File Allocation Table) volume, only the share rights apply (FAT doesn't have object-level security). Pick the most permissive right, and that's what the user can do.*

The exception that proves this rule is that any time No Access appears, it wins the selection process. If a user is assigned No Access by virtue of group membership or account status through share rights or NTFS permissions, the result is that the user has No Access to the requested object.

It's necessary for any user to log on to his or her home domain to obtain any rights or permissions that interdomain trust relationships may provide. If any user logs on to a domain other than his or her home domain, the user becomes a Domain Guest in the foreign domain. The trick to remember is that trusts work only when a user from a trusted domain attempts to access resources in a trusting domain. If users don't log on to a domain where they have true user accounts, they can only function as Domain Guests in the domains they do log on to. This works only when the guest account password is blank, the guest accout is enabled (it's disabled by default), and when no service packs from SP3 or later have been applied.

There are a number of ways to manage user access to network resources. We have explained how trust relationships work, as well as how to define user access in a trust. Now, we move on to explain the use of multiple trust relationships in Windows NT.

Managing Multiple Trusts

As the discussion at the end of the first section of this chapter illustrates, the number and complexity of trust relationships can quickly become mind-numbing, especially when a single or multiple master model is in use. The key to clear thinking is to remember that no matter how many trust relationships may be required to implement a particular usage scenario, such relationships can be defined and managed only between one trusted and one trusting domain at a time.

Understanding how to implement usage scenarios (covered in the next section in some depth) involves cultivating—or perhaps resuscitating—skills in reading "word problems." By inserting the right kinds of relationship arrows to match whatever trust requirements may be implied, you can find ways to understand the necessary requirements and evaluate whatever potential solutions you'll be asked to consider.

If you can remember the following basic rules and requirements, you should be able to get through even the thorniest of scenarios to decide what trusts are necessary to make things work or to decide if the trust arrangement described meets the stated requirements:

- When users in one domain (Domain A) need access to resources in another (Domain B), this means that Domain B must trust Domain A. In other words, this requires B to be a trusting domain and A to be a trusted domain in a trust relationship. Here, you draw the arrow pointing from B to A.
- When users in both domains require access to resources in each other's domains, a two-way trust is required. This means two separate trusts: one where A trusts B and another where B trusts A. Here, you draw a two-headed arrow between A and B.

- When users in a master domain need access to resources in a resource domain, all resource domains must trust the master. Here, draw an arrow that points from each resource domain to the master domain.
- When multiple master domains exist, each master domain must maintain a two-way trust with each and every other master domain, to permit the entire collection of master domains to function as a logical unit.
- When multiple master domains exist, each resource domain must establish a one-way trust with each master domain, to permit all users in all master domains to access resources in all resource domains.

In the section that follows, we'll explore some typical question scenarios. They should help you appreciate how a simple collection of rules and requirements can produce some pretty tricky situations and circumstances that you'll be asked to interpret and understand.

Common Trust Scenarios

This will require additional effort on your part, but be prepared to sketch out the kinds of bubble diagrams you saw earlier in this chapter to match the scenarios we describe. We'll provide the diagrams for the discussions that follow, however.

Three Domains, Interesting Relationships

On a hypothetical network, assume three domains exist: Sales, Marketing, and Engineering. Users in Sales and Marketing need access to each other's resources, but users in Engineering only need access to Sales and Marketing, not vice versa.

Walking through this text description, here's the translation that results:

- Sales and Marketing need access to each other's resources. This key phrase indicates that a two-way trust between the two domains is needed. That's why the diagram shown in Figure 3.4 depicts the trust relationship between these two domains with a two-headed arrow.

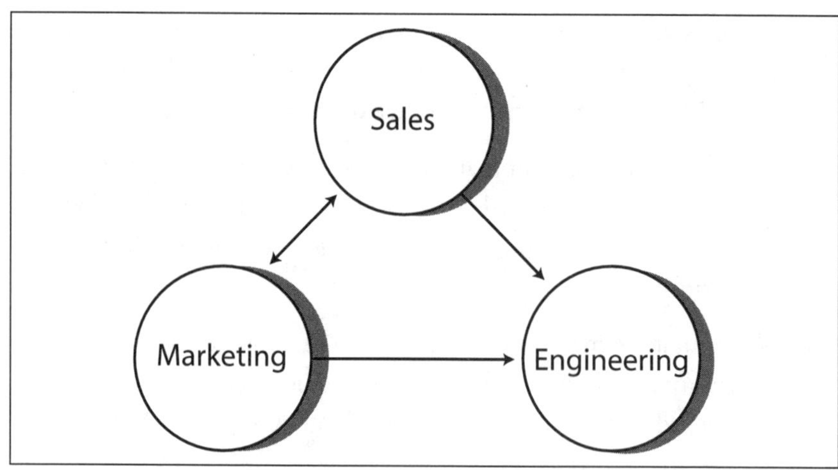

Figure 3.4 Sales and Marketing have a two-way trust between them, but it's only one-way between Sales and Engineering, and Marketing and Engineering.

- Engineering needs access to Sales and Marketing resources, but not vice versa. This means two one-way trusts are required. Because the trusting domain grants access to the trusted domain, and the arrows point from trusting to trusted, we show two arrows—one pointing from Sales to Engineering and another from Marketing to Engineering.

When the phrase "Domain X needs access to Domain Y's resources" occurs, remember that the arrow points from Y to X, not the other way around. That's because Y must trust X to give X access to Y's resources. Got it? You must be able to map out relationships that involve three or more domains that may not involve a clear-cut use of the master or multiple master domain model, too (as in the preceding scenario).

Centralized Administrative Controls

The title of this section is something that is often a code phrase for the kind of relationship that exists between resource domains and the master domain(s) in a master or multiple master domain model. But it can also occur when these models are not invoked by name. The key ingredients to look for, in addition to the phrases "centralized administration" and "centralized administrative controls," are multiple domains (usually three or more), where most are at the periphery of a network and where users (and more importantly, administrators) aggregate in a central or master domain.

In this case, you'll want to be sure to establish one-way trusts from all the peripheral or resource domains to the central or master domain, and to be sure that members of the Domain Administrators group in the central or master domain are added to the local Administrators group on servers in the resource or peripheral domains (this is particularly important for domain controllers). That way, the possibility of administration is not only established (through the trust relationships), but it's assured (through the inclusion of the Domain Administrator's global group from the central or master domain in local groups on individual machines in the peripheral or resource domains). Figure 3.5 shows how to set up shared resources in the master domain model.

Why are these resource and user group shenanigans necessary? Two reasons: Creating a trust doesn't grant authority to do anything with it, and only global groups and users can belong to local groups.

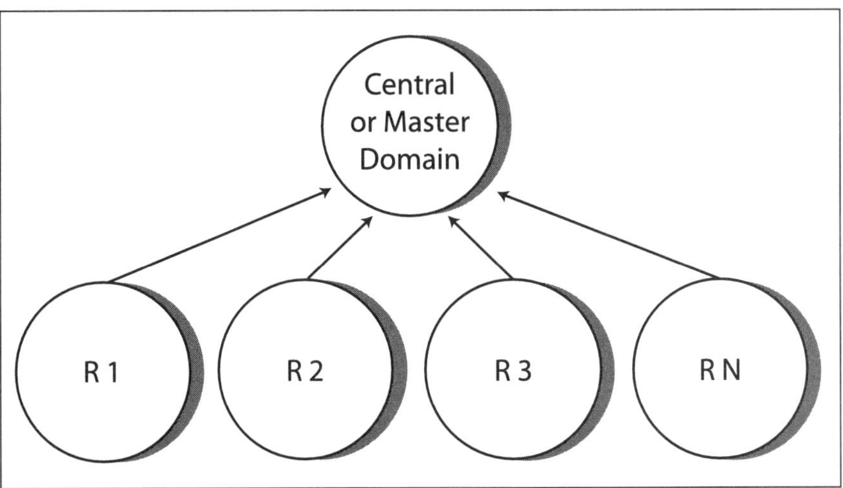

Figure 3.5 For centralized administration, all resource or peripheral domains must trust the central or master domain.

Practice Questions

Question 1

Of the following assertions, which best represents the trust relationships that exist in a multiple master domain model?

❍ a. Two-way trusts exist between all domains in the model.

❍ b. Two-way trusts exist between all master domains, and one-way trusts exist between the master domains to all resource domains.

❍ c. Two-way trusts exist between all master domains, and one-way trusts exist between each resource domain to all master domains.

❍ d. One-way trusts exist between all master domains and between all resource domains; no trust relationships exist between any master and resource domains.

Answer c is correct. The short definition of the trust relationships in a multiple master domain model may be expressed as "two-way trusts between all master domains, and one-way from each resource domain to every master domain." Only answer c meets this definition. Answer a fails because it asserts that all domains share two-way trusts. This defines the complete trust domain model, not the multiple master domain model. Answer b fails because it points the one-way trusts in the wrong direction. It asserts, incorrectly, that the master domains must trust the resource domains, when in fact it should be the other way around. Answer d misses the point of the master domain model completely, in that it fails to make any connection between master and resource domains at all.

Question 2

Trick! question

Assume two domains named "Users" and "Admin" are defined within an organization. Three members of the Users domain have been drafted to work with materials in the Admin domain, prior to their general release to the user community. To assist with prerelease testing, these three users need access to a shared NTFS folder named "\Tests" on a server named "TEST1" in the Admin domain. Admin already trusts Users. Which of the following options is the best way to grant Full Control access to the \TEST1\Tests share for those three individuals from the Users domain?

- ❍ a. Remove the current trust relationship. Add a new trust wherein Admin trusts Users. Create a global group in the Users domain named "Utesters", and add the three individuals' accounts to that group. Create a global group named "Atesters" in the Admin domain, and add the global group Users\Utesters to Atesters. Give Atesters Full Control over the \TEST1\Tests share.
- ❍ b. Create a global group in the Users domain named "Utesters". Assign each of the three Users domain accounts to that group. Create a global group in the Admin domain named "Atesters", and assign Users\Utesters to Atesters. Give Atesters Full Control over the \TEST1\Tests share.
- ❍ c. Create a global group in Users called "Utesters". Add each of the three Users domain accounts to that group. Create a local group on TEST1 called "Utesters", and add the Users\Utesters global group to this local group. Grant Utesters Full Control to the \TEST1\Tests share.
- ❍ d. Remove the current trust relationship. Add a new trust wherein Admin trusts Users. Create a global group in Users called "Utesters". Add each of the three Users domain accounts to that group. Create a local group on TEST1 called "Utesters", and add the Users\Utesters global group to this local group. Grant Utesters Full Control to the \TEST1\Tests share.

Answer c is correct. The key phrase in this question is "the best way," because two answers are actually correct. Answer d, although correct, requires removal and replacement of the existing trust from Admin to Users. This is unnecessary and may break existing trusts established for other uses. Otherwise, d is the same as c, which is correct because it:

- Uses an existing trust
- Creates a global group in the trusted domain
- Puts the global group into a local group on the TEST1 machine in the trusting domain
- Grants the local group the required access to the share

Answer a fails because it breaks an existing trust unnecessarily and because it places one global group inside another (global groups may contain only users, not other groups of any kind, whether local or global). Answer b fails for the latter reason as well, by placing one global group inside another.

Question 3

The XYZ Corporation employs a single master domain model where the name of the master domain is "XYZCorp". The Marketing domain at XYZ already trusts the XYZCorp domain. If a user belonging to the Marketing domain logs on to the XYZCorp domain, what shared resources will the user be able to access?

- ❍ a. All folders in XYZCorp for which Marketing\Domain Users have Read access.
- ❍ b. All folders in either XYZCorp or Marketing for which Marketing\Domain Guests have Read access.
- ❍ c. All folders in either XYZCorp or Marketing for which XYZCorp\Domain Guests have Read access.
- ❍ d. All folders in Marketing for which XYZCorp\Domain Users have Read access.

Answer c is correct. The key phrase to this question—and the reason it's labeled as a trick—is "logs on to the XYZCorp domain." Remember, trust relationships only confer access when a user logs on through his or her home domain. The user in this question belongs to the Marketing domain but logs on to the XYZCorp domain, so the user is automatically treated as a member of the Domain Guests global group in the XYZCorp domain. Once this is understood, the correct answer is easy. It must be c, because the user is treated as a member of the XYZCorp\Domain Guests global group, with access to whatever resources are available to that global group in either the XYZCorp or Marketing domains. Answer a is incorrect because it attributes the login to the wrong domain (Marketing). Answer b is incorrect for the same reason. Answer d is incorrect because it omits the folders in XYZCorp where a Domain Guest might have access and because it puts the user in the Domain Users global group, not the Domain Guests global group.

Question 4

Widgets, Inc. has a network that includes three domains, named "Admin", "Sales", and "Engineering". Users from Sales and Admin need access to resources from Engineering, but they also need access to resources in each other's domains. How must you set up the necessary trust relationships?

- ❍ a. Define two-way trusts between all three domains.
- ❍ b. Set up one-way trusts from Sales to Admin, Admin to Engineering, and Engineering to Sales.
- ❍ c. Define a two-way trust between Sales and Admin, and another two-way trust between Engineering and Sales.
- ❍ d. Set up two one-way trusts from Engineering to Sales and Engineering to Admin, and a two-way trust between Sales and Admin.

Answer d is the only correct answer because it provides both the two-way trust between Sales and Admin that's required and establishes one-way trusts from Engineering to both Sales and Admin, to meet the stated requirement that "users from Sales and Admin need access to resources from Engineering." This means that Engineering must trust both domains, as the answer indicates by specifying two one-way trusts from Engineering to each of the other domains. One good way to eliminate possibilities is to see what's missing in the question when compared to the answers. The question says nothing about Engineering requiring access to anything in Sales or Admin. This automatically knocks out answer a, because it includes two-way trusts from Sales and Admin to Engineering that are not required (and perhaps even unwanted). Likewise, this knocks out answer c because it includes a trust from Sales to Engineering, as well as the required trust from Engineering to Sales. Answer b must be eliminated because it fails to include the two-way trust between Sales and Admin implied by the key phrase "but they also need access to resources in each other's domains."

Question 5

The Sales, Admin, and Engineering domains include 50 user accounts apiece. All 150 users need access to files on a Windows NT Server in a fourth domain named "Resources". How must you configure the trust relationships involved?

- ❍ a. Establish complete trust between all four domains.
- ❍ b. Make the Resources domain the trusting domain, and Sales, Admin, and Engineering the trusted domains.
- ❍ c. Make Sales, Admin, and Engineering all trusting domains, and Resources the trusted domain.
- ❍ d. Establish a two-way trust between Sales and Resources, then establish trusts between Admin and Sales, and Admin and Engineering.

Answer b is correct. Here again, you can begin by eliminating answers that exceed the specifications. The question says nothing that requires two-way trusts, so you can knock answers a and d out immediately. Picking the right answer from the two remaining options requires that you understand that a trusting domain makes resources available to a trusted domain. Because the question requires that users in Sales, Admin, and Engineering obtain access to files in the Resources domain, this means that Sales, Admin, and Engineering are trusted domains, and Resources is the trusting domain. This makes b the only correct answer. Answer c reverses the correct relationship and defines the opposite of what's intended by making Sales, Admin, and Engineering make resources available to Resources.

Question 6

If all other domains on a network trust a domain named "Admin", what kinds of user accounts or groups can be inserted into a global group in the Admin domain?

- ❍ a. User accounts from Admin, plus any user accounts from all trusting domains
- ❍ b. User accounts from Admin only
- ❍ c. User accounts and other global accounts from Admin only
- ❍ d. User accounts from Admin, any user accounts from all trusting domains, plus any local groups from Admin only

Answer b is correct. A global group can contain only users from the domain in which it resides. It's only because of the special default local group Everyone that appearances to the contrary may be believed to exist. The key to understanding this question is to understand what's allowed in a global group—namely, user accounts only. This automatically disqualifies answers c and d, which indicate that a global group in Admin can contain global and local groups, respectively. Even where trust relationships exist, global groups may only include users from the domain in which they're defined. Local groups provide the mechanism for including global groups from other domains because that's where the linkage between groups and resources must reside in any case (in other words, this is a function of a local group's ability to contain local or domain users and global groups, be they from the local domain or some other domain that's trusted by the domain in which the local group resides). This effectively disqualifies answer a.

Question 7

Analyze the following scenario:

Your network includes two domains named "Engineering" and "Admin". Admin is a master domain, and Engineering has a one-way trust with Admin. Each domain includes a single PDC, two BDCs, three member servers, and 200 workstations, all running Windows NT Workstation 4. To ensure the availability of data on the network, you need to create a group named "TotalBack" that can back up all the machines on the network—be they domain controllers, member servers, or workstations.

Required result:

- Members of the TotalBack group must be able to back up all domain controllers, in either Engineering or Admin.

Optional desired results:

- Members of TotalBack should be able to back up all member servers in both domains.
- Members of TotalBack should be able to back up all Windows NT Workstations in both domains.

Proposed solution:

- Create a global group called "TotalBack" in the Admin domain, and add this group to the Backup Operators local group on every domain controller, member server, and Windows NT Workstation in both domains.

Which results does the proposed solution produce?

❍ a. The proposed solution produces the required result and both of the optional desired results.

❍ b. The proposed solution produces the required result but only one of the optional desired results.

❍ c. The proposed solution produces the required result but neither of the optional desired results.

❍ d. The proposed solution does not produce the required result.

Answer a is correct. The key to dealing with this type of question lies in analyzing the proposed solution and deciding where it fits the matrix of possibilities. In this case, defining a global group in Admin is exactly the right thing to do because global groups in a trusted domain can be included in local groups in Admin and in any other domains that trust Admin. Engineering trusts Admin, so the global TotalBack group can be referenced in local groups in both domains. Finally, because all flavors of Windows NT mentioned—namely, domain controllers, member servers, and Windows NT Workstation machines—support the local Backup Operators group, placing a reference to Admin\TotalBack therein creates a situation where members of that group can back up all domain controllers, all member servers, and all Windows NT Workstations in either domain. Thus, the correct answer is a, because the required result and both optional desired results will be produced by the proposed solution.

Question 8

A network includes four domains named “Admin”, “Engineering”, “Marketing”, and “Sales”. Users in the Admin and Sales domains require access to a high-resolution color laser printer to produce proof prints for a sales brochure. Only Marketing and Engineering include such devices. How might you define trust relationships among these domains to grant users in Admin and Sales access to the color laser printers they need?

- ❍ a. Define two-way trusts between all four domains.
- ❍ b. Define two one-way trusts from Admin to Marketing and Engineering, and two more from Sales to Marketing and Engineering.
- ❍ c. Define two one-way trusts from Engineering to Admin and Sales, and two more from Marketing to Admin and Sales.
- ❍ d. Define a two-way trust between Admin and Sales, and another two-way trust between Engineering and Marketing.

Answer c is correct. Here again, you can begin by eliminating unnecessary relationships. So that Admin and Sales can access Engineering and Marketing resources, only one-way trusts are required (because nothing is said about Engineering and Marketing needing access to resources in either Admin or Sales). This eliminates answers a and d, both of which call for two-way trusts. Selecting the correct answer hinges on understanding how the trust relationship works. Because Admin and Sales need access to resources in Engineering and Marketing, Engineering and Marketing must each trust Admin and Sales. This makes answer c the only correct answer, because answer b establishes the trust relationships in the wrong direction.

Question 9

Windows NT Directory Services provides trust relationships to permit secure access to occur across multiple domains. Which Windows NT Server utility provides the tools necessary to define such relationships?

- ❍ a. Server Manager
- ❍ b. User Manager For Domains
- ❍ c. Control Panel, Services applet
- ❍ d. Domain Administration

Answer b is correct. Only one utility includes mention of trust relationships. Trust relationships may only be created using the Policies|Trust Relationships menu entry in User Manager For Domains. Once defined, global groups and accounts from trusted domains may be accessed in User Manager For Domains in the trusting domain. Server Manager includes no options to create or manage trust relationships, nor does the Control Panel's Services applet. Therefore, answers a and c are incorrect. Finally, there is no utility in Windows NT Server called "Domain Administration." Therefore, answer d is incorrect.

Question 10

To facilitate a task group at your company, you're asked to provide temporary access to resources in your Admin domain for a group of auditors in the Auditors domain. For the same reason, you will also have to provide temporary access to the same group of users in other domains in the coming months. There is already a trust relationship where Admin trusts Auditors. Which of the following represents the best way to supply temporary access to Admin for this group of auditors?

❍ a. Create a global group in the Admin domain that includes the auditors' user accounts. Add this group to the Guests local group on all servers in the Admin domain.

❍ b. Create a global group in the Auditors domain that includes the auditors' user accounts. Add this group to the local group on the server (or servers) in the Admin domain that contain(s) the needed resources.

❍ c. Create a local group in the Admin domain that includes the auditors' user accounts on each server where the needed resources reside.

❍ d. Create a local group in the Auditors domain that includes the auditors' user accounts. Add this group to the local group on the server (or servers) in the Admin domain that contain(s) the needed resources.

Answer b is correct. There are two legitimate ways to meet the stated requirements. One of them simply entails adding the users from the Auditors domain into the local group (or groups) in the Admin domain where the needed resources reside. The other puts a global group in-between, by defining a global group in Auditors that may then be placed into local groups in Admin. Both options are legal, because Admin trusts Auditors. This makes answers b and c potentially correct. But because the question mentions a need to put the same group elsewhere in the future, creating a global group will ultimately be less work. That's because when the current temporary situation expires, the reference to the Auditors' global group need only be expunged from the local group (or groups) in Admin. To add this same group into another domain, the global group only needs to be added to the local groups in that domain (provided, of course, that the necessary trust relationship from the new domain to the Auditors domain exists). Thus, answer b represents the best way to meet all requirements. Answer a fails because it assumes that Guests will be able to access the necessary resources, without indicating whether this is true. Answer d fails because it puts one local group within another (only global groups and users may occur within local groups).

Need To Know More?

Heywood, Drew: *Inside Windows NT Server, 2nd Edition*. New Riders, Indianapolis, IN, 1998. ISBN 1-56205-860-6. Pages 148 through 150 cover trust relationships and include interesting details on the subject.

Siyan, Karanjit S.: *Windows NT Server 4 Professional Reference, 2nd Edition*. New Riders, Indianapolis, IN, 1997. ISBN 1-56205-805-3. Chapter 6 covers trust relationships. As usual, Siyan offers the most detailed and thorough coverage of this subject.

The Windows NT Server 4 manuals cover trust relationships only in passing. The *Concepts And Planning Manual* includes the most information on this subject. However, Lesson 10 in the Windows NT 4 Upgrade Training CD-ROM, Microsoft Press, Redmond, WA, 1996, covers this subject in great detail. ISBN 1-57231-528-8.

The *Windows NT Server Resource Kit* contains scattered bits of information about trust relationships and related domain issues. You can search the TechNet CD (or its online version through **www.microsoft.com**), using keywords like "trust relationships" and "interdomain trusts."

Rights, Permissions, And User Access To Resources

4

Terms you'll need to understand:

- √ Authentication
- √ User rights
- √ Permissions
- √ Security Accounts Manager (SAM)
- √ Access token
- √ Objects
- √ Attributes
- √ Services
- √ Access control list (ACL)
- √ Groups
- √ Read
- √ Write
- √ Execute
- √ Delete
- √ Change
- √ Take Ownership
- √ Full Control
- √ No Access
- √ List

Techniques you'll need to master:

- √ Understanding how users are granted access to resources
- √ Assigning permissions
- √ Implementing groups and group access
- √ Knowing Windows NT's built-in groups and the default users of those groups
- √ Understanding the difference between local and global groups, and when to use each
- √ Establishing share permissions
- √ Understanding the effects of combining permissions

Managing a Windows NT Server in an enterprise environment demands a solid working understanding of rights, permissions, and user access. In this chapter, we review these topics and introduce you to the added difficulty of an enterprise-level network. This chapter assumes you've already read and comprehended the previous two chapters on domains and trust relationships.

Logon And User Identification

The first step in understanding Windows NT security must start where every user starts—at logon. By pressing Ctrl+Alt+Del at the initial Windows NT splash screen, you initiate the WinLogon utility. This utility displays the logon dialog box and sends the supplied data to the security manager. The security manager (part of the executive services in the kernel) verifies the name and password, creates an access token, and launches the user's shell (usually Windows NT Explorer). The verification process is the act of comparing the user name and password with the data stored in the Security Accounts Manager (SAM). This database also contains the list of access privileges for each user. The access token is built from this list. Once this process is complete, the user is able to access network resources.

The access token created by the security manager is a collection of identifiers and permissions unique to each individual. It is this access token that the network operating system (NOS) uses to verify authority to access and manipulate every object and resource. The access token is built by combining the individual settings of a user with those of each group to which that user belongs.

The access token is created when a user logs on, and it is not changed until the user logs off and logs on again. This means that any access changes to a user or a group to which that user belongs will not affect those currently logged on. The changes will only affect them the next time they log on.

The access token not only defines what objects and resources with which a user can interact, but it is also attached to every process launched by that user. WinLogon uses the access token it creates to launch the shell for a user. The shell inherits the same access privileges as the user based on the access token. Every process launched by the user or a process initiated by the user can only have the level of access authority granted by the user's access token or less. (In fact, every single process has an access token assigned to it, based on the spawning heritage.) Under Windows NT, it is not normally possible for a user to launch a process or access an object (directly or through a spawned process) that requires a higher level of access than that defined by his or her current access token.

The ultimate purpose of security is to control who has access to what. The WinLogon process determines the "who," and objects are the "what."

Objects

Within the world of Windows NT, everything is an object. An object has a type, a collection of services, and a set of attributes.

The type of an object defines what services and attributes are valid. Object types within Windows NT include files, directories, symbolic links, printers, processes, threads, ports, devices, and even windows.

The services of an object are the activities that can be performed on, with, or by an object. For example, a directory object has services of List, Read, Change, Delete, and so on, but a printer object has services of Print, Manage, Delete, and so forth.

The attributes of an object include the name of the object, the actual data, and the access control list (ACL). Figure 4.1 illustrates a Windows NT object.

An ACL is the attribute of each object that defines which users and groups have what level of services for an object.

Access Control List

An ACL comprises a list of services (Read, Write, Delete) and the associated users and groups who can perform each action (Mary, Bob, Sales group,

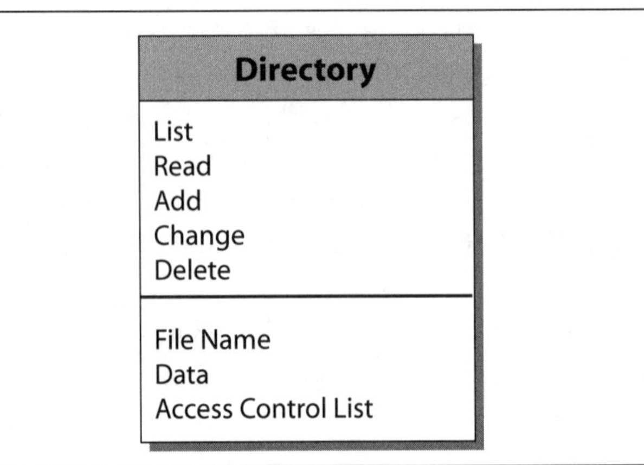

Figure 4.1 A Windows NT object.

Marketing group). Figure 4.2 illustrates an object's access control list along with a user's access token.

When a user attempts to use an object, the user's access token is compared to the ACL of the object. You can think of the access token as a key ring with multiple keys, each related to a group membership or specific permission setting for that user. You can also think of the ACL as a linked group of padlocks for each object. Each lock will open only for a specific user or group key and only allow the specified level of access.

You can set the ACLs on an object in two ways. First, you can use the GUI dialog boxes and your mouse to point and click to make any and all ACL changes you desire. Go check it out for yourself. Right-click on an object, select Properties, click on the Securities tab, and then click on the Permissions button. The second method is to use the **CACLS** command. This command can display or modify one or more files' ACLs in batch mode. Here's the syntax:

```
cacls filename [/t] [/e] [/c] [/g user:r|c|f] [/r user [...]]
[/p user:n|r|c|f [...]] [/d user [...]]
```

The parameters are as follows:

- **filename** Displays ACLs of specified file(s).
- **/t** Changes ACLs of specified files in the current directory and all subdirectories.

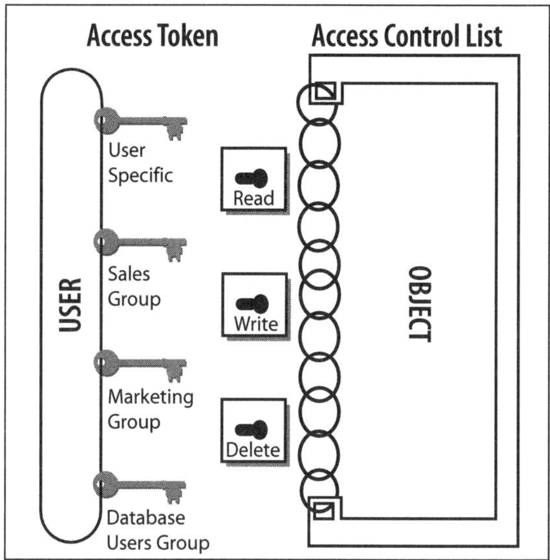

Figure 4.2 A visualization of a user's access token and an object's access control list.

- /e Edits the ACL instead of replacing it.
- /c Continues changing ACLs, ignoring errors.
- /g **user:r|c|f** Grants specified user access rights of Read, Change, or Full Control.
- /r **user** Revokes specified user's access rights.
- /p **user:n|r|c|f** Replaces specified user's access rights of None, Read, Change, or Full Control.

Now that we have defined these parameters, let's continue the discussion with how to ensure that users are assigned the proper access permissions.

Checking Permissions

When a user attempts to access an object, the security system performs a permissions check to determine if the user has proper authority to access the object and with which services he or she can interact. Using the key and lock analogy, the security system tries the keys on the user's key ring (access token) in each of the object's locks (ACL). If a match is found, the user can proceed with the intended activity.

This analogy doesn't quite explain every aspect of the permissions check, but it does give you a good mental image of what takes place. One important facet regarding permissions that the lock and key analogy fails to communicate is the No Access setting. Any user or group can be assigned No Access privileges for an object. If such an assignment is made, then a user cannot gain any access whatsoever.

Putting the lock and key imagery aside, when a user requests access to an object's service, the security system performs the following authority check:

1. Checks for any specified No Access for the user or any groups the user belongs to. If No Access is found, the user is denied access.

2. Checks for any specific granting of access based on the service requested for the user and any groups. If access such as Grant is found, the user is granted access.

3. If neither a specific No Access nor service permission is found, the default of No Access applies. Therefore, the user is denied access.

As you can see, a specific No Access is like a trump card. It overrides any other settings, including specific granting of access. Plus, if no specific permission is given (i.e., no working key is present in the access token), the user cannot gain entry.

Note that No Access under Windows NT prevents a user from using any of the six file operations, but a user is still able to see the name of the object as stored in the Master Browser object list. Now that we have discussed individual user settings, let's examine how group memberships affect permissions for users.

Group Memberships

The use of groups can greatly simplify the feat of assigning access permissions to numerous individuals. Groups are a significant part of the security configuration of Windows NT.

A user can belong to many groups. When a user does belong to multiple groups, the access privileges for that user are a combination of the privileges granted by each group. You can think of group permissions as additive or cumulative. For example, if Sales has read access to an object, Marketing has write access to the same object, and you are a member of both groups, you have read and write access to that object.

The only exception to this addition rule is when any one group has No Access specified for the object. Once again, No Access means *no access* even if every other group offers full access privileges.

Because of the No Access trump, it is important to carefully plan the membership and access patterns of your users. It is common to mistakenly give a user too much access or no access at all through poor planning of group memberships.

Default Groups And Membership Assignments

There are a host of default groups, two default users, and a handful of important membership assignments you need to know about. Table 4.1 describes these groups.

Table 4.1 Default groups and their descriptions.

Group	Type	Description
Account Operators	Local	Administration of domain user and group accounts
Administrators	Local	Full administrative privileges to a domain and the server
Backup Operators	Local	Bypass security restrictions to back up and restore files from network storage devices
Domain Admins	Global	Administration of user and computer accounts within a domain
Domain Guests	Global	Guest access to domain resources

(continued)

Table 4.1 Default groups and their descriptions *(continued)*.

Group	Type	Description
Domain Users	Global	All users in a domain are part of this group
Everyone	Global	Contains all domain and trusted domain users
Guests	Local	Guest access to domain resources
Print Operators	Local	Administration of domain printers
Replicator	Local	Special group for replication
Server Operators	Local	Manage server hardware and configuration, but no access to SAM
Users	Local	Server users

You should remember that global groups can be used across a network on any machine within a domain or a trusted domain. Global groups can also be thought of as network groups. Local groups only apply to a single computer. By Microsoft's recommendation, global groups should contain users and local groups should contain resources. Then, global user groups should be placed into the local resource groups to allow users to access these resources.

The two default user accounts of Windows NT Server are:

- **Administrator** This account has unrestricted access to every object and resource within a domain. This account can be renamed but not deleted or disabled.
- **Guest** This account has limited access to domain resources for a temporary user. This account can be renamed and disabled but not deleted. This account has a blank password by default. Thus, any remote user can log on unless you set a password. This account does not save user preferences or configuration changes. This account is disabled by default.

It is highly recommended that you rename the Administrator and Guest accounts immediately after installing Windows NT. This will improve the security of your network by removing "known" user accounts, thereby thwarting many would-be hackers. It is also a good idea to create separate

Administrator accounts for each administrator within your MIS department. This allows the actions of each person to be tracked individually. Table 4.2 defines the default memberships of the default and new user accounts for Windows NT's built-in groups.

If you add users to these groups, be aware of how the group settings affect that user's access rights. In addition to these rights, there are some settings that are specific to NTFS partitions, which we examine next.

NTFS Permissions

The NTFS file system has a standard set of access permissions for files and directories. Through these permissions, every file and directory within the file system name space can be controlled through the use of access tokens and ACLs. There are six specific operations that can occur on a file or directory:

- R Read. The object's data contents can be accessed.
- W Write. The object's data contents can be changed.

Table 4.2 Windows NT's default members of built-in groups.

Group	Default Members
Account Operators	None
Administrators	Administrators, Domain Admins (global group), Administrator
Backup Operators	None
Domain Admins	Administrator
Domain Guests	Guest
Domain Users	Administrator
Everyone	Every account in a domain and trusted domains
Guests	Domain Guests (global group), Guest
Print Operators	None
Replicator	None
Server Operators	None
Users	Domain Users (global group), Administrator

- X Execute. The object can be executed (in relation to directories, this means the directory can be opened).
- D Delete. The object can be deleted.
- P Change Permissions. The object's access permissions can be altered.
- O Take Ownership. The ownership of the object can be changed.

These six operations are combined into the standard permissions sets for files and directories. The standard permissions for files are:

- **Read (RX)** Allows file to be read and/or executed.
- **Change (RWXD)** Includes read (RX), plus modify and delete.
- **Full Control (RWXDPO)** Includes change (RWXD), plus change permissions and take ownership.
- **No Access ()** Allows absolutely no access.

The standard permissions for directories are (the first parentheses refer to the directory itself, the second refer to the contents of the directory but not the contents in any subdirectories):

- **List (RX)(not specified)** Users can view the names of the contents of this directory. No content-specific settings are specified.
- **Read (RX)(RX)** Users can read and traverse the directory, as well as read and execute the contents.
- **Add (WX)(not specified)** Users can add files to the directory, but they cannot read or change the contents of the directory.
- **Add And Read (RWX)(RX)** Users can add files to and read files from the directory, but they cannot change them.
- **Change (RWXD)(RWXD)** Users can add, read, execute, modify, and delete the directory and its contents.
- **Full Control (RWXDPO)(RWXDPO)** Users have full control over the directory and its contents.
- **No Access ()()** Users have absolutely no access to the directory and its contents.

In addition to these sets of standard file and directory permissions, special access can be defined on a directory or file basis. Special access consists of one or more of the six file/directory object operations (RWXDPO), plus a number of more esoteric operations usually of interest only to system programmers.

Other object types have their own unique set of operations and permissions. For example, print objects have a print operator but do not have a read operator. For each object type, the associated permissions may be slightly different to accommodate the functionality of that object. For the printers permission discussion, please see Chapter 13.

Windows NT uses two types of permission settings to control object access: local and remote. For files and directories, local access is the NTFS permissions we just discussed. Remote access to directories and their contents is controlled by shares.

Shares And Permissions

A share is a network resource that allows remote users to gain access to an object. The share is an object in itself that points to the resource object. The share knows how to translate data from the user (or, more specifically, an application employed by the user) to interact with the resource over the network. Shares enable a local resource to be used anywhere on the network.

Shares have their own set of permission levels:

- **No Access** Absolutely no access.
- **Read (RX)** Read and execute.
- **Change (RWXD)** Read, execute, modify, and delete.
- **Full Control (RWXDPO)** Full control.

Share permissions grant or restrict a user's interaction with the share itself. If a user logs onto a machine locally, the NTFS permissions on the object itself determine what services the user can access. When a share is used to access a resource, the combination of the share restrictions and NTFS restrictions results in granting only the most restrictive permissions common to both the share and the object.

> You can think of a share as a door and the services of an object as boxes. The share will only allow object services to pass through its gateway if they are the same as or less restrictive than the permissions on the share itself. As you can see in Figure 4.3, the "boxes" of NTFS permissions will only fit through the "doors" of a share if the boxes are no bigger than the opening.

Permissions on a share only apply to users attempting to access a resource through that share (i.e., over the network). Local users are not affected by share restrictions because they have direct access to such resources. Thus, local users are only restricted by the NTFS permissions on an object whereas remote or network users are restricted by both the share permissions and the NTFS object permissions.

> Here's an extremely important item to remember about shares: *The initial default settings of all newly created shares is Full Control to the Everyone group.* You'll need to remember this because it can cause some interesting problems if you don't reduce the access range for certain shares.

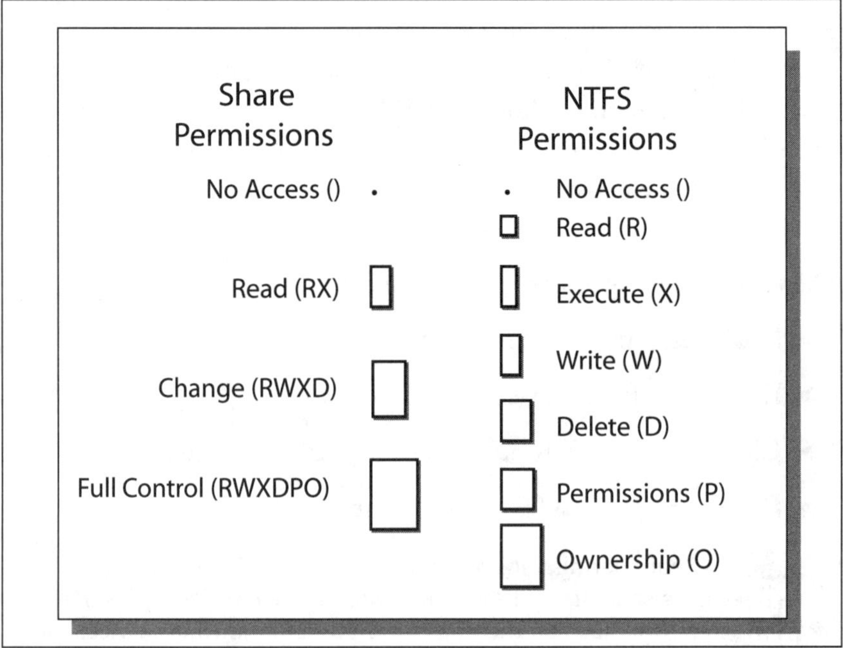

Figure 4.3 A visualization of share permissions in relation to NTFS object permissions.

Permission Combinations

Each time a user attempts to access an object, there are many hurdles that the user's security settings must pass to reach the object. The specified settings of the user account and each group membership must be examined for both the share and the object. Here are some items to keep in mind when deciphering permission combinations:

- No Access on the share or the object prevents all access, even if Full Control is granted by another group membership.
- The permissions from all groups of which a user is a member are cumulative. This applies both to shares and objects.
- The most restrictive set of common permissions between a share and an object apply.

In addition to access tokens and ACLs to control user abilities to access object and resources, Windows NT also provides a set of user rights, which we'll look at in the next section.

User Rights

User rights restrict or grant specific computer-based abilities to a user or group. User rights are assigned through the Policies menu of the User Manager For Domains.

There are 11 basic user rights and an additional 16 advanced rights. Through the User Rights Policy dialog box, you can view any of these rights, in addition to the users and groups to which each right is currently granted. Note that to view the advanced rights, you must check the Show Advanced User Rights option at the bottom of the dialog box.

The basic user rights, their purpose, and their members (in parentheses) are as follows:

- **Access computer from network** Logon or connect to this computer from a client on the network (Administrators, Everyone).
- **Add workstations to domain** Add computers to the domain database in Server Manager (none).

- **Back up files and directories** Back up files or directories on this server and bypass file permissions (Administrators, Backup Operators, System Operators).
- **Change system time** Change the time on the server (Administrators, System Operators).
- **Force remote shutdown** Issue a shutdown command remotely (Administrators, Server Operators).
- **Load/unload device drivers** Load device drivers on this server (Administrators).
- **Log on locally** Direct physical logon to this server (Administrators, Server Operators, Backup Operators, Account Operators, Print Operators).
- **Manage audit and logs** Manage audit details and work with log files (Administrators).
- **Restore files/directories** Restore files or directories from server backups (Administrators, Server Operators, Backup Operators).
- **Shut down the system** Shut down the system from the system console (Administrators, Server Operators, Backup Operators, Account Operators, Print Operators).
- **Take ownership of files or objects** Take ownership of files, directories, or objects (Administrators).

The advanced rights are used for programming and development instead of standard network administration. However, it is a good idea to at least be familiar with the names of these rights:

- Act as part of an operating system
- Bypass traverse checking
- Create a pagefile
- Create a token object
- Create permanent shared objects

- Debug programs
- Generate security audits
- Increase quotas
- Increase scheduling priority
- Lock pages in memory
- Log on as a batch job
- Log on as a service
- Modify firmware environment values
- Profile single process
- Profile system performance
- Replace process-level tokens

Practice Questions

Question 1

You need to gain access to a file named "VENDORS.TXT" in the newly created \\Sales\Documents shared folder in the Sales domain. You are a member of the Marketing domain. There is a trust relationship established so that the Sales domain trusts the Marketing domain. What additional settings must be made to offer you access to the VENDORS.TXT file?

❍ a. Set the Read permission on the Documents folder to your user account.

❍ b. Your user account must be added to the Everyone group in the Sales domain.

❍ c. None, Full Control to all trusted users is the default on all new shares.

❍ d. A new Sales domain-based user account must be created.

Answer c is correct. No action is required because your account becomes a member of the Sales domain Everyone group, which has Full Control to new shares by default. Assigning specific permissions for the object to your user account is not required because your account is a default member of the Everyone group and a new share offers Full Control to this group by default. Therefore, answer a is incorrect. Your user account automatically becomes a member of the Everyone group when your domain is trusted. Therefore, answer b is incorrect. You do not need a new account in the Sales domain to access the file. Therefore, answer d is incorrect.

Question 2

There are two domains within an organization: Sales and Research. New beta software has been deployed on the Research domain for testing, but four members of the Sales domain need to gain access to the beta software to aid in the test process. The beta software resides in an NTFS-based share named "WEBKIT2" on the BETA server in the Research domain. If the Research domain trusts the Sales domain, what additional steps are required to give the four Sales users access to the beta software?

- ❍ a. Create a global group in the Sales domain called "Sales_Beta" and add the four Sales users to this group. Create a local group called "Soft_Test" on server BETA with Full Control over the WEBKIT2 share. Add the Sales_Beta global group to the Soft_Test local group.
- ❍ b. Create new accounts for the Sales users in the Research domain.
- ❍ c. Remove the existing trust. Establish a new trust where the Sales domain trusts the Research domain. Create a global group in the Sales domain called "Sales_Beta" and add the four Sales users to this group. Create a local group called "Soft_Test" on server BETA with Full Control over the WEBKIT2 share. Add the Sales_Beta global group to the Soft_Test local group.
- ❍ d. Create a global group in the Sales domain called "Sales_Beta" and add the four Sales users to this group. Create a global group called "Soft_Test" on server BETA with Full Control over the WEBKIT2 share. Add the Sales_Beta global group to the Soft_Test global group.

Answer a is correct because it provides the proper sequence of steps required to give the Sales users access to the beta software. Adding new accounts to the Research domain is insecure and will result in twice the administration to maintain two accounts for each user. Therefore, answer b is incorrect. The existing trust will allow Sales users to use Research resources. Reversing the trust will prevent access and destroy other possible links currently relying on the trust. Therefore, answer c is incorrect. It is not possible to add a global group to another global group. Plus, Microsoft recommends using local groups to manage resource permissions. Therefore, answer d is incorrect.

Question 3

Your network uses the single master domain model where the CORP domain is the master. One of the resource domains, SALES, trusts the CORP domain. When a user logs on to the CORP domain using a computer attached to the SALES domain, what objects will that user be able to view?

- ❍ a. All objects in both the SALES and CORP domains for which the CORP\Domain Users group has been granted Read access
- ❍ b. All objects in both the SALES and CORP domains for which the SALES\Domain Users group has been granted Read access
- ❍ c. All objects in the SALES domain for which the SALES\Domain Guests group has been granted Read access
- ❍ d. All objects in both the SALES and CORP domains for which the CORP\Domain Guests group has been granted Read access

Answer a is correct. The use of the master domain model implies that all user accounts are present in the CORP domain. Thus, all user accounts are members of the CORP\Domain Users group. Because CORP is trusted by the SALES domain, every user who logs on through a SALES domain workstation will be able to view all objects to which permissions have been granted to the CORP\Domain Users group in either domain. The SALES\DomainUsers group is a null set because all users are in the CORP domain. Therefore, answer b is incorrect. The SALES\Domain Guests and CORP\Domain Guests groups do not have standard users as members. Therefore, answers c and d are both incorrect.

Question 4

Which of the following is not a directory or file standard permission?

- ❍ a. Read
- ❍ b. List
- ❍ c. Create Directory
- ❍ d. Change
- ❍ e. Add

Answer c is correct. Create Directory is not a permission. Read is both a directory and a file permission. Therefore, answer a is incorrect. List is a directory permission. Therefore, answer b is incorrect. Change is both a directory and file permission. Therefore, answer d is incorrect. Add is a directory permission. Therefore, answer e is incorrect.

Question 5

You attempt to add new information into a document stored on a remote server. Using the Documents share, you are able to locate and open the document into your word processor. You have Full Control of the object. You are a member of the Sales group. The Sales group has Read access to the Documents share. You are unable to save your changes to the file, why?

- ❍ a. You cannot edit documents over a network.
- ❍ b. Your resultant permissions for the file object are just Read.
- ❍ c. The Sales group has the Save privilege revoked.
- ❍ d. Only administrators can Save files over the network.

Answer b is correct. Accessing objects through shares results in the most restrictive shared permissions. It is possible to edit documents over a network. The only stipulation is that you must have the proper access level to modify remote objects. Therefore, answer a is incorrect. There is no Save privilege in the Windows NT environment. The Sales group merely has

Read access to the share. Therefore, answer c is incorrect. The ability to save documents (i.e., modify objects) is not limited to administrators. Therefore, answer d is incorrect.

Question 6

What are the recommended actions to increase security for the Administrator account? [Check all correct answers]

- ❑ a. Rename the Administrator account.
- ❑ b. Disable the Administrator account.
- ❑ c. Create user accounts for each system administrator and add them to the Administrators group.
- ❑ d. Use a blank password for the Administrator account.
- ❑ e. Use a difficult password for the Administrator account.

Answers a, c, and e are correct. Renaming the account is an improvement in security. Therefore, answer a is correct. Creating individual administrator accounts for each system admin is a good way to protect your network. Therefore, answer c is correct. Using a difficult password is a good security measure. Therefore, answer e is correct. It is not possible to disable this account. Therefore, answer b is incorrect. Using a blank password for the Administrator account is inviting trouble. Therefore, answer d is incorrect.

Question 7

Which of the following are attributes of an object? [Check all correct answers]

- ❑ a. Data
- ❑ b. ACL
- ❑ c. Services
- ❑ d. Name

Answers a, b, and d are correct. The data associated with an object is an attribute. Therefore, answer a is correct. The ACL of an object is an attribute.

Therefore, answer b is correct. The name of an object is an attribute. Therefore, answer d is correct. The services of an object are services, not attributes. Therefore, answer c is incorrect.

Question 8

You attempt to access a file in the NTFS directory share \UserGuide. Sales has Change access to the share. Marketing has Read access to the share. Accounting has No Access to the share. You have Full Control of the object. You are a member of all three groups. What are your resultant access privileges?

- ❍ a. No Access
- ❍ b. Read
- ❍ c. Change
- ❍ d. Full Control

Answer a is correct. No Access results if any group of which you are a member has No Access. Read is the access for the Marketing group, but you are also a member of the Accounting group, which has No Access. Therefore, answer b is incorrect. Change is the access for the Sales group, but you are also a member of the Accounting group, which has No Access. Therefore, answer c is incorrect. You have Full Control of the object only when accessing it directly. By using a share, you are restricted by your group settings that result in No Access. Therefore, answer d is incorrect.

Question 9

The Administrator account is a default member of what groups? [Check all correct answers]

- ❑ a. Domain Guests
- ❑ b. Domain Users
- ❑ c. Users
- ❑ d. Power Users
- ❑ e. Everyone

Answers b, c, and e are correct. The Domain Users group contains the Administrator account by default. Therefore, answer b is correct. The Users group contains the Administrator account by default. Therefore, answer c is correct. The Everyone group includes the administrator account. Therefore, answer e is correct. The Domain Guests group contains only the Guest account by default. Therefore, answer a is incorrect. Power Users is a group from Windows NT Workstation and Windows NT member servers; it is not present in Windows NT domain controllers. Therefore, answer d is incorrect.

Question 10

A network is comprised of two domains: SALES and CORP. The master domain is CORP, and SALES is the resource domain. SALES trusts CORP. Both domains have numerous servers and workstations. You want to create a group called "NetBack" that can perform backup operations on all computers throughout the network. Which of the following are required steps to accomplishing this goal? [Check all correct answers]

- ❑ a. Create a NetBack global group in the SALES domain.
- ❑ b. Create a NetBack global group in the CORP domain.
- ❑ c. Add the NetBack global group to the Backup Operators local group on each machine in both domains.
- ❑ d. Add the NetBack global group to the CORP\Domain Users group.
- ❑ e. Assign Read access to the NetBack global group for every file object on every machine in the network.

Answers b and c are correct. Creating the global group in the master domain is one of the correct steps. Therefore, answer b is correct. Adding the NetBack group to the local Backup Operators group is a required step. Therefore, answer c is correct. A global group in the resource domain cannot be granted any permissions from the master domain due to the nature of the one-way trust. Therefore, answer a is incorrect. The NetBack group should not be added to the Domain Users group, nor can it be, because both are global groups. Therefore, answer d is incorrect. Assigning Read permissions across the network is an unnecessary and worthless task. The act of adding the NetBack group to the Backup Operators group on each machine in effect performs this activity without compromising security. Therefore, answer e is incorrect.

Question 11

If no configuration changes have been made to a server, what prevents a standard user from logging on to a server by walking up to the local console?

- ❍ a. There is no restriction to prevent users from logging in.
- ❍ b. Servers don't allow anyone to log on to them.
- ❍ c. Log on locally user right is not assigned to standard users.
- ❍ d. The user has No Access permission set for the server object.

Answer c is correct. The log on locally right is not assigned to standard users specifically to prevent them from gaining easy access to the server. There is a default restriction to prevent general users from logging in locally to a server. It is the *log on locally* right, and it is not assigned to users by default. Therefore, answer a is incorrect. Servers allow members of the Administrators, Server Operators, Backup Operators, Account Operators, and Print Operators groups to log on to them. Therefore, answer b is incorrect. There is no server object to which No Access permissions apply. Therefore, answer d is incorrect.

Need To Know More?

Heywood, Drew: *Inside Windows NT Server, 2nd Edition.* New Riders, Indianapolis, IN, 1998. ISBN 1-56205-860-6. Chapters 2, 4, and 5 discuss rights, permission, and gaining access to resources.

Siyan, Karanjit S.: *Windows NT Server 4 Professional Reference, 2nd Edition.* New Riders, Indianapolis, IN, 1997. ISBN 1-56205-805-3. Chapters 7 and 9 have extensive coverage of the Windows NT domain accounts and security system.

The Windows NT Server 4 manuals cover planning, configuration, and installation issues quite well. The *Concepts And Planning Manual* Chapters 1, 2, and 4 contain lots of basic and background information on rights, permissions, and shared resources.

The *Windows NT Server Resource Kit* contains lots of useful information about Windows NT's NTFS, share, user, and group permissions. The TechNet CD or *Resource Kit* CD can be searched using keywords like "user rights," "permissions," and "share." The *Networking Guide* volume, Chapter 2, "Network Security And Domain Planning," is a great place to learn more about configuring users and groups for solid security and controlled access.

5

Optimizing Domain Use

Terms you'll need to understand:

- √ Primary Domain Controller (PDC)
- √ Backup Domain Controller (BDC)
- √ Member server
- √ Stand-Alone server
- √ Authentication
- √ User profiles
- √ System policies
- √ Domain browsers

Techniques you'll need to master:

- √ Establishing server roles
- √ Easing the user authentication load
- √ Setting up user profiles
- √ Managing user, group, and computer policies
- √ Administering the SAM database
- √ Maintaining domain controller synchronization

In Chapter 2, we discussed domain concepts. In this chapter, we continue the domain discussion with information on domain controllers, authentication, user profiles, system policies, and browsers.

Windows NT Server Roles

Windows NT Server can be one of three types of servers within a client/server network. The three server types are Primary Domain Controller (PDC), Backup Domain Controller (BDC), and member server. There is actually a fourth server classification, Stand-Alone server, but this is only used in relation to workgroup networks, and it is the same type of setup as a member server. In fact, the installation screen for Windows NT offers a choice of PDC, BDC, or Stand-Alone server. Thus, you should almost consider the terms "member server" and "Stand-Alone server" interchangeable.

PDCs and BDCs have additional server components installed that a member server does not have. These extra components enable the domain controllers to store and maintain the Security Accounts Manager (SAM) security database, plus handle account administration. A member server is a system that serves network resources to clients, such as files, printers, and applications. Other than the management of the SAM database, there is no difference between domain controllers and member servers.

You select which type of server to configure during installation. Once a server is installed as a domain controller, it cannot be changed to a member server, nor can a member server be changed to a domain controller without reinstalling Windows NT Server. This is due to the way the Registry is constructed for domain controllers. The entire system has to be reinitiated for the domain controller structure to be created or removed. However, PDCs and BDCs can switch roles without any significant hassle. A single domain can have only one PDC and any number of BDCs or member servers.

Just as every user account has a SID (Security ID), so does every server. Once a domain controller has been installed on a domain, it cannot change domains without being reinstalled. The domain itself can be renamed (a significant hassle in itself), but the domain controllers cannot be moved from one domain to another. This is because the SIDs of each domain controller are associated with a specific domain.

The PDC is the central storage and management server for the SAM database. This database maintains all security information for a domain. The SAM database on a PDC can be modified when needed, such as adding new accounts or changing group memberships. At regular intervals, the modifications to the SAM database are pushed out to the BDCs within the domain.

A BDC is a redundant system to protect the integrity and availability of the SAM database. BDCs are not able to make any changes or modifications, but they can use the database to authenticate users. Another benefit of BDCs is load balancing. A BDC shares the burden of authenticating users at logon. The domain controller closest to the machine being booted handles user authentication. If your network is large and uses WAN (wide area network) links, BDCs can be placed in the remote locations to handle local authentication without requiring the logon procedure to tie up the WAN link to communicate with the PDC. If your WAN link goes down, users can still log on through a BDC and access local resources. Having at least one BDC is recommended for redundancy and fault tolerance, even if you do not have a large network or WAN links.

A PDC must be fully installed to establish a network. Once the PDC is fully booted and operational, BDCs can be installed. You should always have a functioning network connection to a PDC when installing a BDC. The BDC must communicate with the PDC to establish a domain-based SID, create a computer account for the BDC computer, gain authority to interact with the SAM database, and make its first copy of the database.

If a PDC is not available, installation of the BDC will fail. Once you've installed one or more BDCs, then you can add member servers and clients. You can add additional BDCs at any time as long as a connection can be established to the PDC.

Domain Controller Synchronization

After the domain controllers have been installed, the PDC will regularly send out updates to the BDCs to keep their copies of the SAM database current. Because any domain controller can authenticate users, it is important for the database stored on each domain controller to be current and accurate. The process of maintaining accurate copies of the accounts database on the BDCs is called "synchronization."

There are two types of synchronization: partial and full. Partial is just the modifications made to the database since the last update. This is the fastest and most common form of synchronization. Full is when the PDC sends out the entire SAM database. This occurs when a new BDC is brought online or at other times. The BDC maintains a change log that lists the changes made to its copy of the database. When the log reaches 64 K (the default size for the log; maximum size is 4 MB)—about 2,000 changes—it requests a full synchronization from the PDC. Full synch can also occur when a BDC's database copy is found to be incomplete or when an administrator forces a full synch. In the following section, we continue our discussion of synchronization, with an eye toward synch management from the Windows NT Registry.

Synchronization Controls In The Windows NT Registry

Depending on the layout, size, and composition of your domain, altering the default settings for synchronization may improve the operation and reliability of your security system. The parameters for the synchronization process are stored in the NetLogon section of the Windows NT Registry.

Using either of the Windows NT Registry Editors—REGEDT32.EXE, or REGEDIT.EXE—open the following key:

```
HKEY_LOCAL_MACHINE\System\CurrentControlSet\Services\Netlogon\Parameters
```

Within this key, you can add or modify the following parameters to change how SAM database synchronization behaves:

- **Pulse (60 through 3,600 seconds)** Defines the typical pulse frequency. All SAM database changes since the last pulse are collected and sent to each BDC when the pulse time has expired. No pulse is sent to up-to-date BDCs. Default=300.

- **PulseConcurrency (1 through 500)** Defines the maximum number of BDCs that the PDC pulses simultaneously. By increasing the setting, you increase the load on the PDC. By decreasing the PulseConcurrency setting, you increase the time it takes to update the BDCs within the domain. Default=20.
- **PulseMaximum (60 through 86,400 seconds)** Sends every BDC a pulse at this interval, whether or not a BDC's SAM database is up-to-date. Default=7,200.
- **PulseTimeout1 (1 through 120 seconds)** Defines the amount of time a PDC will wait for a BDC to respond to a pulse. If the BDC does not respond within the specified time, it is considered nonresponsive. A domain with many nonresponsive BDCs takes longer to finish the synchronization process if the PulseTimeout setting is too high. On the other hand, if the setting is too low, the BDCs may be misjudged as unresponsive. A partial synchronization is received when the BDCs do respond. Default=5.
- **PulseTimeout2 (60 through 3,600 seconds)** Defines how long the PDC waits for a BDC to complete partial synchronization. It is necessary for the BDC to continue to make progress during the process of receiving a database synchronization. The BDC will be thought of as unresponsive if the BDC stops calling the PDC during a synchronization. If the number is too high, the BDC will be slow and take up one of the PulseConcurrency slots, which keeps the PDC from notifying another BDC at that time. If the number is too low, the load on the PDC will be increased if there many BDCs performing partial synchronization. Default=300.
- **Randomize (0 through 120 seconds)** Defines a back-off period for the BDCs. When the BDCs get a pulse from the PDC, they wait the "randomize" number of seconds before they call the PDC. Randomize should always be less than the PulseTimeout1 setting. Default=1.
- **ReplicationGovernor (0 through 100 percent)** Defines the packet size used in the synch process. Synchronization may take up more bandwidth than you are willing to use if it's running over a slow WAN link. To alter the amount of bandwidth consumed by synchronization, the ReplicationGovernor can be used to reduce the packet size used in the synch process to a percentage of the 128 K standard package. Too low a setting prevents synchronization from ever completing. A setting of zero prevents all synchronization from occurring. Default=100. This parameter only applies to BDCs.

That's it for synchronization. To further discuss domain optimization issues, we now turn our attention toward one of the most often used tools in Windows NT management, the Server Manager.

Server Manager Domain Controls

Through the Server Manager tool, you can perform numerous operations on domain controllers that you might find invaluable to the reliability of your network. These operations include controller promotion, synchronization, and adding computer accounts. The Computer menu from the Server Manager is where all of this takes place. First, highlight the server you wish to modify, then choose the appropriate command from the Computer pull-down menu.

Domain controller promotion is used to recover from a PDC failure. In the event of a PDC malfunction, each BDC continues to authenticate users, but it cannot make changes to the SAM database. A BDC can be promoted to a PDC to take over the responsibility of the failed system if the PDC cannot be brought back online quickly. The promoted machine functions as if it were the PDC all along. Once the failed PDC is repaired, it can be brought back online. This may result in two PDCs within a single domain. In such a case, one of the PDCs can be demoted using the Demote To BDC command. Note that this command only appears in the Computer menu when two PDCs are present in a domain.

The original PDC can resume its control over the network if its SID was not changed. Depending on the failure, you may need to completely reinstall Windows NT. In such a case, the old PDC should be installed as a BDC, then promoted back to a PDC once installation is complete. To help make this clearer, review the following section, "Disaster And Recovery Scenario."

Disaster And Recovery Scenario

A domain has SRVR-A as its PDC and SRVR-B as a BDC. The hard drive fails on SRVR-A, and a replacement is not readily available. The administrator promotes SRVR-B to a PDC. Later, SRVR-A is repaired, but the original NOS is destroyed. The administrator attaches SRVR-A to the network and performs a new installation of Windows NT, making

SRVR-A a BDC. After the installation is complete, the administrator forces a synchronization from the PDC SRVR-B. Then, the administrator promotes SRVR-A to a PDC. This restoration is possible without destroying or re-creating the domain because all domain controllers within a single domain share the same SID. In other words, when a BDC is installed into a domain, it assumes the SID of the existing PDC (see Knowledge Base document Q162001).

When Windows NT Server is reinstalled as a member server, that system is assigned a new SID. Even if nothing else about the computer changed (meaning the previous configuration was duplicated), it's considered a completely different computer. The only time a new SID is not assigned on a member server is when an upgrade installation is performed.

Synchronization can be forced. There are two variations to this command: Synchronize Entire Domain and Synchronize With The PDC. When you select a PDC and execute the synch command, the PDC sends out update information to every BDC in the domain. When you select a BDC, the BDC requests an update from the PDC, and no other BDCs are affected.

Creating computer accounts enables new systems to join the domain easily. The Add To Domain command can be used to create accounts for Windows NT Workstations, Windows NT Server member servers, or Windows NT Server BDCs. Every Windows NT Workstation- or Windows NT Server-based computer must have a computer account in a domain to participate as a member of the network. Using Server Manager to add a computer to the domain bypasses the need for the administrator's name and password during the installation of Windows NT on the new computer.

Now that we've covered the details of how PDCs and BDCs work, we continue the discussion with how these domain controllers authenticate users on the network.

Authentication With BDCs And PDCs

To take advantage of distributed authentication, you must duplicate all scripts, profiles, and policies from the PDC to each BDC. This is accomplished using the Replication service. For details on configuring this service, see Chapter 6.

Logon scripts must be stored in the \Winnt\System32\Repl\Export\Scripts directory. Then, as part of configuring replication, make sure you replicate (import) to your export server. This places the scripts in the \Winnt\System32\Repl\Import\Scripts directory, which is shared by the system as NetLogon. Thus, as described in the next section, a user's profile can point to NetLogon\MYSCRIPT.BAT, and the user will always load script from the NetLogon share from the authenticating domain controller.

A User profile must be translated into a roaming profile and stored in a publicly accessible share to be useful for a roaming user. By taking advantage of the existing NetLogon share, roaming profiles can be stored in a subdirectory of \Winnt\System32\Repl\Export, such as \Profiles, and referenced with NetLogon\Profiles\%username%\.

System policies should also be stored in the \Winnt\System32\Repl\Export\Scripts directory. Thus, they can be referenced by the NetLogon share and are present in the import directory of all BDCs (at least those configured to replicate).

The storage of items in the export directory is only useful when the Replication service is being used. All items placed in the export directory will be copied into the import directory. Once in the import directory, the items can be referenced using the NetLogon share, because this share points to the import directory.

The Replication service included on the original Windows NT 4 CD is defective and does not work properly. Install SP3 (or higher) to fix the problem.

Continuing our discussions of how users are authenticated and retain important settings, let's move on to what Microsoft says regarding this important system information.

Domain Database Info

Microsoft recommends that the domain database maintained by the PDCs and BDCs not exceed 40 MB. Each domain database stores three types of information: user accounts, computer accounts, and group accounts. Each user account requires 1 K, and each computer account requires 0.5 K. Global groups require 512 bytes, plus 12 bytes for each user within the group; local groups also require 512 bytes, plus 36 bytes for each user or global group within the group. Therefore, a 40 MB domain database can maintain 25,000 user accounts (25 MB), 25,000 computer accounts (12.5 MB), and 400 group accounts with 400 members each (2.5 MB). (Unfortunately, the only way to determine the size of the SAM or domain database is to calculate it manually.)

With these domain settings in mind, we move forward to explore how to set up access rights and system settings through the use of user profiles.

User Profiles

A user profile is simply the configuration and environmental settings for a user's desktop, menus, network connections, color scheme, and personal applications. User profiles enable a number of people to use a workstation, while retaining each person's customized settings. By default, all user profiles are local, meaning they only apply to a single machine. But user profiles can be configured so they roam with the user to any workstation attached to the domain.

User profiles are either mandatory or customizable. A mandatory profile does not save any changes made by a user, whereas a customizable profile does save changes (hence the name). Mandatory profiles lend themselves well to group usage, because everyone sees the same setup and no user can make changes. Customizable profiles should only be assigned to a single user, so users won't change each other's settings.

A new customizable profile is created when a user logs on for the first time, or a mandatory profile can be assigned by the administrator during the account creation process. All profiles are created by logging in as a user and making whatever changes are desired. During logoff, all changes are saved. If the NTUSER.DAT file is renamed to "NTUSER.MAN", then a customizable profile becomes a mandatory profile. Thus, an administrator can create a user, log in as that user, modify the environment, log off, log back in as administrator, rename the DAT file to ".MAN," then assign the new mandatory profile, as needed.

By default, all user profiles are stored in the \Winnt\ Profiles directory. A subdirectory with the same name as the user's account name is created, and the profile information is stored within the subdirectory. One of the files stored in a profile is the NTUSER.DAT file. If the workstation is a Windows 95 machine, this file is named "USER.DAT". The profiles stored by Windows 95 and Windows NT are not compatible, but by changing USER.DAT to USER.MAN, you get a mandatory Windows 95 user profile.

> Once a profile is created, it can be turned into a roaming profile using the System application located in the Control Panel. The User Profiles tab offers you the ability to copy a profile to an alternate location, such as the \Winnt\System32\Repl\Export directory. Once copied, you can set the copied profile to be a roaming profile.
>
> Once a roaming profile has been created, you can assign that profile to a user (or users, if it is a mandatory profile). This is done through the User Manager For Domains. Open the properties for a user, click the Profile button, then type in the UNC name in the User Profile Path text box, such as \\PDC1\NetLogon\%username%.

Let's move on with our discussion of profiles. In the following section, we explain what happens when a user is unable to download the most recent copy of his or her profile.

Using A Cached Profile On Slow Connections

Roaming user profiles are helpful for maintaining a consistent desktop. However, when users log on to a domain via a slow connection, downloading the user profiles might cause a needless delay (this is especially true if the profiles are the same as they were during their last logon).

Users might want to use a locally cached profile rather than a centrally located profile if the logon process is taking an unusually long time. In the System Properties dialog box, under the User Profiles tab, there is a checkbox for this purpose.

In addition to user profiles, you can also maintain user settings through the use of a system policy, which we discuss next.

Managing Windows NT Policies

A Windows NT system policy is a configuration file that presets the system configuration for a user, group, or computer. System policies actually edit the Registry of the local computer to reflect the changes prescribed by the administrator-defined policy. System policies are created and modified through the System Policy Editor.

Initially, no restrictions are enabled in the default policies. They must be created and implemented by an administrator. This gives you the greatest breadth of freedom with the operation and configuration of your user's network environment. As a general rule, it is unwise to edit a Default User or Default Computer policy. Default policies apply to everyone, including the administrator. It is not too difficult to create a policy that restricts a user and a computer so much that nothing can be done—so much so that you could not even correct your mistake without reinstalling Windows NT.

In addition to the default and system policies, you can also create policies for individual users, computers, and groups, as we explain in the following section.

User, Group, And Computer Policies

User and group policies modify the HKEY_CURRENT_USER section of the Registry, whereas computer policies alter the HKEY_LOCAL_MACHINE section. Once again, policies overwrite existing Registry settings on the local machine to enforce the settings defined in that policy. User policies can apply to a specific user or to all users (called "Default User"). Likewise, computer policies can apply to a specific computer or to all computers (called "Default Computer"). Group policies can only apply to a specific group.

User and group policies can be used to set, alter, or control access to:

- Screen saver
- Appearance
- Wallpaper
- Color scheme
- Shell restrictions (Shut Down, save on exit, Network Neighborhood, hiding drives)
- Registry editing
- Windows application restrictions

- Custom folders
- Explorer access

Computer policies can be used to set, alter, or control access to:

- Network updates
- Simple Network Management Protocol (SNMP) configuration info
- Startup applications
- Hidden drive shares
- Printer settings
- RAS callback settings
- Custom shell settings
- Logon policies
- User profile handling

User, group, and computer policies are automatically applied based on their names. When a new policy is created, you must assign it a name. A user policy should be given a user's name, a group policy a group's name, and a computer policy a computer's name. It is recommended that you first create each user, group, or computer before creating a policy that applies to it.

The logon system looks for system policies in the NetLogon share. All policies are stored in a single file called "NTCONFIG.POL." This should be saved in the \Winnt\System32\Repl\Export \Scripts directory so it can be accessible throughout the domain.

When more than one policy can apply to a user, the following priority order is used:

1. If a user has a user policy, it takes priority over all group-related policies.
2. If a user does not have a user policy, then all group-related policies are merged (see the following).
3. If a user has no specified policies, the default user policy applies.

When more than one group applies to a single user, the predefined group priority settings are used. This is defined through the System Policy Editor's Options|Group Priorities command. Settings in a priority group (i.e., higher in the list) apply to a user instead of the settings on the same parameters from other groups.

Note: *Only a single policy is used on a user except in the case of group policies, where all applicable policies are merged based on priority.*

Hardware Profiles

Hardware profiles are useful for notebook computers with PC Card (previously called PCMCIA) slots and/or docking stations. Multiple hardware profiles can be defined so only the drivers needed for a particular hardware configuration are loaded and system errors may be avoided. Hardware profiles are controlled through the Hardware Profiles tab of the System application, which is located in the Control Panel. The main settings indicate whether the current configuration is docked and if network access is available.

Now that we have discussed how to manage access by users to network resources, let's examine how Windows NT makes those resources available, starting with the Windows NT Browser service.

Browsers

The Windows NT Browser service maintains a list of all network resources within a domain and provides lists of these domains, servers, and resource objects to any Explorer-type interface that requests it (e.g., browse lists).

Each computer within a domain participates in the Browser service. Each time a computer is brought up within the domain, it announces itself and the resources it has to share (if any). This is the most common level of participation for computers within a domain. The most important role within the Browser service is that of the Master Browser. The Master Browser maintains the main list of all available resources within a domain (including links to external domains).

Note: On some TCP/IP networks, another role—the Domain Master Browser (DMB)—is used to enable resource lists to be accessed across subnets within the same domain. By default, the DMB is the PDC. Plus, a Master Browser is present on each subnet.

Two other important roles are the Backup Browser and the Potential Browser. The Backup Browser maintains a duplicate list of the resources and acts within the Browser Service much as a BDC does within a domain. A Backup Browser can serve lists of resources to clients. A Potential Browser is any machine capable of becoming a Backup or Master Browser. As needed, the Browser service changes the role of a machine from Potential Browser to Backup Browser. Within any domain, the Browser service attempts to maintain the maximum of three Backup Browsers, but any number of Potential Browsers can exist.

Only the following computer setups can serve as Potential Browsers:

- Windows NT Server 3.5 or higher
- Windows NT Advanced Server 3.1
- Windows NT Workstation 3.1 or higher
- Windows 95 or Windows 98
- Windows For Workgroups 3.11

Any of these computer setups can also be designated as non-browsers so they will not participate in supporting browser lists, except to announce themselves upon boot-up.

In the next few sections, we continue our discussion of the Browser service. This includes how Master Browsers are chosen (elected), in addition to how the browse list is maintained and how it can be managed through the Windows NT Registry.

Browser Election

When a Master Browser goes offline, or when another machine that has the ability to claim the role of Master Browser comes online, an election occurs. The results of the election determine which machine becomes the active Master Browser. An election packet is transmitted by the new computer or by a Backup once the Master is no longer detected. This packet travels to each potential browser within the domain. The winner of the election is determined by the following hierarchy of criteria (presented in order of priority):

- **Operating System** Windows NT Servers, Windows NT Workstations, Windows 98, Windows 95, WFW
- **Operating System Version** Windows NT 4.0, 3.51, 3.5, Windows 98, Windows 95, WFW 3.11, and Windows NT Advanced Server 3.1.
- **Current Browser Role** Master Browser, Backup Browser, Potential Browser
- **Alphabetical** Further election is resolved through the alphabetical order of the computer names

List Maintenance

When a computer comes online, it announces itself. Initially, it announces itself once a minute, with the interval increasing to once every 12 minutes. This repeated announcement is used by the Master Browser to determine if a resource is still available. The Master Browser maintains the list of resources for any machine for three missed announcements to accommodate performance dips and communication bottlenecks. Thus, after a machine has been up and running for a reasonable time, then goes offline, its resources can remain in the Master Browser's list for up to 36 minutes.

Backup Browsers poll the Master Browser every 15 minutes to request an updated version of the browse list. Therefore, a failed resource can remain in the Backup Browser's list for up to 51 minutes. If a Backup Browser requests an update from the Master and receives no response, it initiates an election.

Browser And The Registry

The status of any Potential Browser can be altered through two Registry parameters. The parameters are located in HKEY_LOCAL_MACHINE\SYSTEM\CurrentControlSet\Services\Browser\Parameters. The first value, **MaintainServerList**, determines whether a machine can be a potential browser. It can have a value of **No, Yes,** or **Auto. No** sets the machine to be a non-browser. **Yes** forces the machine to be a Master or Backup Browser. And, **Auto** allows the Browser Service to determine the role as needed. The second value, **IsDomainMaster,** sets the machine to be the Master Browser. It can take the values of **True** or **False**.

Practice Questions

Question 1

You are the administrator of domain SALES1. There are no BDCs within SALES1. A power outage destroys some system files on the PDC. You attempt to correct the problem by reinstalling a new version of Windows NT onto the PDC machine. After the installation, no workstations are able to connect to SALES1. What could be the problem?

❍ a. The PDC was disconnected from the network.

❍ b. A member server was automatically promoted to PDC status, and it is in conflict with the reinstalled PDC.

❍ c. The new installation of Windows NT created a new SID for the PDC.

❍ d. A BDC in a trusting domain promoted itself to act as the PDC in SALES1. The reinstalled PDC has caused a control conflict.

Answer c is correct. The SID of the PDC is the defining element of a domain, not its name. Thus, the new SID created a new domain in which none of the workstations is a member. The PDC was not disconnected from the network, instead the new SID of the PDC is the culprit. Therefore, answer a is incorrect. Member servers can never be domain controllers. Therefore, answer b is incorrect. BDCs in trusting domains cannot authenticate users nor can they act as PDCs for the trusted domain. Therefore, answer d is incorrect.

Question 2

You want to establish a standard desktop configuration for the entire Sales group. Which of the following tactics will provide you with this result?

- ❍ a. Create a computer policy, and restrict access to change the desktop environment.
- ❍ b. Establish a user profile with the desktop configuration you wish to use, rename the NTUSER.DAT file to "NTUSER.MAN", and set this user profile for each member of the Sales group.
- ❍ c. Create a group policy restricting access to the desktop configuration controls.
- ❍ d. Establish a user profile, and set this profile for each member of the Sales group.

Answer b is correct. Creating a mandatory user profile is the correct method to establish a standard desktop configuration for a group. A computer policy restricts a machine from accessing certain applications to prevent changes or alterations to the environment. A computer policy would prevent users from changing any settings, but it does not establish a common desktop configuration. Therefore, answer a is incorrect. A group policy acts the same as a computer policy, but it restricts members of a group. No matter what machine they are using, group policies do not set a configuration but can be used to prevent change to a configuration. Therefore, answer c is incorrect. A customizable profile, the type created by default, can be altered by users. Thus, it would not create a standard configuration. Therefore, answer d is incorrect.

Question 3

Your network includes five domains in a single master domain model configuration. Where should you place the logon scripts to make administration simplest?

❍ a. On the PDC in the trusted domain

❍ b. In the PDC's \Winnt\System32\Repl\Export\Scripts directory within each trusting domain

❍ c. Within the NetLogon share of each domain

❍ d. On the local workstations

Answer a is correct. The PDC of the trusted domain, i.e., the user domain, is the best place for administration control of user scripts. The PDCs within the trusting domains, i.e., the resource domains, are not used to authenticate users. Plus, there are many of these machines, thereby increasing the administration difficulty. Therefore, answer b is incorrect. The NetLogon share within each domain is the same problem presented in answer b—multiple administration sites within non-authenticating domains. Therefore, answer c is incorrect. A local workstation is not the correct place to store logon scripts, especially for easy administration. Therefore, answer d is incorrect.

Question 4

Bob received a promotion that includes a new office with a great view. The new office has a better computer than he was using before, so he decides to use it instead of dragging his old one in. Previously, Bob had only used one machine and never moved about the organization. But when Bob logs on using his new computer, which runs the same OS as his old computer, he is surprised to find that his wallpaper, Start menu items, drive mappings, and color scheme are different. What could account for this?

- ❍ a. Bob has been reassigned a mandatory user profile.
- ❍ b. Bob mistakenly logs in with the Load Default Profile option selected in the WinLogon box.
- ❍ c. Bob's new computer is not compatible with his previous desktop settings.
- ❍ d. Bob's user profile is not roaming.

Answer d is correct. Bob never moved around the organization previously, so, the administrator probably never bothered to set his profile to roaming. A profile assignment would remove Bob's previous settings from appearing, but this situation does not lean toward this as a solution, because most promotions improve one's computer access and control instead of reduce it. Therefore, answer a is incorrect. There is no such Load Default Profile option anywhere within Windows NT. Therefore, answer b is incorrect. User profiles are not dependent on the computer hardware to function, but rather the OS. Because both machines Bob used supported the same OS, compatibility is not an issue. Therefore, answer c is incorrect.

Question 5

A system administrator installs Windows NT onto a new server. She wants to restrict everyone's ability to use the new server other than herself. She attempts to impose such a restriction by editing the default user policy and restricting all possible options. The next time she logs onto this server, she discovers that she is unable to do anything with the machine. What has happened?

- ❍ a. The new computer hardware has a mechanical fault.
- ❍ b. The default user policy affects the Administrator.
- ❍ c. The system administrator failed to log on using the Administrator account.
- ❍ d. The PAGEFILE.SYS file has been deleted.

Answer b is correct. The default user policy affects even the Administrator, so by restricting everything, the computer is worthless. Windows NT will have to be reinstalled to correct the problem. If the system is able to boot and log a user in, then it is not a hardware-related fault. The system is operational on the current hardware. Therefore, answer a is incorrect. Even if the system administrator failed to log in with the Administrator account, every user attempting to use this computer will be so restricted. Therefore, answer c is incorrect. The PAGEFILE.SYS file is not associated with this problem, but if it was deleted, the system would rebuild it during bootup. Therefore, answer d is incorrect.

Question 6

Users complain that network performance is poor during the early part of the day and right after lunch—the times when users are authenticated by the domain controllers. Currently, there is one PDC and two BDCs within the domain. You inspect the performance levels of the domain controllers and determine that they are operating at acceptable levels. What is the best way to improve network performance?

- ❍ a. Add additional BDCs.
- ❍ b. Increase the RAM on all servers.
- ❍ c. Decrease the Pulse Registry setting on the PDC.
- ❍ d. Install an additional PDC in the domain.

Answer a is correct. Adding additional BDCs will improve network performance by distributing the user authentication. Adding RAM to the servers will not improve the network performance because the performance levels are acceptable. Therefore, answer b is incorrect. Decreasing the Pulse Registry setting would have a negative effect on performance by increasing background network traffic. Therefore, answer c is incorrect. Only one PDC can exist within a domain. Therefore, answer d is incorrect.

Question 7

Which of the following computer systems can act as a Potential Browser? [Check all correct answers]

- ❑ a. Windows NT Server 4
- ❑ b. Windows 3.1
- ❑ c. Windows NT Server 3.51
- ❑ d. Windows For Workgroups 3.11
- ❑ e. Windows NT Workstation 3.5
- ❑ f. OS/2 Warp

Answers a, c, d, and e are correct. Windows NT Server 4, Windows NT Server 3.51, WFW 3.11, and Windows NT Workstation 3.5 are all valid system types that can be Potential Browsers. Windows 3.1 and OS/2 Warp are invalid system types for Potential Browsers. Therefore, answers b and f are incorrect.

Question 8

What is the minimum number of user domains you must have in a multiple master domain model to support 35,000 users, 35,000 computers, and 300 global groups with 600 members each?

- ❍ a. 1
- ❍ b. 2
- ❍ c. 3
- ❍ d. 4

Answer b is correct. Let's start with some math: 35,000 users require 35 MB of storage space at 1 KB per user; 35,000 computers require 17.5 MB of storage space at 512 bytes per computer; 300 global groups with 600 members each require 2.2 MB. This totals 54.7 MB. Because the maximum size for a SAM database is 40 MB, this indicates that two domains will be required, at a minimum. Answer a does not furnish enough space to contain all this data, whereas answers c and d exceed the minimum storage requirement.

Question 9

Your domain consists of two groups of computers connected by a long-distance WAN link. There are multiple BDCs located in each group. The available bandwidth of the WAN link must be maximized. Which of the following changes to the domain controller synchronization will reduce the load placed on the link by the PDC and the BDCs? [Check all correct answers]

- ❑ a. Set Pulse to 60
- ❑ b. Set PulseConcurrency to 1
- ❑ c. Set PulseMaximum to 60
- ❑ d. Set MaintainServerList to Auto
- ❑ e. Set ReplicationGovernor to 50

Answers b and e are correct. Setting PulseConcurrency to its lowest positive value (1) updates one BDC for each Pulse interval, thus reducing WAN traffic. Therefore, answer b is correct. Setting the ReplicationGovernor to 50 percent will reduce the packet size transmitted over the WAN. More packets will be required, but each one uses less bandwidth. Therefore, answer e is correct. Setting Pulse to a low value (60) causes updates to take place too frequently and places extra traffic on the WAN link. Therefore, answer a is incorrect. Setting PulseMaximum low (60) forces a full update more often. Therefore, answer c is incorrect. MaintainServerList is a browser setting, not a domain controller synchronization setting. Therefore, answer d is incorrect.

Question 10

Your network has a single BDC to protect the PDC. During a storm, your PDC's motherboard and hard drives are destroyed. Which of the following activities can help you restore your network to proper working order?

- ❍ a. Promote the BDC to a PDC.
- ❍ b. Restore the data saved to a backup tape from the failed PDC to the current BDC.
- ❍ c. Repair the failed machine, and reinstall Windows NT as a BDC on this machine.
- ❍ d. Repair the failed machine, and reinstall Windows NT as a PDC on this machine.
- ❍ e. Replace the damaged devices, then restore the system from backup.

Answer e is correct. Only replacing the damaged devices and restoring the PDC from backup will bring the network back into proper working order. It's not possible to promote a BDC if the PDC is not present. Therefore, answer a is incorrect. Restoring data from a PDC backup to a BDC machine could render the system DOA, and because you only have a single BDC, it's not worth gambling with the status of the one functioning domain controller that can still authenticate users. Therefore, answer b is incorrect. Reinstalling Windows NT as a BDC will not be possible because a PDC is required to complete the installation. Therefore, answer c is incorrect. Reinstalling Windows NT as a PDC will not be possible because that would create a new domain that does not include the configuration or user accounts from the existing domain. Therefore, answer d is incorrect.

Need To Know More?

Donald, Lisa, and James Chellis: *MSCE: NT Server 4 In The Enterprise Study Guide, 2nd Edition*. Sybex Network Press, San Francisco, CA, 1998. ISBN 0-7821-2221-3. Chapter 1 contains information on domain controllers and server roles. Chapter 7 runs the gamut on domain management. User profiles and system policies are covered in Chapter 5. The Browser service is examined in Chapter 7.

Heywood, Drew: *Inside Windows NT Server, 2nd Edition*. New Riders, Indianapolis, IN, 1998. ISBN 1-56205-860-6. Chapter 5 discusses domain controllers and synchronization. Chapter 10 discusses user profiles and system policies. Brief information about browsers is contained in Chapter 15 on pages 733 through 735.

Siyan, Karanjit S.: *Windows NT Server 4 Professional Reference, 2nd Edition*. New Riders, Indianapolis, IN, 1997. ISBN 1-56205-805-3. Chapters 5 and 6 contain detailed information about domain synchronization, promotion, and other domain issues. Chapter 8 delves into user profiles and system policies. The Browser service is examined in Chapter 19.

The Windows NT Server 4 manuals cover planning, configuration, and installation issues quite well. The *Concepts And Planning Manual* contains domain controller, server role, synchronization, user profiles, system policies, and Browser service issue discussions.

The *Windows NT Server Resource Kit* contains lots of useful information about Windows NT's fault tolerance. The TechNet CD (or its online version at **www.microsoft.com**) can be searched using keywords like "domain controller," "synchronization," "user profiles," "system policies," and "browser service." In the *Networking Guide*, Chapter 2, "Network Security And Domain Planning," contains information on domain controllers and synchronization. Plus, Chapter 3, "Windows NT Browser Service," focuses on the Browser service.

6 Windows NT Redundancy And Fault Tolerance

Terms you'll need to understand:

- √ Fault tolerance
- √ Directory Replication service
- √ Import server
- √ Export server
- √ Partitions
- √ Primary partition
- √ Extended partition
- √ Redundant Array of Inexpensive Disks (RAID)
- √ Volume set

Techniques you'll need to master:

- √ Understanding and implementing fault tolerance
- √ Installing and configuring Windows NT's Directory Replication service
- √ Familiarization with Disk Administrator
- √ Restoring data through fault tolerance
- √ Implementing and configuring backup

The Windows NT operating system is designed to provide reliable network services. The reliability of Windows NT rests upon many specialized features, including domain synchronization, directory replication, fault tolerance, and backup. In this chapter, we cover domain controllers, replication, and fault tolerance.

Domain Controllers

The broad and complex topic of domain controllers is discussed in detail in the previous chapter, but we include it here, as well, to emphasize its role in Windows NT's system reliability.

The Microsoft domain concept prescribes that each domain should have at least one Backup Domain Controller (BDC) to mirror and support the Primary Domain Controller (PDC). Because the PDC is the central control point for the entire Security Accounts Manager (SAM) security database, it is an important component of your network. A BDC is the only reliable method for maintaining a realtime duplicate of the SAM database. If the PDC goes offline for any reason, a BDC will continue to support user authentication in its stead. However, a BDC cannot record new security information, so you need to restore your PDC as quickly as possible or upgrade the BDC to a PDC.

One of the benefits of BDCs when the PDC is still active is that BDCs can still authenticate users. In fact, if a BDC is electronically closer to the user than a PDC, it will most likely handle the authentication and serving of user profiles, logon scripts, and system policies. This results in load balancing that improves the overall performance of the network. However, for this process to really work, you'll need to use the Directory Replication service, as described in the next section.

Note: Please refer to Chapter 5 for complete details on the PDC and BDC relationship, synchronization, and disaster recovery for domain controllers.

Directory Replication

Another aspect of Windows NT redundancy is directory replication. This service is designed to disseminate often-used and regularly updated data (such as user profiles, logon scripts, and system policies) to multiple computers to speed file access and improve reliability. Some early Microsoft documentation also claimed this service was useful for distributing large directory trees, but this suggestion has recently been repealed. The level of traffic caused by the Replication service would affect almost any network adversely if more than 2 MB of data was replicated.

When studying for the Enterprise exam, you need to assume that the Directory Replication service works as advertised. In the real world, Windows NT's original Replication service fails regularly, straight out of the box. But, the Replication service was repaired in Service Pack 3.

Replication is a simple concept, but it's a bit tricky to implement. The Replication service is not enabled or even set up by default. Microsoft left that task up to you. We'll briefly list all the steps you need to know about replication setup.

Replication is the process of duplicating a directory and its contents from an export server to any number of import servers. Any Windows NT Server can act as an export server, but both Windows NT Server and Workstation machines, plus LAN Manager servers, can be import servers.

All data placed in an export server's export directory will be duplicated to all import servers' import directories. By default, the export directory is:

```
\Winnt\System32\Repl\Export\
```

And the default import directory is:

```
\Winnt\System32\Repl\Import\
```

All directories beneath these two directories are under the control of the Replication service. Any files added to the export directory will eventually appear in the import directory. Only subdirectories under the export directory will be replicated, not

> files in the export directory itself. Any files deleted from the export directory tree will be removed from the import directory. In other words, the service performs whatever actions are necessary to ensure that the import directory exactly matches the export directory tree.

Beneath these directories is a default standard directory named "Scripts". This is where logon scripts are usually placed. Plus, the NetLogon share points to the \Import\Scripts directory. This makes defining user profiles easy by allowing the general share name to proceed the script name, such as "NETLOGON\BOB.BAT." Thus, when a BDC or PDC authenticates that user, it knows to grab the file from the closest NetLogon share.

Now that we have covered the basics of what directory replication is and what it does, let's move on to discuss how to get it up and running.

Installing Replication

The steps for initiating replication are as follows:

1. Create a replication user account with the following data:
   - User name: ReplUser
   - Password: (Any will do. The service will change it once it is activated, but you'll need one to get it started.)
   - Deselect: User Must Change Password At Next Logon
   - Select: Password Never Expires
   - Group Membership: Replicator
2. Configure the Directory Replicator service in the Services application in Control Panel using the Startup button:
   - Startup Type: Automatic
   - Logon As: ReplUser
   - Password: (As entered for the account.)
3. Configure directory replication through the Server Manager, open the Properties dialog box for the export

or import server (by double-clicking the computer name), and click the Replication button.

- If Export: Select the Export Directories radio button. The default directory will appear in the From Path field.
- If Import: Select the Import Directories radio button. The default directory will appear in the To Path field.
- Click Add under Export or Import, and select the computer to export to or import from.

4. Place material in the Export directory.
5. Reboot all export and import servers.

A few important items regarding replication:

- Replication will not work if any application is accessing or viewing the export or import directories. This causes the file system to lock and prevents replication. The service treats this as if changes are being made to files, and it is designed to wait until files and directories are inactive before replicating.
- The Manage button found in the Directory Replication on COMPUTERNAME dialog box of the Properties window of a server in Server Manager offers some information about the status of replication:
    - **OK** Replication was successful.
    - **No Master** The import server is not receiving updates from the export server, or the replication service may not be running.
    - **No Sync** This means there was an incomplete replication (e.g., communication errors, locked files, and so forth).
    - **[blank]** No replication has been attempted.
    - The Application log of the Event Viewer displays error messages from the Replication service. The error codes can be deciphered using the following command prompt command:

```
NET HELPMSG <error message number>
```

- The export directory can be hosted on a FAT or NTFS partition.
- Replication will only occur between computers with system clocks that are set within 59 minutes of each other. Thus, servers in different time zones will not replicate.
- All applications should point (or pull) from an import directory only.
- Use the Replication service only for small and important security data. For large or noncritical data, use the **AT** command with an xcopy batch file (or one of the great copy programs in the Resource Kit utilities).
- Always export to the import directory on your export server.

Additional Replication Configuration

Replication from the export server to the import servers will occur every five minutes. This default setting can be changed by editing the following Registry key:

```
HKEY_LOCAL_MACHINE\SYSTEM\CurrentControlSet\Services\Replicator\Parameters
```

The value **Interval** controls how often broadcasts are sent from the export server. **Interval** can have a value of 1 through 60 minutes (it is of data type **REG_DWORD**).

Another important entry in this key is **GuardTime**. This is the number of minutes the export server will wait after a directory becomes stable before attempting to replicate. The default value is two minutes, but it can be set from zero to one-half of **Interval** (it is also of data type **REG_DWORD**).

These are the only two replication items related to the Registry that you need to be aware of. There are additional keys and values referenced in the *Resource Kit* that you should examine if you plan on using this service.

Now that we have covered directory replication, let's move on to discuss keeping your data safe through the use of Windows NT's built-in fault tolerance features.

Fault Tolerance

The specific topics that fall under the heading of fault tolerance for Windows NT Server include: disk mirroring, disk duplexing, and disk striping (both with and without parity). Other relevant fault tolerance topics include disaster recovery, using Windows NT's built-in Disk Administrator utility, and several general storage, controller, and bootup matters.

All the fault tolerant features of Windows NT are focused on, or at least related to, the Disk Administrator utility. This makes it imperative to examine this tool thoroughly so you understand Microsoft's implementation of fault tolerance for Windows NT Server.

Disk Administrator

The better your knowledge of the Disk Administrator's tools and menus (see Figure 6.1), the better you will be able to implement the available disk

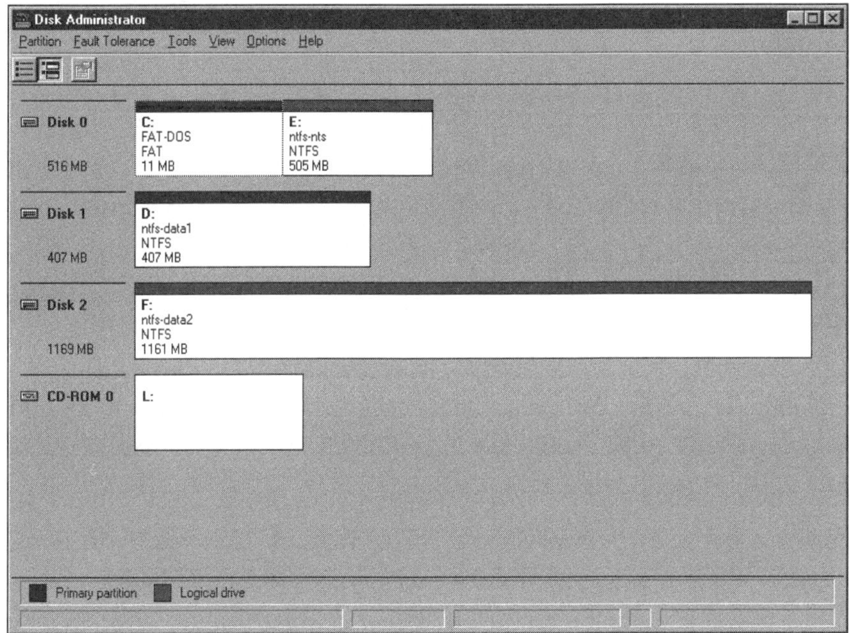

Figure 6.1 The Disk Administrator utility.

configurations. Disk Administrator appears beneath the Start Menu, in the Programs|Administrative Tools (Common) menu.

One important command is the Commit Changes Now option in the Partition menu. This command instructs Windows NT to make your requested changes to the affected storage devices. In other words, partitions and drives will not be created or changed in Disk Administrator until this menu option is chosen.

We have examined the basics of Windows NT's fault tolerance, but let's step back a moment and examine the specifics of setting up a secure disk structure.

Disk Structure 101

Hopefully, you are already familiar with storage devices and the terminology used to describe their configuration and operation. But just to be sure you're equipped with the bare minimum of such information, here's a short refresher on partitions, volumes, drive letters, and the Master Boot Record. In addition, it's important to understand Windows NT's implementation of RAID, which is covered in detail later in the chapter.

Partitions

Hard drives are subdivided into partitions. Each partition can contain one file system, each of which enables an OS or NOS to store and retrieve files. Even though Windows NT only supports FAT and NTFS natively, partitions that support other file systems can reside on a machine that runs Windows NT, even if Windows NT cannot access them. For instance, it's possible that a drive on a dual-boot machine running Windows 98 and Windows NT Server 4 could contain a FAT32 partition. In that case, only Windows 98 could access that partition.

In general, a hard drive can contain from 1 through 32 separate partitions. Thus, a single physical hard drive can appear as multiple logical drives. Hard drives should be partitioned to maximize their usage by the underlying NOS and its applications. If you attempt to change a partition, any information stored in that disk space will be destroyed. If there is free unpartitioned space on a drive, you may create new partitions without damaging existing partitions. Likewise, deleting any one partition does not affect other partitions on a drive.

The NTFS file system supports a variety of partition schemes. A single drive may contain up to four primary partitions, or one through three primary partitions and a single extended partition. An extended partition can be further subdivided into multiple logical drives. But the total number of primary partitions, plus logical drives, cannot exceed 32 on any one physical hard drive under Windows NT's control.

Volumes

A volume is an organizational structure imposed on one or more partitions that support file storage. If you select one or more partitions on a physical drive and format them with a specific file system, the resulting disk structure is a volume. Under Windows NT, volumes can even span multiple partitions on one or more physical drives.

A volume set is a volume comprised of 2 through 32 partitions. An NTFS volume set may be extended at any time by adding another partition to the set without damaging existing data stored therein. However, a volume set and its data must be destroyed to reduce the size of a volume. All the partitions in a volume set must use the same file system, and the entire volume set is assigned a single drive letter. A volume provides no fault tolerance for its data. If any one of the partitions or drives within a volume set fails, all of the volume's data is lost.

The best way to remember the impact of losing a volume set element is the following phrase: You lose one, you lose them all. This also means that the only way to recover data in a damaged volume set is to restore the data from a backup.

Drive Letters

Nearly every volume on a Windows NT machine has an associated drive letter. In fact, Windows NT cannot access a volume unless it has an associated drive letter. Drive letters simplify the identification of an exact physical drive, partition, and volume for any referenced folder or file. Windows NT can assign drive letters to storage devices using the letters C through Z (A and B are reserved for floppy drives). Because this only covers 24 potential drives, and Windows NT supports as many as 32, the assumption is that some volumes will span multiple physical drives (which all share a single drive letter). There is one exception to the floppy drive letter rule. If you do not have a drive B, you can assign a network mapped drive to that letter.

Windows NT automatically assigns the next available drive letter to each new volume that's created. But you can dynamically reassign or shuffle drive letters using the Assign Drive Letter option on the Tools menu in Disk Administrator.

Another exception to the association of volumes with drive letters applies to volumes formatted with file systems not supported by Windows NT. These volumes are generally not assigned drive letters because Windows NT cannot access them anyway.

Master Boot Record

The Master Boot Record (MBR) is a BIOS bootstrap routine used by low-level, hardware-based system code stored in Read-Only Memory (ROM) to initiate the boot sequence on a PC. This in turn calls a bootstrap loader, which then commences loading the machine's designated operating system. The MBR directs the hardware to a so-called "active partition" from whence the designated operating system may be loaded (for more information on this topic, look at Chapter 13).

To be active, a partition must be a primary partition. A primary partition can be made active by using the Mark Active command on the Disk Administrator's Partition menu. The system partition is that partition where the MBR and boot loader reside. For Windows NT, the boot partition is the partition where the Windows NT system files reside.

Now that we have cleared up where Windows NT looks for boot files, let's continue our discussion of Windows NT's fault tolerance features.

System Security Through Fault Tolerance

Fault tolerance describes the resilience of a system in the presence of errors, mistakes, or disasters without causing damage or loss to its data. Windows NT's fault tolerance features vary from disk partition organization, to high-level file system operations, to backup techniques. When these are combined, they make Windows NT a reasonably reliable and solid network operating system.

The NTFS file system supports internal and automatic fault tolerance. Using a method called "hot fixing," every storage device write is monitored and written sectors are checked for integrity. If any verification fails, the questionable sectors are flagged, and the data is rewritten to another working location on disk. This is performed automatically by the file system and does not report error messages to any applications. NTFS also logs all changes to the file system so that changes may be undone or reapplied if a discrepancy is found or if a system failure or power loss causes damage.

Windows NT 4 Server supports three types of fault tolerant disk structures: disk mirroring, disk duplexing, and disk striping with parity. These structures may be implemented using the Fault Tolerance menu in the Disk Administrator utility. Of Windows NT's various stripe and volume sets, only disk striping with parity qualifies as fault tolerant. Disk striping without parity does not qualify as fault tolerant, even though it's another legal way to aggregate multiple partitions in Disk Administrator.

Disk Mirroring

Disk mirroring creates an exact duplicate of one physical and logical storage device on a separate physical storage device. Both the original drive and the "backup," or mirrored drive, are attached to the same hard drive controller. If the original disk fails, there is no loss of data because everything written to the original disk is also written to the mirror. Barring other physical component problems, when the original drive fails, the system automatically switches to the mirrored drive to continue operation.

Drawbacks to disk mirroring include:

- **Slow performance** The act of writing the same data twice takes longer than writing it once.
- **Increased cost** Every mirror must be a separate physical device. Thus, you must purchase twice the storage capacity.
- **No protection from controller failure** If the disk controller fails, the mirrored drive is just as inaccessible as the original drive.

The boot and system partitions can be the original disk in a disk mirror set. But if the original fails, it will be necessary to hand-edit the BOOT.INI file on the boot drive to point to the ARC (Advanced RISC Computing) name for the mirror, instead. (ARC names and BOOT.INI editing are covered in Chapter 13.)

Disk Duplexing

Disk duplexing is similar to disk mirroring, but more robust. Like mirroring, disk duplexing uses a duplicate physical and logical drive on a separate hard disk. Unlike mirroring, however, the drive is connected to the system via a separate controller. If the original drive or controller fails, the system continues to operate using the duplexed drive. Duplexing causes no system performance degradation because writing the same data twice through two disk controllers requires no additional time and both writes occur simultaneously.

One significant drawback to disk duplexing is the cost—it requires double the storage space and a second disk controller.

As with mirroring, the boot and system partitions can be the original disk in a disk duplexing set. But again, if the original fails, you must edit the BOOT.INI file by hand to point to the ARC name for the duplexed drive.

Disk Striping

Disk striping stores data across multiple physical storage devices. In a stripe set, multiple partitions of equal size on separate devices are combined into a single logical device. When data is stored to a stripe set, it is written in 64 K chunks across all partitions in the set. An example of a stripe set is depicted in Figure 6.2. Here, data is written in "stripes" across the drives,

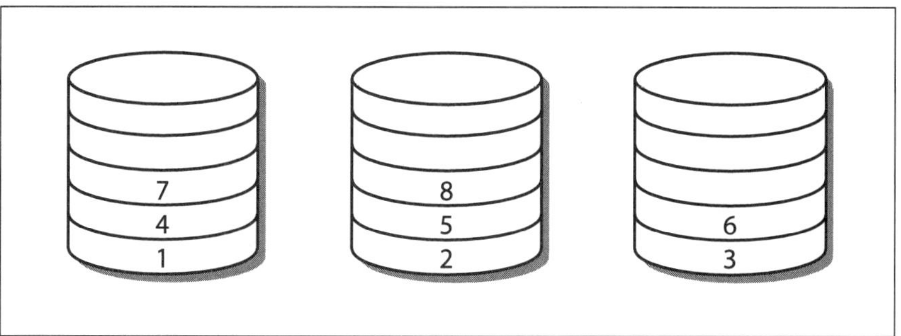

Figure 6.2 A stripe set using three physical disks.

starting at the drive on the left with data block 1, then on the middle drive with data block 2, and so on.

Disk striping is fast, especially when the individual storage devices are attached to separate disk controllers. Disk striping does not have the same cost drawbacks as mirroring and duplexing, because all or most of the storage space you purchase is fully available to you. You only need two devices to create a stripe set without parity, and such a stripe set can include as many as 32 devices. Disk striping can be implemented using either FAT or NTFS.

Disk striping without parity, however, provides no fault tolerance whatsoever. Should any one of the drives in a stripe set without parity fail, all data on all disks is lost. (Once again: If you lose one, you lose them all.) If any of the drive controllers fails, none of the data is accessible until that drive controller is repaired.

The boot and system partitions cannot be part of a disk stripe set without parity (or otherwise, in fact, as you'll see in the next section). Warning! If the documentation says anything about a stripe set but does not mention "parity" (with or without), you must assume that this means a stripe set without parity, and act accordingly.

Disk Striping With Parity

Disk striping with parity offers most of the benefits of parity-free disk striping without the same risk of data loss. Parity defines a storage method where the data that's written across the stripes is recorded so that data stored on any one drive is duplicated across all the other devices in the stripe set. The duplicate data is called "parity information." If any one of the drives in a parity stripe set fails, that data can be rebuilt from the parity information on the remaining devices without loss.

To record parity information within a stripe set, additional space is required. Unfortunately, this means that the total amount of storage capacity is smaller than the sum of the partitions on each member of the stripe set. To calculate the total capacity (T) of a stripe set with parity, use the following formula (where **P** is the size of any single partition, and **n** is the number of partitions in the set):

```
T = P * (n - 1)
```

When you create a stripe set using the Create Stripe Set With Parity option on the Disk Administrator's Fault Tolerance menu, you will be presented with a dialog box that displays the total size of the set. This number is **P * n**, which equals the size of the smallest partition multiplied by the total number of partitions. This number does not reflect the amount of actual usable storage space of a stripe set with parity. (That number is determined by the preceding formula, which takes the space requirements for parity information into account.)

Here are a few important items to remember about disk striping with parity:

- All partitions within a stripe set must be of equal size.
- Each partition must be on a separate physical disk.
- NTFS or FAT can be used as the file system on a stripe set with parity.
- A minimum of 3 devices is required to build a stripe set with parity, and the maximum number of devices is 32.
- Writing performance is slightly slower than disk striping without parity, but faster than disk mirroring.
- If one drive in a set fails, the data set can be rebuilt from the remaining devices.
- Neither the boot nor system partitions can reside in a disk stripe set, even with parity.

In continuing our coverage of fault tolerance, it's important to detail the various levels of RAID security, which we cover in the following section.

RAID

The four partition organizations we've described for Windows NT represent software implementations of RAID (which stands for Redundant Array of Inexpensive—or Individual—Disks). In other words, RAID is a storage method that uses numerous devices in combination to store large amounts of data.

RAID also addresses various levels of fault tolerance and recoverability for specific configurations and storage techniques. There are six distinct levels recognized in RAID subsystems, starting with level 0 and ending with level 5. Windows NT Server supports RAID levels 0, 1, and 5. Here's an explanation of these levels:

- **RAID 0** Disk striping without parity. This level provides no fault tolerance, but it is the fastest method. RAID 0 includes non-striped volume sets as well as disk striping without parity.
- **RAID 1** Disk mirroring. This level provides a reasonable level of data protection, but it has some performance consequences. Disk duplexing is also sometimes categorized as RAID 1, because it provides the same level of data protection with improved performance. Both mirroring and duplexing require twice as much physical storage as the data to be stored (because there are two identical copies of everything).
- **RAID 5** Disk striping with parity. This level provides the highest level of data protection with only a minor dip in performance and modest overhead storage requirements for parity information.

Remember, Windows NT's software implementation of RAID requires additional system overhead, especially when large numbers of devices are involved. Software RAID is convenient and inexpensive because it is included with Windows NT, but hardware RAID is faster and offers more options and reliability (like hot-swappable drives and controllers).

Comparing RAID Levels

You need to be able to designate a level of fault tolerance for a particular system or configuration. Remember, disk striping without parity (RAID 0) offers no fault tolerance whatsoever. In addition to the RAID levels and fault tolerance features of the various partition organizations, remain aware of expense and hardware requirements.

Here's a list of things to consider when comparing disk mirroring (or duplexing) to disk striping with parity:

- Two physical disks per mirror set are required for disk mirroring.
- No less than 3 and no more than 32 physical disks may be used with disk striping with parity.
- You can mirror (or duplex) the volumes where system and boot files for Windows NT are stored (these are the Windows NT boot and system partitions, respectively).
- You cannot use disk striping (with or without parity) for Windows NT system and boot partitions.
- Because it relies on simple duplication, disk mirroring requires half the disk space for copies that might otherwise be used for data storage. The same is true for disk duplexing.
- Disk striping with parity uses **1/n** of the total disk space available to store parity information (where **n** is the number of partitions in the stripe set).
- If a disk stripe set with parity or a mirror set loses more than one physical drive, the entire set's data will be lost. If that happens, the set must be repaired, rebuilt, and the data restored from backup.

It's one thing to make sure that you have backed up your data for later recovery if warranted. The next section explains how to recover stored data.

Recovery

As long as the physical disk(s) that contain the system and boot partitions do not fail, recovery from disk failure is relatively simple. However, recovery without resort to a backup is only possible with a disk mirror, disk duplex, or stripe set with parity. All other partition structures offer no "live recovery" for the data they store. In addition, if the partition that contains Windows NT's system files fails, there are some special boot considerations that you need to address.

Fixing Broken Mirrors And Duplexes

When the primary member of a disk mirror (or duplex) set fails, Windows NT automatically uses the other member of the set to continue operation. But whenever a member of a mirror or duplex set fails, you must replace the failed member and reestablish the mirror. Otherwise, you will no longer benefit from the data protection. In fact, the Windows NT Server will be unable to reboot at all if the primary set member fails, because the BOOT.INI file points to that member (that's why it's necessary to hand-edit the ARC name in the boot file to point to the other member of the set to restart the system).

The first step in repairing a mirrored set is to break the mirror. This is accomplished in the Disk Administrator utility, using the Break Mirror option in the Fault Tolerance drop-down menu. Once the mirror is broken, you must assign the drive letter previously assigned to the set to the remaining member of the now broken mirror set. For example, if Drives 1 and 2 are mirrored and assigned drive letter D, and Drive 1 fails, you must break the mirrored set, and then assign drive letter D to Drive 2.

The second step is to replace the failed drive and create a partition on the new drive equal in size to the drive to be mirrored. Then, you must re-create the mirror by using the Establish Mirror option from the Fault Tolerance drop-down menu. (Note that this effectively switches the roles of the previous original and mirrored drives.) Once Windows NT reboots, the mirror set will be rebuilt using the new member, but the primary drive will now be Drive 2, based on the example in the preceding paragraph.

If the mirror set includes a boot partition and the drive that failed was the primary member of the set, you must boot with a floppy to regain access to the system to run the Disk Administrator utility to repair the set. You must create an up-to-date boot floppy for the system so this process can work. That boot floppy should contain the following files:

- BOOT.INI
- NTLDR
- NTDETECT.COM
- NTBOOTTDD.SYS (only if you are using a SCSI controller with BIOS translation disabled or missing)
- BOOTSECT.DOS (only if you need to boot into MS-DOS or another operating system present on your system)

You may need to edit the BOOT.INI FILE to match new parameters and the new location of boot and system partitions. For further information, read the section titled "Special Boot Considerations" later in this chapter.

RAID Level 5: Disk Striping With Parity

Recovering from a device failure with disk striping with parity is easy. Once the device fails, the system is able to rebuild data on the fly from parity information stored on the still-operational devices. But because regeneration is CPU-intensive, performance slows dramatically. Even so, the system continues to operate, even with a failed set member.

Once a set member fails, it's important to replace it quickly to restore fault tolerance and system performance levels to normal. First, fix the hardware by replacing or repairing the failed drive. Next, using Disk Administrator, create a new partition equal in size to the one that failed (skip this step if the original disk is brought back online without losing its partition structure). Select the stripe set and the partition that replaces the failed member (which could be the original partition if it wasn't destroyed). Then, select the Regenerate command from the Fault Tolerance drop-down menu. After Windows NT reboots, the stripe set will be rebuilt by copying parity information to re-create the new member.

Special Boot Considerations

If the partition that contains Windows NT's system files fails, you will find where those mirrored system files are mapped in BOOT.INI, which uses ARC name syntax to map a path to the system files. This path designation starts by identifying the hard disk controller and finishes with the name of the folder that contains the Windows NT system files.

Here are a couple of examples of BOOT.INI entries:

```
multi(1)disk(0)rdisk(1)partition(2)\WINNT="Windows NT Server
Version 4.00"

scsi(0)disk(0)rdisk(0)partition(1)\WINNT="Windows NT Server
Version 4.00"
```

Should a boot or system partition fail, these entries may need to be changed, especially if the order, number, or configuration of your drives and partitions change, or if the Windows NT system files must be accessed from an alternate location (like the other member of a mirror or duplex set).

If the primary drive in a mirror set fails and that drive was the boot partition, BOOT.INI on the mirror drive (which must now function as the boot partition) must be edited to reflect the new, correct location of these files. You might also edit the BOOT.INI file on a boot floppy to perform the same function, especially if you plan to restore the original drive quickly and return the system to its previous state.

BOOT.INI lives in the system partition on your Windows NT machine, usually on the C drive. BOOT.INI is a text file that you can edit with any text editor. But BOOT.INI attributes are "system" and "read-only". Therefore, you must turn off these attribute settings before you can edit the file. Then, you need to reset those attributes once your changes are complete. Here's an example of a BOOT.INI file:

```
[boot loader]
timeout=10
default=scsi(0)disk(0)rdisk(0)partition(1)\WINNT
[operating systems]
scsi(0)disk(0)rdisk(0)partition(1)\WINNT="Windows NT Server
Version 4.00"
```

```
scsi(0)disk(0)rdisk(0)partition(1)\WINNT="Windows NT Server Version
4.00 [VGA mode]" /basevideo /sos
C:\="MS-DOS 6.22"
```

To edit the BOOT.INI file properly, here are several things you must know about ARC names:

- To change the BOOT.INI file to point to the proper location, you must edit both the **default=** line and the main NOS line (which is **scsi(0)disk(0)rdisk(0)partition(1)\WINNT ="Windows NT Server Version 4.00"** in the preceding example). Both ARC names must match exactly.
- The first four elements of an ARC name are always lowercase in the BOOT.INI file.
- The first element in an ARC name is the controller type. This will be either **scsi** or **multi**. **scsi** indicates that a SCSI disk controller with BIOS translation disabled is being used. If **scsi** appears, it also means that a driver file named "NTBOOTDD.SYS" must appear in the system partition to handle BIOS translation for the controller. **multi** indicates any other controller type support BIOS translation, including IDE and SCSI (with BIOS translation enabled), among others.
- The number immediately following **scsi** or **multi** identifies the position of the controller within the system, defined with ordinal numbers. Thus, the first controller is numbered zero, the second is one, and the third is two.
- The second element in an ARC name, **disk**, designates the device number for a SCSI controller with no BIOS translation abilities. But if **scsi** is the first element in the name, then the number that follows **disk** identifies the storage device, again, with ordinal numbers. Thus, the first device is also numbered zero, the second is one, and so on. If **multi** appears first in an ARC name, **disk** is ignored and will always be set to zero.
- The third element, **rdisk**, designates the device number for a BIOS translating SCSI controller, or for any other controller. **rdisk** always appears in any ARC name. But only if **multi** is its first element does the number following **rdisk** identify the storage device, numbered ordinally. Again, the first device is numbered zero, the second device is one, and so on. If **scsi** appears first in an ARC name, **rdisk** is ignored and is always set to zero.

- The fourth element in an ARC name identifies a disk partition. **partition** indicates the partition where system files reside, numbered cardinally. Unlike the other terms, the first partition is one, the second is two, the third is three, and so on.

- The fifth element in an ARC name is the name of the folder where the system files reside. **\winnt** indicates that the folder (or directory) on the specified partition named "WINNT" is where system information can be found. Whatever the directory is named, this element must reflect the exact name.

- The data following the folder name provides the information that appears in the Windows NT Boot menu. The equal sign and the quotes that enclose the text string must follow the folder name without any additional spaces outside the quotes.

- After the Boot menu name, additional command line parameter switches may be added to control how Windows NT boots. These switches include **/sos** and **/basevideo**. **/sos** causes Windows NT to display the names of drivers on the screen as they load during system boot. **/basevideo** puts Windows NT into VGA Mode, which is useful when troubleshooting video configuration problems.

It is important to note that Microsoft uses the terms *boot partition* and *system partition* in a reversed manner. The boot partition is the partition where the main Windows NT files reside. The system partition is where BOOT.INI and NTLDR reside.

Just remember that it's the opposite of common sense, and you'll do just fine.

Let's continue our discussion of securing data by taking a look at the backup elements available in Windows NT.

Windows NT Backup

Using the Windows NT Backup utility enables you to maintain data, protect an entire network, and restore damaged systems. If you are familiar with the Windows NT Backup interface and the utility's capabilities, you'll be able to protect your network from data loss.

Using a backup to protect data is an additional fault tolerant feature of Windows NT. Backups should be used in addition to BDCs and disk striping (or disk mirror/duplexing). Microsoft suggests that no less than three copies of critical data be maintained, with one copy being kept off-site. These copies can be two sets of backup tapes plus a drive duplication (or stripe set).

Windows NT Backup can access data stored on both local and remote (networked) drives. Plus, it can copy the local system Registry. However, it cannot back up open files and remote Registries, and it includes no built-in scheduling service.

If you'd like more information about Windows NT Backup, you can consult the *Windows NT Resource Kit*, Microsoft TechNet, or the Administering Microsoft Windows NT 4 course material. Otherwise, you can scan the material in *MCSE NT Server 4 Exam Cram* if you are feeling rusty, but we doubt you'll need it.

Practice Questions

Question 1

Using free, unpartitioned space on a SCSI drive, you create a new partition. You highlight the free space, select Create from the Partition menu, specify the size of the partition, and click OK. Now, the new drive appears in the Disk Administrator display. What should you do next in your endeavor to create a new place to store data?

❍ a. Assign a drive letter

❍ b. Select Configuration|Save

❍ c. Format

❍ d. Use the Commit Changes Now command

Answer d is correct. You must use the Commit Changes Now command to save the partition creation changes as your next step. Then, you can proceed to format the partition and assign it a drive letter. A drive letter is automatically assigned to a newly created primary partition or a logical drive within an extended partition. Thus, it is not necessary to assign a drive letter. Therefore, answer a is incorrect. The Configuration|Save command stores the current configuration status as stored in the Registry to an Emergency Repair Disk. This is not a step toward creating a usable volume, so answer b is also incorrect. Formatting a partition to create a volume is required, but this cannot occur until partition creation changes are committed, making answer c incorrect as well.

Question 2

You have two IDE hard drives on a single drive controller in your Windows NT Server computer. There is only one partition on each of the two drives. The first drive's partition is formatted with FAT, and the second drive's partition is formatted with NTFS. The boot files are located on the second drive. What is the ARC name for the system partition?

❍ a. multi(0)disk(1)rdisk(0)partition(1)

❍ b. multi(0)disk(0)rdisk(1)partition(1)

❍ c. multi(1)disk(0)rdisk(1)partition(1)

❍ d. multi(0)disk(0)rdisk(1)partition(0)

❍ e. multi(1)disk(0)rdisk(0)partition(1)

Answer b is correct. It indicates the first partition of the second hard drive on the first **multi** type drive controller, which is indeed the location of the system partition for this configuration. Answer a displays an improperly composed ARC name—when **multi** is used, the **disk(n)** number must be set to zero. Therefore, answer a is incorrect. Answer c points to a second drive controller that doesn't exist in this example. Consequently, answer c is incorrect. Answer d supplies an incorrect number for the partition element—namely, partitions are numbered cardinally, so a partition number can never be zero. Because the first partition is numbered one, answer d is incorrect. Answer e names a second, nonexistent drive controller, and points to the first drive on that controller. Because the system partition for this question is attached to the first (and only) disk controller on the second hard drive, answer e is incorrect.

Question 3

Your network is a single domain, but it connects four remote locations with the central office. What is the best plan of action to maintain reliable performance and user authentication? [Check all correct answers]

- ❑ a. Install a BDC at each location.
- ❑ b. Install four BDCs at the central office.
- ❑ c. Configure disk striping on the PDC machine to protect the SAM database.
- ❑ d. Initiate disk duplexing on the PDC to protect the SAM database.
- ❑ e. Perform regular backups of the PDC.

Answers a, d, and e are correct. Installing a BDC at each location will improve performance and maintain a local copy of the SAM database. Therefore, answer a is correct. Disk duplexing will create a duplicate of the SAM database and will not degrade performance. Therefore, answer d is correct. Performing regular backups will protect all data on the network. Therefore, answer e is correct. Installing four BDCs at the central office will protect the SAM, but it will not improve performance of the network because all authentication will still have to travel over the lengthy communication links. Therefore, answer b is incorrect. Disk striping will not provide fault tolerance, plus the SAM database is stored on the boot partition of the server and cannot be a member of a stripe set. Therefore, answer c is incorrect.

Question 4

What is the best method for implementing fault tolerance on a Windows NT Server computer with two high-speed SCSI drives, each on a separate controller card?

- ❍ a. Disk duplexing
- ❍ b. Disk striping without parity
- ❍ c. Disk mirroring
- ❍ d. Create a volume set across both drives

Answer a is correct. Disk duplexing is the fault tolerance method that utilizes two drives, each on separate controllers. Disk striping without parity offers no fault tolerance, making answer b incorrect. Disk mirroring utilizes two drives on the same controller, making answer c incorrect as well. Finally, a volume set offers no fault tolerance, making answer d incorrect.

Question 5

Which items below describe disk striping with parity? [Check all correct answers]

- ❑ a. Requires three physical drives.
- ❑ b. Can be implemented with FAT.
- ❑ c. Provides fault tolerance.
- ❑ d. Has faster read performance than disk mirroring.
- ❑ e. Data cannot be recovered if a single drive within the set fails.

Answers a, b, c, and d are correct. Disk striping with parity requires a minimum of three physical drives, so answer a is correct. Disk striping with parity can be implemented with either NTFS or FAT, so answer b is correct. Because disk striping with parity is indeed a fault-tolerant storage method, answer c is also correct. Disk striping with parity offers better performance than disk mirroring because it spreads the load across more drives. Thus, answer d is correct as well. Disk striping with parity can recover from a single drive failure. Therefore, answer e is incorrect.

Question 6

Which of the following ARC names indicates the third partition of the fourth SCSI drive on the second controller that has its BIOS disabled?

- ❍ a. multi(1)disk(3)rdisk(0)partition(3)
- ❍ b. multi(1)disk(0)rdisk(3)partition(3)
- ❍ c. scsi(1)disk(3)rdisk(0)partition(3)
- ❍ d. scsi(1)disk(3)rdisk(0)partition(4)

Answer c is correct. It indicates the third partition on the fourth drive on a non-BIOS SCSI controller. Answer a begins with multi(), which indicates a BIOS-enabled controller. Therefore, answer a is incorrect. Answer b does likewise and is equally incorrect. Answer d is close, but indicates the fourth partition and is therefore incorrect.

Question 7

Which type of data should not be distributed via the Replication service?

- ❍ a. Logon scripts
- ❍ b. User profiles
- ❍ c. Relational database files
- ❍ d. System policies

Answer c is correct. Relational database files are often very large and would cause severe performance degradation to the network if their distribution was handled by the replication service. Logon scripts, user profiles, and system policies are the only files that should be distributed by the Replication service. Therefore, answers a, b, and d are incorrect.

Question 8

> You want to implement fault tolerance on your Windows NT Server computer so your data will be protected in the event of a power failure or hardware malfunction. Which of the following techniques will provide you some type of fault tolerance? [Check all correct answers]
>
> - ❑ a. RAID 1
> - ❑ b. Disk duplexing
> - ❑ c. Volume set
> - ❑ d. Disk striping without parity
> - ❑ e. RAID 5

Answers a, b, and e are correct. RAID 1 indicates disk mirroring, which provides some fault tolerance. Therefore, answer a is correct. Disk duplexing is another fault tolerant storage method, so answer b is also correct. RAID 5 is the same thing as disk striping with parity. Because this scheme provides fault tolerance, answer e is also correct. A volume set is not fault tolerant, making answer c incorrect. Likewise, disk striping without parity is not fault tolerant, so answer d is incorrect.

Question 9

> Your Windows NT Server computer has two physical disks. What forms of storage can be implemented with only two drives? [Check all correct answers]
>
> - ❑ a. Disk striping with parity
> - ❑ b. Disk mirroring
> - ❑ c. Disk duplexing
> - ❑ d. Volume set
> - ❑ e. Disk striping without parity

Answers b, c, d, and e are correct. Disk mirroring uses only two drives, but they must be on the same controller, so answer b is correct. Disk duplexing uses only two drives, but they must be on different controllers. Therefore, answer c is also correct. A volume set can consist of anywhere from 2 to 32 partitions on any number of drives. Therefore, answer d is also correct. Disk striping without parity requires a minimum of two drives. Therefore, answer e is also correct. Disk striping with parity requires a minimum of three drives, which makes answer a incorrect.

Question 10

Where does the Replication service place distributed files by default?

- ❍ a. \Winnt\System32\repl\Export of an import server
- ❍ b. \Program Files\Replication of an export server
- ❍ c. \Winnt\System32\repl\Import of an import server
- ❍ d. \Winnt\System32\repl\Export of an export server

Answer c is correct. The directory list in answer c is the correct default destination directory on an import server. The directory listed in answer a is not the default destination server on an import server. Therefore, answer a is incorrect. The directory listed in answer b is not the standard import directory on an import server. Therefore, answer b is incorrect. The directory listed in answer d is the export directory on an export server. This is where files are accessed for distribution. Therefore, answer d is incorrect.

Question 11

Which of the following drive sets supported by Windows NT Server can contain the system and/or boot partitions? [Check all correct answers]

- ❑ a. Disk mirroring
- ❑ b. Disk striping without parity
- ❑ c. Volume set
- ❑ d. Disk duplexing

Answers a and d are correct. Disk mirroring can contain system or boot partitions, or both, on the original disk. Therefore, answer a is correct. Disk duplexing can accommodate either the system or boot partitions, or both, on the original disk, so answer d is also correct. No kind of stripe set can contain either system or boot partitions, so disk striping without parity cannot contain the system or boot partitions. Of course, this means that answer b is incorrect. A volume set cannot contain either system or boot partitions, making answer c incorrect.

Question 12

What files should be placed on a boot disk in order to boot to the duplicate drive of a disk duplex from a floppy in the event of a failure of the original drive? Assume the drive controller is SCSI that does not support BIOS translation. [Check all correct answers]

- ❑ a. NTDETECT.COM
- ❑ b. BOOT.INI
- ❑ c. NTLDR
- ❑ d. WINA20.386
- ❑ e. NTBOOTDD.SYS

Answers a, b, c, and e are correct. NTDETECT.COM is required on the boot floppy. Therefore, answer a is correct. BOOT.INI is required on the boot floppy, making answer b correct. NTLDR is required on the boot floppy. Therefore, answer c is also correct. NTBOOTDD.SYS is the driver for SCSI translation required for non-BIOS controllers, making answer e correct as well. WINA20.386 is a Windows device driver that is not needed on the boot floppy, so answer d is incorrect.

Question 13

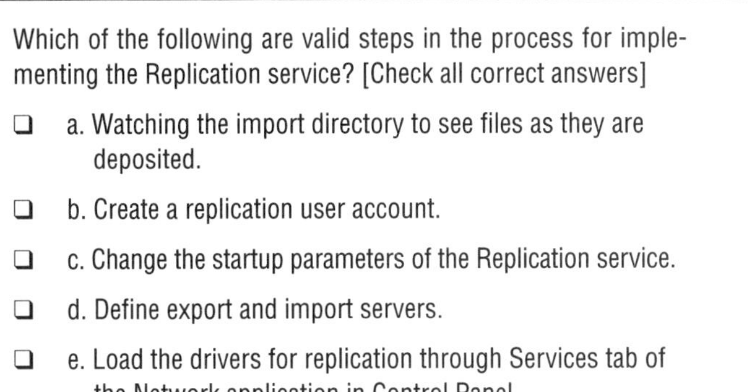

Which of the following are valid steps in the process for implementing the Replication service? [Check all correct answers]

- ❑ a. Watching the import directory to see files as they are deposited.
- ❑ b. Create a replication user account.
- ❑ c. Change the startup parameters of the Replication service.
- ❑ d. Define export and import servers.
- ❑ e. Load the drivers for replication through Services tab of the Network application in Control Panel.

Answers b, c, and d are correct. Creating a replication user account is a required step for implementing replication. Therefore, answer b is correct. Modifying the startup parameters of the Replication service through the Services application of Control Panel is a required step for implementing replication. Therefore, answer c is correct. Defining the servers and destinations for replication is a required step for implementing replication. Therefore, answer d is correct. Answer a is not a step in the implementation process, plus it will prevent replication from occurring by locking the directory. Therefore, answer a is incorrect. The Network application is not involved with the implementation of the replication service. Therefore, answer e is incorrect.

Question 14

The original disk of a disk mirror fails. The mirror did not contain the system or boot partitions. What are the steps required to restore the mirror set?

- ❍ a. Replace the failed disk, reformat both drives, re-create a mirror set, and restore the data from a backup tape.
- ❍ b. Replace the failed disk. Windows NT Server will automatically restore the mirror set.
- ❍ c. Break the mirror set, replace the failed drive, and re-create the mirrored drive.
- ❍ d. Replace the failed disk, select the mirror set and the replaced drive, and select Regenerate from the Fault Tolerance menu.

Answer c is correct. The steps in answer c will properly restore a mirror set, with the roles of the drives reversed. The steps in answer a cause you to perform many long and unnecessary steps—neither formatting the two drives nor restoring from tape backup is required. Therefore, answer a is incorrect. Windows NT will not automatically restore a mirror set, so answer b is also incorrect. The steps in answer d are used to repair a stripe set with parity, so answer d is incorrect.

Question 15

You have a Windows NT Server where the system partition is the original drive of a disk duplex set. If your system partition fails, what modification should you make to a boot floppy to boot to the mirrored partition?

- ❍ a. Add the **/MIRROR** switch to the default line of the BOOT.INI file.
- ❍ b. Edit the ARC name in the BOOT.INI file to reflect the location of the mirrored partition.
- ❍ c. A boot floppy is not needed.
- ❍ d. Change the **PATH** statement in the AUTOEXEC.BAT.

Answer b is correct. Editing the ARC name enables you to boot the mirrored partition. The **/MIRROR** switch is not a valid command parameter, so answer a is incorrect. A boot floppy is indeed required, so answer c is incorrect. There is no AUTOEXEC.BAT file on a Windows NT boot floppy, making answer d incorrect.

Question 16

You add four new drives to your Windows NT Server computer of sizes 800, 600, 500, and 300 MB. You wish to establish a disk stripe set with parity. What is the total size of the largest set you can create using any or all of these drives?

- ❍ a. 1,200 MB
- ❍ b. 1,000 MB
- ❍ c. 800 MB
- ❍ d. 1,500 MB

Answer c is correct. 1,500 MB is the total size of the largest set that may be created from these drives, using only the 800, 600, and 500 MB drives. 1,200 MB would be the size of the set if you used all 4 drives with 300 MB on each one. Because this is not the largest possible sum using this set of drives, answer a is incorrect. 1,000 MB is indeed the amount of data that could be stored on the largest set created from these drives, but the question requested the total size of the set, making answer b incorrect. Likewise, although 800 MB represents the size of the largest individual drive, you must use three drives to create a disk stripe set with parity. Therefore, answer c is incorrect.

Question 17

Windows NT Server is a fault tolerant network operating system. Which of the following are features of Windows NT that support fault tolerance and data redundancy? [Check all correct answers]

- ❑ a. Disk striping
- ❑ b. Software RAID
- ❑ c. Symmetric multiprocessing
- ❑ d. NTFS hot-fixing
- ❑ e. Windows NT Backup
- ❑ f. TCP/IP protocol
- ❑ g. BDCs

Answers b, d, e, and g are correct. Software RAID provides fault tolerance and data redundancy; however, only for RAID 1 and 5. Therefore, answer b is correct. NTFS hot-fixing is a realtime automatic fault tolerant feature of the file system that is hidden from applications. Therefore, answer d is correct. Windows NT Backup, although not useful for large networks, is a fault tolerant feature of Windows NT. Therefore, answer e is correct. BDCs protect the SAM database by duplicating the PDC. Therefore, answer g is correct. Disk striping is not a fault tolerant disk structure. Therefore, answer a is incorrect. Symmetric multiprocessing is a feature of Windows NT, but it is not related to fault tolerance. Therefore, answer c is incorrect. The TCP/IP protocol enables Windows NT to support almost every computer platform in existence as a client, but it is not related to fault tolerance. Therefore, answer f is incorrect.

Question 18

If you do not care about fault tolerance, what is the best method to maximize your data storage space on your Windows NT Server computer?

- ❍ a. Disk mirroring
- ❍ b. Disk striping with parity
- ❍ c. Volume set
- ❍ d. Disk stacking

Answer c is correct. A volume set maximizes storage capacity and allows you to add additional space as needed. Disk mirroring cuts storage capacity in half to implement fault tolerance, making answer a incorrect. Disk striping with parity reduces storage capacity by one full partition to implement fault tolerance, making answer b incorrect. Disk stacking is not a valid Windows NT storage technology, so d is incorrect.

Need To Know More?

Donald, Lisa, and James Chellis: *MSCE: NT Server 4 In The Enterprise Study Guide, 2nd Edition*. Sybex Network Press, San Francisco, CA, 1998. ISBN 0-7821-2221-3. Chapter 1 discusses domain controllers. Chapter 7 looks into directory replication through the Server Manager. Chapter 17 breezes through the disk fault tolerant features of Windows NT.

Heywood, Drew: *Inside Windows NT Server, 2nd Edition*. New Riders, Indianapolis, IN, 1998. ISBN 1-56205-860-6. Chapter 10 discusses fault tolerance issues, implementation tips, and troubleshooting techniques for storage under Windows NT Server. Chapters 2 and 3 discuss PDC and BDC issues. Chapter 11 looks at Windows NT's backup utility. And Chapter 15 examines directory replication.

Siyan, Karanjit S.: *Windows NT Server 4 Professional Reference, 2nd Edition*. New Riders, Indianapolis, IN, 1997. ISBN 1-56205-805-3. Chapter 9 has extensive coverage of Windows NT's storage capabilities and fault tolerant features. Chapters 5 and 6 look into domain controllers and the directory replication service. Chapter 20 looks into Windows NT Backup and the other data protection schemes of Windows NT.

The Windows NT Server 4 manuals cover planning, configuration, and installation issues quite well. The *Concepts And Planning Manual* contains useful fault tolerance, domain controller, directory replication, and backup issue discussions.

The *Windows NT Server Resource Kit* contains a lot of useful information about Windows NT's fault tolerance. The TechNet CD (or its online version through **www.microsoft.com**) can be searched using keywords like "fault tolerance," "replication," "domain controller," and "backup." In the *Resource Guide* volume, Chapter 3, "Disk Management Basics," Chapter 4, "Planning A Reliable Configuration," and Chapter 5, "Preparing For And Performing Recovery," contain useful background, implementation, and reference information on Windows NT's fault tolerance features. The *Networking Guide* Chapter 5, "Network Services—Enterprise Level," contains a great discussion of the replication service, and Chapter 2, "Network Security And Domain Planning," contains information about domain controllers.

Auditing Resources And Access

Terms you'll need to understand:

- √ Auditing
- √ Account Policies
- √ User Rights

Techniques you'll need to master:

- √ Enabling auditing through User Manager For Domains
- √ Using audit information
- √ Establishing policies through User Manager For Domains
- √ Managing user rights through policies

The auditing capabilities of Windows NT Server are part of the overall security system. Auditing, account (and password) policies, and user rights, are all part of the security policies of Windows NT. In this chapter, we take a look at auditing. Account policies are covered briefly at the end of this chapter. User rights are discussed in Chapter 4 of this book.

Auditing

On a computer running Windows NT, the administrator has the option to audit access to resources such as directories, printers, and shares. The audit will inform the administrator if someone attempts to access secured resources or just how often a particular resource is accessed. The information gathered by Windows NT's auditing system applies equally to performance problems, security risks, and expansion planning.

Enabling Auditing

The auditing system is designed to watch every event that occurs on your server. To simplify the act of fine-tuning the areas you wish to audit, there are three levels of switches with which you'll need to work. The master switch is the Audit These Events radio button located on the Audit Policy dialog box (see Figure 7.1). This dialog box is accessed through the User Manager For Domains' Policies pull-down menu.

This master switch turns on or off Windows NT's entire audit system. By default, this switch is set to Do Not Audit.

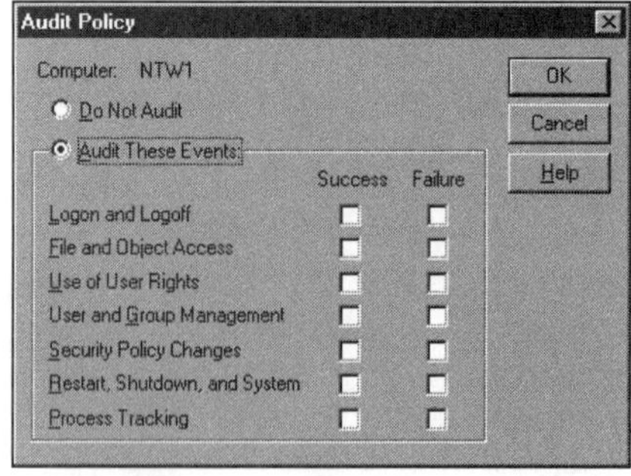

Figure 7.1 The Audit Policy dialog box.

The second level of switches becomes available when you set the master switch. There are seven event types listed in the Audit Policy dialog box. Each of these event types can be audited by tracking its success and/or failure. Here are the seven event types and descriptions of the events they control:

- **Logon And Logoff** Tracks logons, logoffs, and network connections.
- **File And Object Access** Tracks access to files, directories, and other NTFS objects. This includes printers.
- **Use Of User Rights** Tracks when users make use of user rights.
- **User And Group Management** Tracks changes in the accounts of users and groups (password changes, account deletions, group memberships, renaming, and so forth).
- **Security Policy Changes** Tracks changes of user rights, audit policies, and trusts.
- **Restart, Shutdown, And System** Tracks server shutdown and restarts, also logs events affecting system security.
- **Process Tracking** Tracks program activation, program termination, and other object/process access.

The third level of audit switches is at the object level. This level of control only applies to File And Object Access events. These switches reside within the properties of each NTFS-based object, such as files, directories, and printers. Figures 7.2 through 7.4 show the Audit switch screens for file, directory, and print access. Note the differences in the tracking events among the object types. Both the file and directory have Read, Write, Execute, Delete, Change Permissions, and Take Ownership. But the printer object has Print, Full Control, Delete, Change Permissions, and Take Ownership.

A second, important difference to notice is on the directory object. The directory object allows you to change the files and/or subdirectories within the current directory to the same audit settings. Although this is convenient, you should use it with caution because any current audit settings on these objects will be cleared and replaced with the new settings.

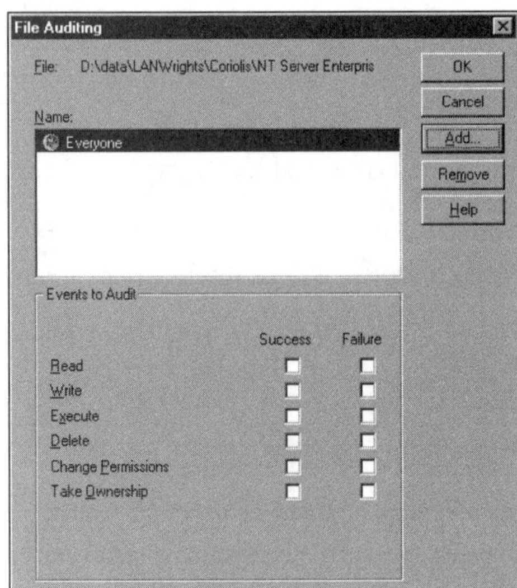

Figure 7.2 The File Auditing dialog box.

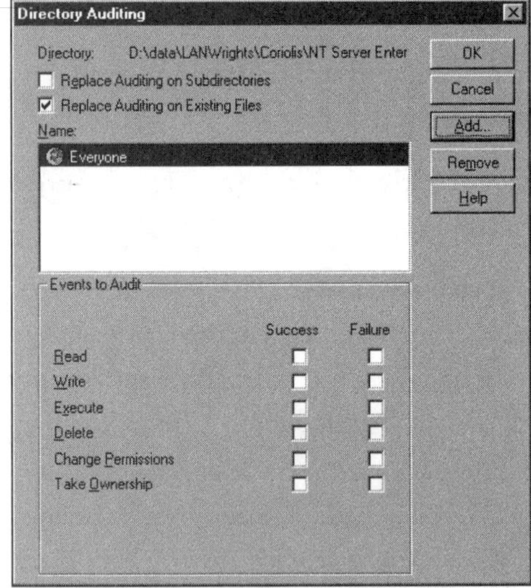

Figure 7.3 The Directory Auditing dialog box.

To get to these dialog boxes, right-click over the object, select Properties from the pop-up menu, select the Security tab, then click the Auditing button. Remember, object auditing is only available to NTFS objects, not FAT objects.

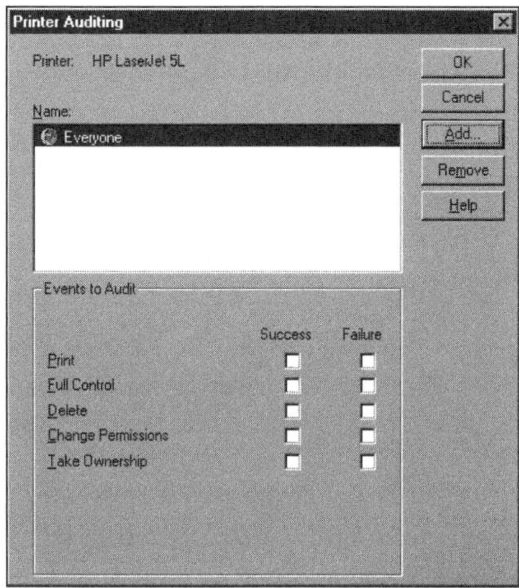

Figure 7.4 The Printer Auditing dialog box.

> *Note: By default, the object level audit switches are all blank with no users or groups present in the Name field. We added the Everyone group before taking these images so the Events list at the bottom of these dialog boxes would become readable instead of their default near-invisible gray.*

The object level audit dialog boxes allow you to set the same success/failure event tracking for all users and groups listed in the Name field. You cannot track success for one group and failure for another.

Let's repeat the steps required to audit:

1. Turn on the master Audit These Events switch.
2. Select one or more of the event types to track success or failure.
3. If you choose the File And Object Access option, you must also edit the auditing settings for each NTFS object.

Auditing Overhead

The activity of auditing system events demands large amounts of computing overhead, especially if the event monitored occurs often, such as file access. It is not recommended to audit any event or object more than is absolutely necessary to track a problem or test equipment. Otherwise, your system will slow down significantly.

Using Audit Information

The information gathered by Windows NT's auditing system is stored in the Security log. You can view this log using the Event Viewer. The Event Viewer lists detailed information about each tracked event. Some of the data recorded includes user logon identification, the computer used, time, date, and the action or event that instigated an audit.

When numerous objects or events are audited, the Security log can grow large quite quickly. You need to monitor the size of this log and possibly implement a size restriction and/or automated new file creation to prevent data loss and maximize the usefulness of the gathered data.

This concludes our discussion of auditing in Windows NT. Let's now discuss how to control access through the use of Policies.

Account Policy

You really don't need to know a whole lot about account policies, but you do need to be familiar with what is possible with this feature. If you need more details than we include here, please consult the Windows NT Server manuals, the *Resource Kit*, or *MCSE NT Server 4 Exam Cram*.

The account policy is set through the Policy menu of the User Manager For Domains. The Account Policy dialog box (see Figure 7.5) is divided into two main sections: Password Restrictions and Account Lockout.

You can use the Account Policy dialog box to set the following parameters:

- Maximum and minimum password age
- Password length
- Password uniqueness
- Account lockout after specified failed attempts
- Failed counter reset

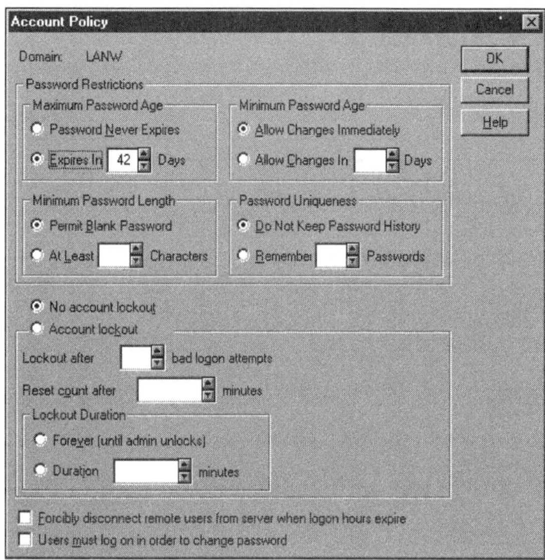

Figure 7.5 The Account Policy dialog box.

- Lockout duration
- Force users off when hours expire
- Require logon before password change

That's all you need to know regarding account policies.

Practice Questions

Question 1

You suspect that an Account group member is accessing a directory that the user should be prevented from reaching. This might mean that you've set up the group memberships incorrectly. You aren't sure who it is, but you do know what directory is being accessed. What feature of Windows NT will let you track who gains access to this directory?

- ❍ a. NTFS file activity logging
- ❍ b. Event auditing
- ❍ c. Event Viewer
- ❍ d. Account lockout

Answer b is correct. Event auditing will track the activity around any object within Windows NT. The NTFS file activity logging is a fault tolerance feature used to ensure the integrity of stored data. It cannot be used to track access. Therefore, answer a is incorrect. The Event Viewer is used to review the Security log created by the auditing system, but it is not the feature that does the actual tracking. Therefore, answer c is incorrect. Account lockout is the feature used to prevent compromised accounts from being used. Therefore, answer d is incorrect.

Question 2

You want to track the activity around a new high-speed color laser printer so you can use the tracking information to restrict and grant privileged and priority access. Which of the following are required steps to implement printer auditing? [Check all correct answers]

- ❑ a. Set the auditing switches on the printer object to track the successful print events for the Everyone group.
- ❑ b. Grant the Everyone group the auditing right through the User Rights policy.
- ❑ c. Set the Audit policy to Audit These Events through the User Manager For Domains.
- ❑ d. Set the audit switch of File And Object Access to Success under Audit These Events.
- ❑ e. Set the priority of the printer to 99 (maximum) under the Scheduling tab on the printer's Properties dialog box.

Answers a, c, and d are correct. Setting the auditing switches on the object is required to enable printer tracking. Therefore, answer a is correct. Setting the master auditing switch to Audit These Events is required to track printer access. Therefore, answer c is correct. Setting the event type switch of File And Object Access to Success is required to track printer usage. Therefore, answer d is correct. There is no auditing right for users. Therefore, answer b is incorrect. Setting a printer's priority has nothing to do with tracking access. Therefore, answer e is incorrect.

Question 3

Which of the following settings cannot be managed through the account policy? [Check all correct answers]

- ❑ a. Password length
- ❑ b. Password history
- ❑ c. User must change password at next logon
- ❑ d. User must log on to change password
- ❑ e. Password age
- ❑ f. User cannot change password

Answers c and f are correct. User Must Change Password At Next Logon and User Cannot Change Password are settings of the user account through the Properties dialog box of each account. Password length, history, age, and User Must Log On To Change Password are all set by using the Account policy. Thus, answers a, b, d, and e are incorrect.

Question 4

An important new custom application is conflicting with an existing utility. The conflict seems to cause both programs to terminate prematurely. Which audit event type should be tracked to record some information about the conflict and which programs are affected?

- ❍ a. File And Object Access
- ❍ b. Security Policy Changes
- ❍ c. Restart, Shutdown, And System
- ❍ d. Process Tracking
- ❍ e. Application Activity

Answer d is correct. Process Tracking tracks threads and process (e.g., applications). File And Object Access is for tracking NTFS objects, such as files and printers. Therefore, answer a is incorrect. Security Policy Changes tracks modifications to security and policies. Therefore, answer b is incorrect. Restart, Shutdown, And System tracks system restarts. Therefore, answer c is incorrect. Application Activity is not a valid selection. Therefore, answer e is incorrect.

Need To Know More?

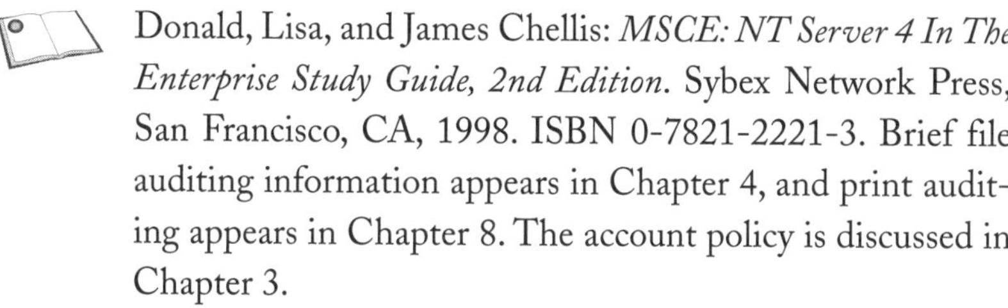

Donald, Lisa, and James Chellis: *MSCE: NT Server 4 In The Enterprise Study Guide, 2nd Edition*. Sybex Network Press, San Francisco, CA, 1998. ISBN 0-7821-2221-3. Brief file auditing information appears in Chapter 4, and print auditing appears in Chapter 8. The account policy is discussed in Chapter 3.

Heywood, Drew: *Inside Windows NT Server, 2nd Edition*. New Riders, Indianapolis, IN, 1998. ISBN 1-56205-860-6. Chapter 12 contains information on the auditing features of Windows NT. Chapter 4 also has a discussion of the Account policy.

Siyan, Karanjit S.: *Windows NT Server 4 Professional Reference, 2nd Edition*. New Riders, Indianapolis, IN, 1997. ISBN 1- 56205-805-3. Chapter 9 covers Auditing as part of the Windows NT Security system. Pages 273 through 275 list the account policy features.

The *Windows NT Server 4 Resource Kit* contains some information about the audit features and account policies of Windows NT. The TechNet CD (or its online version through **www.microsoft.com**) can be searched using keywords like "audit" and "account policy."

8

Network Protocols, Routing, And Relaying

Terms you'll need to understand:

- √ Protocols
- √ Network Basic Input/Output System (NetBIOS)
- √ NetBIOS Extended User Interface (NetBEUI)
- √ Transmission Control Protocol/ Internet Protocol (TCP/IP)
- √ Simple Network Management Protocol (SNMP)
- √ Dynamic Host Configuration Protocol (DHCP)
- √ Windows Internet Name Service (WINS)
- √ Domain Name Service (DNS)
- √ Serial Line Internet Protocol (SLIP)
- √ Point-To-Point Protocol (PPP)
- √ Point-To-Point Tunneling Protocol (PPTP)
- √ File Transfer Protocol (FTP)
- √ Hypertext Transfer Protocol (HTTP)
- √ NWLink Internetwork Packet Exchange/Sequenced Packet Exchange (IPX/SPX)
- √ Client Service For NetWare (CSNW)
- √ Gateway Service For NetWare (GSNW)
- √ File And Print Services For NetWare (FPNW)
- √ Frame types
- √ Data Link Control (DLC)
- √ AppleTalk
- √ Protocol bindings
- √ Multiprotocol Router (MPR)
- √ RIP (Routing Information Protocol)
- √ BOOTP Relay Agent
- √ DHCP Relay Agent

Techniques you'll need to master:

- √ Installing and configuring network protocols
- √ Familiarization with services associated with certain protocols
- √ Establishing a protocol binding order
- √ Manually adjusting the Ethernet frame type

To enable communications on a computer network, you must tell Windows NT how it's supposed to "talk" to other computers and peripheral devices. In the networking world, this is established through the use of protocols. Basically, a protocol is an agreed upon set of standards that defines how computers communicate. In this chapter, we explain the protocols available with Windows NT Server, when to use which protocol, and the properties of each protocol. We also discuss the connectivity and routing features of Windows NT, including RIP and the DHCP Relay Agent. We also provide pointers to additional resources for this topic.

Built-In Windows NT Protocols

Windows NT Server comes with a number of protocols. The following list presents the available protocols:

- Network Basic Input/Output System (NetBIOS)
- NetBIOS Extended User Interface (NetBEUI)
- Transmission Control Protocol/Internet Protocol (TCP/IP)
- NWLink Internetwork Packet Exchange/Sequenced Packet Exchange (IPX/SPX)
- Data Link Control (DLC)
- AppleTalk

In the upcoming sections, we'll define and explain these protocols and their uses.

NetBIOS

NetBIOS was originally developed by IBM in the 1980s, and it provides the underlying communication mechanism for some basic Windows NT functions, such as browsing and interprocess communications between network servers. NetBIOS is an extremely fast protocol that requires very little communications overhead, which is why it's used by Windows NT for basic operations. Unfortunately, it is not a routable protocol; therefore, it cannot be used as the primary protocol for networks that need routing capabilities.

NetBEUI

NetBEUI is a simple Network layer transport protocol that was developed to support NetBIOS networks. Like NetBIOS, NetBEUI is not routable, so it really has no place on an enterprise network. NetBEUI is the fastest transport protocol available to Windows NT. It's great for fast transmission, but it is not usable across routed networks. Benefits of NetBEUI include its speed, good error protection, easy implementation, and small memory overhead. Disadvantages include the fact that it is not routable, has very little support for cross-platform applications, and has very few troubleshooting tools available.

NetBEUI should be selected only when your network is small. NetBEUI is not a useful choice for networks that require routing or involve WAN links.

TCP/IP

TCP/IP is the most widely used protocol in networking today. This is due in part to the vast growth of the global Internet. TCP/IP is the most flexible of the transport protocols and is able to span wide areas. In addition, it has excellent cross-platform support, routing capabilities, and support for the Simple Network Management Protocol (SNMP), Dynamic Host Configuration Protocol (DHCP), Windows Internet Name Service (WINS), Domain Name Service (DNS), and a host of other useful protocols (which we discuss later in this chapter, in the section titled "TCP/IP Connectivity Issues").

TCP/IP can be used in any networking situation; however, it is not recommended for small networks due to its overhead. It can support large heterogeneous networks, but it requires a significant amount of configuration.

NWLink (IPX/SPX)

NWLink is Microsoft's "clean room" implementation of Novell's IPX/SPX protocol suite for NetWare networks. This protocol is included with Windows NT to enable communication with NetWare servers. With NWLink enabled, Windows NT clients can access resources located on a NetWare server, and vice versa.

Put simply, Windows NT Server requires NWLink to be installed to enable communications with NetWare clients and servers. In addition, the File And Print Service For NetWare is also required for NetWare clients and servers to access Windows NT files and printers. The Client Service For NetWare (CSNW) is designed for Windows NT Workstations that require a direct link to NetWare servers. The Gateway Service For NetWare (GSNW) lets Windows NT Servers map a drive to a NetWare server, which provides access to NetWare server resources for Windows NT Workstations (via a gateway). We cover additional details for NWLink later in this chapter, in the section titled "NWLink Connectivity Issues."

NWLink should be used on networks that require NetWare connectivity or on networks that need routing capabilities but can't support the overhead of TCP/IP.

DLC

Windows NT uses the Data Link Control (DLC) protocol primarily for connectivity to SNA (Systems Network Architecture) gateways, and, more importantly, for connecting to network-attached printers, such as JetDirect cards by Hewlett-Packard. This is detailed more in Chapter 13, "Advanced Printing Topics."

AppleTalk

It should come as no surprise that the AppleTalk protocol is used for communication with Macintosh computers. By enabling AppleTalk, you allow Mac clients to store and access files located on a Windows NT Server, print to Windows NT printers, and vice versa. Note that you must first install the Windows NT Services For Macintosh before you can install AppleTalk. Also, Mac support is only available from NTFS partitions.

Connectivity Issues

There are a couple of protocols—namely, IPX/SPX and TCP/IP—that must have special settings changed for them to work properly.

NWLink Connectivity Issues

As mentioned earlier in this chapter, NWLink is IPX for Windows NT—IPX is the protocol, and NWLink is the networking component that provides the protocol. NWLink is provided for connectivity to NetWare networks to allow NetWare clients to access Windows NT Servers, as well as to allow Windows NT clients to access NetWare servers. It is important to note, however, that NWLink by itself does not enable this type of communication. You must first install the Client Service For NetWare and the Gateway Service For NetWare. Basically, CSNW is a redirector, whereas GSNW is what makes file and print sharing on NetWare servers available to Microsoft clients.

IPX has a number of benefits: It supports routing between networks, it's faster than TCP/IP, and it's easy to install and maintain. Unfortunately, IPX doesn't have a sufficient central addressing scheme to prohibit multiple networks from making use of identical addresses, and it doesn't support the Simple Network Management Protocol (SNMP).

Installing NWLink

Installing the NWLink protocol is much like installing other protocols in Windows NT. There are, however, some special issues that must be dealt with. To install NWLink, perform the following steps:

1. Open the Control Panel (Start|Settings|Control Panel).
2. Double-click the Network icon.
3. Click on the Protocols tab in the Network dialog box.
4. Click the Add button.
5. Select NWLink IPX/SPX Compatible Transport from the list of available protocols.
6. Enter the path to the Windows NT Server installation CD in the Path field of the setup dialog box, then click Continue. If you have installed Windows NT's Remote Access Service (RAS), Windows NT will ask if you want to bind NWLink to RAS. Either click OK to enable binding or click Cancel to not enable binding.
7. Click the Close button, then click Yes when Windows NT asks whether to restart computer.

In most cases, it's fine to leave the default frame type (auto) as is; however, some Ethernet adapters don't work well with this setting. For new installations, it's recommended that you set this to the Ethernet 802.2 setting.

Changing The Ethernet Setting

To change the Ethernet frame type and IPX network number, perform the following steps:

1. Open the Control Panel (Start|Settings|Control Panel).
2. Double-click the Network icon.
3. Click the Protocols tab in the Network dialog box.
4. Double-click NWLink IPX/SPX Compatible Transport from the list of available protocols.
5. Click the Manual Frame Type Detection button.
6. Click the Add button.
7. Select your preferred frame type.
8. Enter the IPX network number for the adapter in the Network Number field.
9. Click the Add button.
10. Repeat Steps 7 through 9 for each frame type.
11. Click OK, then click the Close button.
12. Click Yes when asked to restart the computer.

There are more issues to consider when establishing communications between Windows NT and NetWare networks. These details are covered in Chapter 12.

TCP/IP Connectivity Issues

As previously mentioned, TCP/IP is currently the most-used networking protocol as well as the standard protocol of the Internet. The beauty of the TCP/IP protocol suite lies in its ability to link many disparate kinds of computers and peripheral devices. Using this protocol stack, you enable most TCP/IP clients to access Windows NT-based resources, and vice versa.

Windows NT provides for a number of useful TCP/IP services. Included are the following:

- **Dynamic Host Configuration Protocol (DHCP)** This service enables the assignment of dynamic TCP/IP network addresses, based on a specified pool of available addresses. When a network client configured for DHCP logs on to the network, the DHCP service assigns the next available TCP/IP address for that network session. This really simplifies address administration.
- **Windows Internet Name Service (WINS)** This service enables the resolution of NetBIOS network names to IP addresses (similar to the Unix DNS). This way, you don't have to remember the IP address of the client with which you are trying to communicate. You can enter the network name, and Windows NT does the rest. Also, if a TCP/IP-based network does not have a WINS server, then each time one computer tries to access another, it must send a b-node broadcast, which creates a lot of unnecessary network traffic and can bring a busy net work to a crawl. WINS servers provide computer-name-to-IP address resolution, thereby reducing broadcast messages and improving network performance.
- **Serial Line Internet Protocol (SLIP)** SLIP was originally developed for the Unix environment and is still widely used among Internet providers. Although SLIP provides good performance with little system overhead requirements, it does not support error checking, flow control, or security features. SLIP is good for connecting to Unix hosts or Internet providers.
- **Point-To-Point Protocol (PPP)** PPP addresses many of the insufficiencies of SLIP, such as providing the ability to encrypt logons and supporting additional transport protocols, error checking, and recovery. In addition, PPP is optimized for low-bandwidth connections and, in general, is a more efficient protocol than SLIP. Even so, PPP has higher overhead than SLIP, which reflects its more general-purpose capabilities.
- **Point-To-Point Tunneling Protocol (PPTP)** PPTP is a protocol that creates secure connections between private networks over the Internet. Benefits of PPTP include lower administrative, transmission, and

hardware costs than other solutions for this type of connectivity. By taking advantage of the Internet, PPTP drastically reduces costs in these areas.

- **World Wide Web (WWW)** This service comes as a part of Windows NT Server 4 and has the ability to publish Web pages, whether for an Internet based Web site or an intranet.
- **File Transfer Protocol (FTP)** This protocol is great for the fast transfers of files to and from a local hard drive to an FTP server located elsewhere on another TCP/IP-based network (such as the Internet).
- **Gopher** This service serves text and links to other Gopher sites. Gopher predates HTTP (the Web protocol) but has become obsolete (because of HTTP).
- **Hypertext Transfer Protocol (HTTP)** This is the World Wide Web protocol that allows for the transfer of HTML documents over the Internet or intranets, which responds to actions like a user clicking on hypertext links.

Installing TCP/IP

There are a few items you need to have on hand when you install TCP/IP. The following list describes these items:

- **Your server's (Class C) IP address** This is the unique address that identifies your computer on a TCP/IP network. This number consists of four numbers separated by periods (e.g., 125.115.125.48). The first three numbers identify the network on which the computer is located; the remaining number identifies your computer on that network.
- **Your network's subnet masks for each network adapter on the network** The subnet mask is a number mathematically applied to the IP address to determine which IP addresses are a part of the same subnetwork as the computer applying the subnet mask.
- **Your server's default gateway** The gateway is the computer that serves as a router, a format translator, or a security filter for a network.

- **The domain name server for the network** This is a computer that serves as an Internet host, which performs translation of fully qualified domain names into IP addresses.
- **Any DHCP and WINS information about your network** If you already have these services configured, the process of configuring TCP IP is greatly eased.

If you did not install TCP/IP upon the initial installation of Windows NT Server, you must perform the following steps to install and configure this protocol suite:

The steps

1. Open the Control Panel (Start|Settings|Control Panel).
2. Double-click the Network icon.
3. In the Network window, click the Protocols tab.
4. Click the Add button.
5. Select TCP/IP from the list of available protocols. Windows NT may request the installation CD or the location of the installation files.
6. In the Network window, click the Close button.
7. Either enter the TCP/IP address of the computer or select Obtain An IP Address From A DHCP Server, whichever is appropriate for the installation. Then, specify the subnet mask and default gateway.
8. If your network has a DNS server or a constant Internet connection, click the DNS tab, and enter the DNS address.
9. If your network has a WINS server, click the WINS tab, and enter the WINS address.
10. Click OK to close the TCP/IP Properties dialog box. If you did not specify a primary WINS address, Windows NT will display a warning.
11. Click the Close button.
12. Click Yes when asked to restart the computer.

This concludes the installation process for the TCP/IP protocol suite. Now, let's take a look at some of the TCP/IP utilities.

TCP/IP Utilities

The Windows NT version of TCP/IP is bundled with many useful command-line utilities to aid in the configuration and administration of a TCP/IP-based network. Here is a list of those utilities, a brief description, and the syntax (which may be obtained by using the /? parameter at the command line):

- **arp** Address Resolution Protocol. The **arp** utility displays the IP address mapped to a MAC node address. (See Figure 8.1.)
- **hostname** Displays the name of the current computer host.
- **ipconfig** Displays IP configuration details. (See Figure 8.2.)
- **lpq** Displays the status of a print queue only on a computer running DLC.
- **nbtstat** Displays NetBIOS of TCP/IP status. (See Figure 8.3.)
- **netstat** Displays TCP/IP status and statistics. (See Figure 8.4.)
- **ping** Provides a means to test and verify network connections.
- **route** Interacts with routing tables. (For syntax details, see the section titled "Routing And IP RIP," later in this chapter.)
- **tracert** Details the route used by TCP/IP.

```
Command Prompt

ARP -s inet_addr eth_addr [if_addr]
ARP -d inet_addr [if_addr]
ARP -a [inet_addr] [-N if_addr]

  -a            Displays current ARP entries by interrogating the current
                protocol data.  If inet_addr is specified, the IP and Physical
                addresses for only the specified computer are displayed.  If
                more than one network interface uses ARP, entries for each ARP
                table are displayed.
  -g            Same as -a.
  inet_addr     Specifies an internet address.
  -N if_addr    Displays the ARP entries for the network interface specified
                by if_addr.
  -d            Deletes the host specified by inet_addr.
  -s            Adds the host and associates the Internet address inet_addr
                with the Physical address eth_addr.  The Physical address is
                given as 6 hexadecimal bytes separated by hyphens. The entry
                is permanent.
  eth_addr      Specifies a physical address.
  if_addr       If present, this specifies the Internet address of the
                interface whose address translation table should be modified.
                If not present, the first applicable interface will be used.

E:\>_
```

Figure 8.1 The syntax of **arp**.

```
Command Prompt
E:\>ipconfig /?

Windows NT IP Configuration

usage: ipconfig [/? | /all | /release [adapter] | /renew [adapter]]

       /?       Display this help message.
       /all     Display full configuration information.
       /release Release the IP address for the specified adapter.
       /renew   Renew the IP address for the specified adapter.

The default is to display only the IP address, subnet mask and default gateway
for each adapter bound to TCP/IP.

For Release and Renew, if no adapter name is specified, then the IP address
leases for all adapters bound to TCP/IP will be released or renewed.

E:\>
```

Figure 8.2 The syntax of **ipconfig**.

```
Command Prompt
Displays protocol statistics and current TCP/IP connections using NBT
(NetBIOS over TCP/IP).

NBTSTAT [-a RemoteName] [-A IP address] [-c] [-n]
        [-r] [-R] [-s] [-S] [interval] ]

  -a   (adapter status) Lists the remote machine's name table given its name
  -A   (Adapter status) Lists the remote machine's name table given its
                        IP address.
  -c   (cache)          Lists the remote name cache including the IP addresses
  -n   (names)          Lists local NetBIOS names.
  -r   (resolved)       Lists names resolved by broadcast and via WINS
  -R   (Reload)         Purges and reloads the remote cache name table
  -S   (Sessions)       Lists sessions table with the destination IP addresses
  -s   (sessions)       Lists sessions table converting destination IP
                        addresses to host names via the hosts file.

  RemoteName   Remote host machine name.
  IP address   Dotted decimal representation of the IP address.
  interval     Redisplays selected statistics, pausing interval seconds
               between each display. Press Ctrl+C to stop redisplaying
               statistics.

E:\>_
```

Figure 8.3 The syntax of **nbtstat**.

```
Command Prompt
E:\>netstat /?

Displays protocol statistics and current TCP/IP network connections.

NETSTAT [-a] [-e] [-n] [-s] [-p proto] [-r] [interval]

  -a            Displays all connections and listening ports.  (Server-side
                connections are normally not shown).
  -e            Displays Ethernet statistics.  This may be combined with the -s
                option.
  -n            Displays addresses and port numbers in numerical form.
  -p proto      Shows connections for the protocol specified by proto; proto
                may be tcp or udp.  If used with the -s option to display
                per-protocol statistics, proto may be tcp, udp, or ip.
  -r            Displays the contents of the routing table.
  -s            Displays per-protocol statistics.  By default, statistics are
                shown for TCP, UDP and IP; the -p option may be used to specify
                a subset of the default.
  interval      Redisplays selected statistics, pausing interval seconds
                between each display.  Press CTRL+C to stop redisplaying
                statistics.  If omitted, netstat will print the current
                configuration information once.

E:\>
```

Figure 8.4 The syntax of **netstat**.

A cursory knowledge and awareness of these utilities will suffice. The exact details of syntax are not required knowledge but may help you understand the information these utilities display and modify.

NetBEUI Connectivity Issues

NetBEUI is a common protocol for small networks. Here, we'll step through the installation of NetBEUI as a network protocol.

Installing NetBEUI

NetBEUI is by far the easiest protocol to install and configure on a Windows NT network. To install this protocol, perform the following steps:

1. Open the Control Panel (Start|Settings|Control Panel).
2. Double-click the Network icon.
3. In the Network window, click the Protocols tab.
4. Click the Add button.
5. Select NetBEUI from the list of available protocols, and click OK.
6. Enter the path to the installation CD or the location of the installation files.
7. If you have RAS installed, Windows NT asks if you want to support it with this protocol. Click Cancel to leave it unsupported.
8. In the Network window, click the Close button.
9. Select Yes when asked to restart the computer.

That's it for the installation of NetBEUI.

Now that we have discussed the common networking protocols and their special requirements, let's move on to discuss a few general protocol principles. This discussion includes issues such as protocol bindings and routing.

Protocol Bindings

Protocol binding is the process Windows NT uses to link network components from various levels of a network architecture to enable communication among the components. To set the binding order for network protocols, double-click the Network icon in Control Panel, and click the Binding tab. This is where the bindings of installed network components are listed, in order of upper-layer services and protocols to lower-layer network adapter drivers.

Binding should be ordered to enhance a system's use of the network. As an example, if your network has both TCP/IP and NetBEUI installed, and most network devices use TCP/IP, workstation bindings should be set to bind TCP/IP first and NetBEUI second. In other words, the most frequently used protocol should be bound first. This speeds network connections. Servers use whatever protocol is sent to them by each workstation, so the binding order only needs to be changed on the workstations. Network speed is affected by the binding order on the workstations, but not on the servers.

Routing With Windows NT

It is rare for a network to remain isolated. More often than not, multiple networks are aggregated to improve communication and share resources, such as files, applications, and hardware. Microsoft designed Windows NT Server 4 to act as a router to simplify the interconnection of multiple networks. The Multiprotocol Router (MPR) is a service that can dynamically route traffic between different subnets over IPX and TCP/IP. However, to use MPR, the server must have two or more NICs installed and configured in such a way that each NIC is part of a different subnet. In other words, a server must be "multihomed" to implement MPR.

MPR is composed of:

- RIP (Routing Information Protocol) For TCP/IP (a.k.a. IP RIP)
- RIP For IPX
- BOOTP Relay Agent For DHCP (a.k.a. DHCP Relay Agent)

RIP is a protocol used to dynamically exchange routing information between routers. Once RIP is installed, Windows NT routes RIP protocols and dynamically exchanges routing information with other routers running the RIP protocol. Additionally, the BOOTP Relay Agent forwards DHCP requests to DHCP servers located on other subnets over the Windows NT router. Thus, a single DHCP server can support or service multiple subnets.

Routing And IP RIP

A router can exchange routing information with neighboring routers if RIP is enabled. Alterations in the network layout, such as a downed router, are broadcast by routers to neighboring routers. Routers also transmit descriptions of all known routing information by using periodic broadcasts. RIP routers share routing information dynamically.

Windows NT can be a dynamic IP router or a static IP router. Dynamic routers share routing information with other routers to automatically build routing tables. Static routers employ manually configured routing tables.

Dynamic routing is enabled when you install RIP For IP. This is done through the Services tab of the Network applet in the Control Panel. Once it is installed, no further configuration is necessary. The service is started, and the Enable IP Routing option in the Advanced TCP/IP Configuration dialog box is checked automatically. RIP For IP runs as a service. It can be started and stopped via the Control Panel Services icon.

Static routing has the benefit of reduced network traffic. Network traffic is reduced because the static routers don't communicate with each other. The disadvantage of static routing is that the routing tables have to be maintained and created by hand.

To enable static routing, execute the following steps:

1. Go to the Control Panel, and click the Network icon.
2. Select the Services tab.

   If RIP For IP is installed on your computer, you must remove it before enabling static routing.
3. Highlight RIP For IP in the Network Services list located on the Services tab, then click Remove to remove RIP For IP. (If RIP For IP remains installed, dynamic routing will occur.)
4. Select the Protocols tab, highlight TCP/IP Protocol, then click Properties.
5. Select the Routing tab, enable IP Forwarding by marking the checkbox, then click OK.

Using static routing requires manual configuration of the static routing tables. This is done through the command-line command **route**, with syntax of:

```
route [-f] [-p] [command [destination] [MASK netmask] [gateway]
[METRIC metric]]
```

The options are:

- **-f** Removes all gateway entries from the routing table. If this parameter is used with a command, the tables are cleared before the command is run.
- **-p** Implements persistent routes by automatically sustaining routing changes through computer reboots.
- **command** One of the following commands:
  - **print** Prints a route.
  - **add** Adds a route.
  - **delete** Deletes a route.
  - **change** Modifies an existing route.
- **destination** Indicates the host or network to which you want to route.
- **MASK** Specifies that the next parameter is to be interpreted as the *netmask* parameter.
- **netmask** Specifies the subnet mask value to be associated with this route entry. If the value is not specified, this parameter defaults to **255.255.255.255**.
- **gateway** Specifies the default gateway.
- **METRIC** Specifies that the next parameter be interpreted as the *metric* parameter.
- **metric** Defines the hop count for the specified destination. If not defined, metric is set to **1** by default.

A few important items to note about the route utility:

- The subnet mask value of **255.255.255.255** is not accepted on the command line. To set this value, use the default by not specifying MASK.
- The NETWORKS file can be used to convert destination names to addresses, but the network numbers must be appended with trailing **.0** to comply with the full, four-octet, dotted, decimal notation.
- All gateways must be on the same logical network or the route will not be added to the table.
- Only one default gateway should be configured on a server with multiple NICs. Any secondary gateways are useless unless the primary default gateway fails.
- For each route to a new router, the new router must be instructed to reach back to the subnets hosted by the first router.

You don't need to memorize the syntax of the route command, but you need to know its capabilities.

Routing And IPX RIP

Windows NT 4 Server is also equipped with a RIP For NWLink (IPX/SPX) to enable routing over an IPX network. If you are using both TCP/IP and NWLink on your network, you can use both RIP For IP and RIP For IPX on the same network to route both protocols simultaneously.

Enabling RIP For IPX is just as simple as it is for IP—just add the RIP For IPX service on the Services tab of the Network applet of the Control Panel. An additional configuration tab for the NWLink protocol, named "Routing," contains a checkbox labeled "Enable RIP Routing." This checkbox must be marked.

During the installation of RIP For IPX, a dialog box appears that states NetBIOS Broadcast Propagation (packets of broadcast type 20) is currently disabled. If you are using NetBIOS over IPX, click Yes to enable type 20 packet broadcasts.

The SAP Agent For IPX is automatically installed when RIP For IPX is enabled.

DHCP Relay Agent

DHCP (Dynamic Host Configuration Protocol) is used to assign an IP address to a workstation each time it boots. This allows a small set of IP addresses to support a larger number of computers. With the employment of the Windows NT DHCP Relay Agent, a single DHCP server can support multiple subnets connected by the Windows NT Server MPR.

Without the DHCP Relay Agent, routers filter out the DHCP broadcasts instead of passing them through. The Relay Agent intercepts the DHCP broadcasts, then transmits the broadcasts directly to the DHCP server. The router still filters out the DHCP request, but the added Agent intervenes and sends the important boot message to the supporting server.

The following steps describe how to install the DHCP Relay Agent:

1. Add the DHCP Relay Agent through the Services tab of the Network applet in the Control Panel.
2. Specify the IP address of the DHCP server in the IP Address tab of the TCP/IP Properties dialog box.

   The DHCP Relay Agent is enabled automatically and installed as a service.
3. Choose the DHCP Relay tab in TCP/IP Properties dialog to change default values for the DHCP Relay Agent. The values are Seconds Threshold, Maximum Hops, and List Of DHCP Server Addresses.

AppleTalk Routing

If Macintosh clients are used on your network, you can route AppleTalk over Windows NT Server. A Windows NT Server can be a seed router or a non-seed router for AppleTalk networks. A seed router must always be booted before any non-seed routers to establish the proper networking context. AppleTalk routing is a function of the Windows NT Services For Macintosh (SFM) and not part of the MPR. Any Macintosh client on an AppleTalk network routed over a Windows NT Server can access any other network routed through the Windows NT Server.

To enable AppleTalk routing, execute the following steps:

1. Open the Properties of the SFM (Services For Macintosh) from the Services tab of the Network applet in the Control Panel.
2. On the Routing tab, check the Enable Routing box.
3. If the server is to be a seed router, check the Use This Router To Seed The Network box, identify the network range, and define the zones.

AppleTalk routing was not on any of the preparation exams we encountered. So, you can be fairly assured that if you don't know what a seed router is or how to define a zone, there's no need to sweat it. There is a little coverage of this topic in the *Resource Kit*, but unless you use Macintosh clients in the real world, you don't need to know about AppleTalk routing.

Practice Questions

Question 1

There are two TCP/IP-based domains in your company: Marketing and Sales. A Windows NT Server acting as a router joins these two domains together. The Sales domain hosts the DHCP server that manages the IP addressing for workstations. What must be installed on the routing computer so the Marketing domain workstations can obtain IP address assignments from the DHCP server located in the Sales domain?

- ❍ a. NetBEUI
- ❍ b. DHCP Relay Agent
- ❍ c. RIP For IP
- ❍ d. A proxy DHCP server must be installed in the Marketing domain

Answer b is correct. The DHCP Relay Agent will intercept all DHCP calls before they are filtered out by the router and direct them straight to the DHCP server. NetBEUI is a non-routable protocol that does not support DHCP. Therefore, answer a is incorrect. RIP For IP enables routing between two domains, but it does not forward DHCP requests across the link. Therefore, answer c is incorrect. There is no such thing as a proxy DHCP server. The DHCP Relay Agent must be used to allow the Marketing-based workstations to use the Sales-based DHCP server. Therefore, answer d is incorrect.

Question 2

Your TCP/IP-based network is experiencing drastic increases in broadcast traffic. What is the best way to decrease the amount of broadcast traffic on your network?

- ❍ a. Divide your network into two physical subnets, and install a bridge.
- ❍ b. Divide your network into two logical subnets, and install a gateway.
- ❍ c. Install a DHCP server.
- ❍ d. Install a WINS server.

Answer d is correct. If a TCP/IP network does not have a WINS server, each computer on the network has to send a broadcast message to the other computers on the network, which increases network traffic. By making use of a WINS server, you provide computer-name-to-IP address resolution, which reduces the number of broadcast messages.

Question 3

You wish to locate information about the current usage statistics of TCP/IP. Which of the following TCP/IP command-line utilities will display this information?

- ❍ a. lpq
- ❍ b. arp
- ❍ c. netstat
- ❍ d. ping

Answer c is correct. The **netstat** utility will display TCP/IP statistics when the **-e** parameter is used. The **lpq** utility will only display DLC-related print queue information. Therefore, answer a is incorrect. The **arp** utility will only display mappings between IP addresses and MAC addresses. Therefore, answer b is incorrect. The **ping** utility will only list the response time (if any) between the host and a remote system. Therefore, answer d is incorrect.

Question 4

Of the following, which are required for access to a NetWare server from a Windows NT Workstation running Client Service For NetWare? [Check all correct answers]

- ❑ a. A group on the NetWare server called "NTGATEWAY" containing the Windows NT Workstation's user account
- ❑ b. Gateway Service For NetWare
- ❑ c. A user account on the NetWare server
- ❑ d. The NWLink protocol

Answers c and d are correct. Any user accessing a NetWare server directly will need a user account on that NetWare server. Therefore, answer c is correct. A Windows NT Workstation running the Client Service For NetWare can access a NetWare server directly by using the NWLink protocol. Therefore, answer d is also correct. It is only necessary to place user accounts in the NTGATEWAY group on the NetWare server if workstations are accessing the NetWare server via a gateway, which is not the case in this question. Therefore, answer a is incorrect. If a Windows NT Server is to act as a gateway to a NetWare server, the Gateway Service For NetWare must be loaded onto a Windows NT Server. Because this scenario discusses a Windows NT client accessing a NetWare server, answer b is also incorrect.

Question 5

Your network uses multiple protocols. Where in Windows NT is the binding order of the protocols changed to increase network speed?

- ❍ a. Domain controllers only
- ❍ b. Workstations only
- ❍ c. Servers only
- ❍ d. Both the workstations and servers (including the domain controllers)

Answer b is correct. Because Windows NT Servers use the protocol sent to them by workstations, the binding order only needs to be changed on the workstations. Network speed is affected by the binding order on the workstations, but not on the servers. Therefore, answers a, c, and d are all incorrect.

Question 6

Windows NT 4 Server is equipped to be a router between two or more subnets. This can occur only when multiple NICs are installed and configured on a single server computer. The facet of Windows NT that provides the routing function is MPR, or Multiprotocol Router. What is the MPR comprised of? [Check all correct answers]

- ❑ a. NetBEUI
- ❑ b. RIP For IP
- ❑ c. DNS
- ❑ d. RIP For IPX
- ❑ e. DHCP Relay Agent

Answers b, d, and e are correct. RIP For IP, RIP For IPX, and DHCP Relay Agent are all part of MPR. NetBEUI is not contained in MPR. MPR uses IP or MAC addresses to route traffic, not NetBEUI names. Therefore, answer a is incorrect. DNS is a function of TCP/IP but is not part of MPR. Therefore, answer c is incorrect.

Question 7

What is an advantage of SLIP over PPP?

- ❍ a. SLIP supports security, whereas PPP does not support security.
- ❍ b. SLIP supports error checking, whereas PPP does not support error checking.
- ❍ c. SLIP supports flow control, whereas PPP does not support flow control.
- ❍ d. SLIP requires less system overhead than PPP.

Answer d is correct. SLIP does require less system overhead than PPP. SLIP does not support error checking, flow control, or security. These are features of PPP. Therefore, answers a, b, and c are incorrect.

Question 8

You want to install TCP/IP on a member server in a non-routed network. You have already manually assigned an IP address to the server. What other parameter must you specify to install TCP/IP on the server?

- ❍ a. Subnet mask
- ❍ b. Default gateway
- ❍ c. DHCP server IP address
- ❍ d. WINS server IP address

Answer a is correct. When installing TCP/IP on a non-routed network, the IP address and subnet mask parameters must be specified. All other answers are incorrect.

Question 9

You have a TCP/IP-based network that is divided into two subnets using the same cable segment. Your main server is named "SRVR1". The first subnet is comprised of workstations with permanently assigned IP addresses. The second subnet is comprised of workstations that are assigned new IP addresses by a DHCP server each time the workstations boot. What components of MPR should you install to enable routing between these two subnets? [Check all correct answers]

- ❑ a. RIP For IPX
- ❑ b. IPX/SPX
- ❑ c. RIP For IP
- ❑ d. DHCP Relay Agent
- ❑ e. None

Answer e is correct. The situation described in this question does not lend itself to routing based on MPR, because MPR requires two or more NICs in the server across which routing is to occur. This situation has two subnets but only one cable segment, thus, only a single NIC. Because MPR cannot be used on single NIC configurations, no part of MPR should be installed. Some alternate solution is required to route between these subnets. Therefore, only answer e is correct. RIP For IP, RIP For IPX, and DHCP Relay Agent are all part of MPR, but they cannot be used in this situation. Therefore, answers a, c, and d are incorrect. IPX/SPX is a protocol and is not part of MPR. It should not be installed because it will not help with routing and the network is TCP/IP-based. Therefore, answer b is incorrect.

Question 10

Your Ethernet network consists of a Windows NT 4 Server, several Windows NT Workstation clients, a NetWare 3.12 client, and one NetWare 4.1 client. NWLink is running on the network. Each of the NetWare clients is using different frame types. How would you configure the NWLink IPX/SPX Properties dialog box on the Windows NT 4 Server to enable the server to recognize both NetWare clients?

- ❍ a. Enabling Auto Frame Type Detection
- ❍ b. Selecting the Manual Frame Type Detection option, and adding a NetWare client's network number and frame type to the frame type configuration list
- ❍ c. Selecting the Auto Frame Type Detection option, and adding both NetWare clients' network numbers and frame types to the frame type configuration list
- ❍ d. Selecting the Manual Frame Type Detection option, and adding each of the NetWare clients' network numbers and frame types to the frame type configuration list

Answer d is correct. If frame types other than 802.2 are being used on a network, then Manual Frame Type Detection must be enabled. Frame types belonging to each client must be added to the frame type configuration list in the NWLink IPX/SPX Properties dialog box.

Question 11

Your network users need to access your network resources across the Internet. How can you allow Internet-based user access while still providing security?

- ❍ a. Implement the SLIP protocol.
- ❍ b. Implement the FTP protocol.
- ❍ c. Implement the PPP protocol.
- ❍ d. Implement the PPTP protocol.

Answer d is correct. The Point-To-Point Tunneling Protocol (PPTP) uses the Internet as a connection medium while maintaining network security. SLIP simply provides a connection for TCP/IP clients to a host; thus, answer a is incorrect. FTP provides only file transfer without additional security, so answer b is incorrect. PPP provides protocol-neutral access from remote clients to a server, but includes no additional security; thus, answer c is incorrect.

Question 12

To end the process of maintaining user accounts on two different types of servers, you have decided to migrate users from the NetWare server to a Windows NT Server. What must be installed on the Windows NT Server to provide the NetWare clients with access? [Check all correct answers]

- ❑ a. File And Print Services For NetWare
- ❑ b. NWLink protocol
- ❑ c. Client Service For NetWare
- ❑ d. SAP Agent

Answers a and b are correct. File And Print Services For NetWare must be installed on the Windows NT Server. Therefore, answer a is correct. For the Windows NT Server to communicate with the NetWare server, the NWLink protocol must be installed on the Windows NT Server. Therefore, answer b is also correct. The Client Service For NetWare lets Windows NT clients access NetWare servers, but does not let NetWare clients access Windows NT Servers; thus, answer c is incorrect. The SAP agent simply handles NetWare service advertisements and does not provide NetWare clients with access to Windows NT; therefore, answer d is also incorrect.

Need To Know More?

Donald, Lisa, and James Chellis: *MSCE: NT Server 4 In The Enterprise Study Guide, 2nd Edition*. Sybex Network Press, San Francisco, CA, 1998. ISBN 0-7821-2221-3. Chapter 13, "Internetwork Routing," gives brief but useful information regarding MPR. TCP/IP issues are discussed in Chapter 11. NWLink is covered in Chapter 9.

Heywood, Drew: *Inside Windows NT Server, 2nd Edition*. New Riders, Indianapolis, IN, 1998. ISBN 1-56205-860-6. Chapter 9, titled "Using TCP/IP," discusses detailed issues relating to installing and configuring the TCP/IP protocol suite and routing for IP.

Huitema, Christian: *Routing In The Internet*. Prentice Hall, Englewood Cliffs, NJ, 1995. ISBN 0-13-132192-7. This book deals with routing protocols and other general routing topics.

Perlman, Radia: *Interconnections*. Addison-Wesley Professional Computing Series, Reading, MA, 1992. ISBN 0-201-56332-0. This book deals with routing protocols and other general topics.

Siyan, Karanjit S.: *Windows NT Server 4 Professional Reference, 2nd Edition*. New Riders, Indianapolis, IN, 1997. ISBN 1-56205-805-3. Chapters 13 through 16 all discuss various aspects of protocol management. Appendix C, "Bridging and Routing," provides solid background information on routing as well as how to implement MPR.

Search the TechNet CD (or its online version through **www.microsoft.com**) using the keywords "protocol management," "TCP/IP," "NWLink," "internetworking," and "routing."

The *Windows NT Server Resource Kit* contains lots of useful information about shares and share permissions. Here again, you can search the TechNet (either CD or online version) or the *Resource Kit* CD using keywords like "protocols," "binding," "routing," and "networking services."

9 Windows NT Names And Name Services, Plus IIS

Terms you'll need to understand:

- √ NetBIOS names
- √ Dynamic Host Configuration Protocol (DHCP)
- √ MAC address
- √ Domain Name Service (DNS)
- √ Windows Internet Name Service (WINS)
- √ Internet Information Server (IIS)
- √ Fully qualified domain name (FQDN)

Techniques you'll need to master:

- √ Understanding network names and name resolution in Windows NT
- √ Distinguishing between the uses for DNS and WINS
- √ Familiarization with Internet Information Server (IIS)

Computers interact with each other using long strings of complicated address numbers. Fortunately, Windows NT hides most of these unfriendly references behind easy-to-remember names. This chapter discusses many of Windows NT's name resolution features and options. Plus, we include a brief discussion of IIS.

Names And Name Services

Name resolution is the activity of transforming a user-friendly (or otherwise) name for a computer or network share into a computer-friendly network address. This process enables networks to quickly locate and request resources while shielding users from complicated and difficult to remember—much less type in—hardware-level addresses. Within Windows NT, there are three protocol-specific services (NetBEUI, NWLink, and TCP/IP), a base resolution service (NetBIOS), and additional services for TCP/IP (DHCP, DNS, WINS).

NetBIOS Names In Windows NT

NetBIOS is automatically installed upon installation of Windows NT. It is the underlying communication mechanism for many basic Windows NT functions, such as browsing and interprocess communications, between network servers. NetBIOS is an API used by all Windows NT applications. It provides a uniform set of commands to access common low-level services.

All Windows NT resources are identified by a unique NetBIOS name consisting of 15 characters or less. The NetBIOS namespace is not hierarchical, but flat. Thus, every machine on the same network must have a unique NetBIOS name, even if the machines are in different domains. Each time a computer connects to the network, it broadcasts its presence by "shouting" its NetBIOS name. The Master Browser "hears" this broadcast and attempts to register the new machine. If another machine is already using the name broadcasted by the newcomer, the registration is denied. That computer cannot go online until its NetBIOS name is changed or the other computer currently using the name goes offline.

A NetBIOS name is not the same as an IP host name. A host name is a substitute for an IP address of an Internet host. These names are required for communication with the aliased machine (i.e., www.microsoft.com = 207.68.156.53). A NetBIOS name is a mandatory, unique name used by Windows NT for most network functions. Each time an Explorer interface is activated, such as an Open File dialog box, you are interacting with NetBIOS names.

As discussed in Chapter 5 in the section on browsers, NetBIOS names are used to identify and list the resources currently available on a network. A computer announces itself and its resources upon booting up and once every minute thereafter. As it remains up and running, the interval increases to every 12 minutes. If a computer is shut down gracefully, it announces the removal of its resources as it leaves. If a computer goes offline otherwise, its resources may remain listed in the browser service up to 51 minutes until the Master Browser removes the entries and the Backup Browsers are updated. Computers rebroadcast their existence and all their resources every 12 minutes, so the level of traffic can be quite high, even for a small network.

NetBEUI And Name Resolution

All name resolution over NetBEUI is done through NetBIOS. Thus, there is no further configuration or installation required. Both users and computers use the NetBIOS name to call and access network system objects.

With NetBEUI, most of the network overhead is consumed by the NetBIOS announcement broadcasts. This is one of many reasons why NetBEUI should not be used on anything but the smallest of networks.

IPX And Name Resolution

IPX/SPX, or NWLink, uses NetBIOS over IPX (NBIPX) to resolve NetBIOS names into IPX addresses. Because IPX addresses contain the MAC address of the host, no further resolution is required. NWLink caches NetBIOS names to perform the IPX address mappings. NWLink does not use an address mapping file or name service. Unlike Novell's implementation of IPX/SPX, NWLink from Microsoft does not issue Service Advertisement Protocol (SAP) broadcasts. Thus, network overhead is greatly reduced.

IP And Name Resolution

Name resolution under TCP/IP is a complex but important issue. The resolution methods for IP include the Dynamic Host Configuration Protocol (DHCP), the Domain Name Service (DNS), and the Windows Internet Name Service (WINS). These methods are discussed in the upcoming sections.

DHCP

DHCP, or Dynamic Host Configuration Protocol, is not exactly a name resolution system. Instead, it is an IP address-leasing system where a limited number of IP addresses can be shared among numerous computers, usually clients. DHCP dynamically assigns IP addresses to clients on a local subnet.

The details of installing and configuring a DHCP server are beyond the scope of this book. However, you need to be familiar with a few terms and the basic method of operation of DHCP.

When a client boots, it broadcasts a message requesting data from a DHCP server. The receiving DHCP server responds with an IP address assignment for a specified period of time. The client receives the data, integrates it into its configuration, and completes the boot process.

A DHCP server can also distribute subnet masks and default gateway addresses. Each assignment from a DHCP server is for a predetermined length of time, called a "lease period." When a lease expires, a DHCP server can reassign the address to another computer. An operating client can extend its lease simply by indicating that it is still using the address. When half of a lease period is reached, a client requests a lease extension, if needed. It continues to request an extension from the leasing DHCP server until 87.5 percent of its time period has expired. Then, it broadcasts the extension request to all DHCP servers. If no server responds by the time the lease expires, all TCP/IP communications from that client will cease.

A client's IP configuration and lease information can be displayed using **IPCONFIG** with the **/all** parameter. This utility can also terminate a lease by using the **/release** parameter or renew a lease by using the **/renew** parameter.

The 10,000-foot view of DHCP server installation is as follows:

1. Install the service through the Services tab of the Network applet.
2. Define a scope—a pool of valid IP addresses available for assignment.
3. Set the subnet mask.
4. Define any exclusions within the scope.
5. Set the lease duration.

Configuring a client to access a DHCP server is even simpler. To configure a client, all you have to do is open the TCP/IP properties dialog box from the Protocols tab of the Network applet. Then, on the IP Address page, select the radio button labeled Obtain An IP Address From A DHCP Server.

If your DHCP server is located across a router, you'll need to use the DHCP Relay Agent to forward DHCP broadcasts. See Chapter 8 for details.

A DHCP header is simply the response packet from a DHCP server that contains special directional information for the requesting client. Because the client does not yet have an IP address, its MAC address is used to route the response package.

DNS

DNS, or Domain Name Service, is used to resolve host names into IP addresses. Host names are user-friendly conveniences to represent the dotted decimal notation of IP that are not required for operation of communication, unlike NetBIOS names. A host name (such as www.microsoft.com) is much easier to remember than its IP address (207.68.156.51).

Early DNS was a lookup table stored on every machine in a file called HOSTS. As networks expand, maintaining an updated and correct HOSTS file becomes increasingly difficult. To ease administration, centralized DNS was developed. A single server hosts the DNS data for the networks it supports, a hierarchy table of domains, and a list of other DNS servers to which it can refer requests.

DNS operates on user-friendly, fully qualified domain names (FQDNs) to determine the location (IP address) of a system. For example, ftp2.dev.microsoft.com could represent the server named "FTP2" located in the ".dev" subdomain under the ".microsoft" domain within the ".com" top-level domain. This hierarchy structure enables DNS to quickly traverse its database to locate the correct IP address for the host machine.

DNS is essential on large networks, including the Internet. A client is configured to use a DNS server through the TCP/IP Properties dialog box. The DNS tab contains fields to define the host name of the client, the domain where the client resides, the IP addresses of DNS servers, and a search order of domains.

Installing DNS servers is relatively simple in Windows NT. Configuring DNS, however, is much more difficult. The basic steps for a DNS server installation are as follows:

1. Install DNS through the Services tab of the Network applet.
2. After rebooting, launch the DNS Manager that now appears in Administrative Tools in the Start menu.
3. Add a new DNS server object through the DNS menu.
4. Create zones and host records.

The configuration of DNS is complicated and convoluted. Microsoft has done an excellent job of simplifying this task, but it remains difficult. Unix-based DNS, as commonly used on the Internet, can be likened to building an Apollo rocket. Microsoft Windows NT-based DNS can be likened to building a high-performance race car.

WINS

WINS, or Windows Internet Name Service, is a name resolution service for Windows NT-based TCP/IP networks. Similar to DNS, WINS maps NetBIOS names to IP addresses. But unlike DNS, WINS dynamically maintains the mapping database. WINS' main functions include:

- Mapping NetBIOS names to IP addresses.
- Recognizing NetBIOS names on all subnets.
- Enabling internetwork browsing.

WINS reduced NetBIOS background tracking by eliminating NetBIOS broadcasts. A WINS client communicates directly with a WINS server to send a resource notification, to release its NetBIOS name, or to locate a resource.

The original Microsoft solution to reduce NetBIOS broadcast traffic was the LMHOSTS file. This was a static file stored on each client that associated IP addresses with NetBIOS names. Just as with the DNS HOSTS file, it had to be manually maintained. Unfortunately, an LMHOSTS file is useless in a DHCP environment where relationships between IP addresses and NetBIOS names change.

WINS and DHCP work well together. Each time a DHCP client goes online, it can inform the WINS server of its presence. Thus, the dynamic relationship between IP addresses and NetBIOS names can be fully managed by these automatic services.

WINS clients are configured through the TCP/IP Properties dialog box of the Services tab of the Network applet. The WINS Address tab enables you to configure two WINS servers. The second server is for fault tolerance.

The installation and configuration of a WINS server is relatively easy. Here are the basic steps:

1. Add WINS from the Services tab of the Network applet.
2. After rebooting, launch the WINS Manager that now appears in Administrative Tools in the Start menu.
3. Add a WINS server object.
4. Set the renewal and extinction timeouts.
5. Set WINS database replication options.
6. Add static mappings.
7. Set additional preferences.

WINS Vs. DNS

WINS and DNS, although similar, have significant differences that define when each should be used for name resolution. Table 9.1 displays a comparison chart to highlight the differences between WINS and DNS.

Within many private networks, both DNS and WINS are installed. This provides support for both NetBIOS and FQDN resolution. Both DNS and WINS can be configured to pass resolution requests to the opposing resolution service if the referenced name is not listed in the respective database.

Now that we have detailed the various network naming schemes, let's move on to discuss how to hook your Windows NT network to the Internet using Microsoft's Internet Information Server (IIS).

Internet Information Server

The Internet Information Server (IIS) is another important component. Windows NT ships with IIS version 2, but version 3 is the current standard for real-world implementation. You only need to know the basics of this application in its version 2 form. There is a separate test for IIS version 4 that covers this software in much greater detail.

Table 9.1 Differences between WINS and DNS.

WINS	DNS
Maps NetBIOS names to IP addresses	Maps IP addresses to fully qualified domain names (FQDNs)
Automatic client data registration	Manual configuration
Flat database name space	Uses FQDN's hierarchical structure
Used on Microsoft clients and networks	Used on TCP/IP-based hosts and networks
Only one entry per client	Each host can have multiple aliases
Enables domain functions such as logon and browsing	N/A

IIS is a file and application server that provides Web, FTP, and Gopher services. If you are not already familiar with the Internet and these three services, you should reference:

- *Internet For Dummies*, by John R. Levine, Carol Baroudi, and Margy Levine-Young, Harper Audio, 1996. ISBN: 0-69451-667-8.
- *The Internet Complete Reference*, by Harley Hahn, Osborne McGraw-Hill, 1996. ISBN: 0-07882-138-X.

These resources will bring you up to speed on the topics considered as prerequisites for using IIS to host Internet services.

IIS can be used to support Web and FTP (and Gopher in older versions of IIS) Internet services within a private TCP/IP-based network or over the Internet. The bulk of IIS focuses on the Web service, but you need to be at least minimally aware of the FTP and Gopher services.

Web

The Web, or World Wide Web, is a service based on the Hypertext Transfer Protocol (HTTP). HTTP is a client/server interprocess communications protocol that can deliver text, graphics, multimedia, and other forms of data as content. A Web server, such as IIS, sends out requested documents to Web clients, such as Internet Explorer. IIS's Web service offers numerous configuration options, including:

- Anonymous access
- Windows NT user account restricted access
- Activity logging
- IP or domain name restricted/granted access
- Virtual server configuration

Two important configuration features in IIS's Web service are custom directory roots and virtual servers. Multiple Web sites can be hosted on a single installation of IIS. Each Web site is stored in its own root directory. In addition, each hosted Web site can be identified with its own FQDN and IP address. To host multiple IP addresses on the same IIS server, additional IP addresses are assigned to the server's NIC through the TCP/IP properties (for older versions, that is; IIS 4.0 can handle multihoming through a single IP address).

If IIS is used on a network with Internet connectivity, no additional services are required. DNS is handled by Internet-based servers, and WINS will not be needed at all. However, if IIS is used within a private isolated network, both DNS and WINS might be needed to support local name resolution.

FTP

The File Transfer Protocol (FTP) is the service and protocol used on the Internet to transfer files from one machine to another. IIS offers this service to improve file distribution over the Internet and within large private networks. IIS's FTP service can host multiple sites, each stored in a separate directory, but they must all be referenced by a common base domain name. Version 2 of IIS does not support FTP virtual servers, so you may need to look elsewhere if you want to provide FTP services to your users (or get the newest version of IIS).

Gopher

Gopher is a text-based, menu-like hierarchical organization of data. This service was extremely popular before the development of the Web. Because of this, bastions of Gopher sites can still be found on the Internet. There is no compelling reason to use Gopher within a private network. Like FTP, multiple Gopher sites can exist, but they are all referenced by a common base domain name.

Practice Questions

Question 1

What is the primary function of a Dynamic Host Configuration Protocol server?

- ❍ a. To maintain a dynamic relationship database between IP addresses and NetBIOS names
- ❍ b. To route IP packets across routers to other subnets
- ❍ c. To assign IP addresses to clients
- ❍ d. To resolve FQDNs into IP addresses

Answer c is correct. The service that assigns IP addresses to clients is DHCP. The service that maintains a dynamic relationship database between IP addresses and NetBIOS names is WINS. Therefore, answer a is incorrect. The service that routes IP packets is RIP for IP. Therefore, answer b is incorrect. The service that resolves FQDNs to IP addresses is DNS. Therefore, answer d is incorrect.

Question 2

All Windows NT internal basic network server and service communications occur using what protocol?

- ❍ a. TCP/IP
- ❍ b. AppleTalk
- ❍ c. NetBIOS
- ❍ d. DLC

Answer c is correct. NetBIOS is the protocol or API used for all of Windows NT's basic internal network communications. TCP/IP is a supported protocol of Windows NT, but it is not the one used for basic internal communication. Therefore, answer a is incorrect. AppleTalk is a supported protocol, but it is not used in this manner. Therefore, answer b is incorrect. DLC is a protocol used for IBM mainframe and network-attached printers. Therefore, answer d is incorrect.

Question 3

What type of a frame header identifies network packets that contain information used to assign subnet masks and gateways to clients?

❍ a. DNS header

❍ b. DHCP header

❍ c. WINS header

❍ d. NetBEUI header

Answer b is correct. A DHCP header is the header type that identifies network packets used to assign subnet masks and gateways to clients. None of the other services mentioned handles this role, including DNS, WINS, and Net BEUI. Therefore, answers a, c, and d are all incorrect.

Question 4

A DNS server links what types of information together? [Check all correct answers]

❑ a. NetBEUI names

❑ b. FQDNs

❑ c. Subnet masks

❑ d. IP addresses

❑ e. MAC addresses

Answers b and d are correct. DNS maintains a relationship between FQDNs and IP addresses in such a way that both forward and reverse lookups are possible. NetBEUI names are stored by WINS. Therefore, answer a is incorrect. Subnet masks can be distributed by a DHCP server, but a link table does not exist. Therefore, answer c is incorrect. MAC addresses are linked through NWLink's and NetBEUI's cached name resolution. Therefore, answer e is incorrect.

Question 5

You need to set up four new virtual Web servers to be hosted on your private network using only a single installation of IIS. Each Web site will require its own directory, a unique URL, and a unique IP address. What should you do to implement this configuration? [Check all correct answers]

- ❑ a. Install RIP For IP on the IIS server.
- ❑ b. Assign each of the IP addresses to be used to the NIC in the IIS server via the Network applet, then associate each IP address with the appropriate Web directory.
- ❑ c. Set up the DHCP Relay Agent.
- ❑ d. Configure DNS so it contains the FQDN for each server and correlates that name to its IP address.
- ❑ e. Configure WINS by adding the NetBIOS names and IP addresses of the sites to the static list of servers.

Answers b, d, and e are correct. Assigning additional IP addresses to the server's NIC is an important step. Therefore, answer b is correct. Because this site is within a private network, you will need both DNS and WINS to support name resolution. Therefore, answers d and e are correct. RIP For IP should not be used in this situation, nor do you know if there is more than one NIC in the server. Therefore, answer a is incorrect. The DHCP Relay Agent does not apply to this situation. Therefore, answer c is incorrect.

Question 6

What are the functions of WINS? [Check all correct answers]

- ❑ a. Enables internetwork browsing
- ❑ b. Maps FQDNs to IP addresses
- ❑ c. Maps NetBIOS names to IP addresses
- ❑ d. Maps NetBIOS names to MAC addresses
- ❑ e. Assigns clients IP addresses

Answers a and c are correct. Enabling internetwork browsing and mapping NetBIOS names to IP addresses are two of the three functions of WINS; the third function is recognizing NetBIOS names on all subnets. Mapping FQDNs to IP addresses is a function of DNS. Therefore, answer b is incorrect. Mapping NetBIOS names to MAC addresses happens in both NWLink and NetBEUI. Therefore, answer d is incorrect. Assigning clients IP addresses is a function of a DHCP server. Therefore, answer e is incorrect.

Question 7

What is an LMHOSTS file?

- ❍ a. A static list of NetBIOS names mapped to IP addresses
- ❍ b. A dynamic list of NetBIOS names mapped to IP addresses
- ❍ c. A static list of FQDNs mapped to IP addresses
- ❍ d. A dynamic list of FQDNs mapped to IP addresses

Answer a is correct. LMHOSTS is the predecessor to WINS and is a static list of NetBIOS names mapped to IP addresses. A dynamic list of NetBIOS names mapped to IP addresses is WINS. Therefore, answer b is incorrect. The HOSTS file is a static list of FQDNs mapped to IP addresses. Therefore, answer c is incorrect. There is no dynamic list of FQDNs mapped to IP addresses, but this is a decent explanation of DNS. Therefore, answer d is incorrect.

Question 8

Which of the following services are best matched for reducing administration of multiple clients? [Check all correct answers]

- ❑ a. DNS
- ❑ b. DHCP
- ❑ c. LMHOSTS
- ❑ d. WINS
- ❑ e. HOSTS

Answers b and d are correct. DHCP and WINS are the best matched pair of services for maintaining a dynamic list of changing client mappings. DNS, LMHOSTS, and HOSTS are all administration intensive. Therefore, answers a, c, and e are incorrect.

Question 9

On a network with Internet access, you wish to host six Web sites from a single implementation of IIS. Which of the following must you do to accomplish this?

- ❍ a. Install RIP For IP on the IIS server.
- ❍ b. Assign each of the IP addresses to be used to the NIC in the IIS server, then associate each IP address with the appropriate Web directory.
- ❍ c. Set up the DHCP Relay Agent.
- ❍ d. Configure DNS so it contains the FQDN for each server and correlates that name to its IP address.
- ❍ e. Configure WINS by adding the NetBIOS names and IP addresses of the sites to the static list of servers.

Answer b is correct. The only activity required to host multiple Web sites on IIS when connected to the Internet is to assign multiple IP addresses to the server and to associate each address with its respective directories. RIP For IP and DHCP Relay Agent are unrelated to this situation. Therefore, answers a and c are incorrect. DNS and WINS are not required because an Internet-hosted DNS will support the name resolution. Therefore, answers d and e are incorrect.

Question 10

On a private network not attached to the Internet, what are the benefits of using WINS over DNS? [Check all correct answers]

- ❑ a. Dynamic automated updates of NetBIOS and IP address correlation
- ❑ b. Reverse lookup capabilities
- ❑ c. Hierarchical database structure
- ❑ d. Supports domain functions
- ❑ e. Platform-independent

Answers a and d are correct. The advantages WINS has over DNS include the dynamic automated updates of its address correlation tables and its support for domain functions. WINS does not support reverse lookup, uses a flat namespace structure, and is limited to Microsoft platforms. Therefore, answers b, c, and e are incorrect.

Question 11

How are the HOSTS and LMHOSTS files different?

- ❍ a. A HOSTS file maps host names to IP addresses, whereas an LMHOSTS file maps IP addresses to NetBIOS names.
- ❍ b. An LMHOSTS file maps host names to IP addresses, whereas a HOSTS file maps IP addresses to NetBIOS names.
- ❍ c. A HOSTS file maps host names to IP addresses, whereas an LMHOSTS file maps host names to NetBIOS names.
- ❍ d. An LMHOSTS file maps host names to IP addresses, whereas a HOSTS file maps host names to NetBIOS names.

Answer a is correct. A HOSTS file maps host names to IP addresses, whereas an LMHOSTS file maps IP addresses to NetBIOS names. HOSTS has nothing to do with NetBIOS names, so answer b is incorrect. LMHOSTS maps IP addresses to NetBIOS names, not host names to NetBIOS names, so answer c is incorrect. Answer d reverses the correct role of these two files, so it is also incorrect.

Need To Know More?

Donald, Lisa, and James Chellis: *MSCE: NT Server 4 In The Enterprise Study Guide, 2nd Edition*. Sybex Network Press, San Francisco, CA, 1998. ISBN 0-7821-2221-3. Chapter 11 discusses TCP/IP-based name resolution, including DNS, WINS, LMHOSTS, HOSTS, and DHCP. Chapter 12 focuses on IIS.

Heywood, Drew: *Inside Windows NT Server, 2nd Edition*. New Riders, Indianapolis, IN, 1998. ISBN 1-56205-860-6. Chapter 9 has a limited discussion of name resolution and DHCP. Chapter 18 looks at IIS.

Siyan, Karanjit S.: *Windows NT Server 4 Professional Reference, 2nd Edition*. New Riders, Indianapolis, IN, 1997. ISBN 1-56205-805-3. Chapters 13 through 16 discuss various aspects of protocol TCP/IP, name resolution, DHCP, and WINS. Chapter 23 discusses DNS. This book does not discuss IIS.

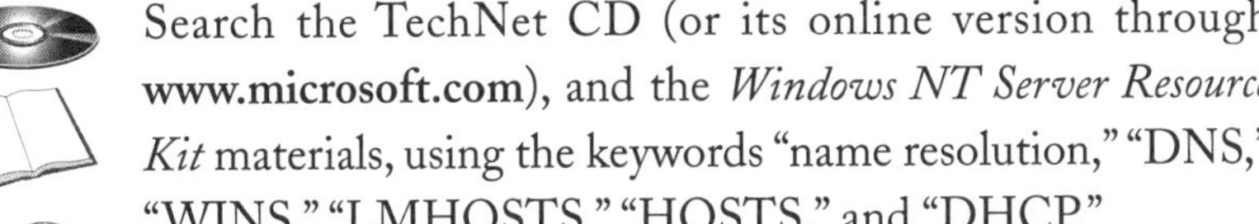

Search the TechNet CD (or its online version through **www.microsoft.com**), and the *Windows NT Server Resource Kit* materials, using the keywords "name resolution," "DNS," "WINS," "LMHOSTS," "HOSTS," and "DHCP."

Windows NT Network Monitor

Terms you'll need to understand:

- √ Network monitoring
- √ Capture filters
- √ Capture triggers
- √ Buffer space
- √ Dedicated mode captures

Techniques you'll need to master:

- √ Installing and configuring Network Monitor
- √ Analyzing Network Monitor data
- √ Capturing network data by protocol, address, and data pattern
- √ Recognizing security issues

Windows NT Server 4 is the first Microsoft operating system to include a network sniffer as a built-in utility. However, this version of Network Monitor is not fully functional. Instead, it is a scaled-down version of the Microsoft Systems Management Server (SMS) Network Monitor tool.

Even with its limitations, Network Monitor is a handy tool for investigating network-related problems. For example, the Network Monitor can monitor the number of network frames that are dropped by a network card. Frames dropped by a network card might signify a faulty adapter. In this chapter, we examine the details of Network Monitor.

Installing And Configuring Network Monitor

Network Monitor is not one of the utilities automatically installed during the initial Windows NT setup. You must use the Services tab of the Network applet in Control Panel to add Network Monitor Tools and Agent to your system. Once installed, Network Monitor appears in the Administrative Tools menu and the Monitoring Agent appears in the Control Panel.

While installing Network Monitor, you might notice that there is a Network Monitor Agent entry right above the Network Monitor Tools and Agent. This allows you to install just the Agent portion of Network Monitor to help identify a system to a Network Monitor operating on another machine and to distribute Performance Monitor metrics when monitoring the performance of a system remotely. If you don't select the Tools version from the Services tab, you won't be able to capture and view data on the server where it's installed.

Analyzing Network Monitor Data

Because the version of Network Monitor included with Windows NT is a scaled-down version, it's not as capable as the Systems Management Server (SMS) version, and this limited functionality is not unexpected. On the other hand, this "limitation" offers a performance advantage. The server NIC does not have to be placed in promiscuous mode because all supported frame types are captured by the card due to the support for NDIS 4. This saves up to 30 percent in CPU performance over a system with a NIC in promiscuous mode.

Network Monitor is only able to capture four types of data:

- Frames sent from the server
- Frames sent to the server
- Broadcast frames
- Multicast frames

To capture data using Network Monitor, simply launch the application, then select the Start command in the Capture pull-down menu (or press F10). At any time, you can stop or pause the data capture through this menu. Once the capture process has been stopped or paused, you can view the contents of any frame.

During and after the capture session, you can view four collections of information gathered by Network Monitor:

- Bar graphs
- Session statistics
- Station statistics
- Total statistics

These options appear by default in the sectioned display window, as shown in Figure 10.1.

Bar graphs display information in realtime as it is gathered by the utility. The graphs include:

- Percent network utilization
- Frames per second
- Bytes per second
- Broadcasts per second
- Multicasts per second

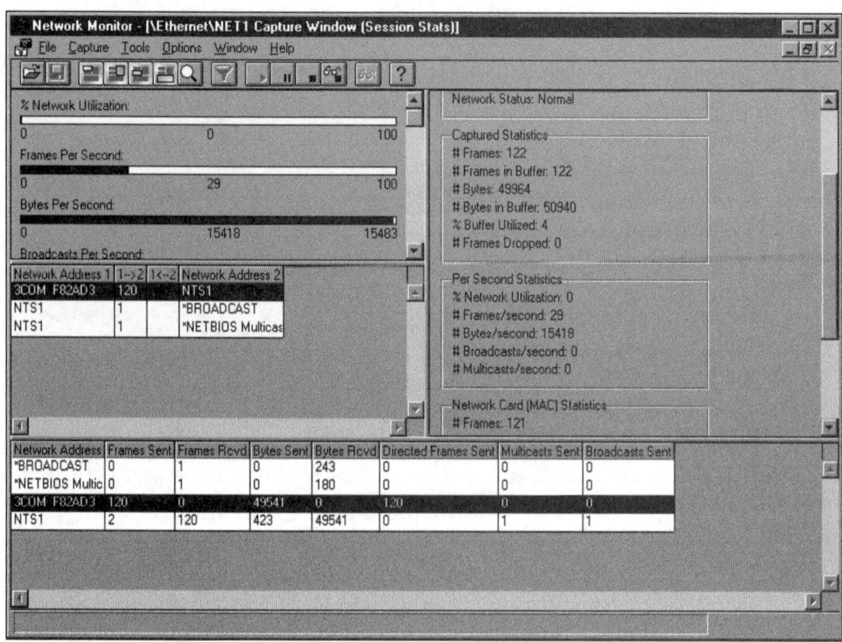

Figure 10.1 The Network Monitor.

The network utilization metric is significant because it gives you a direct visual guide to how traffic to and from the server is affecting overall network performance.

Session statistics detail the conversations going on over the network. This information is real time and cumulative during each capture session. Remember, due to the limitations of this application, the network conversations listed in this section are only those that involve the server.

Station statistics are cumulative data on the dynamics of each network conversation. The information displayed here includes:

- MAC or network address (sometimes replaced by a NetBIOS name)
- Sent frames
- Received frames
- Bytes sent
- Bytes received

- Directed frames sent
- Multicasts sent
- Broadcasts sent

Total statistics are cumulative data sets on a wide variety of metrics, including:

- Network
- Captured
- Per second
- MAC
- MAC errors

During a capture session, all of the intercepted frames are stored in the server's memory buffer. Once you complete your examination, wish to start another capture session, or are exiting Network Monitor, you can save the captured data to a CAP file for later investigation. By default, these files are placed in the \System32\Netmon\Captures directory. It is a good idea to name your captures by date to help identify them in the future.

Capture Filters

Capture filters are designed through the Capture Filter dialog box, reached by selecting the Filter command from the Capture drop-down menu (shown in Figure 10.2), or by pressing F8. This dialog box displays a decision tree that graphically represents the logic of the filter.

The Network Monitor is only able to capture as much information as will fit in whatever system memory is available. Capture information accumulates rapidly. If you attempt to gather all data points over an extended period of time, you'll have a difficult job of isolating (or even locating) any one element. Because of this, it is a good idea to limit the extent of any network capture. Through the use of filters, you can limit and fine-tune the data you gather to focus on one type of packet or data to and/or from one machine. A capture filter acts much like a database query: It specifies what results you want without dumping everything in your lap. Once you create a capture filter, it can be saved and reused.

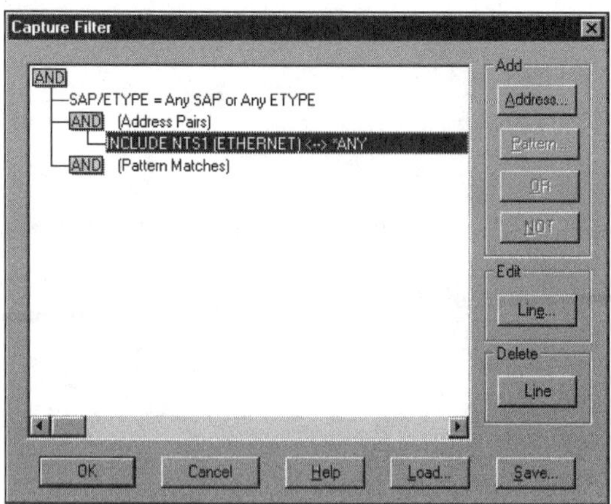

Figure 10.2 The Capture Filter dialog box.

Capture filters can gather data based on protocol, address pairs, and data patterns. The following sections discuss each technique available to filter and capture data.

Capturing By Protocol

A protocol-based filter is created by adding the filter line:

```
SAP/ETYPE={protocol}
```

The filter can be set to identify many different protocol types, including those listed in Table 10.1. The SMS version of Network Monitor supports additional protocols. Figure 10.3 shows the Capture Filter SAPs And ETYPEs dialog box.

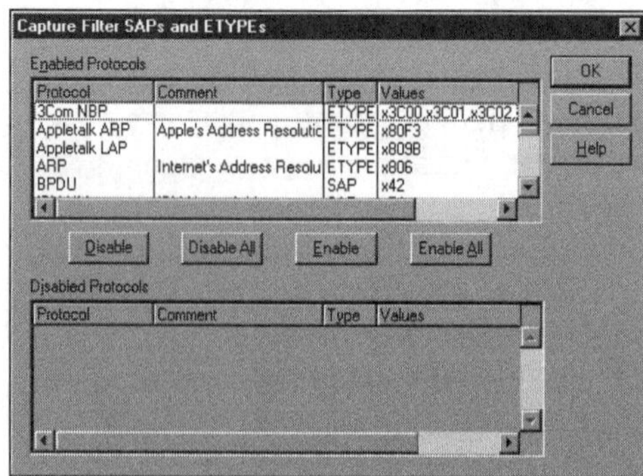

Figure 10.3 The Capture Filter SAPs And ETYPEs dialog box.

Table 10.1 The supported protocols for capture in Network Monitor.

AARP	FINGER	NBT	RPC
ADSP	FRAME	NCP	RPL
AFP	FTP	NDR	RTMP
ARP_RARP	ICMP	NetBIOS	SAP
ASP	IGMP	NETLOGON	SMB
ATP	IP	NFS	SMT
BONE	IPCP	NMPI	SNAP
BPDU	IPX	NSP	SPX
BROWSER	IPXCP	NWDP	TCP
CBCP	LAP	OSPF	TMAC
CCP	LCP	PAP	TOKEN_RING
DDP	LLC	PPP	UDP
DHCP	MSRPC	PPPCHAP	XNS
DNS	NBFCP	PPPPAP	ZIP
ETHERNET	NBIPX	RIP	
FDDI	NBP	RIPX	

Capturing By Address

Communication between the server and a specific computer can be tracked using an address pair in the capture filter (see Figure 10.4). Up to four address pairs can be monitored simultaneously.

An address pair is:

- The MAC address of the two computers
- An arrow specifying the direction of traffic to monitor (<- -, - ->, or <- ->)
- The **INCLUDE** or **EXCLUDE** keyword to instruct Network Monitor to track the frame or to ignore it

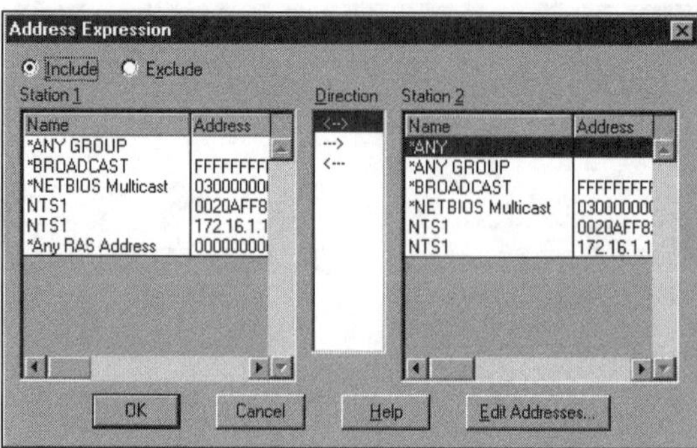

Figure 10.4 The Address Expression dialog box.

The order of the one to four address pairs is not significant. However, **EXCLUDE** statements are processed first. If the same frame is represented by both an **EXCLUDE** and an **INCLUDE** address pair, then **INCLUDE** is ignored (i.e., **EXCLUDE** takes precedence).

If you do not specify an address pair, the default address pair of ***<your computer>* <- -> ANY** is used.

Capturing By Data Pattern

Communications can also be traced using pattern matching within the capture filter (see Figure 10.5). Pattern matching limits a capture to frames that contain a specific ASCII or hexadecimal pattern that occurs within the entire frame or a specified depth into the frame (called an "offset") in bytes (from either the beginning of the frame or the end of the topology header). Two logical operations can be used with pattern matching filters: OR and NOT. These operators enable you to identify multiple patterns to capture or ignore.

In addition to Pattern Matching, you can set Capture Triggers, as explained in the following section.

Capture Triggers

Capture triggers are defined through the Capture Trigger dialog box, shown in Figure 10.6. You access the Capture Trigger dialog box through the Trigger command in the Capture pull-down menu.

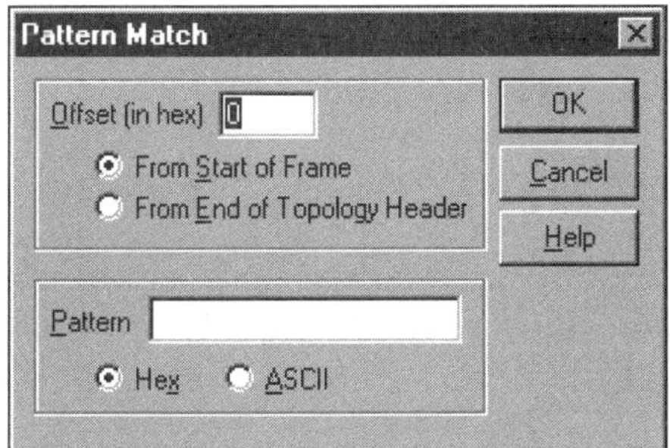

Figure 10.5 The Pattern Match dialog box.

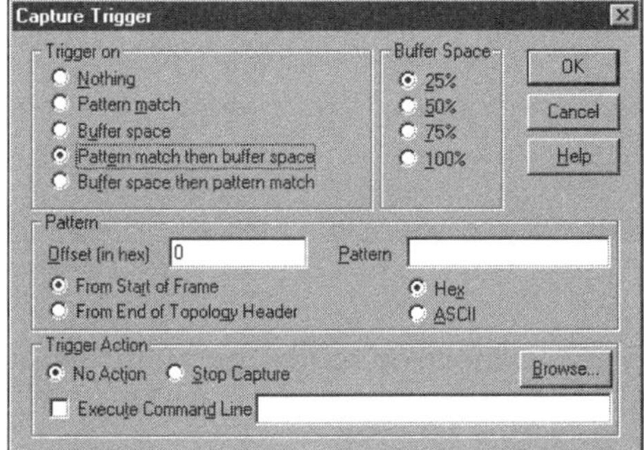

Figure 10.6 The Capture Trigger dialog box.

A capture trigger is a set of conditions that initiates an action when the conditions are met. Capture triggers allow you to automate some of the tasks associated with gathering network communications data, such as stopping the capture, executing a batch file, or even launching an application.

From this dialog box, the following selections can be used to define a custom trigger:

- **Nothing** Default setting of no trigger.
- **Pattern Match** Trigger is a matched pattern within a captured frame. The Pattern area is used to define the pattern matching conditions. The settings are the same as those present in the pattern match filter.

- **Buffer Space** Trigger is the percentage level of used buffer space. The Buffer Space area is used to set the percentage level.
- **Pattern Match Then Buffer Space** Trigger is a pattern match followed by a percentage of used buffer space.
- **Buffer Space Then Pattern Match** Trigger is a percentage of used buffer space followed by a pattern match.

Once the trigger has occurred, the settings in the Trigger Action area define what occurs:

- **No Action** By default, no action is taken other than a computer beep when the trigger occurs.
- **Stop Capture** Capture is halted.
- **Execute Command Line** A command line pointing to an application or batch file is launched.

Now that we have explained triggers, let's move on to discuss capturing in dedicated mode.

Dedicated Mode Captures

You can put the Network Monitor into dedicated mode to reduce the load on the CPU. This mode prevents the Network Monitor from updating and displaying Capture window statistics. The Dedicated Mode can be chosen from the Network Monitor Capture menu.

The Dedicated Mode dialog box only displays the total number of captured frames. In this dialog box, you will also find control buttons enabling you to stop, stop and view, or pause the capture. There is also a button called Normal Mode that takes the Network Monitor back to normal mode.

That's all you need to know about Network Monitor. Now let's move on and explore setting up security on your Windows NT network.

Addressing Security Issues

Windows NT Network Monitor captures only the frames that are sent to or from the local computer (this includes multicast and broadcast frames). This is for security reasons. To prevent nonauthorized users from gaining access to Network Monitor's data, two passwords can be configured for this application.

Through the Monitoring Agent utility in the Control Panel, a Display password and a Capture password can be set to restrict access. The Display password requires validation before any captured data files can be viewed. The Capture password requires validation before data can be gathered or viewed.

If the Network Monitor Agent is installed but no password is set, anyone using the SMS version of Network Monitor can connect to the machine and capture data.

As an added security precaution, you can use the Network Monitor to find different installations of Network Monitor on the local segment. This helps administrators limit unauthorized network monitoring. If the Network Monitor Agent is being used remotely, the Network Monitor detects all instances of this as well as SMS Network Monitor and Performance Monitor remote usage.

The Identify Network Monitor Users command on the Tools menu searches the local segment, then displays the computer's name, user name, state of the Network Monitor, version number, and network adapter address. This feature is not able to detect usage across routers that do not forward multicasts.

Displaying Data

Captured data can be examined on a frame-by-frame basis through the Display Captured Data command in the Capture menu. This command switches Network Monitor into Display Mode and presents an ordered list of all frames currently in the buffer. The frame captured number, time of capture, MAC source and destination address, protocol, description, and more can be viewed by scrolling through this list.

Any frame can be examined even closer by double-clicking it. This action opens two additional panes that display the protocol delivery details and a hexadecimal and ASCII representation of the captured data.

Similar to capture filters, display filters can be used to limit or restrict the frames displayed to a specific source address, protocol, or various protocol-specific properties and values. Display filters are created through the Filter command in the Display menu. The Display menu only appears when Network Monitor is in Display Mode. The syntax for display filters is as follows (note that a GUI interface is present to simplify the construction of these expressions):

- **Protocol** Protocol == {INCLUDE or EXCLUDE list of protocols}
- **Address Filter** Address1 <- -> Address2 or Address1- -> Address2 (the default is ANY <- -> ANY)
- **Property** Protocol:Property [Relation] Value (each property can vary, but this is the standard syntax)

For a property filter, each of the supported protocols has a lengthy list of commands, properties, and events. Each of these properties often has two or more possible relations, such as **==**, **<>**, **>**, **=<**, **CONTAINS**, **EXISTS**, **INCLUDES**, and so forth. Furthermore, the value is determined by the property and the relation. The most common value is a hex, decimal, or ASCII number, but it can also be a selection from a predefined list of expressions, events, or NetBIOS names. We recommend you spend a little time reviewing the thousands of possible settings. Other than the common patterns listed previously, we can't offer any shortcut to this material.

Other Features

There are a handful of other features and functions of which you should be aware:

- All of the addresses intercepted by Network Monitor can be viewed through the Addresses command in the Capture menu. From this dialog box, you can review all the addresses currently stored in Network Monitor's database. You can edit entries to alter the type, address, name, or comment for each entry. Plus, you can manually add and delete entries. This address database is used to associate the MAC address with a user friendly name.

- The buffer size used by Network Monitor to store captured frames can be controlled through the Buffer Settings command in the Capture menu. By default, the buffer is set to 1 MB. The size of the buffer can be increased to a maximum of 8 MB less than the total amount of RAM installed on your server. Once the buffer is full, old frames are dropped to accommodate new ones, instead of storing the frames in the swap file. A further setting in this dialog box is the amount of data to store from each frame. This can be set to the entire frame or from 64 to 65,472 bytes. This does not change the size of frames used by the network, but changes how much of each frame is stored in the memory buffer.
- Through the Network command in the Capture menu, you can track multiple network segments attached to separate NICs. Each NIC installed on the server is listed in the Select Capture Network dialog box. Each listed NIC can be Connected (captured from) or Suspended (not captured from). To capture two networks simultaneously without combining the data requires two instances of Network Monitor, each set to watch a different segment.
- The Find All Names command from the Capture menu will search each captured frame for a NetBIOS name assigned to MAC addresses. All names found are added to the address database and used in the display sections to simplify the identification of computers for humans. In other words, found names replace corresponding instances of MAC addresses in the statistics panes.
- The commands Find Routers and Resolve Addresses From Name do not work in the Network Monitor version that ships with Windows NT. These work only in the SMS version.

Practice Questions

Question 1

While using the Network Monitor, you decide to implement a display filter to aid in your search for the NetBIOS Add Group Name command. What is the proper syntax of a properties-based display filter?

- ❍ a. NETBIOS:Command == 0x0 (Add Group Name)
- ❍ b. NETBIOS <= Add Group Name Command
- ❍ c. Add Group Name > NETBIOS
- ❍ d. NETBIOS<- ->Add Group Name

Answer a is correct. It contains the proper syntax for the properties display filter. It contains Protocol:Property [Relation] Value. Answer b is incorrect because the four elements of the properties-based display filter are scrambled. Answer c is incorrect because it is missing the property and the remaining elements are out of order. Answer d is incorrect because it is missing the property element, the other elements are out of order, and the relation is not valid for a property relation.

Question 2

Which application is best suited for detecting which computer on a local segment is causing the most network traffic?

- ❍ a. Performance Monitor
- ❍ b. Network Monitor
- ❍ c. Server Manager
- ❍ d. Traffic Analyzer

Answer b is correct. Network Monitor is able to identify individual machines based on their MAC addresses, and it can track their contributions to network traffic if that traffic is sent to the server. The Performance Monitor is not able to identify a single machine from the bulk of network traffic. Therefore, answer a is incorrect. The Server Manager does not have the ability to monitor network traffic. Therefore, answer c is incorrect. There is no utility called Traffic Analyzer in Windows NT. Therefore, answer d is incorrect.

Question 3

You are working with Network Monitor to evaluate your network usage. You want to capture all frames inbound to your server, except any traffic sent from John's computer. The name of your server is "Admin1", and the name of John's computer is "Sales5". What is the best way to set up the capture filter?

- ❍ a. INCLUDE Admin1 <- -> NOT (Sales5)
- ❍ b. INCLUDE Admin1 <- -> ANY; EXCLUDE Admin - -> Sales5
- ❍ c. EXCLUDE Admin1 <- - Sales5
- ❍ d. EXCLUDE Admin1 <- -> Sales5

Answer c is correct. Answer c is an **EXCLUDE** statement that ignores traffic from the Sales5 computer. Answer a is not a proper construction. The relation indicates both inbound and outbound traffic, plus the **NOT** logical operator is used outside of the filter statement. Therefore, answer a is incorrect. Answer b lists the default **INCLUDE** statement, which does not need to be repeated, and the **EXCLUDE** statement applies to traffic sent to Sales5. Therefore, answer b is incorrect. Answer d excludes both inbound and outbound traffic for Sales5. Therefore, answer d is incorrect.

Question 4

What types of information can be tracked with the version of Network Monitor that ships with Windows NT Server? [Check all correct answers]

- ❑ a. Multicast packets
- ❑ b. All packets on a network
- ❑ c. Packets sent to or from the monitoring server
- ❑ d. Broadcast packets
- ❑ e. Packets from one workstation to another
- ❑ f. NetBIOS packets sent over a router

Answers a, c, and d are correct. As it ships with Windows NT Server, Network Monitor can only track packets that include the monitoring server as the destination or origination address; this includes broadcast and multicast packets. Answers b, e, and f are incorrect. Network Monitor cannot capture packets that are not addressed to or from the server, plus NetBIOS is not a routable protocol.

Question 5

Which product from Microsoft also includes a Network Monitor, where that version also includes additional features and functions?

- ❍ a. SQL Server
- ❍ b. SNA Server
- ❍ c. Systems Management Server
- ❍ d. Exchange Server

Answer c is correct. Systems Management Server includes a Network Monitor with more capabilities than the version shipped with Windows NT. SQL Server is a database system and does not include a Network Monitor. Therefore, answer a is incorrect. SNA Server is a mainframe integration product and does not include a Network Monitor. Therefore, answer b is incorrect. Exchange Server is an email system and does not include a Network Monitor. Therefore, answer d is incorrect.

Question 6

You installed Windows NT Server with the default configuration onto your C drive and subsequently installed Network Monitor Tools and Agent from the Services tab of the Network Control Panel application. When you save sets of captured data, where will the CAP files be placed by default?

- ❍ a. C:\Winnt\System32\Netmon\Captures
- ❍ b. C:\Program Files\Netmon\Captures
- ❍ c. C:\Admin\Netmon\Captures
- ❍ d. C:\Winnt\System32\Repl\Export\Netmon\Captures

Answer a is corect. The directories listed in answers b, c, and d are not the default directories for storing the CAP files from Network Monitor. Therefore, answers b, c, and d are incorrect.

Question 7

Network Monitor's security feature of searching out other users of the Network Monitor Agent can detect what applications? [Check all correct answers]

- ❑ a. Network Monitor from SMS
- ❑ b. HP's OpenView
- ❑ c. Event Viewer from Windows NT Workstation
- ❑ d. Network Monitor from Windows NT Server
- ❑ e. Performance Monitor

Answers a, d, and e are correct. Network Monitor can detect instances of Network Monitor from SMS. Therefore, answer a is correct. Network Monitor can detect both Windows NT Server's Network Monitor and Performance Monitor. Therefore, answers d and e are also correct. Network Monitor cannot detect HP's OpenView or Event Viewer, and neither of these applications accesses the Network Monitor Agent. Therefore, answers b and c are incorrect.

Question 8

How would you protect captured data from being viewed by unauthorized users? [Check all correct answers]

- ❑ a. Set a Display password through the Monitoring Agent applet.
- ❑ b. Set an Access password on the Network Monitor application.
- ❑ c. Set a Capture password through the Monitoring Agent applet.
- ❑ d. Set a Display password through the Security menu of Network Monitor.
- ❑ e. There are no features to restrict Network Monitor access.

Answers a and c are correct. Setting a Display password through the Monitoring Agent applet will restrict users from viewing captured data. Therefore, answer a is correct. Setting a Capture password through the Monitoring Agent applet will restrict both capturing and viewing data. Therefore, answer c is correct. There is no command named "Access Password." Therefore, answer b is incorrect. There is no Security menu in Network Monitor. Therefore, answer d is incorrect. There are two passwords used to restrict access to Network Monitor configured through the Monitoring Agent applet in the Control Panel. Therefore, answer e is incorrect.

Need To Know More?

Donald, Lisa, and James Chellis: *MSCE: NT Server 4 In The Enterprise Study Guide, 2nd Edition.* Sybex Network Press, San Francisco, CA, 1998. ISBN 0-7821-2221-3. Chapter 16 is dedicated to the Network Monitor. Its coverage is mediocre, and details about filtering are virtually nonexistent.

The Windows NT Server 4 manuals cover planning, configuration, and installation issues quite well. The *Concepts And Planning Manual* contains the only useful documentation we could find on the Network Monitor, in Chapter 10, "Monitoring Your Network."

For further details on the Network Monitor, please consult the Windows NT Server online help. It provides at least some details for each command.

11

Managing Windows NT Performance

Terms you'll need to understand:

- √ Task Manager
- √ Objects
- √ Instances
- √ Counters
- √ Alerts
- √ Logging
- √ Baselining
- √ Paging file
- √ Process priorities

Techniques you'll need to master:

- √ Using Task Manager to view and control system processes
- √ Using Performance Monitor to capture and analyze network statistics
- √ Monitoring and examining disk performance
- √ Configuring administrative alerts
- √ Viewing network statistics logs
- √ Assigning process priorities
- √ Optimizing Windows NT Server settings

Performance management on Windows NT Server involves numerous applications and configuration screens. In this chapter, we look into many of the tools and methods used to monitor and increase performance. Specifically, we look at the Task Manager, Performance Monitor, and the Windows NT paging file. In addition, we look at managing process priorities and optimizing server settings.

Task Manager

The Task Manager is a new utility to the Windows NT environment. This tool enables you to view and control the processes currently active on your machine. Three types of information are available through the Task Manager (each displayed on its own display tab).

The three types of information available through the Task Manager are:

- **Applications** This tab shows a list of the applications currently in use and their status, whether running or nonresponsive (see Figure 11.1).
- **Processes** This tab displays a list of all processes in memory, with details on the CPU and memory usage (see Figure 11.2).
- **Performance** This tab shows a graphical and numerical display of system performance metrics, including CPU and memory usage graphs; totals for handles, threads, and processes; physical memory stats; committed memory changes (memory allocated to the system or an application); and kernel memory stats (see Figure 11.3).

The Task Manager can be launched using two different methods:

- Press Ctrl+Alt+Del, then click the Task Manager button.
- Right-click over a blank area of the taskbar, then select the Task Manager from the pop-up menu.

The Task Manager is an invaluable tool for fast investigation of system activity and instant corrective actions, such as:

- Identifying nonresponsive applications, and terminating them to release their hostage resources (Applications tab).

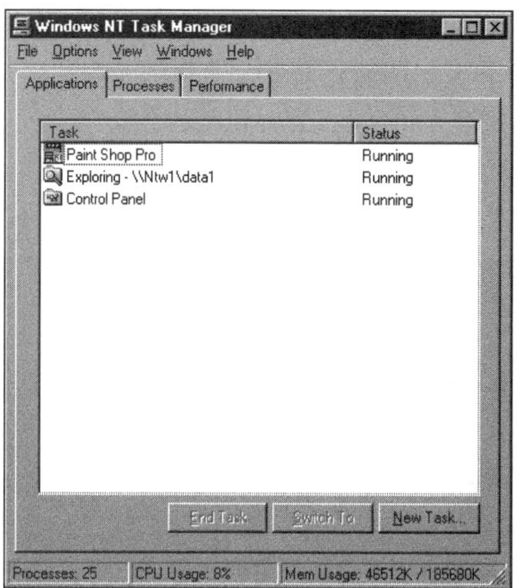

Figure 11.1 The Task Manager's Applications tab.

Windows NT Task Manager

File Options View Help

Applications Processes Performance

Image Name	PID	CPU	CPU Time	Mem Usage
System Idle Process	0	87	360:53:53	16 K
System	2	00	0:05:16	120 K
smss.exe	21	00	0:00:00	120 K
csrss.exe	30	00	0:00:08	224 K
WINLOGON.EXE	35	00	0:00:01	20 K
SERVICES.EXE	41	00	0:00:50	2144 K
LSASS.EXE	46	00	0:00:17	764 K
SPOOLSS.EXE	71	00	0:00:07	756 K
DkService.exe	83	00	0:00:00	0 K
FINDFAST.EXE	88	00	2:30:05	1724 K
Control.exe	95	00	0:11:57	2580 K
LLSSRV.EXE	97	00	0:00:14	580 K
LOCATOR.EXE	104	00	0:00:00	0 K
wfxctl32.exe	114	05	17:13:39	3084 K
RPCSS.EXE	120	00	0:00:01	176 K
wfxsvc.exe	125	00	0:00:00	0 K
wfxmod32.exe	130	00	0:01:24	1148 K
inetinfo.exe	133	00	0:07:47	760 K
TAPISRV.EXE	166	00	0:00:01	120 K

End Process

Processes: 25 CPU Usage: 15% Mem Usage: 46672K / 185680K

Figure 11.2 The Task Manager's Processes tab.

- Identifying runaway processes, and terminating them to return the system to normal operational levels (Processes tab).
- Ascertaining the memory use levels to determine the need for additional RAM (Performance tab).

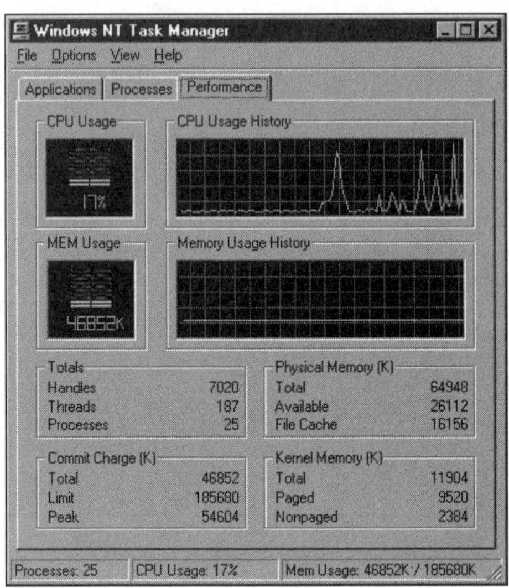

Figure 11.3 The Task Manager's Performance tab.

The Task Manager also enables you to launch new processes (applications), switch to a new foreground application, view separate graphs for each CPU, display the kernel access time, and alter the priority of processes (see the "Managing Process Priorities" section, later in this chapter).

Performance Monitor

The Windows NT Performance Monitor (PerfMon) is an analytical utility that you can use to inspect the performance and activity of processes, resources, physical components, networks, and remote machines. The use and operation of Performance Monitor is rather simple. However, knowing what metrics or counters to watch and what to do about them is not always so easy. We'll take a look at the controls and commands of PerfMon, then look into how to use it to evaluate Windows NT's performance.

Performance Monitor has four views: Chart, Alert, Log, and Report.

- **Chart view** Allows users to view realtime data in a line graph or histogram form (see Figure 11.4).
- **Alert view** Allows users to set and view alerts and alert statistics.

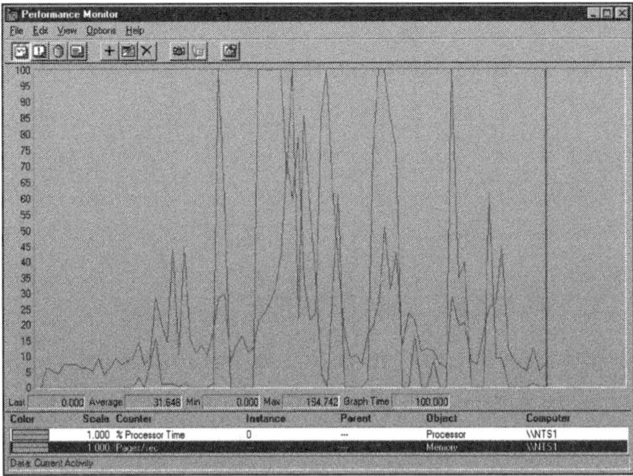

Figure 11.4 The Performance Monitor in Chart view monitoring processor time and memory page swaps.

- **Log view** Allows users to create and save a log of system performance.
- **Report view** Allows users to create custom reports of Performance Monitor data.

All four views revolve around counters. A counter is a measurable aspect of an object used to evaluate the performance of that object. No matter which view you use, the Add To command in the Edit menu is how you add counters. When you initiate this command, a dialog box appears that allows you to select counters based on the counter's computer, object, and instance.

- **Computer** Most computers on the network provide counters that PerfMon can read and display; however, as the operating system on the remote machine gets farther away from Windows NT, the number of useful counters decreases.
- **Objects** Any component on the specified computer that can be measured is listed as an object, such as processor, memory, physical disk, and so forth.
- **Instances** This identifies which instance of an object should be monitored. Instance **0** is the first or only occurrence of an object, instance **1** is the second occurrence, and so on. If it is not possible for an object to have multiple instances, such as the Server service, then this area is blank.

➤ **Counters** This identifies the available counters for a specific instance of an object on the chosen computer.

A cursory interaction with PerfMon may leave you baffled as to which counters are important. The next section looks at counters that are used most frequently.

Common Objects And Counters

In the real world of networking, you may have to be familiar with more counters than the ones listed in this section. Fortunately, if you don't quite understand any counter, you can highlight it in the Add To dialog box and click the Explain button to get a brief but helpful definition for each counter.

The following PerfMon counters are the most frequently used:

➤ **Processor: %Processor Time** When you suspect a processor upgrade may be necessary, measure this counter. If the processor counter measures 80 percent or more for an extended period of time, this could be a good indication that the processor is in need of an upgrade.

➤ **System: Processor Queue Length** This can also be measured to figure out if a processor upgrade is necessary. If the number of threads waiting to be processed is greater than two, the processor may be a bottleneck for the system.

➤ **Processor: Interrupts/sec.** When you suspect a hardware device is malfunctioning in the system, measure this counter. If the Processor-Interrupts/sec. increases and the processor time does not, a hardware device could be sending bogus interrupts to the processor. Locate the hardware device and replace it.

➤ **Memory: Cache Faults, Page Faults, and Pages/sec.** When you suspect that there is not enough memory in the system, these counters should be measured. They indicate the frequency your system needs to swap pages to the hard disk swap file. If any of these counters is high, chances are the need for memory is high as well.

- **PhysicalDisk/LogicalDisk: %Disk Time** When you suspect the hard disk is a system bottleneck, measure this counter. This counter shows you how much processor time is being spent servicing disk requests. Measure this counter against Processor: % Processor Time to see if the disk requests are using up a notable amount of processor time.
- **PhysicalDisk/LogicalDisk: Disk Bytes/Transfer** When you are trying to find out how fast your hard disks are transferring data, measure this counter.
- **PhysicalDisk/LogicalDisk: Current Disk Queue Length** When you are thinking about upgrading your hard disk, measure this counter. This counter shows you how much data is waiting to be transferred to the disk. If the disk queue is long (2 or greater), processes are being delayed by disk speed.

Note: The PhysicalDisk object counters apply to the entire physical storage device and are best used for hardware troubleshooting. The LogicalDisk object counters focus on a specific volume and are best used for read/write performance investigations.

Monitoring Disk Performance

By default, the physical and logical disk counters are not activated. The process of gathering disk counters has a significant effect on the performance of storage devices. To turn on the disk counters, you need to execute **diskperf -y**, then reboot your system. Once you complete your monitoring, turn off the disk counters with **diskperf -n** and reboot. You must be logged on as the Administrator to execute either of these commands. Until **diskperf** is executed, all Physical and Logical Disk counters will display a reading of **0** (zero).

Using The PerfMon Views

In the following sections, we explore the various views you can use in Performance Monitor to examine network data. These views include Chart, Alert, Log, and Report.

Using Charts

Once you've selected and added counters to your Chart view, you can make some adjustments through the Options|Chart command. This brings up a dialog box where you can alter the maximum value of the vertical axis, change between graph and histogram, add grid lines, and change update intervals.

Configuring Alerts

You can use the Windows NT Performance Monitor to configure system alerts. For example, an administrator could be informed when a storage device approaches 85 percent capacity. To work with alerts, you must switch to the Alert view from the View menu. Just as in the Chart view, you add counters through the Edit|Add To Alert command. The Add To Alert dialog box is the same as that for a chart, with the addition of an alert trigger level and program/script to run when an alert occurs.

The remaining alert configuration options are accessed through the Options|Alert command. From there, you can instruct PerfMon to switch to Alert view when an alert is triggered, write the alert in the Application log, and send a notification message to a user or machine.

Working With Logs

The Log view is used to create a stored record of the performance of one or more objects to be analyzed or compared to at another time. Just as in the Chart view, you must use the Edit|Add To Log command to add objects for the Log to record. Note that Log does not offer a selection at the counter level. It records all possible counters for the selected objects.

Once you've selected the objects to log, you need to define the update interval and file name of the log file. This is done through the Options|Log command. You will be prompted for a file name and how often to capture the counters for the objects.

Creating A Report

A report of your gathered metrics can be created through the Report view. Counters to include in a report are added in a similar manner as counters are added in the other views, through the Edit|Add To Report command.

After you select the counters to list in the report, you need to set the update interval using the Options|Report command.

Miscellaneous Commands And Controls

All PerfMon view selections have numerous commands in common, including:

- **File|Save [View] Settings As** Saves a view's settings to be used at another time.
- **File|Save Workspace** Saves all view settings in a single file.
- **File|Export** Saves the current view's captured data in a tab- or comma-delimited file.
- **Add|Edit** Edits the counter parameters or settings.
- **Add|Delete** Removes the counter.
- **Options|Data From** Displays data from the active network or from a log file.

> *Note: No matter which view is being used, Performance Monitor must remain up and running (i.e., an active process) to display realtime charts, record a log, send alerts, or create reports.*

Now that we have discussed the Performance Monitor's views, let's move on to the process of baselining.

Baselining

Baselining, or establishing a baseline, is the process of recording the parameters of a fully functional system. This is done through the Log view. Once you've recorded a log of an operating system with "normal" parameters, you can use the log in the future to evaluate the performance of the system. Some objects you should include in your baseline are:

- Processor
- Physical disk
- Memory

- Server
- System
- Any installed protocols

However, just grabbing a short interval of data won't provide a useful baseline for comparison. Instead, you should record a log file for each counter over a 24-hour interval with a counter reading 5, 10, or 15 minutes, and repeat this for a few days or even a week. This provides you with a look into the network's performance during an entire day, covering both peak and off-peak hours. Furthermore, it is a good idea to repeat the process of collecting a baseline once a month. This not only establishes a timeline of "normal" performance, but also provides a regular interval to investigate the activity of your network. The regular inspection may help reveal new bottlenecks or failures, which you would otherwise not be aware of until production came to a standstill.

Windows NT Paging File

Windows NT uses disk space to expand the available memory for the system. The Virtual Memory Manager (VMM) swaps pages from physical RAM to the swap or paging file stored on a hard drive. Generally, the VMM handles everything about the paging file automatically, but you can control its maximum size and destination drive.

Changes to the paging file are made through the Performance tab of the System applet in the Control Panel. There is an area in the middle of this display tab labeled Virtual Memory (see Figure 11.5) that indicates the total size of the pagefile. Click the Change button to alter this setting.

Through the Virtual Memory dialog box, you can change the size of the paging file on any storage device. The paging file can reside on a single drive or in areas on multiple drives. However, the overall speed of Windows NT is determined by how fast the VMM can swap sections of memory from physical RAM to the swap file. Thus, the speed of the storage device is important.

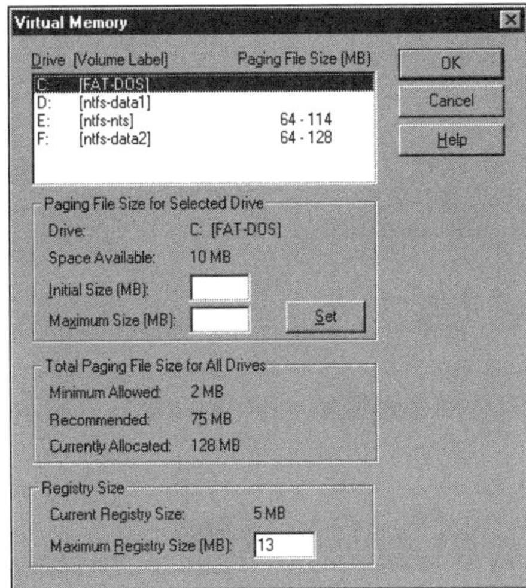

Figure 11.5 The Virtual Memory dialog box.

The two parameters you must define for each drive that will support a pagefile are "initial size" and "maximum size." The initial size is the space VMM initially allocates and uses for the swap file. The maximum size is the most space the VMM will use on the drive for the swap file. The VMM is able to expand and shrink the swap file as needed between these two settings. However, neither of these settings guarantees that the disk will have enough free space for a pagefile of the specified size.

Here are some hints on how to speed up the paging file:

- If your system includes multiple physical disks, the paging file may be spread across these disks. This is called "disk striping," which automatically spreads the paging file across multiple physical disks. Disk striping increases the speed of the paging file because it uses the read/write heads of multiple disks instead of a single disk.

- If you move the paging file off the drive that contains the Windows NT system files, it keeps the paging files from competing with the operating system files.

- The pagefile should not be placed within a disk mirror because the double-writing of data in such a configuration causes a significant delay in pagefile access. Also, a pagefile shouldn't be placed in a duplex set because the temporary storage of memory data would require more CPU cycles to write twice (even over two controllers), once again increasing access time.

The second control is accessed via the Task Manager. By selecting any of the listed processes on the Processes tab, you can change the priority to low, normal, high, or realtime via the Set Priority menu, accessed through the right-click pop-up menu.

While Windows NT is operating, the PAGEFILE.SYS (the name of the swap file) cannot be deleted. If for some reason the swap file is deleted, Windows NT will re-create it during boot-up.

Managing Process Priorities

Windows NT's multiprocessing environment requires that some processes have a higher execution priority than others. The kernel handles the setting of priorities for each process and has the ability to increase or decrease the priority of a process to improve or alter how it executes. There are 32 priority levels (0 through 31). The higher-numbered priorities are executed before the lower numbered priorities.

Although the system has the ability to use all 32 levels directly, you have only a limited ability to set priorities. By default, all user- and administrator-launched applications are assigned a base priority of **8** (**/normal**). However, users can launch applications with **4** (**/low**) or **13** (**/high**) priority and an administrator can launch with **24** (**/realtime**) priority. To launch an application with an alternate priority level, use the following syntax at a command prompt:

```
start [/low|/normal|/high|/realtime] application
```

Windows NT offers two other priority controls to alter the levels of running processes. The first is a slide bar to control the performance boost for foreground applications. A foreground application is the process that is the active window on your screen, usually indicated by a colored title bar. This slide control is located on the Performance tab in the System applet in the Control Panel. By default, foreground applications have a priority of **10** (maximum). You can move the slider to set foregrounds with an additional priority level of **1** (middle tick) or **0** (none).

The second control is accessed via the Task Manager. By selecting any of the listed processes on the Process tab, you can change the priority to low, normal, high, or realtime via the Set Priority menu accessed through the right-click pop-up menu.

Optimizing Server Settings

The Server service is the process that distributes data to requesting clients. You can select one of four settings to fine-tune or optimize how this service operates.

The dialog box shown in Figure 11.6 is reached through the Properties Of The Server Service listed on the Services tab of the Network applet in the Control Panel. The choices are:

- **Minimize Memory Used** This setting provides the best performance for less than 10 users.
- **Balance** This setting provides the best performance for 10 through 64 users.
- **Maximize Throughput For File Sharing** This setting provides the best performance for more than 64 users, by maximizing the memory available for file sharing. This is the default setting.
- **Maximize Throughput For Network Applications** This setting is used for supporting distributed applications, such as SQL Server.

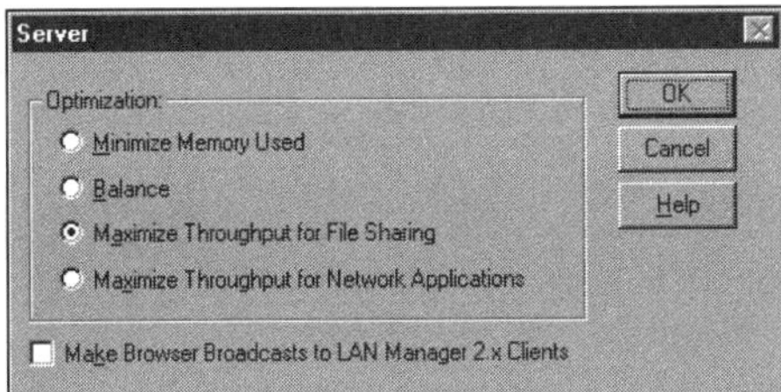

Figure 11.6 Selecting Maximizing Throughput For File Sharing on a Windows NT Server.

Practice Questions

Question 1

Which of the following is the best way to establish a baseline for Server service performance counters?

- ❍ a. Capture performance counters from the Server object for 30 minutes during nonworking hours.
- ❍ b. Capture performance counters from the Server object for 30 minutes during the peak hour, capture performance counters from the Service object for 30 minutes during a nonworking hour, then average these two measurements.
- ❍ c. Capture performance counters from the Server object for 30 minutes each day at a pre-selected time for a week.
- ❍ d. Capture performance counters from the Server object at regular intervals throughout the day for three days.

Answer d is correct. Answer d will provide an adequate baseline because the data collected will represent all levels of use over a multiple-day period. Answer a will not provide an adequate baseline because the captured data covers only a brief off-peak interval. Therefore, answer a is incorrect. Answer b will not provide an adequate baseline because the captured data represents only a brief off-peak and peak interval. Furthermore, the averaging of the times makes the data even more useless. Therefore, answer b is incorrect. Answer c will not provide an adequate baseline because recording a brief period every day does not reflect the overall picture of the network activity. Therefore, answer c is incorrect.

Question 2

You want to monitor the physical disk performance of a server remotely. With a standard installation of Windows NT Server on both machines, network connectivity, and membership in the same domain, what additional operation must be performed to enable the monitoring of the disk counters remotely?

- ❍ a. Install Network Monitor Agent on the machine to be observed.
- ❍ b. Run the **diskperf** utility with the **-y** option on the machine to be observed.
- ❍ c. Install Network Monitor Agent, and run the **diskperf** utility with the **-y** option on the machine to be observed.
- ❍ d. No additional operations are required. The physical disk counters are remotely accessible by default.

Answer b is correct. The **diskperf -y** command is needed to enable the physical disk counters, but all performance counters can be accessed remotely without further configuration. The Network Monitor Agent is not required to remotely monitor performance counters. It is only needed to access Network Monitor elements remotely. Therefore, answer a is incorrect. The Network Monitor is not required, but the **diskperf** command is. Therefore, answer c is incorrect. The **diskperf** command is required because all disk counters are not enabled by default. They must be turned on before PerfMon can access them locally or remotely. Therefore, answer d is incorrect.

Question 3

Users on your network are experiencing upwards of twice the normal time to access files from the Windows NT Server, but all other activities are relatively unaffected. Your server has three physical hard disks with two partitions on each. Which of the following is the best type of object counter to monitor to investigate this problem?

- ❍ a. System object counters
- ❍ b. Logical Disk object counters
- ❍ c. Server object counters
- ❍ d. Physical Disk object counters
- ❍ e. Memory object counters

Answer b is correct. Logical Disk object counters are the best selection because they will provide data on space usage and level of read/write activities on volumes. System, Server, and Memory object counters will provide little help toward a storage device performance problem. Therefore, answers a, c, and e are incorrect. Physical Disk object counters are useful for hardware troubleshooting and affect an entire drive. The question focuses on the time to access files within a partition and not necessarily the entire drive, making the Logical Disk counters more effective. Therefore, answer d is incorrect.

Question 4

Which of the following utilities can be used to display the current level of CPU utilization? [Check all correct answers]

- ❑ a. Performance Monitor
- ❑ b. Network Monitor
- ❑ c. Task Manager
- ❑ d. Windows NT Diagnostics
- ❑ e. Server Manager

Answers a and c are correct. The Performance Monitor can display the Processor CPU Utilization counter. Therefore, answer a is correct. The Task Manager displays CPU utilization. Therefore, answer c is correct. Network Monitor does not have a CPU utilization display ability. Therefore, answer b is incorrect. Neither Windows NT Diagnostics nor Server Manager can display CPU utilization. Therefore, answers d and e are incorrect.

Question 5

Which view available through Performance Monitor should you use to create a baseline?

- ❍ a. Chart
- ❍ b. Log
- ❍ c. Report
- ❍ d. Graph

Answer b is correct. Log view records object counters and should be used to create a baseline. Chart view displays the realtime values of counters but cannot record the data as it is gathered. Therefore, answer a is incorrect. Report view creates a snapshot of the performance levels of counters from realtime gathering or a recorded log. Therefore, answer c is incorrect. Graph is not a view but a display selection in the Chart view. Therefore, answer d is incorrect.

Question 6

Which of the Server service optimization selections is recommended for use with fewer than 10 users?

- ❍ a. Minimize Memory Used
- ❍ b. Balance
- ❍ c. Maximize Throughput For File Sharing
- ❍ d. Maximize Throughput For Network Applications

Answer a is correct. Minimize Memory Used is the recommended setting for 10 users or less. Balance is the recommended setting for 10 through 64 users. Therefore, answer b is incorrect. Maximize Throughput For File Sharing is the recommended setting for more than 64 users. Therefore, answer c is incorrect. Maxamize Throughput For Network Applications is the recommended setting for a server hosting a distributed application. Therefore, answer d is incorrect.

Question 7

After an application has been launched, which of the following are possible settings for the priority level on the Processes tab of the Task Manager? [Check all correct answers]

- ❑ a. Low
- ❑ b. Realtime
- ❑ c. System
- ❑ d. Normal
- ❑ e. Kernel
- ❑ f. High

Answers a, d, and f are correct. Low, Normal, and High are three of the four selections available on the Processes tab; the fourth is Pause. Realtime is only available on the Processes right-click pop-up menu. Therefore, answer b is incorrect. There is no such priority setting of System or Kernel. Therefore, answers c and e are incorrect.

Question 8

Which are possible functions of the Task Manager? [Check all correct answers]

- ❑ a. Switch the foreground application
- ❑ b. View committed memory changes
- ❑ c. Launch new processes
- ❑ d. Set the increase in priority for foreground applications
- ❑ e. View multiple CPUs in separate graphs

Answers a, b, c, and e are correct. The Task Manager is able to switch the foreground application, view committed memory changes, launch new processes, and view multiple CPUs in separate graphs. The Task Manager cannot set the increase in priority for foreground applications. This is done through the System applet. Therefore, answer d is incorrect.

Question 9

You just doubled the size of your server's physical RAM to 128 MB. If you have disk striping with parity implemented on a set of high-speed SCSI drives and are duplexing the boot partition, what change should you make to the pagefile settings?

- ❍ a. No change to the pagefile size is recommended, but it should be placed on the stripe set.
- ❍ b. The pagefile should be increased to 140 MB and placed on the boot duplexed drive.
- ❍ c. The pagefile should be increased by 12 MB and placed on the stripe set.
- ❍ d. The pagefile should be increased to 140 MB and placed on the stripe set.

Answer d is correct. The pagefile should be 140 MB and placed on the fastest storage set available. The pagefile size is recommended to be the size of physical RAM plus 12 MB. Therefore, answer a is incorrect. The pagefile should not be placed within a duplex set, especially on the duplexed drive. Therefore, answer b is incorrect. The pagefile should be the size of physical RAM plus 12 MB. Therefore, answer c is incorrect.

Need To Know More?

Donald, Lisa, and James Chellis: *MSCE: NT Server 4 In The Enterprise Study Guide, 2nd Edition.* Sybex Network Press, San Francisco, CA, 1998. ISBN 0-7821-2221-3. Chapter 15 contains information on Performance Monitor, Task Manager, and Server service optimizations. But, process priority settings are not listed.

Heywood, Drew: *Inside Windows NT Server, 2nd Edition.* New Riders, Indianapolis, IN, 1998. ISBN 1-56205-860-6. The Performance Monitor is discussed in Chapter 15. Virtual Memory is given a brief look in Chapter 14. The Task Manager and the Server service optimization settings are not discussed.

Siyan, Karanjit S.: *Windows NT Server 4 Professional Reference, 2nd Edition.* New Riders, Indianapolis, IN, 1997. ISBN 1-56205-805-3. A lengthy discussion of the Performance Monitor, Task Manager, process priority settings, and Server Service optimization is contained in Chapter 21.

The Windows NT Server 4 manuals cover planning, configuration, and installation issues quite well. The *Concepts And Planning Manual* contains useful documentation on the Performance Monitor in Chapter 8, "Monitoring Performance."

The *Windows NT Server Resource Kit* only mentions the Network Monitor in passing. It is not a useful resource for this topic. The *RK Supplement #1* contains many discussions on using Performance Monitor to investigate all aspects of a network.

Advanced NetWare Topics

Terms you'll need to understand:

- √ NetWare
- √ NWLink Internetwork Packet Exchange/Sequenced Packet Exchange (IPX/SPX)
- √ SubNetwork Access Protocol (SNAP)
- √ Gateway Service For NetWare (GSNW)
- √ Client Service For NetWare (CSNW)
- √ File And Print Services For NetWare (FPNW)
- √ NWCONV.EXE

Techniques you'll need to master:

- √ Installing and configuring NWLink IPX/SPX
- √ Configuring CSNW, GSNW, and FPNW
- √ Using Microsoft's Migration Tool For NetWare

By making NetWare connectivity part and parcel of Windows NT Server, Microsoft makes it possible to integrate its products directly and easily with existing networks all over the world. Considering its built-in NetWare access capabilities, and the add-ins available at low cost from Microsoft for Windows NT Server to enhance these capabilities, it's clear that NetWare interoperability is an important concern in Redmond.

Even if you don't have any NetWare servers on your Windows NT network, you must still understand what Microsoft offers by way of NetWare compatibility and access. If you work in hybrid NetWare/Windows NT environments, much of this chapter's material might be familiar to you. On the other hand, if you don't have the benefit of direct exposure, you should study this chapter carefully.

Protocols And Compatibility Issues

To avoid paying fees to Novell, Microsoft built its own implementation of the Internetwork Packet Exchange/Sequenced Packet Exchange (IPX/SPX) protocols. Surprisingly, comparisons between Novell's own IPX/SPX client implementations and Microsoft's NWLink (which is what it calls the protocols to avoid using Novell trade names) show Microsoft's implementation as slightly faster than Novell's. In other words, these guys are serious about NetWare compatibility and have done a good job of it.

Although NetWare supports multiple protocols—primarily IPX/SPX and TCP/IP—it's most common to find IPX/SPX as the protocol used between NetWare's clients and servers. In fact, Novell itself supports no protocols other than IPX/SPX for versions of NetWare older than 3.x (which usually means version 2.2). Thus, if you encounter NetWare 2.2, it's safe to assume that IPX/SPX is the protocol used to communicate between the NetWare server and its clients.

When Novell implemented IPX/SPX, it also used a special frame format for the protocol on Ethernet and other network types. Even though the emerging standard at the time (which has since become official) was to use 802.2 frame formats for networked communications, Novell elected to use what's often called a "raw 802.3" frame format for its implementation of IPX/SPX on Ethernet.

To make a long and complex story short, the upshot of Novell's initial decision and its subsequent divergence from industry standard frame types, introduced the possibility of a frame type mismatch when using IPX/SPX (or NWLink, in Microsoft parlance).

Here's what you need to know to deal with such questions:

- Although NWLink is provided primarily to enable NetWare access and interoperability, Windows NT-based networks can use NWLink, even when NetWare is absent.
- Until NetWare 3.12 shipped, NetWare's default frame type was raw 802.3, which Microsoft calls simply 802.3 frame type.
- For NetWare 3.12 and all later versions (including IntranetWare, a.k.a. 4.11, and NetWare 5.0), the default frame type uses 802.2 headers, atop the native frame type for the network technology in use. Microsoft calls this the 802.2 frame type, without regard to technology.
- The total battery of frame types you're likely to encounter is:
    - **802.2 frame type** Industry standard; default for NetWare 3.12 and higher-numbered versions.
    - **802.3 frame type** So-called "raw 802.3 header" format, developed by Novell; default for older, pre-3.12 versions of NetWare.
    - **802.3 with SNAP header** Sometimes called "Ethernet_SNAP" frame type in Microsoft terminology.
    - **802.5 frame type** The native format for Token Ring networks.
    - **802.5 frame type with SNAP header** Sometimes called Token_Ring_SNAP in Microsoft terminology.

> ***Note:*** *SNAP stands for SubNetwork Access Protocol, and it provides a mechanism to permit nonstandard, higher-level protocols to appear within a standard IEEE logical link control frame, like the frame types listed in the preceding bulleted item. SNAP is often used to transport AppleTalk or SNA in IP network environments. It's not necessary to understand the subtleties of this technology.*

- If any workstation (or server) is configured for an incorrect IPX frame type (one that doesn't match the rest of the population), an improperly configured machine can't interact with the network. This might occur even though the network otherwise works properly and all other machines communicate successfully.
- Autodetect will select the first frame type seen during its initial inspection period. Autodetect functions predictably only in a homogeneous frame environment. If no IPX traffic is detected, it will default to 802.2. Manual setting should be used in heterogeneous environments.
- Windows NT Server can support a so-called SAP agent, which is necessary if the Server is to route IPX from one network interface to another as part of its duties. Otherwise, this functionality is not needed.
- For client/server applications (like SQL Server database access) or NetBIOS-based applications, native NetWare clients using IPX/SPX can communicate directly with a Windows NT Server running such an application. This can be done without requiring anything other than NWLink and the server side of the application to be installed on that machine. In essence, the client side of the client/server application supplies everything clients need to communicate, with one requirement—the clients and servers must have a common protocol. Because the assumption is that native NetWare clients use IPX/SPX, a Windows NT Server must install NWLink to communicate with NetWare clients across a network.

Now that we've given you the heads-up on IPX/SPX compatibility issues, let's continue the NetWare discussion with some coverage on Windows NT's Gateway Service For NetWare (GSNW).

Gateway Service For NetWare

Microsoft often refers to this software component by its acronym, GSNW. But there's more to GSNW than meets the eye, and it can be the occasion for some confusion. Examine the listing in Figure 12.1 carefully. Notice that the complete name of the software component—Gateway (and Client) Services For NetWare—appears in the Add dialog box, generated from the Services tab on the Control Panel's Network applet.

Unless you've actually looked at this on screen at some point or have been warned about it, you may be surprised to learn that GSNW includes Client Service For NetWare (CSNW), which is covered in detail later in this chapter. This means that any Windows NT Server with GSNW installed can also function as a NetWare client. This explains why you must remove existing NetWare client software—especially Novell's NetWare Client For Windows NT—from any Windows NT Server before installing GSNW.

Dealing with GSNW requires that you understand what GSNW does and what's involved in installing the software. The next couple of sections provide key information aimed at increasing your understanding of GSNW features, installation procedures, and configuration issues.

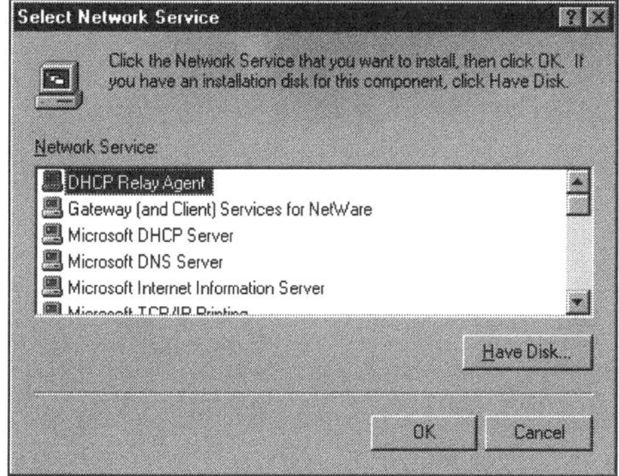

Figure 12.1 The unabridged expansion for GSNW is actually Gateway (and Client) Services For NetWare.

Understanding GSNW

Speaking generically, the term "gateway" refers to a software component that permits computers that do not share a common set of protocols and services to communicate with one another. In other words, a gateway translates between two incompatible protocol and service worlds.

GSNW is no exception. GSNW makes it possible for ordinary Microsoft network clients (be they PCs running Windows 3.x, Windows 95, Windows 98, or even Windows NT Workstation or Server) to access resources on a NetWare server. GSNW translates client requests stated in Microsoft network terms into NetWare terms, and then translates the resulting responses of a NetWare server from NetWare terms back into Microsoft network terms. The gateway is in the middle of any communication that goes from one protocol and service world to another.

The "trick" that makes GSNW translations work is that the Windows NT Server where GSNW runs exports a logical volume from the NetWare server through a gateway that Microsoft network clients can access as if it were any other Windows NT-based network share. The gateway can also create a similar fiction for NetWare-based printers, making NetWare-based print services available to Microsoft network clients. The chief selling point for GSNW is that it provides access to NetWare resources for Microsoft network clients without requiring any additional software or software changes to be made to the clients themselves.

Installing, Configuring, And Enabling GSNW

Gateway Service For NetWare is an optional network service included as part of Windows NT Server 4. This means it's included with the distribution media for the product, but not installed by default when you install the core OS. To install GSNW, you must open the Network applet in Control Panel, select the Services tab, and then click the Add button in the resulting display. This produces the screen shown earlier in Figure 12.1, where GSNW appears as the second choice in the list. To begin installing GSNW, highlight its entry, then click the OK button at the bottom of the window. This prompts you for the Windows NT Server CD, from whence it reads the necessary code.

NWLink may be referenced separately from GSNW. It's important to note that if you elect to install GSNW on a Windows NT Server that does not already have NWLink running, it automatically installs NWLink during GSNW installation. Thus, although NWLink is required for GSNW to run, it's not necessary to install it in advance, nor is it a problem if NWLink has already been installed when installing GSNW.

Here's a high-level overview of the GSNW installation process, emphasizing installation elements and information most likely to appear in GSNW-related test questions.

1. Before installing and configuring GSNW, you must create the following accounts on the NetWare server where the gateway will connect:
   a. User account on the NetWare server with rights to the NetWare file system directories that gateway users from the Windows NT side will need.
   b. Group account named "NTGATEWAY" on the NetWare server with rights to all file and print resources that gateway users will need.

   Note: All users who share a GSNW gateway have the same access and rights to NetWare resources. The only way to create different collections of access and rights is to set up multiple gateways (keep in mind that only one instance of GSNW per individual Windows NT Server is permitted).

2. To install GSNW, you must log in to the Windows NT Server as an Administrator.
   a. In the Network applet in Control Panel, select the Services tab, click the Add button, and select the entry that reads Gateway (And Client) Services For NetWare.
   b. Supply the Windows NT Server CD or point to a copy of the \i386 directory where the necessary source code files reside. The software will more or less install itself.

3. To configure GSNW, double-click the GSNW icon in Control Panel. The Gateway Service For NetWare dialog box appears.
   a. Click the Gateway button to elicit the Configure Gateway dialog box.
   b. Check the Enable Gateway box to enable the Gateway service.
   c. In the Gateway Account field, enter the NetWare user name you created in Step 1a. Enter the password into the Password field, and then confirm the password in the Confirm Password field.
   d. Click the Add button to create a NetWare share for use by Microsoft networking clients. A New Share dialog box appears.
   e. In the Share Name field, enter a name through which the NetWare directory will be shared.
   f. In the Network Path field, enter a UNC name for the NetWare directory that's being shared. For the SYS:Public directory on a server named "NETONE," the syntax is \\NETONE\SYS\PUBLIC.
   g. In the Comment field, you can add an optional descriptive phrase that will appear in the Browse window for Microsoft clients on the network.
   h. In the Use Drive field, select a drive letter on the Windows NT Server to be assigned to the NetWare directory. This drive letter remains taken as long as GSNW runs on the Windows NT Server. By default, Z is the letter assigned to the first share name.
   i. The User Limit box permits administrators to limit the number of users who can simultaneously access the NetWare share. Because the gateway bogs down under increased loads, try to limit the number of users to 10 or so (unless the server's fast or only lightly loaded).

j. Click OK to save your configuration changes. You'll return to the Configure Gateway dialog box. Click OK again to exit the Gateway Service For NetWare dialog box. All changes will take effect upon the next system logon.

4. The only way to create NetWare shares is through the interface described in Steps 3d through 3j (not through Explorer or My Computer, as for normal Windows NT Server shares). Likewise, you must use the GSNW applet in Control Panel to set permissions for such shares.
   a. From an administrative logon, launch GSNW from Control Panel.
   b. When the Gateway Service For NetWare dialog box appears, choose the Gateway button.
   c. In the Configure Gateway dialog box that appears, highlight the NetWare share name, and choose the Permissions button. Use this interface to set permissions for the NetWare share.
5. Using NetWare Print Resources through the gateway requires no such special handling. Instead, configure NetWare print queues through the Printers icon in Control Panel (as with any other Windows NT Server-attached printer).
   a. From an administrative logon, launch the Printers applet. Select the Add Printer icon. This will display the Add Printer Wizard window.
   b. Select the Network Printer radio button, and then click the Next button. This brings up the Connect To Printer dialog box.
   c. In this dialog box, you will see an icon labeled NetWare Or Compatible Network as well as Microsoft Windows Network. You can expand and navigate this directory tree the same way you expand the Microsoft Windows Network tree, simply by double-clicking the network, selecting a server, double-clicking that server's name, and then selecting the

printer you wish to manage. Otherwise, the procedure is exactly the same as installing an ordinary Windows NT network printer (covered in Chapter 13 of this book).

The important points to remember about this process are that it's necessary to map a drive on the Windows NT Server for the NetWare share and that NetWare shares and their permissions can only be managed through the GSNW applet (not through ordinary file management tools). NetWare printers, on the other hand, work like any other network printers through the Printers applet after GSNW has been installed.

That's it for the server side of dealing with NetWare, let's take a look at what needs to take place on the client end.

Client Service For NetWare

GSNW makes NetWare resources available to ordinary Microsoft network clients. CSNW works with Windows NT machines so they can act as native clients to NetWare servers on the network. This system component is called CSNW only on Windows NT Workstation 4, which ships without GSNW. But, CSNW is part and parcel of GSNW on Windows NT Server. In either case, CSNW lets Windows NT machines link up to and browse NetWare resources alongside Microsoft Windows network resources.

Now, let's take a look at the requirements for sharing files and resources between Windows NT and NetWare.

File And Print Services For NetWare

FPNW, as it's usually called, is not included with Windows NT Server 4. It must be purchased separately (but it only costs $149 in the U.S. market). What GSNW is to Microsoft network clients, FPNW is to native NetWare clients—it makes resources from a Windows NT Server available to NetWare clients, without requiring additional software or configuration changes. Another way to think about FPNW is that it makes a Windows NT Server look like a NetWare 3.11 server to any native NetWare clients on a network.

Now that you know how to set up file and print sharing with NetWare, let's take a look at a handy tool Microsoft included with Windows NT to help you migrate from the NetWare NOS to Windows NT.

Microsoft's Migration Tool For NetWare

The name of this program, which ships as an optional element in the Windows NT Server 4 distribution media, is NWCONV.EXE. This program takes user and group data from a NetWare server, along with most of the associated rights and permissions that pertain to them, and re-creates that information on a Windows NT Server 4 machine.

Likewise, NWCONV can also grab volumes, directories, and files from a NetWare server and copy them to a Windows NT Server, while translating and preserving most of the file system permissions involved. This program is fairly sophisticated. It offers lots of bells and whistles for dealing with duplicate accounts and for converting information from its NetWare server incarnation to a reasonable Windows NT Server facsimile.

The aspects of NWCONV's behavior you're most likely to encounter touch on the Migration Tool's following capabilities:

- When duplicate account names are encountered during migration (which means identical account names already exist on both the NetWare and Windows NT Server machines), the default is to skip the account and not migrate any additional information from the NetWare server to the Windows NT Server.
- The Migration Tool includes options to permit duplicates to be transferred by adding a prefix to the old account name, thereby creating a unique name that captures the transferred information from the NetWare server on the Windows NT Server.
- If multiple NetWare servers that include identical account names are to be migrated to a single Windows NT domain controller, a mapping file that renames NetWare account

names to Windows NT account names may be created to drive this process. Otherwise, only the first such account will transfer (if it's not already a duplicate). Microsoft recommends mapping files to achieve the best results when migrating account information from NetWare to Windows NT (consult the Siyan reference at the end of this chapter for details not covered here). One of the mapping file's most important functions is to preserve NetWare passwords on a Windows NT Server so that users need not learn another password once migration occurs. Because the Migration Tool cannot read NetWare passwords (they're encrypted), this is the only way to transfer such information successfully.

- If migration on a network involves replacing NetWare completely with Windows NT, it's important to remember that additional software changes may be necessary. To permit NetWare clients to browse Windows NT resources, it is necessary to install a Microsoft redirector on those clients. To permit NetWare clients to access resources on a Windows NT Server without replacing their client software completely, it is necessary to install FPNW on a Windows NT Server to permit it to look like a NetWare server to those clients.
- Only NTFS supports object-level file and directory security in the Windows NT environment; therefore, only NTFS can provide a reasonable equivalent to the file and directory security available from NetWare's own file system. In other words, NTFS provides the underlying support necessary to preserve as much security information from the NetWare environment as the two dissimilar security models will permit.
- For the Migration Tool to work, GSNW must be installed on the Windows NT PDC where account and group information will be transferred.

Unless you work in a mixed NetWare/Windows NT environment, you should review the basics about GSNW, CSNW, FPNW, the Migration Tool, and NWLink, covered earlier in this chapter. If it sounds like gibberish, check the Glossary first, then reread this chapter (and at least one of the references listed at the end of this chapter). For those who feel like they're better-prepared, here are some questions for you to study.

Practice Questions

Question 1

Windows NT Server includes a Migration Tool to move data and accounts from NetWare to Windows NT Servers. It can be especially helpful when moving user accounts from one or more NetWare servers to a Windows NT PDC. Which of the following requirements is most likely to benefit from use of a mapping file to guide the migration process?

- ❍ a. When migrating unique user accounts from several NetWare servers to a Windows NT domain controller.
- ❍ b. To make sure that existing domain accounts will not be affected by migration of identical user accounts from NetWare.
- ❍ c. To migrate accounts from NetWare servers that do not have corresponding accounts in the Windows NT domain.
- ❍ d. To supply passwords for migrated accounts in the Windows NT domain that match the previous NetWare passwords.

Answer d is correct. This is another question—and a corresponding set of answers—that requires careful reading to ferret out the "most likely" requirement. Answer d lets administrators supply the same passwords for Windows NT accounts as NetWare accounts, which is not an automatic feature of the Migration Tool. This is the only behavior described in any of the answers that absolutely requires a mapping file. Therefore, answer d is definitely the best answer to this question. Answer a falls within the capabilities of a mapping file, but matches the default behavior of the Migration Tool, in that unique accounts (that is, those that are not duplicated, neither on the NetWare side nor the Windows NT side) are the easiest to migrate. Answer b relies on the default behavior of the Migration Tool where existing accounts will not be affected by identical accounts on a NetWare server. Answer c also works fine without a mapping file, because the Migration Tool can handle such accounts automatically.

Question 2

To support a client/server application for NetWare clients to access a Windows NT Server on your network, which of the following additional software components must be present on the Windows NT Server?

- ❍ a. Gateway Service For NetWare
- ❍ b. File And Print Services For NetWare
- ❍ c. The Migration Tool For NetWare
- ❍ d. An NWLink SAP Agent
- ❍ e. The NWLink protocol

Answer e is correct. Client/server applications normally include whatever client- and server-side high-level capabilities and protocols that may be required within the applications themselves. The only absolute requirement is that clients and servers share a transport protocol in common. In this case, that protocol is NWLink. Therefore, answer e is the only correct answer. Answer a, GSNW, is incorrect because it permits Microsoft network clients to communicate with NetWare, not NetWare clients with Windows NT Server. Answer b, FPNW, is incorrect only because the client/server application itself provides the service-level access from NetWare clients to Windows NT Server. Answer c, the Migration Tool, is irrelevant because it applies only when moving accounts and data from a NetWare server to Windows NT Server. Finally, answer d, the NWLink SAP Agent, is incorrect because it is needed only when a Windows NT Server must be able to forward IPX Service Advertisement Protocol (SAP) packets from one network segment to another (which is not stated as a requirement in Question 2).

Question 3

To facilitate a move from NetWare to Windows NT Server, XYZ Corp. plans to use the Migration Tool For NetWare. If the Tool encounters user account names on the NetWare server that match existing accounts in the target Windows NT domain, what will the Migration Tool do by default?

- ❍ a. Prompt the administrator with an option to overwrite existing account information, or block the account information from the transfer.
- ❍ b. The account will be transferred to the Windows NT domain, but a prefix will be added to all duplicate names.
- ❍ c. All duplicate NetWare account information will be ignored.
- ❍ d. The incoming NetWare account information replaces all existing Windows NT domain account information.

Answer c is correct. By default, the Migration Tool ignores any user account name on a NetWare server that matches an existing account name in the target Windows NT domain database. Answer a is incorrect because the Tool does not prompt when duplicates are encountered. Answer b is incorrect because a mapping file must be defined to assign such prefixes (the Tool does not perform this action by default, nor would it know what prefix to assign). Answer d is flat wrong. The Migration Tool has been designed to take the safest action by default, which is to leave existing domain database entries untouched.

Question 4

On a Windows NT Server where the Migration Tool For NetWare is to be run, which software components must be explicitly installed, assuming that no NetWare-related capabilities are already present on that machine?

- ❍ a. NWLink
- ❍ b. Gateway Service For NetWare
- ❍ c. File And Print Services For NetWare
- ❍ d. The Migration Tool For NetWare
- ❍ e. Client Service For NetWare

Answer b is correct. As indicated in the discussion of the Migration Tool earlier in this chapter, Gateway Service For NetWare must be installed on a machine where the Migration Tool is to be used. Answer a is incorrect because installing GSNW on a machine where NWLink is not already installed will automatically install that protocol. Answer c is incorrect because the Migration Tool does not require NetWare clients to be able to access the Windows NT Server (although it might be a good idea to do so, after the migration is complete). Answer d is incorrect because the Migration Tool will be automatically installed by the system when GSNW is installed. Answer e is incorrect because installing GSNW on a Windows NT Server automatically installs CSNW (and CSNW is not available for installation on a Windows NT Server as a separate option). The trick in this question lies in remembering that GSNW includes CSNW, and that it will automatically install NWLink and the Migration Tool on a machine where they are not already present.

Question 5

XYZ Corp. has just finished migrating files and accounts from its NetWare server to a Windows NT Server on the network. That Windows NT Server already uses NWLink. NetWare clients complain that they cannot access the migrated files. What is probably missing on the Windows NT Server and on the NetWare client machines? [Check all correct answers]

- ❑ a. Gateway Service For NetWare
- ❑ b. Client Service For NetWare
- ❑ c. File And Print Services For NetWare
- ❑ d. Account permissions for the NetWare clients
- ❑ e. Microsoft redirectors for the NetWare clients

Answers c and e are correct. For NetWare clients to access files on a Windows NT Server, FPNW is the required software component. Therefore, answer c is one correct answer to this question. On the other hand, the NetWare clients must have a way to send requests to the Windows NT domain controller to browse available resources and request access to those resources. This is where the Microsoft redirectors for the NetWare clients come into play. These will permit the clients to browse network resources directly. Therefore, answer e is also correct. Answer a is incorrect because it lets Microsoft network clients access a NetWare server, which is irrelevant to these circumstances. Answer b is incorrect because it lets Windows NT Workstations and Servers act as clients to a NetWare server, also irrelevant. Finally, answer d is incorrect because the question clearly states that accounts were migrated from NetWare to Windows NT.

Question 6

Select all the protocols and file systems necessary on a Windows NT Server to accommodate the Migration Tool For NetWare when transferring files and folders, and their security information, from a NetWare server to a Windows NT Server. [Check all correct answers]

- ❑ a. NWLink
- ❑ b. TCP/IP
- ❑ c. NetBEUI
- ❑ d. FAT
- ❑ e. NTFS

Answers a and e are correct. NWLink provides the transport mechanism for moving files from the NetWare server to the Windows NT Server machine. NTFS provides the object-level security needed to accommodate NetWare's file and directory security information. Answer b is incorrect because the Migration Tool does not work with TCP/IP. Likewise, for answer c, the Migration Tool doesn't work with NetBEUI. Answer d is incorrect because FAT does not support file- and folder-level security as a file system.

Need To Know More?

Gaskin, James E.: *The Complete Guide To NetWare 4.11/ IntranetWare, 2nd Edition*. Sybex Network Press, Alameda, CA, 1997. ISBN 0-7821-1931-X. For a comprehensive look at NetWare networking, there's no better reference than this one. Use it to deal with NetWare specifics and the NetWare side of any NetWare-to-Windows NT connection. Look for a new edition of this book aimed at NetWare 5.0 in the near future.

Heywood, Drew: *Inside Windows NT Server, 2nd Edition*. New Riders, Indianapolis, IN, 1998. ISBN 1-56205-860-6. Chapter 19, "Windows NT Server And NetWare," explains the salient software, communications issues, and connectivity concerns related to NetWare.

Minasi, Mark, and Peter Dyson: *Mastering Windows NT Server 4, 5th Edition*. Sybex Network Press, Alameda, CA, 1997. ISBN 0-7821-163-2. Minasi has been a Windows NT guru since it all began. His experience and practical orientation show in Chapter 13, "Novell NetWare In An NT Server Environment."

Siyan, Karanjit S.: *Windows NT Server 4 Professional Reference, 2nd Edition*. New Riders, Indianapolis, IN, 1998. ISBN 1-56205-805-3. Chapter 12, "Integrating NetWare With Windows NT Server," brings Siyan's usual depth of coverage and details to this topic. It's the best available preparation material for NetWare issues.

Strebe, Matthew, Charles Perkins, and James Chellis: *MSCE: NT Server 4 Study Guide*. Sybex Network Press, San Francisco, CA, 1996. ISBN 0-7821-1972-7. Chapter 13, "Interoperating With NetWare," covers this ground well (only Siyan offers more details).

Search the TechNet CD (or its online version through **www.microsoft.com**) using the keywords "NetWare," "NWLink," "Gateway Services," "GSNW," and related

product names. The Windows NT *Concepts And Planning Manual* also includes useful information on making Windows NT-to-NetWare connections, and vice versa.

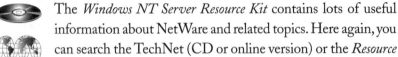

The *Windows NT Server Resource Kit* contains lots of useful information about NetWare and related topics. Here again, you can search the TechNet (CD or online version) or the *Resource Kit* CD, using the same keywords mentioned in the preceding paragraph. Useful NetWare-related materials occur throughout the *Networking Guide* volume of the *Resource Kit*.

Advanced Windows NT Printing

Terms you'll need to understand:

- √ Client application
- √ Connecting to a printer
- √ Creating a printer
- √ Network interface card (NIC)
- √ Print client
- √ Print device
- √ Print job
- √ Print resolution
- √ Print server
- √ Print Server services
- √ Print spooler
- √ Printer/logical printer
- √ Queue/print queue
- √ Graphics Device Interface (GDI)
- √ Print auditing

Techniques you'll need to master:

- √ Installing and configuring a printer
- √ Managing printing clients
- √ Managing the print spooler
- √ Setting up print priorities
- √ Establishing logical printers and printing pools
- √ Creating and maintaining printer shares

To manage a Windows NT Server in an enterprise environment, you need to be aware of many issues regarding printing. For your convenience, we've repeated most of the printing material from *MCSE NT Server 4 Exam Cram* here, with additional enterprise-level printing topics. You should note that these additional topics are listed under the heading "Advanced Printing."

As a network administrator, it's your job to make sure that users have access to needed resources. One of the most often used resources is the printer. With many other network operating systems, one of the biggest complaints is the lack of the ability to effectively and efficiently handle printers. Microsoft developed an intuitive and simple way to manage these much-used resources. This chapter focuses on Microsoft's approach to printing and defines a few Microsoft-specific printing terms.

The Windows NT Print Lexicon

There is some Microsoft-specific printing terminology that must be mastered. This section defines some terms as a prelude to the "meat and potatoes" discussion of printing with Windows NT Server 4.

These are the printing terms you should know:

- **Client application** A network program that originates print jobs (this can be located on a print server or client computer on the network).
- **Connecting to a printer** The process of attaching to a network share that resides on the computer on which the logical printer was created (performed through the Add Printer Wizard—accessed from the Start|Printers option).
- **Creating a printer** The process of naming, defining settings for, installing drivers for, and linking a printing device to the network. In Windows NT, this process is performed through the Add Printer application (also called the Add Printer Wizard).

- **Network interface card** These are built-in network interface cards for print devices that are directly attached to the network (such as the Hewlett-Packard JetDirect). Either DLC or TCP/IP must be installed to communicate with directly attached print devices.
- **Print client** This is a computer on a network (called a "client computer") that transmits print jobs to the print server to be produced by the physical printing device.
- **Print device** The print device is what is commonly referred to as a printer. In other words, a print device is the physical hardware device that produces printed material. This is very confusing to most people. Just remember that the print device is the piece of hardware that actually spits out paper with your material printed on it.
- **Print job** This is the actual code that defines the print processing commands as well as the actual file to be printed. Windows NT defines print jobs by data type, depending on what adjustments must be made to the file for it to print accurately.
- **Print resolution** Resolution is the measurement of pixel density that is responsible for the smoothness of any image or text being printed. This is measured in dots per inch (DPI). When it comes to printing, the higher your DPI, the better the quality of the printed material.
- **Print server** This is the server computer that links physical print devices to the network and manages sharing those devices with computers on the network.
- **Print server services** These are software components located on the print server that accept print jobs and send them to the print spooler for execution. These components, such as Services For Macintosh, enable a variety of client computers to communicate with the print server to process print jobs.
- **Print spooler** The print spooler is the collection of dynamic link libraries (DLLs) that acquires, processes, catalogs, and disburses print jobs. Print spooling is the procedure of writing a print job to disk,

called a "spool file." Print despooling is the process of reading what is contained in the spool file and transmitting it to the physical printing device.

- **Printer driver** This is a program that enables communication between applications and a specific print device. (Most hardware peripherals, like printers, require the use of a driver to process commands.)

- **Printer/logical printer** The logical printer (what Microsoft calls the "printer") is the actual software interface that communicates between the operating system and the physical printing device. The logical printer is what handles the printing process from the time the print command is issued. Its settings determine things such as the physical printing device that renders the file to be printed, as well as how the file to be printed is sent to the printing device (e.g., via a remote print share or local port, and so forth). Just remember that what Microsoft calls the printer is the software interface, not the physical printing device.

- **Queue/print queue** Literally defined, a queue is a line (that is, like standing in line). In printing terms, a queue is a series of files waiting to be produced by the printing device.

- **Rendering** The rendering process in Windows NT is as follows: A client application sends file information to the Graphics Device Interface (GDI), which receives the data, communicates that data to the physical printing device driver, and produces the print job in the language of the physical printing device. The printing device then interprets this information and creates a file (a bitmap) for each page to be printed.

It is very important that you know and fully understand all of these terms and concepts. Troubleshooting printing problems can be tricky, especially with this specialized terminology.

Printing With Windows NT Server

Windows NT print settings are managed through the Printers folder, which is accessible from the Control Panel or the Start menu. The Printers folder replaces the old Windows NT 3.51 Print Manager. This has simplified a number of printing aspects, such as print device installation and maintenance, as well as print permission management. This approach is extremely straightforward when compared to earlier versions of Windows NT and other network operating systems.

Windows NT takes a modular approach to printing. Each component has a specific use and interfaces with the other components in the print architecture.

The following list defines each component of the Windows NT printing architecture, and Figure 13.1 shows a visual of the architecture:

- **Graphics Device Interface (GDI)** This component provides network applications with a system for presenting graphical information. The GDI works as a translator between an application's print request and the device driver interface (DDI) so the job is rendered accurately.
- **Print device** This is the physical hardware device that produces printed output.
- **Print driver** This is the software component that enables communication between the operating system and the physical printing device.

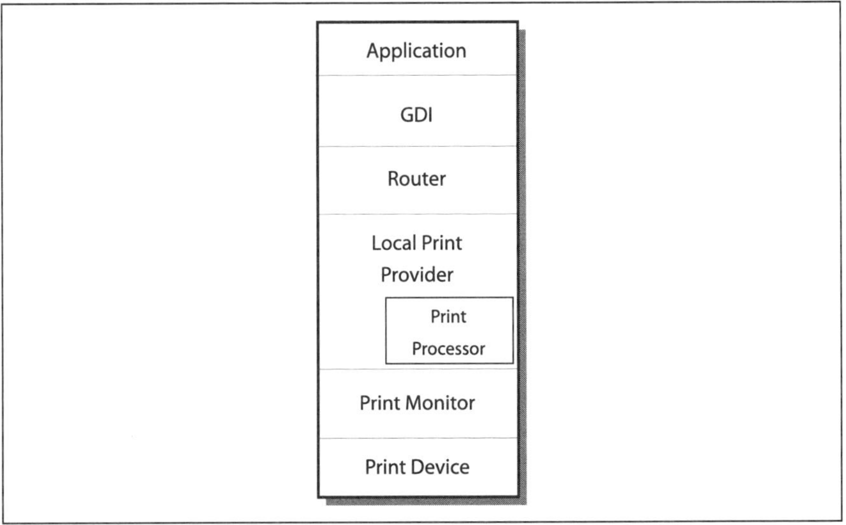

Figure 13.1 The Windows NT print architecture components work together to render print jobs for the user.

- **Print monitor** This component passes the print job (which has been translated to the print device's language) to the physical printing device.
- **Print processor** This component is responsible for making any necessary modifications to the print job before passing the job to the print monitor. Windows NT actually has two print processors: one for the Windows platform and one for the Macintosh.
- **Print router** This component directs the print job to the appropriate printing device.
- **Print spooler** This component, also called the "print provider," accepts print jobs from the router, calls the processor to make any needed changes to the print job, and transfers the jobs one at a time to the print monitor.

Printing Clients

The following list examines how to set up printing for various types of clients:

- **Printing from Windows NT clients** This is where Windows NT's approach to printing really shines. Windows NT-based client computers need access to print devices, so they must add the printer (via the Add Printer Wizard). Previously, all client computers required that the print driver be installed on each client machine that needed access to a printing device. No more! All that is needed for printing from a Windows NT client is that the driver be installed on the print server. This simplifies the printing process, because, if an updated print driver is released, it just needs to be installed on the server, not on every Windows NT-based client machine.
- **Printing from Windows 95 and Windows 98 clients** This process is the same as for Windows NT clients. All that is needed is a connection between the Windows 95-based client computer and the print device, and for the print driver to be installed on the server.
- **Printing from MS-DOS and Windows 3.x clients** Unfortunately, the simplicity of printing from Windows NT and 95 clients does not extend to older client machines, such as DOS, Windows 3.x, and

Macintosh clients. The best idea for these computers is to create a central repository for print drivers. You can then use the central repository for any clients that must load the print drivers locally.

That's it for setting up clients to print to a Windows NT print server. Now let's move on to some general printing topics, such as spooling issues and setting print priorities.

Spooling

As previously mentioned, when a user sends a print job, it goes to the print spooler. As a reminder, the spooler is the interface between the application and the print monitor. It is responsible for sending print jobs to the printing device. It is also responsible for tracking the print job through the printing process, routing jobs to the correct ports by tracking what printers are connected to what ports, and assigning priorities to print jobs. This section discusses spooling concepts, including setting print priorities, creating separate spool files, stopping and starting the spooler service, and changing the spool location.

Print Priorities

By default, the spooler prints jobs in the order in which they are received. It is possible, however, to ensure that print jobs from certain users are printed before any other job. To adjust priority levels for individual users or groups, you must create a different logical printer to a particular printing device (this is discussed in detail later in this chapter, in the section titled "Logical Printers And Printing Pools"). To assign higher priority to print jobs from certain users (such as the CEO, for example), perform the following steps on a logical printer:

1. Go to the Printers folder (Start|Settings|Printers).
2. Select Server Properties from the File menu for the logical printer to be adjusted.
3. Select the Scheduling tab.
4. Adjust the slide bar to assign a higher priority (this setting can range from 1 through 99, with 1 being the lowest, as well as the default, setting.

Separate Spool Files

If the printers on your network are hit pretty hard with many print jobs at a time, the print spooler can get to be fairly large. It is important to make sure that the spooler file is large enough to handle the jobs that are sent to it. Therefore, it may become necessary to create individual spool files for each printer on the network. This is performed through the Registry by creating files under the following Registry key:

```
HKEY_LOCAL_MACHINE\SYSTEM\CurrentControlSet\Control\Print\Printers
```

Stopping And Restarting The Spooler Service

It is possible for print jobs to get stuck in the spooler. To remedy this situation, you may be required to stop and restart the spooler service.

To stop and restart the spooler service, perform the following steps:

1. Go to the Control Panel (Start|Settings|Control Panel).
2. Double-click the Services icon.
3. Highlight the entry labeled Spooler in the list of services.
4. Click the Stop button, and confirm that you want to stop the service.
5. Click the Start button.
6. Click Close on the Services dialog box.

This should remedy the problem of stalled print jobs in the spooler.

Changing The Spool Location

The default directory for the print spooler is \Winnt\System32\Spool. To change the location of the spooler directory, perform the following steps:

1. Go to the Printers folder (Start|Settings|Printers).
2. Select Server Properties from the File menu.

3. Select the Advanced tab.
4. Enter the path to the new spool directory in the Spool Folder text box.

One reason you might want to change this setting is that the drive for the default path has limited storage space for storing print jobs. Note that you must restart the print server before these changes take effect.

Now that we have covered spooling and priorities issues, let's move on to discuss setting up multiple printers and grouping print devices.

Logical Printers And Printing Pools

As previously defined, a logical printer (the printer in Microsoft-speak) is the software interface that enables communication between Windows NT and the physical printing device. You can create multiple logical printers that send print jobs to a single print device (and, conversely, a single logical printer that sends jobs to multiple print devices).

It is necessary to create different logical printers (with different share names) to assign varying priorities for print jobs from various groups and users to a single print device. All of this is defined through the Add Printer Wizard in the Printers folder. You simply provide different settings (such as access rights, access times, and priorities) for different shares that attach to the same physical print device.

When a printer services multiple printing devices, this is called a "printer pool." Put simply, a single logical printer spools out jobs to the next available printing device in the printer pool. It is necessary for the print devices in a printer pool to be of the same type. With this setup, the printer assigns files to be printed to whichever print device is free in the printer pool.

Now that we have discussed basic printing issues, we'll move on to explain a few issues that must be understood for printing in an enterprise environment.

Advanced Printing

Understanding enterprise printing builds on your existing knowledge of server-level printing and adds a few twists. This section pinpoints these topics, encompassing discussions concerning the following:

- Print commands and controls
- Print shares
- Multiple physical and logical printers
- Print auditing
- Ownership
- DLC
- TCP/IP and Unix printers

The Print Commands And Controls

Solid knowledge of the common print controls and the Printers folder commands is important. Take the time to review the multiple tabs of printer controls found in the properties of any locally installed printer.

Here are a few items on which you need to focus:

General Tab

- **New Driver** Installs or replaces existing printer driver.
- **Print Processor** Changes the data type used by the print system.
- **Separator Page** Defines a document to be inserted between print jobs.

Ports Tab

- **Enable Printer Pooling** Assists in configuring identical printers to share a single print queue.

Scheduling Tab

- **Available** Defines the time frames when a printer is active. If a user sends a print job to a logical printer when it is not available, that job is stored in the spooler and printed in priority order when the available time period arrives.

- **Priority** Sets the priority of a logical printer against other logical printers for the same physical printer (priority has no effect if there is only one logical printer serving a physical printer).

- **Spool Print Documents So Program Finishes Printing Faster** Tells the spooler to store print jobs on a hard drive before or during printing. The alternate selection, Print Directly To The Printer does not save the print job at all. To reduce the time a large print job occupies the printer, select Start Printing After Last Page Is Spooled. Thus, the printer doesn't have to wait for the application to completely send the job over the network. It is stored in the spool file before printing begins.

Some of the Printers folder commands are just as important to remember as the controls, such as those listed in the file drop-down menu:

- **Pause Printing** Halts the activity of the selected logical printer when deselected activity resumes where it left off.

- **Purge Print Documents** Flushes all waiting, paused, and printing print jobs from the selected printer.

- **Server Properties** Launches a dialog box where you can create new forms (paper sizes), modify ports, or perform advanced configurations. The Advanced tab has six important controls:

  - Path to the spool
  - Log spool errors
  - Log spool warnings
  - Log spool events
  - Beep on document errors
  - Notify completion of remote printing

You should remember to take a look at the individual logical Printers folders, as well. The Printer menu contains some of the Pause Printing and Purge Print Documents commands, as does the main Printers folder. The Document menu is the most important drop-down menu at the individual logical Printers folder level.

The important commands on the Document menu are:

- **Pause** Allows users to manage print jobs in the queue, does not grant the ability to print.
- **Resume** Continues printing where paused.
- **Restart** Starts the current print job over. Any document can be restarted if it has not been deleted from the spooler.

Printer Shares

One of the most useful abilities of a network is that of sharing a single printer with multiple users. The process of enabling other network users to access a printer is just as simple as giving users network access to a directory or a drive—you create a printer share. This is done through the Sharing command located in the File menu of the main Printers folder or the Printer menu of the individual Printers folder. All you need to do is assign a share name. Now, everyone on the network can print to that printer (provided they have the printer drivers available).

To tighten security on a printer, you must access the Permissions button located on the Security tab of a printer's Properties dialog box. The Printer Permissions dialog box acts the same way as the File Permissions version. The only real change is the types of access possible with printers:

- **No Access** Grants absolutely no access other than viewing the NetBIOS name.
- **Print** Enables users to print and manage their own documents, but they can only see the documents of others.
- **Manage Documents** Allows users to manage print jobs in the queue; does not grant the ability to print.
- **Full Control** Allows users to print, manage print jobs, change permissions, and install drivers.

The default settings for a newly created printer share are:

- **Full Control** Administrators, Server Operators, and Print Operators
- **Manage Documents** Creator owner
- **Print** Everyone

To restrict access to a printer, you must remove the Everyone group, and then add group(s) and user(s) as needed.

Multiple Printers: Physical And Logical

Many of the problem areas that deal with printers involve multiple groups requiring printer access, with one of the groups printing large non-urgent documents. These situations are often resolved by defining multiple logical printers for a single physical printer and altering the priority or access times.

Keep in mind that:

- A single physical printer can be served by multiple logical printers.
- A single logical printer can serve multiple physical printers (pooling).
- Multiple logical printers can serve multiple physical printers.

Print Auditing

A printer is just another Windows NT object. Therefore, you can use Windows NT's audit system to monitor access, use, and errors. (For more details about Windows NT's audit system, refer to Chapter 7.) You need to enable File And Object Access level auditing (Success and/or Failure) to track printer events. To set the events to Audit By User/Group, go to the Audit button on the Security tab of the Properties of a printer. This dialog box operates the same as the File version.

The events you can audit are:

- Print
- Full Control
- Delete
- Change Permissions
- Take Ownership

Events captured through print auditing are listed in the System or Security log, depending on the nature of the event.

Ownership

The creator of a logical printer is the owner of that printer. Only an administrator or a user with Full Control can take ownership of a printer (just like every other object within Windows NT). In addition to the ability to change permissions on an owned printer, the owner can also modify form-to-tray assignments, install font cartridges, and adjust the halftone settings.

DLC

The DLC protocol is typically used to interoperate with IBM mainframes, but it is also used to provide connectivity to network-attached print devices. Most commonly, the DLC protocol is used for Hewlett-Packard network-attached printers and/or JetDirect interfaces (e.g., a printer NIC).

The DLC protocol is installed using the Protocol tab of the Network Control Panel applet. There are no configuration options; however, the binding order of DLC is important. The order in which adapters are bound (i.e., priority) to DLC is the reference number used by DLC applications—the first adapter is value **0**, the second is value **1**, and so on. Windows NT DLC can support up to 16 physical adapters.

To use DLC for printing, you must install both the DLC protocol and the Hewlett-Packard Network Port monitor on the server designated as the print server. You can designate any server to be the print server because the print device is attached to the network directly and not through a parallel cable to a computer. The DLC protocol must be installed first, then the HP Network Port monitor (HPMON.DLL) should be installed through the Add Printer Wizard Add Port command. Once installation is complete, the logical printer on the print server can be shared across the network and used as any other printer.

The Hewlett-Packard Network Port monitor can be configured so the managed ports are either "job-based" or "continuous connection," which are set at port creation. A job-based setting disconnects from a printer when the print job is complete. Thus, other print servers can connect and print. A continuous connection setting does not release the printer, so other servers cannot connect.

TCP/IP And Unix Printers

If your network has Unix workstations or you don't want to use the DLC protocol to communicate with network-attached printers, you can use Windows NT's TCP/IP Printing service. TCP/IP only needs to be installed on the print server where the print device resides. TCP/IP printing services rely on the LPD (Line Printer Daemon) and LPR (Line Printer Remote) services. LPD servers and LPR clients are often Unix systems, but these utilities are available for most platforms, including Windows NT.

The TCP/IP Printing service is installed through the Services tab of the Network, Control Panel applet. After installation, you can change its startup settings in the Services applet from Manual (the default) to Automatic. If a print device resides on a Windows NT machine, use the New Printer Wizard to create a new port of type "LPR Port" and direct it to the proper location of the printer, whether a Windows NT print share or a Unix-hosted queue.

Logical printers are created to send documents to the TCP/IP printer through the Add Printer Wizard by using the IP address of the print server and the name of the print device, as defined by the print server.

Practice Questions

Question 1

A single printer is shared by the Sales, Marketing, and Accounting departments. The Accounting users print large documents that tie up the printer for hours, but these documents are rarely needed the same day they are sent to the printer. You want to alter the printing situation so that the print jobs of the Sales and Marketing users will take priority and the Accounting print job will not tie up the printer. Which of the following steps are necessary? [Check all correct answers]

- ❑ a. Give the Sales and Marketing groups Full Control over the printer.
- ❑ b. Create three logical printers, and assign each printer to a single department.
- ❑ c. Set the Accounting group's logical printer so that it is only available from 8 P.M. to 6 A.M.
- ❑ d. Set the Accounting group's printer to send directly to the printer.
- ❑ e. Set the Accounting group's print priority to 99.

Answers b and c are correct. Creating separate logical printers isolates the print jobs of the departments, giving you finer control over access privileges. Therefore, answer b is correct. Setting the Accounting printer to print jobs overnight will prevent tying up the device during the day. Therefore, answer c is correct. Giving users Full Control over anything is a bad idea, but doing so over the printer will invite them to delete the Accounting group's print jobs. Therefore, answer a is incorrect. Sending the files directly to the printer will take longer to print than if they were spooled. Plus, if the printer is not available (off hours only), the print job would be lost because it would not be stored in the spool. Therefore, answer d is incorrect. Giving the Accounting group top priority will place its long jobs at the front of the queue. Therefore, answer e is incorrect.

Question 2

You have a large bank of printers. You have enough money in the budget to purchase two printers to replace two of the existing printers. How can you determine which printers receive the most usage (page count and print jobs) so you can replace them?

- ❍ a. Audit File And Object Access events.
- ❍ b. Use Performance Monitor to create a Printer object report.
- ❍ c. Set the Application log to tally printer events.
- ❍ d. Use the Printer Wizard to gather statistics.

Answer a is correct. You must use File And Object Access audits to record print activities, which in turn can be used to tally the number of pages and jobs sent to each printer. The Performance Monitor does not have a Printer object that you can use to create a report. Therefore, answer b is incorrect. There is no way to set the Application log to tally anything. The Application log records information an application sends to it to record. Therefore, answer c is incorrect. The Printer Wizard is used to create logical printers. It does not have any statistical abilities. Therefore, answer d is incorrect.

Question 3

During the printing of a 43-page document, your printer jams on the second page. You pause the printer through the Printers folder. After you remove the jam and reset the physical printer, what command should you enter?

- ❍ a. Open the Printers folder for the printer, and select Resume from the Document menu.
- ❍ b. Open the Printers folder for the printer, and select Restart from the Document menu.
- ❍ c. Open the Printers folder for the printer, and select Resume from the Printer menu.
- ❍ d. Open the Printers folder for the printer, and select Restart from the Printer menu.

Answer b is correct. Restart will start the print process over again from the beginning. Resume will start printing from the last place in the print job and will not resend the destroyed page or the data lost from the printer buffer. Therefore, answer a is incorrect. Resume is located in the Document menu, not the Printer menu, and it is the wrong command. Therefore, answer c is incorrect. Restart is located in the Document menu, not the Printer menu. Therefore, answer d is incorrect.

Question 4

Both the Sales group and the regional sales manager's secretary use the same network printer. How can you adjust the printing environment so the secretary's print jobs are processed quickly so she can keep up with her boss's hectic routine?

- ❍ a. Set the Sales groups print jobs to print directly to the printer.
- ❍ b. Give the secretary Full Control over the printer.
- ❍ c. Create a separate logical printer for the secretary, and assign it priority level 99.
- ❍ d. Create a separate logical printer for the secretary, and set it to use the Print Processor data type of RAW.

Answer c is correct. Creating a logical printer with priority level 99 will place her print jobs at the front of the print queue. Sending the Sales group's print jobs directly to the printer will not improve the print time for the secretary. Therefore, answer a is incorrect. Giving the secretary Full Control will allow her to rearrange the print queue, but the added manual control will only slow her down by requiring her to perform administrative functions. Therefore, answer b is incorrect. Setting the logical printer to use the RAW data type may prevent some graphical data from printing correctly and will not improve the print time. Therefore, answer d is incorrect.

Question 5

A user is attempting to print to a printer attached to the network using an HP JetDirect card. The print server and the user's client machine both have DLC properly installed. But the user is repeatedly denied access to the printer, even after the printer has been physically reset. What is the most likely cause of this?

❍ a. The print server is disconnected from the network.

❍ b. The JetDirect card is not compatible with the DLC protocol.

❍ c. Another user is printing to the device using the Microoft TCP/IP Printing service.

❍ d. Another print server is configured with DLC set to continuous connection mode.

Answer d is correct. If DLC is set to continuous connection mode, no other access to that printer is possible. If the print server is offline, the NetBIOS name of the resource would not be present instead of a denial of service. Therefore, answer a is incorrect. The JetDirect card is designed to handle DLC. Therefore, answer b is incorrect. If the TCP/IP Printing service were in use by another user, that would not deny access via DLC. Therefore, answer c is incorrect.

Question 6

Several users are trying to print to a print server. You receive many complaints from users that they have sent several jobs to the print server but the jobs have not printed and cannot be deleted. How do you resolve this problem?

❍ a. Verify that the Pause Printing option is not checked on the print server.

❍ b. Delete the stalled printer from the print server, create a new printer, and tell your users to resend their jobs to the new printer.

❍ c. Delete all files from the spool folder on the print server, and tell your users to resend them.

❍ d. Stop the spooler service, and then restart it.

Answer d is correct. This scenario is a quintessential case of stalled print spooler. To fix the problem, select Services in Control Panel, stop the spooler service, and then restart it. If pause printing were active, those jobs could be deleted; because they cannot be deleted, answer a is incorrect. Answer b involves way too much work, which may in fact be unnecessary and probably won't fix the problem anyway. Answer c implies that users must resend their print jobs, but that doesn't restart the spooler, so it will delete their pending jobs without fixing the problem.

Question 7

You have a Windows NT Server that provides print services to 20 Windows NT computers on your network. You have an HP LaserJet attached to the Windows NT print server. Hewlett-Packard has just released an updated printer driver. What must be done to provide the updated driver for the computers that print to this print server?

- ❍ a. Install the updated driver on all client computers. There is no need to update the server.
- ❍ b. Install the updated driver on the print server, and do nothing more.
- ❍ c. Install the updated driver on the print server and on all client computers.
- ❍ d. Create a separate logical printer with the updated driver on the print server, and tell all your users to print to the new printer.
- ❍ e. Install the updated driver on the print server, and instruct all client computers to download the updated driver from the server.

Answer b is correct. The best way to update a printer driver is simply to update the driver on the print server. There is no need to manually update the driver on each client computer that is running Windows NT. When a client computer sends a print job to the print server, the updated driver is automatically copied to the client. Therefore, answers a, c, and e are incorrect because it's not necessary to define a new logical printer simply to update a driver.

Question 8

You run a network for a small consulting firm. You only have a single printer on the network. The company executives have asked that you configure printing so documents from the executives print before other users' documents. How is this performed?

- ❍ a. Create a separate logical printer, assign rights to the executive group, and set the printer priority to 1.
- ❍ b. Create a separate logical printer, assign rights to the executive group, and set the printer priority to 99.
- ❍ c. Create a separate logical printer for the executive group, and configure the printer to start printing immediately.
- ❍ d. Create a separate logical printer for the executive group, and configure the printer to print directly to the physical print device.

Answer b is correct. It is possible to set priorities between groups of documents by creating different logical printers for the same physical print device and setting different priority levels on the printers. To set printer priority, select the Scheduling tab in Printer Properties. The highest priority is 99. Answer a is incorrect because it sets the priority at the default level, which confers no advantage when executives access the printer. Printing immediately may confer a slight advantage when printing, but won't get the executives ahead in the queue, so answer c is incorrect. Printing directly simply avoids saving the spool file on disk, so it doesn't get executives ahead in the queue either; therefore, answer d is also incorrect.

Question 9

You have just installed a new printer on your print server. You send a print job to the printer, but it comes out as pages of nonsense words. What is the most likely cause of the problem?

- ❍ a. The DLC protocol is not installed.
- ❍ b. The print spooler is corrupt.
- ❍ c. An incorrect printer driver is installed.
- ❍ d. There is not enough hard disk space for spooling.

Answer c is correct. If an incorrect printer driver is installed, documents may print illegibly. If DLC or another protocol needed to access the printer wasn't installed, nothing would print—not even nonsense; therefore, answer a is incorrect. If the print spooler were corrupt, nothing would print either; therefore, answer b is also incorrect. If there wasn't enough disk space for spooling, the job would never be stored, and could never get to the printer (not to mention error messages to that effect). That's why answer d is incorrect as well.

Question 10

You want to create a printer pool with five print devices. Which must be true for you to create a printer pool?

- ❍ a. All print devices must use the same protocol.
- ❍ b. All physical print devices must be connected to the same logical printer.
- ❍ c. All print devices must use the same printer port.
- ❍ d. All print devices must be located in the same room.

Answer b is correct. To create a printer pool, all print devices must be connected to the same logical printer. All print devices should also be identical. The logical printer handles protocol issues, even when multiple protocols are used; therefore, answer a is incorrect. The logical printer also handles multiple printer ports with ease for pooled printers (which cannot be the same, unless each printer is attached to a separate machine). Therefore, answer b is also incorrect. The logical printer doesn't care where the devices are located, so answer d is incorrect as well.

Question 11

You have a printer pool that consists of Printer 1 and Printer 2. Printer 1 is printing a job, and Printer 2 is idle. A paper jam occurs on Printer 1's print device. What will happen to the rest of the job that was being printed?

- ❍ a. The print job will be completed on Printer 2.
- ❍ b. The print job is canceled.
- ❍ c. The print job will be completed on Printer 2 because Printer 2 has a higher priority level.
- ❍ d. The print job is held for completion by Printer 1 until the device is fixed.

Answer d is correct. If a physical print device in a printer pool fails in the middle of a print job, the print job is retained at that physical print device until the device is fixed. This explains why answers a and c are incorrect. Answer b is incorrect because the job is not flushed from the queue if it doesn't complete.

Question 12

You want to configure a Windows NT computer as a print server for an HP network-attached print device that uses DLC. However, you can't locate the option to install a port for the printer. Why?

- ❍ a. PostScript printing is enabled on the print device and must be disabled.
- ❍ b. You didn't install the print driver on the print server.
- ❍ c. The print processor is corrupt and must be fixed.
- ❍ d. The DLC protocol is not installed on the print server.

Answer d is correct. For Windows NT to provide support for this HP network interface print device, you must install DLC. You can't install a printer driver if Windows NT cannot recognize the print device. PostScript printing has nothing to do with port availability; therefore, answer a is incorrect. You couldn't access the Printers folder for this printer unless a driver was installed; therefore, answer b is incorrect. Print processors have nothing to do with port availability either, so answer c is incorrect as well.

Need To Know More?

Donald, Lisa, and James Chellis: *MSCE: NT Server 4 In The Enterprise Study Guide, 2nd Edition*. Sybex Network Press, San Francisco, CA, 1998. ISBN 0-7821-2221-3. Chapter 8 focuses on printing, print shares, and print management.

Heywood, Drew: *Inside Windows NT Server, 2nd Edition*. New Riders, Indianapolis, IN, 1998. ISBN 1-56205-860-6. Chapter 8, entitled "Managing Print Services," details the issues relating to printing and printer permissions and management.

Siyan, Karanjit S.: *Windows NT Server 4 Professional Reference, 2nd Edition*. New Riders, Indianapolis, IN, 1997. ISBN 1-56205-805-3. A nice discussion of using Windows NT print services is located in Chapter 17, "Windows NT Printing."

Strebe, Matthew, Charles Perkins, and James Chellis: *MSCE: NT Server 4 Study Guide, 2nd Edition*. Sybex Network Press, San Francisco, CA, 1997. ISBN 0-7821-2222-1. Chapter 14 contains detailed information about creating and maintaining your printing environment.

The *Windows NT Server Resource Kit* contains lots of useful information about printers and printer management. Some places to start out are: *The Networking Guide* Chapter 14, "Using DLC With Windows NT" and *The Resource Guide* Chapter 2, "Printing." There are scattered documents about the TCP/IP Printing service and DLC.

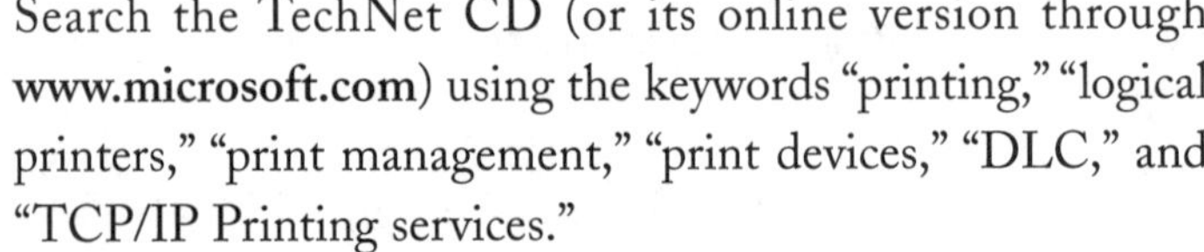

Search the TechNet CD (or its online version through **www.microsoft.com**) using the keywords "printing," "logical printers," "print management," "print devices," "DLC," and "TCP/IP Printing services."

Advanced Remote Access Service (RAS)

14

Terms you'll need to understand:

- √ Remote Access Service (RAS)
- √ RAS clients
- √ Telephony Application Programming Interface (TAPI)
- √ RAS Phonebook
- √ Encryption
- √ AutoDial
- √ Logging
- √ Null modem
- √ Name resolution

Techniques you'll need to master:

- √ Installing and configuring RAS
- √ Configuring the RAS Phonebook
- √ Implementing RAS security measures

RAS is an important topic to understand if you want to enable remote communication in Windows NT. In this chapter, we explore Windows NT's Remote Access Service.

What Is RAS?

RAS, or Remote Access Service, is a secure and reliable method of extending a network across communication links to remote computers. Modems and other communication devices act just like a network interface card (NIC) over a RAS connection. Everything a standard network-attached client is able to access and operate, a remote RAS client can do as well.

RAS in Windows NT 4 is a significant improvement over the capabilities in 3.5x. Many of its advances are borrowed from Windows 95, including the ease of installation, process of configuration, and the look and feel. RAS is able to support 256 simultaneous connections; act as a firewall, a gateway, or a router; and maintain tight security.

The following is a list of communication links through which RAS can connect:

- Public Switched Telephone Networks (PSTN)
- Integrated Service Digital Networks (ISDN)
- X.25 packet switching network

Standard local area network (LAN) protocols are used over the RAS connection. Thus, TCP/IP, IPX, and NetBEUI can be used for network communication over the link established by RAS. Because the actual network protocol is used, the remote RAS client acts just as if it were connected locally to the network. The only difference is in speed of data transfer—the RAS connection is slower than a network-attached connection. Always remember: A client is a client is a client, no matter if it is connected locally or uses RAS.

RAS Clients

A RAS client is any machine that is able to dial-in or connect to a RAS server and establish an authorized connection. Although optimized to integrate Microsoft-based operating systems, other types of systems can gain access with the proper software, protocols, and configuration.

The links established between a client and a server using RAS are often called wide area network (WAN) links. This is because RAS is most often used to connect a computer (or an entire LAN) to a centrally located network over a long distance. It should not be too much of a stretch to think of the communication protocols used to establish a RAS connection as WAN protocols. Windows NT supports two WAN protocols:

- **SLIP** The Serial Line Internet Protocol connection supports TCP/IP, but does not support IPX or NetBEUI. SLIP does not support DHCP. Thus, every client must have an assigned IP address. SLIP does not support encrypted passwords. It is provided only as a means for a Windows NT Server to act as a client when dialing into a Unix server, and it cannot be used to accept inbound connections on Windows NT.
- **PPP** The Point-To-Point Protocol supports numerous protocols, including AppleTalk, TCP/IP, IPX, and NetBEUI. It was designed as an improvement to SLIP. PPP supports DHCP and encrypted passwords, and it is the most common and most widely supported WAN protocol.

Windows NT Server can act as a RAS client whenever it dials out over a modem (or other communication device) to establish a connection with another server or computer system. The most common situation where Windows NT is a client is when a LAN connects to the Internet.

RAS Servers

Windows NT Server can support up to 256 simultaneous incoming RAS connections.

Here are the important points to remember about Windows NT as a RAS server:

- Only supports inbound PPP clients. SLIP is not supported for dial-up.

- A NetBIOS gateway is established between the server and PPP-attached RAS client to sustain standard Windows NT network operations.
- Supports both IP and IPX routing.
- Supports NetBIOS and Windows Sockets applications.
- Supports Point-To-Point Tunneling Protocol (PPTP) connections, which makes it possible for Windows NT computers to communicate securely over the Internet.
- Supports Multilink PPP (MP), where numerous connections can be aggregated.

Let's discuss these last two bullets in more detail.

Point-To-Point Tunneling Protocol (PPTP)

PPTP enables "tunneling" of IPX, NetBEUI, and TCP/IP inside PPP packets in such a way as to establish a secure link between a client and server over the Internet. PPTP connections are useful for establishing VPNs (virtual private networks) in small companies that cannot afford to obtain expensive leased-lines for wide area network communications. PPTP provides users anywhere in the world with a secure connection back to the home office's network. PPTP uses a powerful encryption security scheme that is more secure than the standard communications over the network itself. Thus, all traffic over the Internet using PPTP is considered safe and secure.

PPTP must be installed using the Protocols tab in the Network applet.

Multilink PPP (MP)

Windows NT has the capability to combine the bandwidth of multiple physical links, which increases the total bandwidth that could be used for a RAS connection. This aggregation of multiple communication links can be used as an inexpensive way to increase the overall bandwidth with the least amount of cost. MP must be supported by both the client and server systems.

MP cannot be used with the callback security feature (covered later in this chapter). The MP callback feature can only control a single modem device to return a client's call. The only exception to this rule is a multichannel

ISDN modem. A single ISDN line consists of three individual lines: a D channel and two B channels. An MP callback can reestablish a connection using both B channels of an ISDN line because a phone number is used and the linking process usually is the responsibility of the ISDN interface itself.

The checkbox to enable MP is located on the Network Configuration dialog box, which is displayed in Figure 14.1 (seen later in the chapter).

When you install a modem or the RAS components of Windows NT, the Telephony Application Programming Interface (TAPI) is automatically installed. TAPI is required to control any communications device.

Telephony API (TAPI)

In Windows NT, the Telephony Application Programming Interface provides a standard method of controlling communications over voice, data, and fax. Although the hardware is not provided with Windows NT, TAPI can be used to control many PBX systems and communication devices for automated activity.

As mentioned, TAPI is required to control any communications device. This includes modems. Each time a system attempts a dial-out connection, TAPI controls the modem and moderates the connection. Once a connection is established, TAPI continues to oversee the operation of the communication link.

The Dialing Properties dialog box (reached through the Modems applet) controls how TAPI uses your modem to place calls. You can control long-distance dialing, calling card use, prefix numbers, and tone/pulse dialing. You can also define multiple configurations based on physical location. If you travel with a Windows NT Server notebook, you can define a dialing property profile for each of the cities you visit regularly.

TAPI also controls the Phonebook entries used to establish RAS connections. All the functions and features of the modem and the communication types established over a modem are configured through a TAPI-controlled interface (see the section entitled "RAS Phonebook" later in this chapter).

Now that we have discussed the RAS basics, let's move ahead to RAS installation and configuration.

Installing RAS

RAS is installed through the Services tab of the Network applet. Installing RAS takes some preparation and know-how to perform correctly. Following are the important elements to remember when performing the installation:

- Physically install or attach the modem.
- Install RAS through the Services tab of the Network applet.
- During the installation, if a modem has not already been installed, you will be forced to install one.
- Part of installing a modem requires the selection of the communications port.
- An installed modem must be added as a RAS device.
- The port must be configured for:
  - Dial out only
  - Receive calls only
  - Dial out and receive calls
- The LAN network protocols must be selected.
  - If dial out was selected, only the outbound protocols can be chosen.
  - If receive calls was selected, only the inbound protocols can be configured.
  - If dial out and receive calls was selected, both outbound and inbound protocols can be configured.
- Each inbound protocol requires protocol-specific configuration, as shown in Figures 14.2 and 14.3.

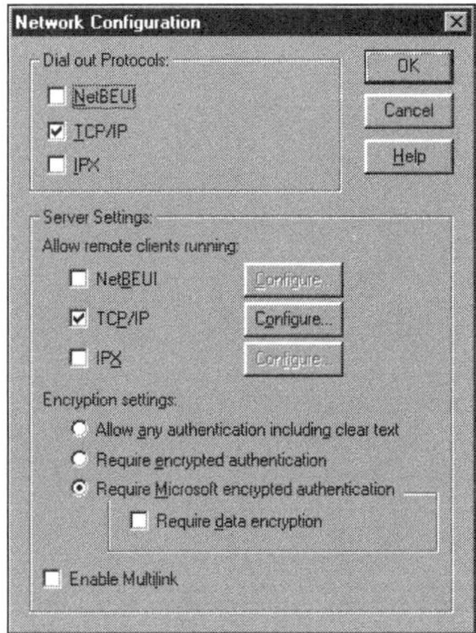

Figure 14.1 The Network Configuration dialog box for RAS.

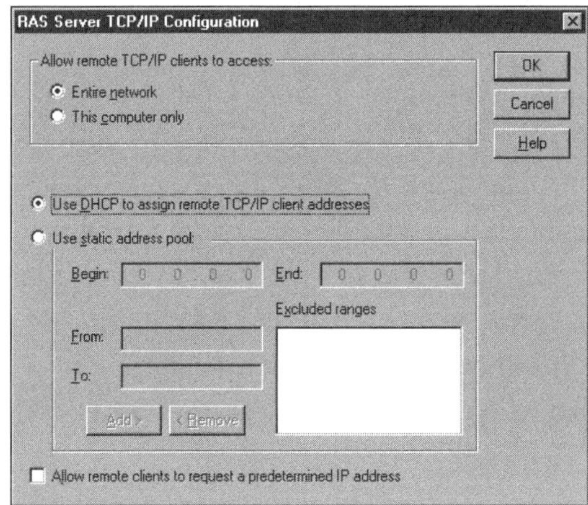

Figure 14.2 The TCP/IP inbound configuration dialog box for RAS.

- Once RAS itself is installed, you need to check your port and modem configuration through the Ports and Modems applets in the Control Panel.
- If RAS is configured to receive calls, the port and modem cannot be used by any other application. RAS locks the port to maintain control to monitor for inbound calls.

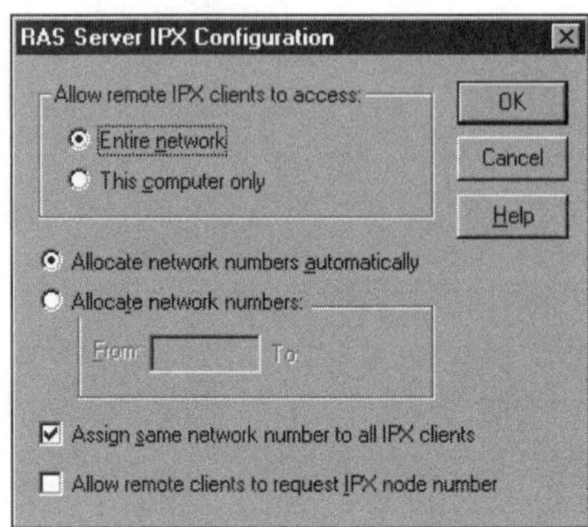

Figure 14.3 The IPX/SPX inbound configuration dialog box for RAS.

Now that we have discussed what RAS is and how to configure it, let's examine some RAS features.

RAS Features

RAS is a broad subject with many associated tie-ins to most of the standard network operations of Windows NT. There is much more to RAS than what is listed in this chapter. You'll need to review the reference materials listed at the end of this chapter for more RAS information. However, we have included some important features and options about RAS. The remaining sections in this chapter discuss topics such as RAS routing, gateways, and firewalls; the RAS Phonebook; RAS security, including encryption and callback features; RAS logon; AutoDial; and a number of other RAS features.

RAS Routing, Gateway, And Firewall

On the dialog boxes to configure the network protocols for inbound calls, you can select whether to let RAS clients using the protocol to access just the RAS server or the entire network. If you allow RAS clients to access the entire network, you are using RAS as a router. When NetBEUI is the only protocol in use, RAS acts as a gateway to enable NetBEUI—a non-routable protocol—to access the network. When you limit RAS clients to the RAS server, you are using RAS as a firewall. No access of any kind is permitted from the RAS server to the rest of the network.

RAS Phonebook

The dial-out capabilities of RAS are controlled and accessed through the RAS Phonebook. This utility is found in the Programs|Accessories folder of the Start menu, under the name Dial-Up Networking (DUN). The first time DUN is launched, you will be presented with a wizard to create your first Phonebook entry. Otherwise, the Phonebook dialog box will appear. Through this interface, you can create and modify dialup parameters for every RAS connection.

Phonebook entries consist of:

- Name
- Phone number
- Modem to use
- Server type
- Protocol settings
- Connection scripts
- Security settings
- X.25 settings (if applicable)

RAS Security

RAS offers numerous levels and types of security to protect your network from unauthorized remote access. The following sections highlight RAS encryption and callback features.

RAS Encryption

Windows NT can be configured to increase or decrease connection security through the:

- Security Tab of a Phonebook entry for outbound RAS links.
- Network Configuration dialog box for inbound RAS links (shown earlier in Figure 14.1).

Three settings are available for RAS data encryption:

- **Allow Any Authentication Including Clear Text** This is the most permissive setting. It should be used when the user is not concerned about passwords. This option allows a connection using any authentication provided by the server; therefore, it is useful when connecting to a non-Microsoft server. This selection uses Password Authentication Protocol (PAP), a clear-text authentication protocol.
- **Require Encrypted Authentication** This option is beneficial when the transmission of a clear-text password is not desired and when you're connecting to a non-Microsoft server. This selection uses Challenge Handshake Authentication Protocol (CHAP) or Shiva Password Authentication Protocol (SPAP).
- **Require Microsoft Encrypted Authentication** For this setting, the Microsoft Challenge Handshake Authentication Protocol (MS-CHAP) must be used. It is useful when calling a Microsoft server from a Microsoft client. (Also included here is Require Data Encryption. If this box is checked, data sent over the wire will be encrypted. Data encryption is provided by Windows NT using the RSA [Rivest-Shamir Adleman Data Security] Incorporated RC4 algorithm. If the data sent fails to encrypt, the connection is automatically terminated.)

RAS Callback

Callback is a security feature where a RAS connection is only established after the server has disconnected the inbound call and then called the user back. Setting callback is done via the properties of a user through the User Manager For Domains or the User|Properties command of the Remote Access Manager. The following three callback settings are available:

- **No Call Back** This is the default setting. No Call Back means that when users establish a RAS connection, they will not be called back.
- **Set By Caller** This means that callback can be set by the user. This is a good way to save on long-distance charges because the server calls the client back at the number that is set by the caller.

- **Preset To** This means you can configure the callback for a preset number. This heightens security because the user must call from a predetermined phone number.

The RAS Logon Process

In Windows NT Server 4, you can log on to a domain via RAS at the Logon prompt by selecting the Connect Via Dial-in and the proper domain. This allows you to establish a RAS connection to the remote network without requiring you to log on locally, first.

When you use TCP/IP via a slow RAS connection, an LMHOSTS file might speed up network access and name resolution. Place an LMHOSTS file on the RAS client. Ensure that LMHOSTS entries have the **#PRE** tag so that the IP addresses will be cached.

AutoDial

AutoDial is the ability of Windows NT to remember the location of resources accessed through a RAS connection. Windows NT maintains a map that correlates a network address to a Phonebook entry. When a resource is referenced, RAS reestablishes the WAN connection to regain access to the resource without additional user interaction. AutoDial is enabled by default. AutoDial does not yet function over IPX/SPX, but it works with TCP/IP and NetBEUI.

Logging

Troubleshooting RAS difficulties is much simpler when the logging capabilities are employed. There are two logging features of Windows NT that record RAS-related activities. The first is the MODEMLOG.TXT file that records the modem's activities. This is enabled through a modem's properties in the Modems applet in the Advanced Connections Settings area. This file is placed in the Windows NT root directory.

The second log file is DEVICE.LOG. DEVICE.LOG can only be enabled through the Registry. The "Logging" value located in \HKEY_LOCAL_MACHINE\SYSTEM\CurrentControlSet\Services\RasMan\Parameters should be set to **1**. The DEVICE.LOG file is stored in the \Winnt\System32\ras directory.

The Event Viewer captures some RAS information that may be useful for troubleshooting and deciphering RAS. By default, all server errors, user connect attempts, disconnects, and so forth, are logged in the System Log.

Null Modem

A null modem is a serial cable that enables two computers to connect without the need for any modems. These special cables are common peer-to-peer attachment devices, but they can be used by Windows NT RAS to establish a standard Windows NT network connection. A null modem can be installed through the Modems applet by selecting it from the standard modems. A cable is not actually required for the setup, which offers you a way out when installing RAS if you don't have a modem on hand. Once installed, a null modem cable can be used just like a modem, which is itself used by RAS just as if it was a NIC (meaning a null modem cable-attached workstation can fully participate in a domain, but at a slower data transfer rate).

Name Resolution

In situations where static lookups occur, the most optimal configuration for resolution speed and WAN link traffic is to store the HOSTS (DNS) and the LMHOSTS (WINS) files on the local hard drives of the RAS clients. This presents some difficulty in maintaining the newest version of the files on multiple remote clients. PPP will support DHCP and IP-based access to DNS, however, so dynamic lookups are supported for PPP clients as well.

DUN Monitor

The Dial-Up Networking Monitor offers you a realtime assessment of the activity over RAS connections. Device statistics, connection statistics, and errors are some of the data sets presented by the utility.

Practice Questions

Question 1

If no standards are in place for the operating system, protocol, or the method of access for your remote clients, what is the highest level of security you can implement and still allow your users to connect via RAS?

- ❍ a. Allow Any Authentication Including Clear Text
- ❍ b. Require Encrypted Authentication
- ❍ c. PGP Encryption
- ❍ d. Require Microsoft Encrypted Authentication

Answer a is correct. With nonstandardized configurations, implementing any encryption security other than Allow Any Authentication Including Clear Text results in some clients being restricted from accessing the network via RAS. Require Encrypted Authentication and Require Microsoft Encrypted Authentication are encryption security schemes that require special configuration or operating systems. Therefore, answers b and d are incorrect. PGP Encryption is not a native option of Windows NT. Therefore, answer c is incorrect.

Question 2

Which of the following statements about PPP and SLIP are true? [Check all correct answers]

- ❑ a. PPP supports encrypted passwords. SLIP does not.
- ❑ b. SLIP supports NetBEUI, IPX/SPX, and TCP/IP. PPP only supports TCP/IP.
- ❑ c. PPP supports DHCP. SLIP does not.
- ❑ d. SLIP is used to access Unix servers.
- ❑ e. PPP is the most commonly used WAN protocol.

Answers a, c, d, and e are correct. PPP supports encrypted passwords, and SLIP does not. Therefore, answer a is correct. PPP supports NetBEUI, IPX/SPX, and TCP/IP. PPP supports DHCP, and SLIP does not. Therefore, answer c is correct. SLIP is used to access Unix servers. Therefore, answer d is correct. PPP is the most commonly used WAN protocol. Therefore, answer e is correct. SLIP only supports TCP/IP. Therefore, answer b is incorrect.

Question 3

Which of the following Windows NT networking activities are supported by a PPP RAS connection? [Check all correct answers]

- ❑ a. Printer share access
- ❑ b. Named pipes
- ❑ c. WinSOCK API applications over TCP/IP
- ❑ d. InterProcess Communications (IPC)
- ❑ e. User Logon Authentication

All answers—a, b, c, d, and e—are correct. Because a RAS-connected client is no different from a directly connected client, other than speed of data transfer, all standard network activities still occur over the WAN link.

Question 4

While connected to the office LAN, you create a shortcut on your desktop that points to a documents folder located on the LAN's file server. After working with a few files from this folder, you close your RAS session. Later, you attempt to reopen one of the files you edited earlier. What happens?

- ❍ a. Access is denied because no link to the LAN exists.
- ❍ b. The file is pulled from the network cache.
- ❍ c. A file with a similar name on your local hard drive is accessed instead.
- ❍ d. RAS AutoDial attempts to reconnect to the office LAN.

Answer d is correct. RAS maintains a list of the resources accessed over WAN links. When one of these resources is referenced, RAS will attempt to AutoDial to regain a connection to the server hosting the resource. Answer a would be the result if AutoDial was not enabled, but you should always assume the default configuration for computers unless indicated otherwise. Therefore, answer a is incorrect. Answers b and c are fictitious activities that do not occur. Therefore, answers b and c are incorrect.

Question 5

Where can you find information related to RAS problems to aid in troubleshooting? [Check all correct answers]

- ❑ a. Event Viewer
- ❑ b. DEVICE.LOG
- ❑ c. Dr. Watson
- ❑ d. MODEMLOG.TXT
- ❑ e. Windows NT Diagnostics

Answers a, b, and d are correct. The Event Viewer, DEVICE.LOG, and MODEMLOG.TXT can be useful troubleshooting tools for RAS problems. Dr. Watson does not track RAS events. Instead, it focuses on applications. Therefore, answer c is incorrect. Windows NT Diagnostics does not provide useful information related to RAS. Therefore, answer e is incorrect.

Question 6

What is the best method for offering reliable and secure access to your network over the Internet for your remote users?

- ❍ a. Internet Information Server (IIS)
- ❍ b. Serial Line Internet Protocol (SLIP)
- ❍ c. Point-To-Point Tunneling Protocol (PPTP)
- ❍ d. Require Encrypted Authentication

Answer c is correct. PPTP offers a reliable and secure network connection over the Internet. IIS only offers WWW, FTP, and Gopher services, without access to the entire network or additional security. Therefore, answer a is incorrect. SLIP will not offer access over the Internet, it cannot be used to dial into a Windows NT Server, and it does not support encryption. Therefore, answer b is incorrect. Require Encrypted Authentication is a midlevel security setting, but it does not directly offer connection over the Internet nor does this setting imply access to the network. Therefore, answer d is incorrect.

Question 7

You have a field technician who travels extensively around the country. Her schedule changes often, and she rarely visits the same place twice. It is important that she is able to connect to the office LAN periodically, but your organization's security policy requires callback security on all RAS connections. How can you configure her account so she is able to gain access while supporting your organization's security?

- ❍ a. Set the callback security to No Call Back only for her account.
- ❍ b. Enable callback security with Set By Caller selected.
- ❍ c. Set the callback security to Preset To with her home phone number.
- ❍ d. Set the callback security to Roaming, and give her the page number to remotely configure the callback number.
- ❍ e. Turn on the callback Caller ID capture.

Answer b is correct. Setting the Set By Caller option will allow the technician to input the callback number each time she needs to connect. Setting the No Call Back option will violate the organization's security policy. Therefore, answer a is incorrect. Setting the Preset To number will not allow her to gain access to the network because she is never in the same place. Therefore, answer c is incorrect. There is no Roaming callback setting. Therefore, answer d is incorrect. Windows NT does not have a Caller ID capture setting, but this can be obtained through third-party software; however, Caller ID capture is not required for this situation. Therefore, answer e is incorrect.

Question 8

Which protocols can be used over a RAS connection?

- ❍ a. TCP/IP, NetBEUI, but not NWLink
- ❍ b. TCP/IP, NWLink, but not NetBEUI
- ❍ c. Only TCP/IP
- ❍ d. TCP/IP, NetBEUI, and NWLink

Answer d is correct. TCP/IP, NetBEUI, and NWLink can all be used over RAS. TCP/IP, NetBEUI, but not NWLink is the restriction for the AutoDial feature but not a limitation of RAS as a whole. Therefore, answer a is incorrect. TCP/IP, NWLink, but not NetBEUI are the protocols that can be routed over RAS, but not a limitation as to which protocols can be used. Therefore, answer b is incorrect. Only TCP/IP can be used over SLIP, but RAS is not limited to SLIP. Therefore, answer c is incorrect.

Question 9

What are the possible uses for a null modem cable? [Check all correct answers]

- ❑ a. Attach a workstation to a domain
- ❑ b. Enable subnet routing
- ❑ c. Test a RAS server locally
- ❑ d. Establish a VPN over the Internet
- ❑ e. Temporarily connect two LANs

Answers a, c, and e are correct. Attaching a workstation to a domain is a use for a null modem cable. Therefore, answer a is correct. A RAS server can be tested using a null modem cable to simulate a remote client. Therefore, answer c is correct. Two closely adjacent LANs can be connected over a null modem cable. Therefore, answer e is correct. Subnet routing can only be implemented when two NICs are installed on the same machine. Therefore, answer b is incorrect. A VPN over the Internet can only be established with

PPTP and a connection to the Internet. An Internet connection requires a modem. Therefore, answer d is incorrect.

Question 10

If a user who is able to access resources on a Windows NT Server through a dial-in RAS connection is unable to access resources on a NetWare server on the same network, what is the most likely cause of his or her access problems?

❍ a. Nothing; RAS does not allow access to NetWare servers.

❍ b. The user's connection needs to be reconfigured to support NetWare access.

❍ c. The user's machine must be checked to make sure a NetWare-compatible protocol (such as NWLink or IPX/SPX-compatible protocol) and a NetWare-compatible client (such as the Microsoft Client for NetWare networks) is installed and working.

❍ d. The user's machine must add support for IPX/SPX or a compatible protocol.

Answer c is correct. The client must be checked to make sure the proper protocol and client support is available to connect to a NertWare server, or that the protocol and client are properly configured. RAS allows NetWare resources to be accessed using NetBEUI, IPX/SPX, and TCP/IP, and includes the ability to access NetWare-based resources. Therefore answer a is incorrect. RAS requires no special configuration to support access to NetWare. Therefore, answer b is incorrect. In addition to a common protocol with a NetWare server, the cliet also requires client software to create a connection with a NetWare server. Because this latter element is missing from answer d, it is incorrect.

Question 11

If static name resolution is used, what is the proper location of the HOSTS and LMHOSTS to optimize the lookup time?

- ❍ a. Both HOSTS and LMHOSTS should be stored on the RAS clients.
- ❍ b. HOSTS should be stored on the RAS server, and LMHOSTS should be stored on the RAS clients.
- ❍ c. Both HOSTS and LMHOSTS should be stored on the RAS server.
- ❍ d. HOSTS should be stored on the RAS clients, and LMHOSTS should be stored on the RAS server.

Answer a is correct. The fastest lookup time will occur when the HOSTS and LMHOSTS files are stored on the local hard drive of each RAS client because no WAN traffic needs to occur to resolve a resource location. Answers b, c, and d all involve one or both of these files being stored on the server, so they are all incorrect.

Need To Know More?

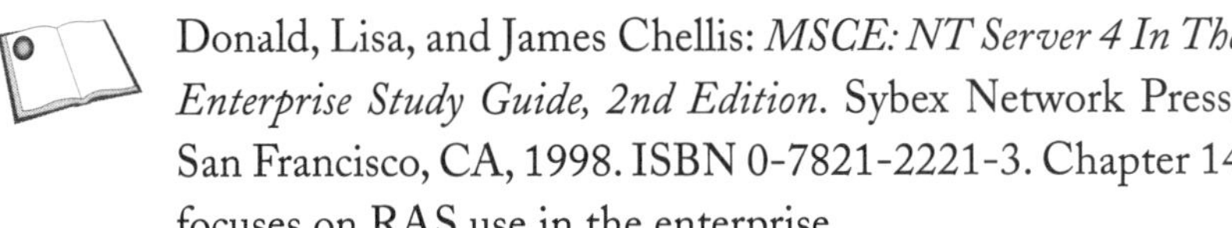

Donald, Lisa, and James Chellis: *MSCE: NT Server 4 In The Enterprise Study Guide, 2nd Edition.* Sybex Network Press, San Francisco, CA, 1998. ISBN 0-7821-2221-3. Chapter 14 focuses on RAS use in the enterprise.

Heywood, Drew: *Inside Windows NT Server, 2nd Edition.* New Riders, Indianapolis, IN, 1998. ISBN 1-56205-860-6. Chapter 16 discusses the installation, configuration, and use of RAS.

Siyan, Karanjit S.: *Windows NT Server 4 Professional Reference, 2nd Edition.* New Riders, Indianapolis, IN, 1997. ISBN 1-56205-805-3. Chapter 18 covers RAS in great detail.

Strebe, Matthew, Charles Perkins, and James Chellis: *MSCE: NT Server 4 Study Guide, 2nd Edition.* Sybex Network Press, San Francisco, CA, 1998. ISBN 0-7821-2222-1 RAS is examined in Chapter 11.

Search the TechNet CD (or its online version through **www.microsoft.com**) using the keywords "RAS," "Remote Access," "PPP," and "modems." The *Windows NT Server Resource Kit* contains some discussion of RAS, such as Appendix E, "RAS Reference," in the *Networking Guide*.

15

Advanced Troubleshooting

Terms you'll need to understand:

- √ Troubleshooting
- √ Boot failures
- √ NTLDR
- √ NTOSKRNL
- √ BOOT.INI
- √ BOOTSECT.DOS
- √ NTDETECT.COM
- √ Event Viewer
- √ Last Known Good Configuration (LKGC)
- √ Registry
- √ Emergency Repair Disk (ERD)
- √ Dr. Watson
- √ Kernel Debugger

Techniques you'll need to master:

- √ Understanding the troubleshooting process
- √ Troubleshooting media errors, domain controller communication difficulties, STOP message errors or halt on blue screen, hardware problems, and dependency failures
- √ Recognizing installation failures
- √ Troubleshooting boot failures
- √ Using Windows NT's built-in repair tools

The arena of troubleshooting Windows NT is both extensive and immense. In this chapter, we focus on a number of troubleshooting issues that you should be aware of, including installation failures, boot failures, repair tools, printing solutions, and a collection of other pertinent issues.

Installation Failures

During the initial installation of Windows NT, there are five common types of errors: media errors, domain controller communication difficulties, stop message errors or halt on blue screen, hardware problems, and dependency failures. Following is a short synopsis of each type of error:

- **Media errors** Media errors are problems with the distribution CD-ROM, the copy of the CD-ROM hosted on a network drive, or the communication between the installation and the distribution files. The only way to resolve a media error is to attempt to switch media, such as from one server's CD-ROM to another or copy the CD-ROM files to a network drive. If media errors are encountered, always restart the installation process from the beginning.
- **Domain controller communication difficulties** Any inability to communicate with a working domain controller prevents the current installation from joining the domain. This is especially a problem when installing a BDC. This error is often due to a mistyped name, network failure, or a domain controller being offline. Verify the viability of the domain controller directly and with other workstations (if present).
- **Stop message errors or halt on blue screen** Stop messages and halting on the blue screen during installation are usually caused by the wrong driver for a controller card. If any information is presented to you about the error, try to determine if the proper driver is being used. If not, or if you can't tell, double-check your hardware and the drivers required to operate them under Windows NT.
- **Hardware problems** Hardware problems should only occur if you failed to verify your hardware with the Hardware Compatibility List (HCL) or a physical defect has surfaced in supposedly operational devices. In

such cases, replacing the device is the only solution. However, it is not uncommon for a device to be improperly configured or installed. Always double-check the setup of your hardware before seeking a replacement.

- **Dependency failures** Dependency failures are when one or more dependent services fail due to the absence of a foundational service, hard ware, or driver. An example of a dependency failure is when the server and workstation services fail because the NIC fails to initialize properly. If Windows NT even boots with such errors, check the Event log.

Now that we have covered some caveats pertaining to installation, let's move on to discuss common errors in the boot process.

Boot Failures

Boot failures are problems during the startup of Windows NT.

NTLDR Error Message

If NTLDR is damaged or missing, the following error occurs:

```
BOOT: Couldn't find NTLDR. Please insert another disk.
```

Resolve using ERD to repair or replace.

Boot Error Due To Floppy In Drive A:

If a Windows NT bootable floppy with a defective BOOT.INI is in Drive A:, the following error occurs:

```
BOOT: Couldn't find NTLDR. Please insert another disk.
```

If the floppy is not bootable, the following error occurs:

```
Invalid system disk. Replace the disk, and then press any key.
```

In either case, eject the floppy and then reboot or press any key.

NTOSKRNL Missing Error Message

If NTOSKRNL is corrupt, missing, or the BOOT.INI points to the wrong partition, the following error occurs:

```
Windows NT could not start because the following file is missing
or corrupt:
\winnt\System32\ntoskrnl.exe
Please re-install a copy of the above file.
```

Repair the NTOSKRNL file using the ERD repair process, or edit and correct the BOOT.INI.

BOOT.INI Missing Error Message

If no BOOT.INI is present, NTLDR will launch Windows NT from \winnt of the current partition. If this fails, the following error occurs:

```
BOOT: Couldn't find NTLDR. Please insert another disk.
```

To alleviate this problem, replace the BOOT.INI file from a backup or use the ERD to repair.

BOOTSECT.DOS Missing Error Message

If the BOOTSECT.DOS file is not present to boot to MS-DOS or another operating system (not Windows NT), an error message appears as follows:

```
I/O Error accessing boot sector file
multi(0)disk(0)rdisk(0)partition(1):\bootsect.dos
```

This indicates that the BOOT.INI file has been changed, the partition numbering has changed, or the partition is missing, inactive, or inaccessible. To attempt to repair or replace the BOOTSECT.DOS file, use the ERD repair procedure.

NTDETECT.COM Missing Error Message

If the NTDETECT.COM file is not present, the following error message appears:

```
NTDETECT V1.0 Checking Hardware...
NTDETECT failed
```

This error must be repaired using the ERD repair process.

Repair Tools

Fortunately, Windows NT does not leave you high and dry when you encounter errors. There is a handful of invaluable tools you can use to repair and correct operational difficulties. In the next few sections, we detail how to use Event Viewer, Last Known Good Configuration, Registry, and ERD.

Event Viewer

The Event Viewer, located in Programs|Administrative Tools, is used to inspect the three logs created by Windows NT automatically. These logs are:

- **System** Records information and alerts about Windows NT's internal processes.
- **Security** Records security-related events.
- **Application** Records Windows NT application events, alerts, and system messages.

Each log records a different type of information, but all the logs collect the same information about each event: date, time, source, category, event, user ID, and computer. Plus, each event recorded has, at worst, an error code number or, at best, a detailed description with a memory HEX buffer capture.

Most system errors, including stop errors that result in the blue screen, are recorded in the System log. This allows you to review the time and circumstances around a system failure.

Last Known Good Configuration

The Last Known Good Configuration (LKGC) is a recording made by Windows NT of all the Registry settings that existed the last time a user successfully logged on to the server. Every time a login completes, Windows NT records a new LKGC. If a system error occurs or the Registry becomes corrupted so that booting or logging in is not possible, the LKGC can be used to return to a previously operational state. The LKGC is accessed during bootup when the following message displays: "Press the spacebar now to boot with the Last Known Good Configuration." A menu will appear where you can select to load using the LKGC (by pressing L) or other stored configurations.

The Registry

Editing the Registry by hand should be your last resort. A single, improperly configured Registry entry can render an installation of Windows NT DOA. There are two Registry editing utilities: REGEDIT and REGEDT32. Both of these utilities must be launched from the Run command or a DOS prompt. REGEDIT displays all the hives of the Registry in a single display window, and the entire Registry can be searched at one time. REGEDT32 displays each of the five hives in a separate display window, but it offers more security- and control-related functions.

It is a good idea to back up your Registry regularly. You can do this using any of these tools:

- Windows NT Backup
- Disk Administrator (SYSTEM key only)
- Either Registry editing tool (REGEDIT or REGEDT32)
- REGBACK utility from the Resource Kit

The best times to make a backup are just before and after any significant changes are made to your system, such as hardware installation, software installation, or service pack application. If Windows NT fails to operate properly but boots up, you can attempt a repair by restoring the Registry from a backup.

There are a few things you should note about working with the Registry. When you edit the Registry, you are working with it in memory. This means that the instant you make a Registry change, it goes into effect. However, in some cases, a reboot is required to correct memory settings and launch applications to fully comply with the changes. It is always a good idea to reboot after editing the Registry. Also, when a key of the Registry is saved (or backed up), you capture all the subcontents of that key. This is important to remember when restoring portions of the Registry from backup. All subkeys below the point at which restoration occurs will also be overwritten by the saved version. Any and all changes made since the backup will be lost in the sections restored.

Emergency Repair Disk

The Emergency Repair Disk (ERD) is the miniature first-aid kit for Windows NT. This single floppy contains all the files needed to repair system-partition and many boot-partition problems. The ERD is most often used to repair or replace files that are critical to the boot process of Windows NT. An ERD is usually created during the installation of Windows NT, but additional and updated ERDs can be created using the RDISK.EXE utility. At the Run command, **RDISK /S** will force Windows NT to save to disk all current Registry settings in memory to \Winnt\System32\Config, then prompt you for a preformatted disk. The ERD will contain the files listed in Table 15.1.

The ERD does not contain the entire Registry but just enough to fix the most common errors. To use the ERD to make repairs, you need the three setup disks used to install Windows NT. The repair process is depicted in the following steps:

1. Reboot the computer using Windows NT setup Disks 1 and 2.
2. Select "R" for Repair. A menu appears containing the following options:
   - Inspect Registry files
   - Inspect startup environment
   - Verify Windows NT system files
   - Inspect boot sector

Table 15.1 The contents of an ERD.

File	Contents
SYSTEM._	HKEY_LOCAL_MACHINE\SYSTEM compressed
SOFTWARE._	HKEY_LOCAL_MACHINE\SOFTWARE compressed
SECURITY._	HKEY_LOCAL_MACHINE\SECURITY compressed
SAM._	HKEY_LOCAL_MACHINE\SAM compressed
NTUSER.DA_	Default profile, compressed
AUTOEXEC.NT	Winnt\System32\autoexec.nt
CONFIG.NT	Winnt\System32\config.nt
SETUP.LOG	List of installed files and their checksums
DEFAULT._	HKEY_USERS\DEFAULT compressed

3. Deselect any options you do not wish to use, then continue.
4. Insert Disk 3 and the ERD when prompted.

Now that we have discussed some common system problems, let's move on to everyone's favorite—printing.

Printing Solutions

When working with printers, there seems to be an infinite number of issues to resolve before normal operation is restored after an error. Many printer problems are either simple or obvious, so always check the obvious before moving on to more complicated solutions. Here is a short list of tasks you can perform when digging for a printer solution:

- Always check the physical aspects of the printer—cable, power, paper, toner, and so on.
- Check the logical printer on both the client and server.
- Check the print queue for stalled jobs.
- Make sure the printer driver has not become corrupted by reinstalling it.
- Attempt to print from a different application or a different client.
- Print using Administrator access.
- Stop and restart the spooler using the Services applet.
- Check the status and CPU usage of the SPOOLSS.EXE using the Task Manager.
- Check the free space on the drive hosting the spooler file, and change its destination.

There are a number of topics that don't really fall into any one category, the following sections discuss this hodgepodge of troubleshooting considerations.

Miscellaneous Troubleshooting Issues

The following sections cover a handful of great troubleshooting items that just don't fit well into any particular section.

Permissions Problems

If a permissions problem is suspected, attempt the action using the Administrator account or temporarily add the user account to the Administrators group. Double-check group memberships for conflicting access levels, especially No Access. Check the access control list (ACL) on the object in question for group and No Access assignments. Check the permissions on the share if appropriate. Check user, group, or computer policies for access restrictions.

Re-Creating The Setup Disks

If you need a new set of installation floppies, run WINNT.EXE (or WINNT32.EXE) from the installation CD with the **/ox** parameter. This creates the three floppies without initializing the actual installation process. However, you will need to preformat these diskettes beforehand.

Master Boot Record

If the Master Boot Record (MBR) fails on the system partition (the section of the disk that contains BOOT.INI, NTLOADER, and Windows NT DETECT), the ERD will not help with its restoration. Instead, you'll need to use the first diskette from DOS 6.0 (or higher). Executing **FDISK /MBR** re-creates the MBR and allows the system to boot.

The DOS FDISK will overwrite the existing disk signature. This is a problem only when the drive is a member of a fault tolerant set (mirror, duplex, stripe, or multi-partition volume). Otherwise, Windows NT will still boot and function properly. The next time Disk Administrator is run, the disk signature will be corrected automatically (i.e., a Windows NT MBR is written instead of a DOS MBR).

Dr. Watson

Dr. Watson is Windows NT's application error debugger. It detects application errors, diagnoses the error, and logs the diagnostic information. Most of the information gathered by Dr. Watson is only useful when working with a Microsoft technical professional to diagnose an application error. Data captured by Dr. Watson is stored in the DRWTSN32.LOG file. Dr. Watson can also be used to create a binary crash dump file of the memory where the failing application operates.

Dr. Watson launches itself automatically whenever an application error occurs. However, to configure Dr. Watson, you can launch it by executing DRWTSN32 at the command prompt or in the Run dialog box. The configuration options of Dr. Watson are fairly obvious, the only two that may cause some confusion are:

- **Dump Symbol Table** Adds the corresponding symbol data to the dump file, greatly increasing its size.
- **Dump All Thread Contexts** Forces a dump file to be created for all active threads, not just those owned by the failed application.

BOOT.INI Switches

To improve the troubleshooting abilities of the bootup, you can use one of the following switches after each OS line in the BOOT.INI file (remember those are the ones with the ARC name followed by the displayable name in quotes):

- **/BASEVIDEO** Boots using the standard VGA video driver.
- **/BAUDRATE=*n*** Sets the debugging communication baud rate when using the Kernel Debugger. Default is 9,600 for a modem and 19,200 for a null modem cable.
- **/CRASHDEBUG** Loads the debugger into memory, where it remains inactive unless a Kernel error occurs.
- **/DEBUG** Loads the debugger into memory to be activated by a host debugger connected to the computer. See the section titled "Kernel Debugger" later in this chapter.
- **/DEBUGPORT= com*x*** Sets the debugging COM port.
- **/MAXMEM:n** Sets the maximum amount of RAM that Windows NT can use.

- /NODEBUG Indicates that no debugging information is being used.
- /NOSERIALMICE=[COM*x* | COM*x,y,z*...] Disables serial mouse detection of the specified COM port(s).
- /SOS Specifies to display each driver name when it is loaded.

VGA Mode

If you set your video driver to something that prevents a readable display, you can select VGA Mode from the boot menu to boot with the standard VGA driver loaded. Then, you can modify the display drivers to correct the problem.

NTDETECT Debugged

If NTDETECT fails to detect the proper hardware, it may be corrupted or damaged or your hardware may not be functioning properly. A debugged or checked version of NTDETECT is stored on the CD in the Support \Debug\I386 directory. First, rename NTDETECT.COM to NTDETECT.BAK, then copy the file named NTDETECT.CHK to the system partition, and rename it to NTDETECT.COM. Then, you can reboot. This version of NTDETECT will give a verbose display of all detection activities to help isolate the problem. NTDETECT.COM has the attributes of Hidden, System, and Read Only set. You need to deselect these attributes before renaming the file, and reset them after the renaming process. Once you've solved the hardware detection problem, return the original NTDETECT from NTDETECT.BAK or the ERD.

ESDI Hard Drives

Some ESDI hard drives are not supported by Windows NT. ESDI hard drives are pre-IDE storage devices that can be low-level formatted using various values to assign the number of sectors per track. Owing to special formatting geometry and drive controllers, Windows NT may be able to access cylinders beyond 1,024. If Windows NT has direct access to cylinders numbered higher than 1,024, only Windows NT, not DOS, can access these areas. If the controller handles a sector translation transparently, both Windows NT and DOS can access cylinders numbered above 1,024.

A determination whether Windows NT can even use an ESDI disk cannot be made until an installation is attempted. If Windows NT fails to install on an ESDI disk properly, a Fatal System Error:0x0000006b message may be displayed after NTLDR starts. When this occurs, you can deduce that the ESDI drive is not supported by Windows NT.

Now that we've wrapped up many of troubleshooting's loose ends, let's take a look at some advanced troubleshooting issues.

Advanced Troubleshooting

In addition to the tools and utilities listed earlier in this chapter, there are three more troubleshooting mechanisms that require a professional support engineer to interpret. The three mechanisms—blue screen, Kernel Debugger, and memory dump—are listed here only for your general understanding.

Blue Screen

No matter what "they" tell you, Windows NT has GPFs, but that's not what they're called. When a GPF (General Protection Fault) occurs under Windows NT, the blue screen "of death" appears. This displays the STOP message error. There are lots of details included on this screen, such as the error's location, type of the error, and whether a memory dump is created. Unfortunately, most of this data is in hex or a strange acronym shorthand that you won't be able to read.

Kernel Debugger

The Kernel Debugger records Windows NT's activity during bootup and when a stop error occurs. To employ the Kernel Debugger, two computers with the same version of Windows NT connected by a null modem cable or RAS must be used. One computer is designated as the host, and the other as the target. The host machine must have the symbol files installed from the Windows NT CD-ROM (or the version associated with the installed Service Pack). The debugging software is located on the CD in the \support\debug\platform directory. This path must be copied onto the host machine, as well.

Memory Dump

A memory dump is the act of writing the entire contents of memory to a file when a STOP error occurs. The contents of this file can be inspected to determine the cause of the failure. Memory dumps are configured on the Startup/Shutdown tab of the System applet. The options are:

- Write the error event to the System log
- Send an Administrative alert
- Write a dump file
- Automatically reboot

The default location and the name of the memory dump file is Winnt\MEMORY.DMP. You can use the DUMPEXAM.EXE utility to view the contents of a memory dump file. However, most of the contents will require a Microsoft technical professional to interpret.

Practice Questions

Question 1

Which of the following can be corrected by the repair process using the three installation disks and a recent Emergency Repair Disk? [Check all correct answers]

- ❑ a. Boot sector corruption
- ❑ b. Unable to locate Master Boot Record
- ❑ c. NTLDR not found
- ❑ d. Corrupt NTOSKRNL

Answers a, c, and d are correct. The ERD repair process can often correct boot sector problems, replace the NTLDR, and repair the NTOSKRNL. The MBR cannot be repaired using the ERD or the installation floppies—that requires a DOS setup disk. Therefore, answer b is incorrect.

Question 2

Your Windows NT Server experiences a STOP error due to a run-away process from a custom application developed in-house. Where can information about this error be found once the server has been rebooted?

- ❍ a. Kernel Debugger
- ❍ b. Performance Monitor
- ❍ c. Event Viewer
- ❍ d. Windows NT Diagnostics

Answer c is correct. The Event Viewer can be used to view the System log where all STOP errors are recorded. The Kernel Debugger is only able to view STOP error information when specifically configured and installed on two connected machines. That situation was not indicated in this question. Therefore, answer a is incorrect. The Performance Monitor and Windows NT Diagnostics are not able to record any information about a STOP error. Therefore, answers b and d are incorrect.

Question 3

Which two parameter switches are present by default on the VGA Mode selection ARC name line in the BOOT.INI file? [Check two answers]

- ❑ a. /nodebug
- ❑ b. /basevideo
- ❑ c. /noserialmice
- ❑ d. /sos
- ❑ e. /vgavideo

Answers b and d are correct. The parameters **/basevideo** and **/sos** are present on the VGA Mode line by default. The parameters **/nodebug** and **/noserialmice** are not present on the VGA Mode line by default. Therefore, answers a and c are incorrect. The parameter **/vgavideo** is not a valid parameter. Therefore, answer e is incorrect.

Question 4

The **SYSTEM** Registry key contains errors. You do not have a recent ERD, but you do have a copy of the **SYSTEM** key itself on floppy. Which of the following programs should you use to restore the **SYSTEM** key from the floppy disk?

- ❍ a. Disk Administrator
- ❍ b. System applet
- ❍ c. Network Client Administrator
- ❍ d. Server Manager

Answer a is correct. The Disk Administrator is the correct utility to use to restore the SYSTEM key if you have a stored copy. The other three utilities do not offer Registry restoration options. Therefore, answers b, c, and d are incorrect.

Question 5

Your Windows NT Server has recently been experiencing numerous STOP errors. Where should you configure Windows NT so a memory dump will occur before the system reboots to help pinpoint the problem?

- ❍ a. The server properties within Server Manager
- ❍ b. The recovery option in Dr. Watson
- ❍ c. The Tracking tab of the Task Manager
- ❍ d. On the Startup/Shutdown tab of the System applet

Answer d is correct. The Startup/Shutdown tab of the System applet is the location of the memory dump options for Windows NT. The Server Manager does not offer memory dump configuration options. Therefore, answer a is incorrect. Dr. Watson is used to perform memory dumps on application faults, not for Windows NT Server itself. Therefore, answer b is incorrect. The Task Manager does not have a Tracking tab nor does it offer memory dump options. Therefore, answer c is incorrect.

Question 6

After installing a new SCSI driver, Windows NT will not boot. No other changes have been made to the system. What is the easiest way to return the system to a state where it will boot properly?

- ❍ a. Use the repair process with the ERD.
- ❍ b. Use the Last Known Good Configuration.
- ❍ c. Launch the Kernel Debugger.
- ❍ d. Boot to DOS, and run the setup utility to change the installed drivers.

Answer b is correct. The LKGC is the fastest way to return to a bootable configuration, especially because only a single change was made to the system. The ERD repair process will restore the system so it can boot; however, this requires a recent ERD and all three installation disks. In addition, this process can take upwards of 30 minutes. Therefore, answer a is incorrect. The Kernel Debugger will not help this situation, especially because it was not preconfigured to watch the boot process before the new driver was installed. Therefore, answer c is incorrect. There is no DOS setup utility, that utility was only available for Windows 3.x. Therefore, answer d is incorrect.

Question 7

During the boot process, you receive the following error message after the Last Known Good Configuration prompt:

"Windows NT could not start because the following file is missing or corrupt: \WINNT\SYSTEM32\NTOSKRNL.EXE. Please reinstall a copy of the above file."

What are the possible explanations for this error? [Check all correct answers]

- ❑ a. NTOSKRNL.EXE is missing.
- ❑ b. BOOT.INI points to the wrong partition.
- ❑ c. NTOSKRNL.EXE is corrupt.
- ❑ d. BOOT.INI file is missing.

Answers a, b, c, and d are correct. All of these explanations can result in the given error message. When the boot process cannot find NTOSKRNL.EXE, it does not indicate if the problem is with the file itself, its location, or the pointers to it.

Question 8

Which of the files on the ERD lists the files installed during setup and the checksums of each of these files?

- ❍ a. INSTALLED.DAT
- ❍ b. CONFIG.NT
- ❍ c. DEFAULT._
- ❍ d. SOFTWARE._
- ❍ e. SETUP.LOG

Answer e is correct. SETUP.LOG is the only file on the ERD that lists the files installed during setup and their corresponding checksums. INSTALLED.DAT is not a file present on an ERD. Therefore, answer a is incorrect. The CONFIG.NT, DEFAULT._, and SOFTWARE._ are all files on an ERD, but they do not contain installed file and checksum information. Therefore, answers b, c, and d are incorrect.

Question 9

Your Windows NT Server experiences yet another STOP error. Fortunately, you enabled the memory dump option through the System applet. What utility can you use to view the contents of the DMP file?

- ❍ a. Event Viewer
- ❍ b. Debug Inspector
- ❍ c. DUMPEXAM.EXE
- ❍ d. Windows NT Diagnostics

Answer c is correct. Only DUMPEXAM.EXE can be used to view the contents of DMP files. The Event Viewer and Windows NT Diagnostics are not able to view the contents of a memory dump file. Therefore, answers a and d are incorrect. There is not a Debug Inspector. Therefore, answer b is incorrect.

Question 10

Which of the following are valid ways to make full or partial backups of the Registry? [Check all correct answers]

- ❑ a. Create an ERD using the **rdisk /s** command
- ❑ b. Use Windows NT Backup
- ❑ c. Copy all of the contents of the \Winnt\System32\Config directory
- ❑ d. Use the Disk Administrator
- ❑ e. Use REGEDT32

Answers a, b, c, d, and e are correct. All of these methods are valid ways to create full or partial backups of the Windows NT Registry. However, it should be noted that the files stored in \Winnt\System32\ Config are only as current as the last reboot or execution of **rdisk /s**.

Need To Know More?

Donald, Lisa, and James Chellis: *MSCE: NT Server 4 In The Enterprise Study Guide, 2nd Edition.* Sybex Network Press, San Francisco, CA, 1998. ISBN 0-7821-2221-3. Chapter 18 covers most of the issues discussed in this chapter. It is a great resource for troubleshooting information. The remainder of the book contains some problem-resolving data.

Heywood, Drew: *Inside Windows NT Server, 2nd Edition.* New Riders, Indianapolis, IN, 1998. ISBN 1-56205-860-6. This book does not have a chapter focused on troubleshooting. However, tips and tricks about resolving problems are scattered throughout the text.

Strebe, Matthew, Charles Perkins, and James Chellis: *MSCE: NT Server 4 Study Guide, 2nd Edition.* Sybex Network Press, San Francisco, CA, 1998. ISBN 0-7821-2222-1. Chapter 17 contains lots of great troubleshooting information. In addition, other tips and tricks are scattered through the rest of the text.

Search the TechNet CD (or its online version through **www.microsoft.com**) and the *Windows NT Server Resource Kit* CD. Using the keyword "troubleshooting" will result in numerous hits on relevant materials. However, for more focused searching, use keywords associated with the topic or subject in question, such as "boot," "installation," "printing," "Emergency Repair Disk," or "Registry."

Sample Test #1

In this chapter, we provide pointers to help you develop a successful test-taking strategy, including how to choose proper answers, how to decode ambiguity, how to work within the Microsoft testing framework, how to decide what you need to memorize, and how to prepare for the test. At the end of the chapter, we include 60 questions on subject matter pertinent to Microsoft Exam 70-068: "Implementing and Supporting Microsoft Windows NT Server 4.0 in the Enterprise." After this chapter, you'll find the answer key to this test; after that, you'll find yet another sample test, followed by another answer key. In addition, we provide you with some practice scenario questions in the Scenarios section following Chapter 19. This gives you three opportunities to prepare!

Also, remember that you can take adaptive practice exams on Windows NT Server 4.0 in the Enterprise online at www.coriolis.com/cip/core4rev/ to help you prepare even more. Good luck!

Questions, Questions, Questions

There should be no doubt in your mind that you are facing a test full of specific and pointed questions. Currently, the Windows NT Server 4.0 in the Enterprise test may be a fixed-length, adaptive, short-form, or combination exam. See Chapter 1 for more information on the various exam types.

Whichever type of test you take, for this exam, questions belong to one of six basic types:

- Multiple-choice with a single answer
- Multiple-choice with one or more answers
- Multipart with a single answer
- Multipart with one or more answers
- Graphical organization questions that present numerous alternatives and ask you to rank, organize, or prioritize them as the question directs
- Simulations

Always take the time to read a question at least twice before selecting an answer, and always look for an Exhibit button as you examine each question. Exhibits include graphics information related to a question. An exhibit is usually a screen capture of program output or GUI information that you must examine to analyze the question's contents and formulate an answer. Thus, the Exhibit button brings up graphics and charts used to help explain a question, provide additional data, or illustrate page layout or program behavior.

Not every question has only one answer; many questions require multiple answers. Therefore, it's important to read each question carefully, to determine how many answers are necessary or possible, and to look for additional hints or instructions when selecting answers. Such instructions often occur in brackets, immediately following the question itself (as they do for all multiple-choice, questions in which one or more answers are possible).

Picking Proper Answers

Obviously, the only way to pass any exam is to select enough of the right answers to obtain a passing score. However, Microsoft's exams are not standardized like the SAT and GRE exams; they are far more diabolical and convoluted. In some cases, questions are strangely worded, and deciphering them can be a real challenge. In those cases, you may need to rely on answer-elimination skills. Almost always, at least one answer out of the possible choices for a question can be eliminated immediately because it matches one of these conditions:

- The answer does not apply to the situation.
- The answer describes a nonexistent issue, an invalid option, or an imaginary state.
- The answer may be eliminated because of the question itself.

After you eliminate all answers that are obviously wrong, you can apply your retained knowledge to eliminate further answers. Look for items that sound correct but refer to actions, commands, or features that are not present or not available in the situation that the question describes.

If you're still faced with a blind guess among two or more potentially correct answers, reread the question. Try to picture how each of the possible remaining answers would alter the situation. Be especially sensitive to terminology; sometimes the choice of words ("remove" instead of "disable") can make the difference between a right answer and a wrong one.

Only when you've exhausted your ability to eliminate answers, but remain unclear about which of the remaining possibilities is correct, should you guess at an answer. An unanswered question offers you no points, but guessing gives you at least some chance of getting a question right; just don't be too hasty when making a blind guess.

If you're taking a fixed-length or a short-form test, you can wait until the last round of reviewing marked questions (just as you're about to run out of time, or out of unanswered questions) before you start making guesses. If you're taking an adaptive test, you'll have to guess to move on to the next question if you can't figure out an answer some other way. Either way, guessing should be your technique of last resort!

Decoding Ambiguity

Microsoft exams have a reputation for including questions that can be difficult to interpret, confusing, or ambiguous. In our experience with numerous exams, we consider this reputation to be completely justified. The Microsoft exams are tough, and deliberately made that way.

The only way to beat Microsoft at its own game is to be prepared. You'll discover that many exam questions test your knowledge of things that are not directly related to the issue raised by a question. This means that the answers you must choose from, even incorrect ones, are just as much a part of the skill assessment as the question itself. If you don't know something about most aspects of Windows NT Server 4.0, you may not be able to eliminate obviously wrong answers because they relate to a different area of Windows NT Server than the one that's addressed by the question at hand. In other words, the more you know about the software, the easier it will be for you to tell right from wrong.

Questions often give away their answers, but you have to be Sherlock Holmes to see the clues. Often, subtle hints appear in the question text in such a way that they seem almost irrelevant to the situation. You must realize that each question is a test unto itself and that you need to inspect and successfully navigate each question to pass the exam. Look for small clues, such as the mention of times, group permissions and names, and configuration settings. Little things like these can point at the right answer if properly understood; if missed, they can leave you facing a blind guess.

Working Within The Framework

The test questions appear in random order, and many elements or issues that receive mention in one question may also crop up in other questions. It's not uncommon to find that an incorrect answer to one question is the correct answer to another question, or vice-versa. Take the time to read every answer to each question, even if you recognize the correct answer to a question immediately. That extra reading may spark a memory, or remind you about a Windows NT Server feature or function, that helps you on another question elsewhere in the exam.

If you're taking a fixed-length test, you can revisit any question as many times as you like. If you're uncertain of the answer to a question, check the box that's provided to mark it for easy return later on. You should also mark questions you think may offer information that you can use to answer other questions. On fixed-length or short-form tests, we usually mark somewhere between 25 and 50 percent of the questions on exams we've taken. The testing software is designed to let you mark every question if you choose; use this framework to your advantage. Everything you will want to see again should be marked; the testing software can then help you return to marked questions quickly and easily.

For fixed-length or short-form tests, we strongly recommend that you first read through the entire test quickly, before getting caught up in answering individual questions. This will help to jog your memory as you review the potential answers and can help identify questions that you want to mark for easy access to their contents. It will also let you identify and mark the really tricky questions for easy return. The key is to make a quick pass over the territory to begin with, so that you know what you're up against; and then to survey that territory more thoroughly on a second pass, when you can begin to answer all questions systematically and consistently.

If you're taking an adaptive test, and you see something in a question or one of the answers that jogs your memory on a topic, or that you feel you should record if the topic appears in another question, write it down on your piece of paper. Just because you can't go back to a question in an adaptive test doesn't mean you can't take notes on what you see early in the test, in hopes that it might help you later in the test.

For adaptive tests, don't be afraid to take notes on what you see in various questions. Sometimes, what you record from one question, especially if it's not as familiar as it should be or reminds you of the name or use of some utility or interface details, can help you on other questions later on.

Finally, some Microsoft tests combine 15 to 25 adaptive questions with 10 fixed-length questions. In that case, use our recommended adaptive strategy for the adaptive part, and the recommended fixed-length or short-form strategy for the fixed-length part.

Deciding What To Memorize

The amount of memorization you must undertake for an exam depends on how well you remember what you've read, and how well you know the software by heart. If you are a visual thinker, and you can see the drop-down menus and dialog boxes in your head, you won't need to memorize as much as someone who's less visually oriented. The tests will stretch your recollection of commands and functions of Windows NT Server.

At a minimum, you'll want to memorize the following kinds of information:

- Windows NT installation switches and options
- How to set up and manage users and groups within workgroups and domains
- Trust relationships between domains
- The various domain models that Microsoft recognizes

If you work your way through this book while sitting at a machine with Windows NT Server installed, and try to manipulate the environment's features and functions as they're discussed throughout, you should have little or no difficulty mastering this material. Also, don't forget that The Cram Sheet at the front of the book is designed to capture the material that is most important to memorize; use this to guide your studies as well.

Preparing For The Test

The best way to prepare for the test—after you've studied—is to take at least one practice exam. We've included one here in this chapter for that reason (and another in Chapter 18); the test questions are located in the pages that follow (and unlike the preceding chapters in this book, the answers don't follow the questions immediately; you'll have to flip to Chapter 17 to review the answers separately [see Chapter 19 for the answers to Chapter 18's sample test]).

Give yourself 90 minutes to take the exam, keep yourself on the honor system, and don't look at earlier text in the book or jump ahead to the answer key. When your time is up, or you've finished the questions, you can check your work by consulting Chapter 17 or 19. Pay special attention to the explanations for the incorrect answers; these can also help to reinforce your knowledge of the material. Knowing how to recognize correct answers is good, but understanding why incorrect answers are wrong can be equally valuable.

Taking The Test

Relax. Once you're sitting in front of the testing computer, there's nothing more you can do to increase your knowledge or preparation. Take a deep breath, stretch, and start reading that first question.

There's no need to rush, either. You have plenty of time to complete each question and to return to those questions that you skip or mark for return (if you are taking a fixed-length or short-form test). If you read a question twice and remain clueless, you can mark it if you're taking a fixed-length or short-form test; if you're taking an adaptive test, you'll have to guess and move on. Both easy and difficult questions are intermixed throughout the test in random order. If you're taking a fixed-length or short-form test, don't cheat yourself by spending too much time on a hard question early in the test, thereby depriving yourself of the time you need to answer the questions at the end of the test. If you're taking an adaptive test, don't spend more than five minutes on any single question—if it takes you that long to get nowhere, it's time to guess and move on.

On a fixed-length or short-form test, you can read through the entire test, and before returning to marked questions for a second visit, figure out how much time you've got per question. As you answer each question, remove its mark. Continue to review the remaining marked questions until you run out of time, or you complete the test.

On an adaptive test, set a maximum time limit for questions (we recommend no more than five minutes if you're completely clueless), and watch your time on long or complex questions. If you hit your limit, it's time to guess and move on. Don't deprive yourself of the opportunity to see more questions by taking too long to puzzle over questions, unless you think you can figure out the answer. Otherwise, you're limiting your opportunities to pass.

That's it for pointers. Here are some questions for you to practice on!

Sample Test #1

Question 1

Which of the following are valid ways to make full or partial backups of the Registry? [Check all correct answers]

- ❑ a. Create an ERD using the **RDISK /s** command
- ❑ b. With Windows NT Backup
- ❑ c. Copy the contents of the \Winnt\System32\Config directory
- ❑ d. Use the Disk Administrator
- ❑ e. Use REGEDT32

Question 2

A small company with a few departments wants to deploy a domain model network. It wants to be able to access all servers and resources from each department and maintain centralized management of user accounts. Which domain model is best suited for this purpose?

- ❍ a. Single domain model
- ❍ b. Master domain model
- ❍ c. Multiple master domain model
- ❍ d. Complete trust domain model

Question 3

Analyze the following scenario:

Your network includes two domains: Production and General. General is a master domain, and Production has a one-way trust with General. Each domain includes several Windows NT Servers configured as follows: a single PDC, two BDCs, three member servers, and 100 Windows NT Workstation 4 clients. To ensure the availability of data on the network, you need to create a group named "TotalBack" that can back up all the machines on the network—be they domain controllers, member servers, or workstations.

Required result:

- Members of the TotalBack group must be able to back up all domain controllers, in either Production or General.

Optional desired results:

- Members of TotalBack should be able to back up all member servers in both domains.
- Members of TotalBack should be able to back up all Windows NT Workstations in both domains.

Proposed solution:

- Create a global group called "TotalBack" in the General domain, and add this group to the Backup Operators local group on every domain controller, member server, and Windows NT Workstation in both domains.

Which results does the proposed solution produce?

❍ a. The proposed solution produces the required result and both of the optional desired results

❍ b. The proposed solution produces the required result but only one of the optional desired results

❍ c. The proposed solution produces the required result but neither of the optional desired results

❍ d. The proposed solution does not produce the required result.

Question 4

Which view available through Performance Monitor should you use to create a historical baseline?

❍ a. Chart

❍ b. Log

❍ c. Report

❍ d. Graph

Question 5

You want to track the activity around a new high-speed color laser printer so you can use the tracking information to restrict and grant privileged and priority access. What steps are required to implement printer auditing? [Check all correct answers]

❑ a. Set the auditing switches on the printer object to track successful print events for the Everyone group.

❑ b. Grant the Everyone group the auditing right through the User Rights policy.

❑ c. Set the audit policy to Audit These Events through the User Manager For Domains.

❑ d. Set the audit switch of File And Object Access to Success under Audit These Events.

❑ e. Set the priority of the printer to 99 (maximum) under the Scheduling tab on the printer's Properties dialog box.

Question 6

You attempt to add new information into a document stored on a remote server. Using the Documents share, you are able to locate and open the document into your word processor. You have Full Control of the object. You are a member of the Sales group. The Sales group has Read access to the Documents share. You are unable to save your changes to the file. Why?

❍ a. You cannot edit documents over a network.

❍ b. Your resultant permissions for the file object are Read.

❍ c. The Sales group has the Save privilege revoked.

❍ d. Only administrators can save files over the network.

Question 7

You have a Windows NT Server that provides print services to 20 Windows NT computers on your network. You have an HP LaserJet attached to the Windows NT print server. Hewlett-Packard has just released an updated printer driver. What must be done to provide the updated driver for the computers that print to this print server?

❍ a. Install the updated driver on all client computers. There is no need to update the server.

❍ b. Install the updated driver on the print server, and do nothing more.

❍ c. Install the updated driver on the print server and on all client computers.

❍ d. Create a separate logical printer with the updated driver on the print server, and tell all your users to print to the new printer.

❍ e. Install the updated driver on the print server, and instruct all client computers to download the updated driver from the server.

Question 8

You have a network that has five domains in a single master domain model configuration. Where should the logon scripts be placed for simplified administration?

❍ a. On the PDC in the trusted domain

❍ b. In the PDC's \Winnt\System32\Repl\ Export\Scripts directory within each trusting domain

❍ c. Within the NETLOGON share of each domain

❍ d. On the local workstations

Question 9

ExecuCorp has 50,000 users and many branch offices. You have been hired to set the network up so that there is central administration of users but decentralized control of resources. Security is important. Which of the following domain models is best suited for this situation?

- ❍ a. Single domain model
- ❍ b. Single master domain model
- ❍ c. Multiple master domain model
- ❍ d. Complete trust domain model

Question 10

You have two IDE hard drives on a single drive controller in your Windows NT Server computer. There is only one partition on each of the two drives. The first drive's partition is formatted with FAT, and the second drive's partition is formatted with NTFS. The system files are located on the second drive. What is the ARC name for the boot partition?

- ❍ a. multi(0)disk(1)rdisk(0)partition(1)
- ❍ b. multi(0)disk(0)rdisk(1)partition(1)
- ❍ c. multi(1)disk(0)rdisk(1)partition(1)
- ❍ d. multi(0)disk(0)rdisk(1)partition(0)
- ❍ e. multi(1)disk(0)rdisk(0)partition(1)

Question 11

A user is attempting to print to a printer attached to the network using an HP JetDirect card using the DLC protocol. The print server and the user's client machine both have DLC properly installed. But the user is repeatedly denied access to the printer, even after the printer has been physically reset. What is the most likely cause of this?

❍ a. The print server is disconnected from the network.

❍ b. The JetDirect card is not compatible with the DLC protocol.

❍ c. Another user is printing to the device using the Microsoft TCP/IP Printing service.

❍ d. Another print server is configured with DLC set to continuous connection mode.

Question 12

You have noticed that users complain of poor network performance in the morning and right after lunch—the times when users are authenticated by the domain controllers. Currently, there is one PDC and two BDCs within the domain. You inspect the performance levels of the domain controllers and determine that they are operating at acceptable levels. What is the best way to improve network performance?

❍ a. Add additional BDCs.

❍ b. Increase the RAM on all servers.

❍ c. Decrease the Pulse Registry setting on the PDC.

❍ d. Install an additional PDC in the domain.

Question 13

Which of the following Windows NT networking activities are supported by a PPP RAS connection? [Check all correct answers]

❑ a. Printer share access

❑ b. Named pipes

❑ c. WinSock API applications over TCP/IP

❑ d. InterProcess Communications (IPC)

❑ e. User Logon Authentication

Question 14

You want to install TCP/IP on a member server in a non-routed network. You have already manually assigned an IP address to the server. What other parameter must you specify to install TCP/IP on the server?

❍ a. Subnet mask

❍ b. Default gateway

❍ c. DHCP server IP address

❍ d. WINS server IP address

Question 15

Windows NT Server includes a Migration Tool to move data and accounts from NetWare to Windows NT Servers. It can be especially helpful when moving user accounts from one or more NetWare servers to a Windows NT PDC. Which of the following requirements is most likely to benefit from use of a mapping file to guide the migration process? [Choose the single best answer]

❍ a. To migrate unique user accounts from several NetWare servers to a Windows NT domain controller.

❍ b. To make sure existing domain accounts will not be affected by migration of identical user accounts from NetWare.

❍ c. To migrate accounts from NetWare servers that do not have corresponding accounts in the Windows NT domain.

❍ d. To supply passwords for migrated accounts in the Windows NT domain that match the previous NetWare passwords.

Question 16

Which of the following options are object attributes? [Check all correct answers]

❑ a. Data

❑ b. ACL

❑ c. Services

❑ d. Object name

Question 17

Which type of data should not be distributed via the Directory Replication service?

❍ a. Logon scripts

❍ b. User profiles

❍ c. Relational database files

❍ d. System policies

Question 18

To facilitate a move from NetWare to Windows NT Server, XYZ Corp. plans to use the Migration Tool for NetWare. If the Migration Tool encounters user account names on the NetWare server that match existing accounts in the target Windows NT domain, what will the Migration Tool do by default?

- ❍ a. Prompt the administrator with an option to overwrite existing account information, or block the account information from the transfer.
- ❍ b. Transfer the account to the Windows NT domain, but add a prefix to all duplicate names.
- ❍ c. Ignore all duplicate NetWare account information.
- ❍ d. Replace all existing Windows NT domain account information with the incoming NetWare account information.

Question 19

You have a field technician who travels extensively around the country. Her schedule changes often and she rarely connects from the same place twice. It is important that she is able to connect to the office LAN periodically, but your organization's security policy requires callback security on all RAS connections. How can you configure her account so that she is able to gain access while supporting your organization's security?

- ❍ a. Set the callback security to No Call Back only for her account.
- ❍ b. Enable callback security with Set By Caller selected.
- ❍ c. Set the callback security to Preset To with her home phone number.
- ❍ d. Set the callback security to Roaming, and give her the page number to remotely configure the callback number.
- ❍ e. Turn on the Callback Caller ID Capture.

Question 20

An important new custom application is conflicting with an existing utility. The conflict seems to cause both programs to terminate prematurely. Which audit event type should be tracked to record some information about the conflict and which programs are affected?

- ❍ a. File And Object Access
- ❍ b. Security Policy Changes
- ❍ c. Restart, Shutdown, And System
- ❍ d. Process Tracking
- ❍ e. Application Activity

Question 21

Your Windows NT Server experiences a STOP error owing to a runaway process from an application developed in-house. Where can information about this error be found once the server has been rebooted?

- ❍ a. Kernel Debugger
- ❍ b. Performance Monitor
- ❍ c. Event Viewer
- ❍ d. Windows NT Diagnostics

Question 22

Where does the Directory Replication service place distributed files by default?

- ❍ a. \Winnt\System32\repl\Export of an import server
- ❍ b. \Program Files\Replication of an export server
- ❍ c. \Winnt\System32\repl\Import of an import server
- ❍ d. \Winnt\System32\repl\Export of an export server

Question 23

The SYSTEM Registry key contains errors. You do not have a recent ERD, but you have a floppy of the SYSTEM key itself. Which of the following programs should you use to restore the SYSTEM key from the floppy?

- ❍ a. Disk Administrator
- ❍ b. System applet
- ❍ c. Network Client Administrator
- ❍ d. Server Manager

Question 24

What files should be placed on a boot disk to boot to the duplicate drive of a disk duplex from a floppy in the event of a failure of the original drive? Assume the drive controller is a SCSI that does not support BIOS translation. [Check all correct answers]

- ❑ a. NTDETECT.COM
- ❑ b. BOOT.INI
- ❑ c. NTLDR
- ❑ d. WINA20.386
- ❑ e. NTBOOTDD.SYS

Question 25

What are the functions of WINS? [Check all correct answers]

- ❑ a. Enable internetwork browsing
- ❑ b. Map FQDNs to IP addresses
- ❑ c. Map NetBIOS names to IP addresses
- ❑ d. Map NetBIOS names to MAC addresses
- ❑ e. Assign client IP addresses

Question 26

You are an administrator of a domain that consists of two groups of computers connected by a long-distance WAN link. There are multiple BDCs located in each group. The available bandwidth of the WAN link must be maximized. Which of the following changes to the domain controller synchronization will reduce the load placed on the link by the PDC and the BDCs? [Check all correct answers]

- ❑ a. Set Pulse to 60
- ❑ b. Set PulseConcurrency to 1
- ❑ c. Set PulseMaximum to 60
- ❑ d. Set MaintainServerList to Auto
- ❑ e. Set ReplicationGovernor to 50

Question 27

Of the following, which are required for access to a NetWare server from a Windows NT Workstation running Client Service For NetWare? [Check all correct answers]

- ❑ a. A group on the NetWare server called "NTGATEWAY" containing the Windows NT Workstation's user account
- ❑ b. Gateway Service For NetWare
- ❑ c. A user account on the NetWare server
- ❑ d. The NWLink protocol

Question 28

Tech Toys, Inc. has a network with three domains: Admin, Sales, and Production. Users from the Sales and Admin domains need access to resources from the Production domain, but they also need access to resources in each other's domains. How should you set up the trust relationships among the domains?

❍ a. Define two-way trusts between all three domains.

❍ b. Set up one-way trusts from Sales to Admin, Admin to Production, and Production to Sales.

❍ c. Define a two-way trust between Sales and Admin, and another two-way trust between Production and Sales.

❍ d. Set up two one-way trusts from Production to Sales and Production to Admin, and a two-way trust between Sales and Admin.

Question 29

All Windows NT internal basic network server and service communications occur using what type of communication?

❍ a. TCP/IP

❍ b. AppleTalk

❍ c. NetBIOS

❍ d. DLC

Question 30

You want to monitor the physical disk performance of a server remotely. With a standard installation of Windows NT Server on both machines, network connectivity, and membership in the same domain, what additional operation must be performed to enable the monitoring of the disk counters remotely?

❍ a. Install Network Monitor Agent on the machine to be observed.

❍ b. Run the **diskperf** utility with the **-y** option on the machine to be observed.

❍ c. Install Network Monitor Agent, and run the **diskperf** utility with the **-y** option on the machine to be observed.

❍ d. No additional operations are required. The physical disk counters are remotely accessible by default.

Question 31

While using the Network Monitor, you decide to implement a display filter to aid in your search for the NetBIOS Add Group Name command. What is the proper syntax of a properties-based display filter?

❍ a. NETBIOS:Command == 0x0 (Add Group Name)

❍ b. NETBIOS <= Add Group Name Command

❍ c. Add Group Name > NETBIOS

❍ d. NETBIOS<—>Add Group Name

Question 32

Assume two domains named "Users" and "Admin" are defined within an organization. Three members of the Users domain have been drafted to work with materials in the Admin domain prior to their general release to the user community. To assist with prerelease testing, these three users need access to a shared NTFS folder named "\Tests" on a server named "TEST1" in the Admin domain. Admin already trusts Users. Which of the following options is the best way to grant Full Control access to the \\TEST1\Tests share for those three individuals from the Users domain?

- ❍ a. Remove the current trust relationship. Add a new trust wherein Admin trusts Users. Create a global group in the Users domain named "Utesters," and add the three individuals' accounts to that group. Create a global group named "Atesters" in the Admin domain, and add the global group Users\Utesters to Atesters. Give Atesters Full Control over the \\TEST1\Tests share.
- ❍ b. Create a global group in the Users domain named "Utesters." Assign each of the three users' domain accounts to that group. Create a global group in the Admin domain named "Atesters," and assign Users\Utesters to Atesters. Give Atesters Full Control over the \\TEST1\Tests share.
- ❍ c. Create a global group in Users called "Utesters." Add each of the three users' domain accounts to that group. Create a local group on TEST1 called "Utesters," and add the Users\Utesters global group to this local group. Grant Utesters Full Control to the \\TEST1\Tests share.
- ❍ d. Remove the current trust relationship. Add a new trust wherein Admin trusts Users. Create a global group in Users called "Utesters." Add each of the three users' domain accounts to that group. Create a local group on TEST1 called "Utesters," and add the Users\Utesters global group to this local group. Grant Utesters Full Control to the \\TEST1\Tests share.

Question 33

Your Ethernet network consists of a Windows NT 4 Server, several Windows NT Workstation clients, a NetWare 3.11 client, and one NetWare 4.1 client. NWLink is running on the network. Each of the NetWare clients is using different frame types. How would you configure the NWLink IPX/SPX Properties dialog box on the Windows NT 4 Server to enable the server to recognize both NetWare clients?

❍ a. Enabling Auto Frame Type Detection

❍ b. Selecting the Manual Frame Type Detection option and adding a NetWare client's network number and frame type to the frame type configuration list

❍ c. Selecting the Auto Frame Type Detection option and adding both NetWare clients' network numbers and frame types to the frame type configuration list

❍ d. Selecting the Manual Frame Type Detection option and adding both of the NetWare clients' network numbers and frame types to the frame type configuration list

Question 34

You need to set up four new virtual Web servers to be hosted on your private network using only a single installation of IIS. Each Web site will require its own directory, a unique URL, and a unique IP address. What should you do to implement this configuration? [Check all correct answers]

❑ a. Install RIP For IP on the IIS server.

❑ b. Assign each of the IP addresses to be used to the NIC in the IIS server, then associate each IP address with the appropriate Web directory.

❑ c. Set up the DHCP Relay Agent.

❑ d. Configure DNS so that it contains the FQDN for each server and correlates that name to its IP address.

❑ e. Configure WINS by adding the NetBIOS names and IP addresses of the sites to the static list of servers.

Question 35

You're asked to provide temporary access to resources in your Accounting domain for a group of auditors in the Auditors domain. For the same reason, you must also provide temporary access to the same group of users in other domains in the coming months. There is already a trust relationship in which Accounting trusts Auditors. Which of the following represents the best way to supply temporary access to Accounting for this group of auditors?

❍ a. Create a global group in the Accounting domain that includes the auditors' user accounts. Add this group to the Guests local group on all servers in the Accounting domain.

❍ b. Create a global group in the Auditors domain that includes the auditors' user accounts. Add this group to the local group on the server (or servers) in the Accounting domain that contain(s) the needed resources.

❍ c. Create a local group in the Accounting domain that includes the auditors' user accounts on each server where the needed resources reside.

❍ d. Create a local group in the Auditors domain that includes the auditors' user accounts. Add this group to the local group on the server (or servers) in the Accounting domain that contain(s) the needed resources.

Question 36

To end the process of maintaining user accounts on two different types of servers, you have decided to migrate users from the NetWare server to a Windows NT Server. What must be installed or present on the Windows NT Server to provide the migrated clients with NetWare access? [Check all correct answers]

❑ a. Gateway Service For NetWare

❑ b. NWLink protocol

❑ c. Client Service For NetWare

❑ d. SAP Agent

Question 37

Where can you find information related to RAS problems to aid in troubleshooting? [Check all correct answers]

- ❑ a. Event Viewer
- ❑ b. DEVICE.LOG
- ❑ c. Dr. Watson
- ❑ d. MODEMLOG.TXT
- ❑ e. Windows NT Diagnostics

Question 38

On a network with Internet access, you wish to host six Web sites from a single implementation of IIS. Which of the following must you do to accomplish this?

- ❍ a. Install RIP For IP on the IIS server.
- ❍ b. Assign each of the IP addresses to be used to the NIC in the IIS server, then associate each IP address with the appropriate Web directory.
- ❍ c. Set up the DHCP Relay Agent.
- ❍ d. Configure DNS so that it contains the FQDN for each server and correlates that name to its IP address.
- ❍ e. Configure WINS by adding the NetBIOS names and IP addresses of the sites to the static list of servers.

Question 39

You installed Windows NT Server with the default configuration onto your C drive and subsequently installed Network Monitor Tools and Agent from the Services tab of the Network Control Panel applet. When you save sets of captured data, where will the CAP files be placed by default?

- ❍ a. C:\Winnt\System32\Netmon\Capture
- ❍ b. C:\Program Files\Netmon\Capture
- ❍ c. C:\Admin\Netmon\Capture
- ❍ d. C:\Winnt\System32\Repl\Export\Netmon\Capture

Question 40

Your TCP/IP-based network is experiencing a drastic increase in broadcast traffic. What is the best way to decrease the amount of broadcast traffic on your network?

- ❍ a. Divide the network into two physical subnets and install a bridge.
- ❍ b. Divide the network into two logical subnets and install a gateway.
- ❍ c. Install a DHCP server.
- ❍ d. Install a WINS server.

Question 41

You just doubled the size of your server's physical RAM to 128 MB. If you have disk striping with parity implemented on a set of high-speed SCSI drives and are duplexing the boot partition, what change should you make to the pagefile settings?

- ❍ a. No change to the pagefile size is recommended, but it should be placed on the stripe set.
- ❍ b. The pagefile should be increased to 140 MB and placed on the boot duplexed drive.
- ❍ c. The pagefile should be increased by 12 MB and placed on the stripe set.
- ❍ d. The pagefile should be increased to 140 MB and placed on the stripe set.

Question 42

During the boot process, you receive this error message after the Last Known Good Configuration prompt:

"Windows NT could not start because the following file is missing or corrupt: \Winnt\System32\NTOSKRNL.EXE. Please reinstall a copy of the above file."

What are the possible explanations for this error? [Check all correct answers]

- ❑ a. NTOSKRNL.EXE is missing.
- ❑ b. BOOT.INI points to the wrong partition.
- ❑ c. NTOSKRNL.EXE is corrupt.
- ❑ d. BOOT.INI is missing.

Question 43

If no standards are in place for the operating system, protocol, or method of access for your remote clients, what is the highest level of security you can implement and still allow your users to connect via RAS?

- ❍ a. Allow Any Authentication Including Clear Text
- ❍ b. Require Microsoft Encrypted Authentication
- ❍ c. PGP Encryption
- ❍ d. Require Encrypted Authentication

Question 44

Your firm has five branch offices scattered across the globe. They are located in Houston, Moscow, Paris, Geneva, and Hong Kong. Each office has about 750 users. The corporate headquarters is located in Los Angeles. Each branch office is linked to the corporate office via a T1 WAN link. You have been asked to implement a domain model for this company.

Required results:

- All Los Angeles users must be able to access resources in Hong Kong and Moscow.
- Users in Houston, Paris, and Geneva must be able to access resources in Los Angeles.
- Security and logon validation traffic must be minimized over the WAN links.

Optional desired results:

- Centralized management of all user accounts.
- Each branch office is able to manage local resources.

Proposed solution:

- Use a complete trust model.
- Place all users in the Los Angles domain.
- Use all branch office domains as resource domains.

Which results does the proposed solution produce?

❍ a. The required results and both of the optional results.

❍ b. The required results and only one of the optional results.

❍ c. The required results but none of the optional results.

❍ d. The required results are not all met.

Question 45

XYZ Corp. has just finished migrating files and accounts from its NetWare server to a Windows NT Server on the network. The Windows NT Server already uses NWLink. NetWare clients complain that they cannot access the migrated files. What might be missing on that Windows NT Server and on the NetWare client machines? [Check all correct answers]

- ❑ a. Gateway Service For NetWare
- ❑ b. Client Service For NetWare
- ❑ c. File And Print Services For NetWare
- ❑ d. Account permissions for the NetWare clients
- ❑ e. Microsoft redirectors for the NetWare clients

Question 46

You have a large bank of printers. You have enough money in the budget to purchase two printers to replace two existing printers. How can you determine which printers receive the most usage (page count and print jobs) so you can replace them?

- ❍ a. Audit File And Object Access events.
- ❍ b. Use Performance Monitor to create a printer object report.
- ❍ c. Set the Application log to tally printer events.
- ❍ d. Use the Printer Wizard to gather statistics.

Question 47

You are the administrator of domain ADMIN1. There are no BDCs within ADMIN1. A power outage destroys some system files on the PDC, and you attempt to correct the problem by reinstalling Windows NT on the machine. After the installation, none of the workstations is able to connect to ADMIN1. What could be the problem?

- ❍ a. The PDC was disconnected from the network.
- ❍ b. A member server was automatically promoted to PDC status, and it is in conflict with the reinstalled PDC.
- ❍ c. The new version installation of Windows NT created a new SID for the PDC.
- ❍ d. A BDC in a trusting domain promoted itself to act as the PDC in ADMIN1. The reinstalled PDC has caused a control conflict.

Question 48

There are two domains within an organization: Admin and Research. New beta software has been deployed on the Research domain for testing, but four members of the Admin domain need to gain access to the beta software to aid in the test process. The beta software resides in an NTFS-based share named "TEST2" on the BETA server in the Research domain. If the Research domain trusts the Admin domain, what additional steps are required to give the four Admin users access to the beta software?

❍ a. Create a global group in the Admin domain called "Admin_Beta," and add the four Admin users to this group. Create a local group called "Soft_Test" on server BETA with Full Control over the TEST2 share. Add the Admin_Beta global group to the Soft_Test local group.

❍ b. Create new accounts for the Admin users in the Research domain.

❍ c. Remove the existing trust. Establish a new trust where the Admin domain trusts the Research domain. Create a global group in the Admin domain called "Admin_Beta," and add the four Admin users to this group. Create a local group called "Soft_Test" on server BETA with Full Control over the TEST2 share. Add the Admin_Beta global group to the Soft_Test local group.

❍ d. Create a global group in the Admin domain called "Admin_Beta," and add the four Admin users to this group. Create a global group called "Soft_Test" on server BETA with Full Control over the TEST2 share. Add the Admin_Beta global group to the Soft_Test global group.

Question 49

If static name resolution is used, what is the proper location of HOSTS and LMHOSTS to optimize the lookup time?

- ❍ a. Both HOSTS and LMHOSTS should be stored on the RAS clients.
- ❍ b. Both HOSTS and LMHOSTS should be stored on the RAS server.
- ❍ c. LMHOSTS should be stored on the RAS clients, and HOSTS should be stored on the RAS server.
- ❍ d. HOSTS should be stored on the RAS clients, and LMHOSTS should be stored on the RAS server.

Question 50

You want to configure a Windows NT Server to be the print server for an HP network interface print device. However, you are unable to locate the option to install a port for the printer. Why is this?

- ❍ a. PostScript printing is enabled on the print device and must be disabled.
- ❍ b. You didn't install the print driver on the print server.
- ❍ c. The print processor is corrupt and must be fixed.
- ❍ d. The DLC protocol is not installed on the print server.

Question 51

You add 4 new drives to your Windows NT Server computer of sizes 800, 600, 500, and 300 MB. You wish to establish a disk stripe set with parity. What is the total size of the largest set you can create using any or all of these drives?

- ❍ a. 1,200 MB
- ❍ b. 1,000 MB
- ❍ c. 800 MB
- ❍ d. 1,500 MB

Question 52

You are working with Network Monitor to evaluate your network usage. You want to capture all frames inbound to your server, except those sent from John's computer. The name of your server is "Admin1," and the name of John's computer is "Sales5." What is the best way to set up the capture filter?

- ❍ a. INCLUDE Admin1 <--> NOT (Sales5)
- ❍ b. INCLUDE Admin1 <--> ANY; EXCLUDE Admin --> Sales5
- ❍ c. EXCLUDE Admin1 <-- Sales5
- ❍ d. EXCLUDE Admin1 <--> Sales5

Question 53

If no configuration changes have been made to a server, what prevents a standard user from logging on to a server by walking up to the local console?

- ❍ a. There is no restriction to prevent users from logging on.
- ❍ b. Servers don't allow anyone to log on to them.
- ❍ c. Log on locally user right is not assigned to standard users.
- ❍ d. The user has No Access permission set for the server object.

Question 54

Which items below describe disk striping with parity? [Check all correct answers]

- ❑ a. Requires three physical drives
- ❑ b. Can be implemented with FAT
- ❑ c. Provides fault tolerance
- ❑ d. Has faster read performance than disk mirroring
- ❑ e. Data cannot be recovered if a single drive within the set fails

Question 55

You have a printer pool that consists of Printer 1 and Printer 2. Printer 1 is printing a job, and Printer 2 is idle. A paper jam occurs on Printer 1's print device. What will happen to the rest of the job that was being printed?

❍ a. The print job will be completed on Printer 2.

❍ b. The print job is canceled.

❍ c. The print job will be completed on Printer 2 because Printer 2 has a higher priority level.

❍ d. The print job is held for completion by Printer 1 until the device is fixed.

Question 56

The XNY Company, located in New York, acquires the MNO Group, based in Singapore. Each company already operates a Windows NT-based network based on the single domain model. Both XNY and MNO currently handle fewer than 500 users in their present domains. Given that administrators at XNY need to manage their users and resources separately from how administrators at MNO handle their users and resources, but that centralized user management and a single login are still required, which of the following approaches to merging the two networks will work the best?

❍ a. Merge all of the MNO users into the XNY domain and replace the MNO PDC and all BDCs with XNY BDCs.

❍ b. Set up a single master domain that combines all XNY and MNO users, and then create resource domains for the XNY site and the MNO site.

❍ c. Set up user domains for XNY users and another for MNO users to create a multiple master domain with resource domains at each location.

❍ d. Set up user domains and resource domains at XNY and MNO. Establish complete trust between all domains.

Question 57

Which of the following actions or activities can result in network traffic, which is related to creation or use of trust relationships between domains? [Check all correct answers]

- ❑ a. Assigning permissions to users from a trusted domain to resources in a trusting domain
- ❑ b. Adding users from a trusting domain to a local group in a trusted domain
- ❑ c. Requesting resources in a trusting domain by a user in a trusted domain
- ❑ d. Requesting resources in a trusting domain by a user in a trusting domain

Question 58

You've been asked to implement Windows NT on a heavy-duty database server. The machine includes four CPUs, 512 MB RAM, and three SCSI disk controllers. It also includes seven SCSI disk drives, each 4 GB in size or larger. Which of the following disk configurations is likely to produce the best system performance?

- ❍ a. Allocate one drive for the boot and system partitions, plus the paging file. Place that drive on its own controller. Use the six remaining drives and both remaining controllers to duplex three drives for database use.
- ❍ b. Allocate one drive for the boot and system partitions. Place that drive on its own controller. Allocate another drive for the paging file and place that drive on its own controller. Place the remaining five drives on the last controller and set up a stripe set with parity. Run the database on the stripe set.
- ❍ c. Allocate two drives and two controllers to create a duplexed drive set for the boot and system partitions plus the paging file. Use the remaining five drives and the last controller to set up a stripe set with parity. Run the database on the stripe set.
- ❍ d. Allocate two controllers and two drives to create a duplexed drive set for the boot and system partitions. Use the remaining controller to create a stripe set with parity. Run the database on the stripe set and put the paging file on the stripe set.

Question 59

Which of the following server optimizations offers the biggest performance gain for the smallest investment?

- ❍ a. Adding more RAM
- ❍ b. Replacing a slower disk controller with a faster one
- ❍ c. Removing unused applications
- ❍ d. Removing unneeded protocols and protocol bindings
- ❍ e. Replacing a slower CPU with a faster one

Question 60

Which of the following statements about Windows NT's Directory Replicator service are true? [Check all correct answers]

- ❑ a. One or more export servers can handle the same directories for one or more import servers.
- ❑ b. Any Windows NT Server 4 machine can be an export server within its domain.
- ❑ c. Any Windows NT 4 machine can be an import server within its domain.
- ❑ d. If the content of the replication directory changes on the export server, all changes propagate automatically to all import servers.
- ❑ e. Events related to the Directory Replicator service appear in the System log.
- ❑ f. To load the Directory Replicator service, you must use the Add button on the Services tab in the Network applet in Control Panel.

Answer Key #1

1. a, b, c, d, e
2. a
3. a
4. b
5. a, c, d
6. b
7. b
8. a
9. c
10. b
11. d
12. a
13. a, b, c, d, e
14. a
15. d
16. a, b, d
17. c
18. c
19. b
20. d
21. c
22. c
23. a
24. a, b, c, e
25. a, c
26. b, e
27. c, d
28. d
29. c
30. b
31. a
32. c
33. d
34. b, d, e
35. b
36. a, b
37. a, b, d
38. b
39. a
40. d
41. d
42. a, b, c, d
43. a
44. d
45. c, e
46. a
47. c
48. a
49. a
50. d
51. d
52. c
53. c
54. a, b, c, d
55. d
56. c
57. a, c
58. b
59. d
60. b, c, d

Here are the answers to the questions presented in the sample test in Chapter 16.

Question 1

Answers a, b, c, d, and e are correct. All of these methods are valid ways to create full or partial backups of the Windows NT Registry. However, it should be noted that the files stored in \Winnt\System32\Config are only as current as the last reboot or execution of **RDISK /s**.

Question 2

Answer a is correct. The single domain model is the best solution for this situation. It offers centralized management, access to all resources, and support for small networks. The master domain model has separate domains for resources and users. This design is too much work for a small network. Therefore, answer b is incorrect. The multiple master domain model is too complicated for such a small network. Therefore, answer c is incorrect. The complete trust domain model is also unnecessarily complex for this situation. Therefore, answer d is also incorrect.

Question 3

Answer a is correct. Defining a global group in General is exactly the right action to take because global groups in a trusted domain can be included in local groups in General and in any other domains that trust General. Production trusts General, so the global TotalBack group can be referenced in local groups in both domains. Finally, because all flavors of Windows NT mentioned—domain controllers, member servers, and Windows NT Workstation machines—support the local Backup Operators group, placing a reference to General\TotalBack creates a situation where members of that group can back up all domain controllers, member servers, and Windows NT Workstations in either domain. Therefore, answer a is correct because the required result and both optional desired results will be produced by the proposed solution.

Question 4

Answer b is correct. Log view records object counters and should be used to create a baseline. Chart view displays the realtime values of counters but cannot record the data as it is gathered. Therefore, answer a is incorrect. Report view creates a snapshot of the performance levels of counters from realtime gathering or a recorded log. Therefore, answer c is incorrect. Graph is not a view but a display selection in the Chart view. Therefore, answer d is incorrect.

Question 5

The correct answers are a, c, and d. Setting the auditing switches on the object is required to enable printer tracking. Therefore, answer a is correct. Setting the master auditing switch to Audit These Events is required to track printer access. Therefore, answer c is correct. Setting the event type switch of File And Object Access to Success is required to track printer usage. Therefore, answer d is correct. There is no auditing user right. Therefore, answer b is incorrect. Setting a printer's priority has nothing to do with tracking access. Therefore, answer e is incorrect.

Question 6

Answer b is correct. Accessing objects through shares results in the most restrictive shared permissions. It is possible to edit documents over a network. The only stipulation is that you must have the proper access level to modify remote objects. Therefore, answer a is incorrect. There is no Save privilege in the Windows NT environment. The Sales group merely has Read access to the share. Therefore, answer c is incorrect. The ability to save documents (i.e., modify objects) is not limited to administrators. Therefore, answer d is incorrect.

Question 7

Answer b is the only correct answer. The best way to update a printer driver is simply to update the driver on the print server. There is no need to manually update the driver on each client computer running Windows NT. When a client computer sends a print job to the print server, the updated driver is automatically copied to the client. Therefore, answers a, c, and e are incorrect. You don't have to create a new logical printer to update a driver. Therefore, answer d is also incorrect.

Question 8

Answer a is correct. The PDC of the trusted domain (i.e., the user domain) is the best place for administration control of user scripts. The PDCs within the trusting domains (i.e., the resource domains) are not used to authenticate users. Plus, there are many of these machines, thereby increasing the administration burden. Therefore, answer b is incorrect. The NETLOGON share within each domain is the same problem presented in answer b—multiple administration sites within non-authenticating domains. Therefore, answer c is incorrect. A local workstation is not the correct place to store logon scripts, especially for easy administration. Therefore, answer d is also incorrect.

Question 9

Answer c is correct. The multiple master domain model can support 50,000 users with its multiple user domains, and each branch office can manage its own local resources. The single domain model cannot support 50,000 users. Therefore, answer a is incorrect. The single master domain model cannot support 50,000 users in its single user domain either. Therefore, answer b is incorrect. The complete trust domain model does not offer centralized management of user accounts and does not adequately support security. Therefore, answer d is incorrect.

Question 10

Answer b is correct. It indicates the first partition of the second hard drive on the first multi type drive controller. Because this is indeed the location of the system partition for this configuration, answer b is correct. Answer a displays an improperly composed ARC name—when **multi** is used, the **disk(n)** number must be set to zero. Therefore, answer a is incorrect. Answer c points to a second drive controller that doesn't exist in this example. Consequently, answer c is incorrect. Answer d supplies an incorrect number for the partition element. Partitions are numbered cardinally, so a partition number can never be zero. Because the first partition is numbered one, answer d is incorrect. Answer e names a second, nonexistent drive controller, and points to the first drive on that controller. Because the system partition for this question is attached to the first (and only) disk controller on the second hard drive, answer e is incorrect.

Question 11

Answer d is correct. If DLC is set to continuous connection mode, no other access to that printer is possible. If the print server is offline, the NetBIOS name of the resource would not be present instead of a denial of service. Therefore, answer a is incorrect. The JetDirect card is designed specifically for the DLC protocol. Therefore, answer b is incorrect. The TCP/IP Printing service in use by another user would not deny access via DLC. Therefore, answer c is incorrect.

Question 12

Answer a is correct. Adding additional BDCs improves network performance by distributing the user-authentication load. Adding RAM to the servers will not improve the network performance because the performance levels are acceptable. Therefore, answer b is incorrect. The Pulse Registry setting would have a negative effect on performance by increasing background network traffic. Therefore, answer c is incorrect. Only one PDC can exist within a domain. Therefore, answer d is incorrect.

Question 13

All answers—a, b, c, d, and e—are correct. Because a RAS-connected client is no different from a direct-connected client (other than speed of data transfer), all standard network activities still occur over the WAN link.

Question 14

Answer a is correct. When installing TCP/IP on a non-routed network, the IP address and subnet mask parameters must be specified. The default gateway is used for routing non-local requests from the local subnet to another destination; because this network is not routed, answer b is incorrect. If you've assigned an IP address manually, there's no need for the DHCP server's address, so answer c is incorrect. There's no need for a WINS server on a single-segment network; therefore, answer d is also incorrect.

Question 15

Answer d lets administrators supply the same passwords for Windows NT accounts as NetWare accounts, which is not an automatic feature of the Migration Tool. Because this is the only behavior described in any of the answers that absolutely requires a mapping file, answer d is definitely the best answer to this question. Keep in mind that to accomplish this, you have to know what the original passwords are, but this is at least a real process that can be used to define the same passwords for the migrated accounts. This is another question and corresponding set of answers that requires careful reading to ferret out the best answer. Answer a falls within the capabilities of a mapping file, but matches the default behavior of the Migration Tool in that unique accounts (i.e., accounts that are not duplicated, neither on the NetWare side nor the Windows NT side) are the easiest to migrate. Answer b relies on the default behavior of the Migration Tool, where existing accounts will not be affected by identical accounts on a NetWare server. Answer c also works fine without a mapping file, because the Migration Tool can handle such accounts automatically.

Question 16

Answers a, b, and d are correct. The data associated with an object is one of that object's attributes. Therefore, answer a is correct. The ACL of an object is an attribute. Therefore, answer b is correct. The name of an object is an attribute. Therefore, answer d is correct. The services of an object are services, not attributes. Therefore, answer c is incorrect.

Question 17

Answer c is correct. Relational database files are often very large and would cause severe performance degradation to a network if their distribution was handled by the Replication service. Logon scripts, user profiles, and system policies are the only files that should be distributed by the replication service. Therefore, answers a, b, and d are incorrect.

Question 18

Answer c is correct. By default, the Migration Tool ignores any user account name on a NetWare server that matches an existing account name in the target Windows NT domain database. Answer a is incorrect because the Migration Tool does not prompt when duplicates are encountered. Answer b is incorrect because a mapping file must be defined to assign such prefixes (the Migration Tool does not perform this action by default, nor would it know what prefix to assign). Answer d is flat wrong. The Migration Tool has been designed to take the safest action by default, which is to leave existing domain database entries untouched.

Question 19

Answer b is correct. Setting the Set By Caller option will allow the field technician to input the callback number each time she needs to connect. Setting the No Call Back option violates the organization's security policy. Keep in mind that allowing the caller to define the callback number is not really a secure option. If this were a real organization, it would need to rethink its security policy. Therefore, answer a is incorrect. Setting the Preset To number does not allow the tech to gain access to the network because she is never in the same place. Therefore, answer c is incorrect. There is no Roaming callback setting. Therefore, answer d is incorrect. Windows NT does not have a Caller ID capture setting, but this can be obtained through third-party software; however, caller ID capture is not required for this situation. Therefore, answer e is incorrect.

Question 20

Answer d is correct. Process Tracking tracks threads and process (e.g., applications). File And Object Access is for tracking NTFS objects, such as files and printers. Therefore, answer a is incorrect. Security Policy Changes tracks modifications to security and policies. Therefore, answer b is incorrect. Restart, Shutdown, And System tracks system restarts. Therefore, answer c is incorrect. Application Activity is not a valid selection. Therefore, answer e is incorrect.

Question 21

Answer c is correct. The Event Viewer can be used to view the System log where all STOP errors are recorded. The Kernel Debugger is only able to view STOP error information when specifically configured and installed on two connected machines. The configuration was not indicated in this question. Therefore, answer a is incorrect. Performance Monitor and Windows NT Diagnostics are not able to record any information about a STOP error. Therefore, answers b and d are incorrect.

Question 22

Answer c is correct. The directory listed in answer c is the correct default destination directory on an import server. The directory listed in answer a is not the default destination server on an import server. Therefore, answer a is incorrect. The directory listed in answer b is not the standard import directory on an import server. Therefore, answer b is incorrect. The directory listed in answer d is the export directory on an export server. This is where files are accessed for distribution. Therefore, answer d is incorrect.

Question 23

Answer a is correct. The Disk Administrator is the correct utility from this list to use to restore the SYSTEM key if you have a stored copy. The other three utilities do not offer Registry restoration options. Therefore, answers b, c, and d are incorrect.

Question 24

The correct answers are a, b, c, and e. NTDETECT. COM is required on the boot floppy. Therefore, answer a is correct. BOOT.INI is required on the boot floppy, making answer b correct. NTLDR is required on the boot floppy. Therefore, answer c is also correct. NTBOOTDD.SYS is the driver for SCSI translation required for non-BIOS controllers, making answer e correct as well. WINA20.386 is a Windows device driver that is not needed on the boot floppy, so answer d is incorrect.

Question 25

Answers a and c are correct. Enabling internetwork browsing and mapping NetBIOS names to IP addresses are two of the three functions of WINS. The third function is recognizing NetBIOS names on all subnets. Mapping FQDNs to IP addresses is a function of DNS. Therefore, answer b is incorrect. Mapping NetBIOS names to MAC addresses happens in both NWLink and NetBEUI. Therefore, answer d is incorrect. Assigning clients IP addresses is a function of a DHCP server. Therefore, answer e is incorrect.

Question 26

Answers b and e are correct. Setting PulseConcurrency low (1) updates a fewer number of BDCs on each Pulse interval, thus reducing WAN traffic. Therefore, answer b is correct. Setting the ReplicationGovernor to 50 percent will reduce the packet size transmitted over the WAN. More packets will be required, but each one will use less bandwidth. Therefore, answer e is correct. Setting Pulse low (60) causes updates to take place too frequently and places extra traffic on the WAN link. Therefore, answer a is incorrect. Setting PulseMaximum low (60) forces a full update more often. Therefore, answer c is incorrect. MaintainServerList is a browser setting, not a domain controller synchronization setting. Therefore, answer d is incorrect.

Question 27

Answers c and d are correct. Any user accessing a NetWare server directly will need a user account on that NetWare server. Therefore, answer c is correct. A Windows NT Workstation running the Client Service For NetWare can access a NetWare server directly by using the NWLink protocol. Therefore, answer d is also correct. It is only necessary to place user accounts in the NTGATEWAY group on the NetWare server if workstations are accessing the NetWare server via a gateway, which is not the case in this question. Therefore, answer a is incorrect. If a Windows NT Server is to act as a gateway to a NetWare server, the Gateway Service For NetWare must be loaded onto a Windows NT Server. Because this scenario discusses a Windows NT client accessing a NetWare server, answer b is also incorrect.

Question 28

Answer d is the only correct answer because it provides the two-way trust required between Sales and Admin, and establishes one-way trusts from Production to both Sales and Admin (thereby meeting the stated requirement that users from Sales and Admin need access to resources from Production). Production must trust both domains, as the answer indicates, by specifying two one-way trusts from Production to each of the other domains. One good way to eliminate possibilities is to see what's missing in the question when compared to the answers. This question says nothing about Production requiring access to anything in Sales or Admin. This automatically knocks out answer a because it includes two-way trusts from Sales and Admin to Production that are not required (and perhaps even unwanted). Likewise, this knocks out answer c because it includes a trust from Sales to Production, as well as the required trust from Production to Sales. Answer b must be eliminated because it fails to include the two-way trust between Sales and Admin implied by the key phrase "but they also need access to resources in each other's domains."

Question 29

Answer c is correct. NetBIOS is the protocol or API used for all of Windows NT's basic internal network communications. TCP/IP is a supported protocol of Windows NT, but it is not the protocol used for basic internal communication. Therefore, answer a is incorrect. AppleTalk is a supported protocol, but it is not used in this manner. Therefore, answer b is incorrect. DLC is a protocol used for IBM mainframe and network attached printers. Therefore, answer d is incorrect.

Question 30

Answer b is correct. The **diskperf -y** command is needed to enable the physical disk counters, but all performance counters can be accessed remotely without further configuration. The Network Monitor Agent is not required to remotely monitor performance counters; it is only needed to access Network Monitor elements remotely. Therefore, answer a is incorrect. The Network Monitor is not required, but the **diskperf** command is. Therefore, answer c is incorrect. The **diskperf** command is required because all disk counters are not enabled by default. Disk counters must be turned on before PerfMon can access them locally or remotely. Therefore, answer d is incorrect.

Question 31

Answer a is correct. It contains the proper syntax for the properties display filter and Protocol:Property [Relation] Value. Therefore, answer a is correct. Answer b is incorrect because the four elements of the properties display filter are scrambled. Answer c is incorrect because it is missing the property element and the remaining elements are out of order. Answer d is incorrect because it is missing the property element, the other elements are out of order, and the relation is not valid for a property relation.

Question 32

The correct answer is c. The key phrase in this question is "the best way" because two answers are actually correct: c and d. Answer d, although correct, requires removing and replacing the existing trust from Admin to Users. This is unnecessary and could break existing trusts established for other uses. Otherwise, d is the same as c, which is correct because it:

- Uses an existing trust.
- Creates a global group in the trusted domain.
- Puts the global group into a local group on the TEST1 machine in the trusting domain.
- Grants the local group the required access to the share.

Answer a fails because it breaks an existing trust unnecessarily and because it places one global group inside another (global groups can contain only users, not other groups of any kind, whether local or global). Answer b fails for the latter reason as well—it places one global group inside another.

Question 33

Answer d is correct. If multiple frame types are being used on a network, then Manual Frame Type Detection must be enabled. Frame types belonging to each client must be added to the frame type configuration list in the

NWLink IPX/SPX Properties dialog box. Answer a is incorrect because Auto Frame Type Detection uses only the first frame type it sees, which results in ignoring all other frame types in use. Answer b is incorrect because it doesn't include entering information for all NetWare clients. Answer c is incorrect because automatic frame type detection does not require entry of client network numbers or frame types.

Question 34

The correct answers are b, d, and e. Assigning the additional IP addresses to the server's NIC is an important step. Therefore, answer b is correct. Because this site is within a private network, you will need both DNS and WINS to support name resolution. Therefore, answers d and e are correct. RIP For IP should not be used in this situation, plus you do not know if there is more than one NIC in the server. Therefore, answer a is incorrect. The DHCP Relay Agent does not apply to this situation. Therefore, answer c is incorrect.

Question 35

Answer b is correct. There are two legitimate ways to meet the stated requirements. One way simply entails adding the users from the Auditors domain into the local group (or groups) in the Accounting domain (where the needed resources reside). The other way to meet the stated requirements is to put a global group between the two domains by defining a global group in Auditors that can be placed into local groups in Accounting. Both options are legal because Accounting trusts Auditors. This makes answers b and c potentially correct. But because the question mentions a need to put the same group elsewhere in the future, creating a global group will ultimately be less work. That's because when the current temporary situation expires, the reference to the Auditor's global group only needs to be expunged from the local group (or groups) in Accounting. To add this same group into another domain, the global group only needs to be added to the local groups in that domain (provided, of course, that the necessary trust relationship from the new domain to the Auditors domain exists). Therefore, answer b represents the best way to meet all requirements. Answer a fails because it assumes that Guests will be able to access the necessary resources, without indicating whether this is true. Answer d fails because it puts one local group within another (only global groups and users can occur within local groups).

Question 36

Answers a and b are correct. Gateway Service For NetWare must be installed on the Windows NT Server. Therefore, answer a is correct. For the Windows NT Server to communicate with the NetWare server, the NWLink protocol must be installed on the Windows NT Server. Therefore, answer b is also correct. CSNW is only required when a Windows NT client needs access to a NetWare server. Therefore, answer c is incorrect. The SAP agent is only necessary when Windows NT Server is routing IPX traffic; here again, that's not part of the scenario, so answer d is also incorrect.

Question 37

Answers a, b, and d are correct. The Event Viewer, DEVICE.LOG, and the MODEMLOG.TXT can be useful troubleshooting tools for RAS problems. Dr. Watson focuses on applications and does not track RAS events. Therefore, answer c is incorrect. Windows NT Diagnostics will not provide useful information related to RAS. Therefore, answer e is incorrect.

Question 38

Answer b is correct. The only activity required to host multiple Web sites on IIS when connected to the Internet is to assign the multiple IP addresses to the server and the re-spective directories. RIP For IP and DHCP Relay Agent are unrelated to this situation. Therefore, answers a and c are incorrect. DNS and WINS are not required because an Internet hosted DNS will support the name resolution. Therefore, answers d and e are incorrect.

Question 39

Answer a is correct. The directory listed in answer a is the default location for storing the CAP files from Network Monitor. The directories listed in answers b, c, and d are not the default directories. Therefore, answers b, c, and d are incorrect.

Question 40

Answer d is correct. If a TCP/IP network does not have a WINS server, each computer on the network has to send a broadcast message to the other computers on the network. This increases network traffic. By making use of a WINS server, you provide computer-name-to-IP address resolution, which reduces the number of broadcast messages. A bridge will forward broadcasts and exacerbate the problem. Therefore, answer a is incorrect. A gateway can't route between subnets. Therefore, answer b is incorrect. DHCP only handles IP addresses and related configuration data, not routing between subnets. Therefore, answer c is also incorrect.

Question 41

Answer d is correct. The pagefile should be 140 MB and placed on the fastest storage set available. The pagefile size is recommended to be set equal to the amount of RAM installed in the server plus 12 MB. Therefore, answer a is incorrect. The pagefile should not be placed on the duplex set, especially on the duplexed BOOT/SYSTEM drive. Therefore, answer b is incorrect. The pagefile should be set equal to the amount of RAM plus 12 MB. Therefore, answer c is incorrect.

Question 42

Answers a, b, c, and d are correct. All these factors can result in the stated error message. When the boot process cannot find NTOSKRNL.EXE, it does not indicate if the problem is with the file itself, its location, or the pointers to the file.

Question 43

Answer a is correct. With non-standardized configurations, implementing any encryption security other than Allow Any Authentication Including Clear Text results in some clients being restricted from accessing the network via RAS. Require Microsoft Encrypted Authentication and Require Encrypted Authentication are encryption security schemes that require special configuration or operating systems. Therefore, answers b and d are incorrect. PGP Encryption is not a native option for Windows NT. Therefore, answer c is incorrect.

Question 44

The correct answer is d. The complete trust model can be used as a modified master domain model with good success. However, this solution does not reduce validation traffic over the WAN links. By placing all users in the Los Angeles domain, each time a branch office user logs on, he or she will connect to the corporate domain. Thus, heavy loads on the WAN links will result from this security traffic. To make this solution work, a Los Angeles domain BDC should be physically placed in each of the branch offices. Then, all users would access the BDC for authentication and minimize WAN usage.

Question 45

The correct answers are c and e. For NetWare clients to access files on a Windows NT Server, FPNW is the required software component. Therefore, answer c is one correct answer to this question. On the other hand, the NetWare clients must have a way to send requests to the Windows NT domain controller, browse available resources, and request access to those resources. This is where the Microsoft redirectors for the NetWare clients come into play. The redirectors will permit clients to browse network resources directly. Therefore, answer e is also correct. Answer a is incorrect because it lets Microsoft network clients access a NetWare server, which is irrelevant to the circumstances. Answer b is incorrect because it lets Windows NT Workstations and Servers act as clients to a NetWare server, also irrelevant. Finally, answer d is incorrect because the question clearly states that accounts were migrated from NetWare to Windows NT.

Question 46

Answer a is correct. You must use File And Object Access audits to record print activities, which in turn can be used to tally the number of pages and jobs sent to each printer. The Performance Monitor does not have a printer object that you can use to create a report. Therefore, answer b is incorrect. There is no way to set the Application log to tally anything. The Application log records information sent by an application. Therefore, answer c is incorrect. The Printer Wizard is used to create logical printers. It does not have any statistical abilities. Therefore, answer d is incorrect.

Question 47

Answer c is correct. The SID of the PDC is the defining element of a domain, not its name. Thus, the new SID created a new domain of which none of the workstations is a member. The PDC was not disconnected from the network. Instead, the new SID of the PDC is the culprit. Therefore, answer a is incorrect. Member servers can never be domain controllers. Therefore, answer b is incorrect. BDCs in trusting domains cannot authenticate users nor can they act as PDCs for a trusted domain. Therefore, answer d is incorrect.

Question 48

Answer a is correct. It contains the proper sequence of steps required to give the Admin users access to the beta software. Adding new accounts to the Research domain is insecure and will result in twice the administration to maintain two accounts for each user. Therefore, answer b is incorrect. The existing trust will allow Admin users to use Research resources, reversing the trust will prevent access and destroy other possible links currently relying on the trust. Therefore, answer c is incorrect. It is not possible to add a global group to another global group, plus Microsoft recommends using local groups to manage resource permissions. Therefore, answer d is incorrect.

Question 49

Answer a is correct. The fastest lookup time will occur when the HOSTS and LMHOSTS files are stored on the local hard drive of each RAS client because no WAN traffic needs to occur to resolve a resource location. The other options do not result in optimized lookup time. Therefore, answers b, c, and d are incorrect.

Question 50

Answer d is correct. For Windows NT to provide support for DLC-based HP network interface print devices, you must install DLC (Data Link

Control). You can't install a printer driver if Windows NT cannot recognize the print device.

Question 51

Answer d is correct. As it happens, 1,500 MB is the total size of the largest set that can be created from these drives, using only the 800, 600, and 500 MB drives. 1,200 MB would be the size of the set if you used all 4 drives with 300 MB on each one. Because this is not the largest possible sum using this set of drives, answer a is incorrect. 1,000 MB is indeed the amount of data that could be stored on the largest set created from these drives, but the question requested the total size of the set, making answer b incorrect. Likewise, although 800 MB represents the size of the largest individual drive, you must use 3 drives to create a disk stripe set with parity. Therefore, answer c is incorrect.

Question 52

Answer c is correct. Answer c is an **EXCLUDE** statement that restricts traffic from the Sales5 computer. Answer a is not a proper construction. The relation indicates both inbound and outbound traffic, plus the **NOT** logical operator is used outside of the filter statement. Therefore, answer a is incorrect. Answer b lists the default **INCLUDE** statement, which does not need to be repeated, and the **EXCLUDE** statement applies to traffic sent to Sales5. Therefore, answer b is incorrect. Answer d excludes both inbound and outbound traffic from Sales5. Therefore, answer d is incorrect.

Question 53

Answer c is correct. The log on locally right is not assigned to standard users specifically to prevent them from gaining easy access to the server. There is a default restriction to prevent general users from logging in locally to a server—it is the log on locally right, and it is not assigned to users by default. By extension, answer a must therefore be incorrect. Servers allow members of the Administrators, Server Operators, Backup Operators, Account Operators, and Print Operators groups to log on to them. Therefore, answer b is incorrect. There is no server object to which you could assign No Access permissions. Therefore, answer d is incorrect.

Question 54

The correct answers are a, b, c, and d. Disk striping with parity requires a minimum of three physical drives, so answer a is correct. Disk striping with parity can be implemented with either NTFS or FAT. Therefore, answer b is correct. Because disk striping with parity is indeed a fault-tolerant storage method, answer c is also correct. Disk striping with parity offers better performance than disk mirroring because it spreads the load across more drives. Therefore, answer d is correct, as well. Disk striping with parity can recover from a single drive failure. Therefore, answer e is incorrect.

Question 55

Answer d is correct. If a physical print device in a printer pool fails in the middle of a print job, the print job is retained at that physical print device until the device is fixed. Any other print jobs sent to the printer pool will continue to print to other physical print devices in the printer pool.

Question 56

Answer c is correct. Using a multiple master domain model lets XNY administrators concentrate on the XNY-based user and resource domains, and MNO administrators do likewise with their user and resource domains. Given the minimal needs for domain controller synchronization in this situation (a single BDC on either side of the connection for the other domain will suffice) and the relative independence of the two sites, plus the 13-hour time difference, this is the best solution. Replication traffic from New York to Singapore could be a problem, and the 13-hour time difference could cause coordination problems, so a single domain will probably cause more problems than it solves. Therefore, answer a is incorrect. Although a single master domain would work, it would require that the PDC for that domain operate in one location or the other, and incur replication overhead. Also, it would enable MNO administrators to manage XNY users, and vice-versa. Therefore, answer b is incorrect. Complete trust is overkill, and it prevents separation of resource and user management. Therefore, answer d is incorrect.

Question 57

Answers a and c are correct. When a trust relationship exists, users from a trusted domain may be assigned permissions to resources in a trusting domain. When such assignments occur, traffic related to the trust relationship occurs. When a trust relationship exists and users in a trusted domain request resources in a trusting domain, a process called *pass-through authentication* occurs. This involves traffic from the PDC of the trusted domain to the PDC of the trusting domain. When a trust relationship exists, users come from trusted domains to resources in trusting domains, not vice-versa. Therefore, answers b and d are incorrect. (However, if the direction in answer b were stated correctly, that option would indeed state a cause of trust-related network traffic.)

Question 58

Answer b is correct. The two principles that apply here are to separate the paging file from the boot partition whenever possible, and to avoid placing a paging file on a stripe set. Answer b is correct because it adheres to both principles. The reason the system files and the paging file should be on separate drives is to avoid contention between the two. The reason the paging file should not be placed on a stripe set is to allow Windows NT to maximize both read and write performance (stripe sets with parity are faster for reading, but slower for writing, especially for 4 KB memory pages). Answer a is incorrect because it leaves the paging file and the system files (on the boot partition) on the same drive. Answer c is incorrect because it keeps the paging file and the boot partition on the same drive. Answer d is incorrect because it puts the paging file on a stripe set with parity.

Question 59

Answer d is correct. Removing unneeded protocols and protocol bindings speeds the search order for network communications. It can provide a noticeable performance improvement, and its only cost is the time it takes to do the job. Although adding more memory is often thought of as a panacea for server problems, it does cost something, so it's not the correct answer. Therefore, answer a is incorrect. Replacing a disk controller costs money.

Therefore, answer b is incorrect. Removing unused applications may free up disk space, but otherwise does nothing to optimize a server. Therefore, answer c is incorrect. Replacing a slower CPU with a faster one will almost always improve performance, but it does cost money (and may require upgrading other parts of a system as well). Therefore, answer e is incorrect.

Question 60

Answers b, c, and d are correct. Any Windows NT Server, be it a domain controller or a member server, can act as an export server for a Windows NT domain. Any Windows NT Workstation can act as an import server within its domain. The Directory Replicator service regularly polls the export directory's subdirectories for changes, and it automatically copies any changes it finds to its import partners. Although more than one export server can be active on a Windows NT network, it's not recommended that more than one export server handle any particular set of directories. Therefore, answer a is incorrect. Events related to the Directory Replicator service appear in the Application log, not the System log. Therefore, answer e is incorrect. The Directory Replicator service is installed automatically when Windows NT is installed and must be activated in the Services applet in Control Panel before it can be used. It's not necessary to add the service in the Network applet. Therefore, answer f is incorrect.

Sample Test #2

See Chapter 16 for Sample Test #1 and pointers to help you develop a successful test-taking strategy, including how to choose proper answers, how to decode ambiguity, how to work within the Microsoft testing framework, how to decide what you need to memorize, and how to prepare for the test. In this chapter, we include another sample test on subject matter pertinent to Microsoft Exam 70-068: "Implementing and Supporting Microsoft Windows NT Server 4.0 in the Enterprise." After this chapter, you'll find the answer key to this test.

Also, remember that you can take adaptive practice exams on Windows NT Server 4.0 in the Enterprise online at www.coriolis.com/cip/core4rev/ to help you prepare even more. Good luck!

Question 1

A user has left the company and you need to take ownership of her files. From the following list, which default built-in groups permit you to take ownership of files?

- ❍ a. Server Operators
- ❍ b. Backup Operators
- ❍ c. Account Operators
- ❍ d. Administrators
- ❍ e. Domain Guests

Question 2

Which of the following special groups includes users who can log on locally to a Windows NT Server?

- ❍ a. Creator/Owner
- ❍ b. Interactive
- ❍ c. Network
- ❍ d. Everyone

Question 3

National Herbal Products has three domains: Accounting, Marketing, and Sales. Users in each of the domains need access to a Windows NT Server in the Gensing domain. What trust relationships need to exist to allow access from all three domains?

- ❍ a. Configure Accounting, Marketing, and Sales to trust the Gensing domain.
- ❍ b. Configure Accounting, Marketing, and Sales to be trusted by the Gensing domain.
- ❍ c. Configure two one-way trusts between Accounting, Marketing, and Sales and Gensing.
- ❍ d. No trust relationships are required.

Question 4

You think your server is being hacked and you want to check the number of current users connected to one of your shares. Where would you look?

- ❍ a. Server Manager|Properties|In Use
- ❍ b. Server Manager|Properties
- ❍ c. Server Manager|Properties|Replication
- ❍ d. Server Manager|Properties|Shares
- ❍ e. Server Manager|Properties|Alerts

Question 5

One of your new employees is confused about NetLogon and has asked you for an explanation. What functions does NetLogon provide? [Check all correct answers]

- ❑ a. Logon validation
- ❑ b. Pass-through authentication
- ❑ c. Server management
- ❑ d. Resource share management
- ❑ e. PDC/BDC synchronization

Question 6

You create an NTCONFIG.POL file that you wish to apply to all Windows NT users. Where should this file be placed? [Check all correct answers]

- ❑ a. Winnt\System32\repl\import\scripts
- ❑ b. Winnt\System32\repl\export\scripts
- ❑ c. Netlogon share
- ❑ d. Users share

Question 7

You are setting up directory replication and you want to ensure that the replicated file is not transmitted while in use. What option should you select to achieve this?

- ❍ a. Lock
- ❍ b. Stabilize
- ❍ c. You cannot control this; it is automatic
- ❍ d. Locked Since

Question 8

Your company is based in Chicago and has branch offices in New York City, San Francisco, Atlanta, Washington, D.C., and Seattle. Each of the six offices has 200 users. Each branch office is connected to the Chicago office via T1 lines. You are asked to implement a domain model for your company.

Required results:

- Users from Chicago must be able to access resources in Seattle and Atlanta.
- Users from San Francisco and New York City must be able to access resources in Chicago.
- Logon validation traffic over the WAN links must be minimized.

Optional desired results:

- You want centralized administration of all user accounts.
- Each branch office wants to be able to manage its own resources.

Proposed solution:

- Implement the single domain model. Place the PDC and at least one BDC in Chicago. Place at least one BDC in each branch office. Manage all user accounts from Chicago.

Which result does the proposed solution satisfy?

❍ a. Meets the required results and both optional desired results.

❍ b. Meets the required results and one of the optional desired results.

❍ c. Meets the required results and none of the optional desired results.

❍ d. Does not meet the required results.

Question 9

What is the Registry parameter that specifies whether the server will maintain a browse list or not?

❍ a. MaintainServerList

❍ b. IsDomainMaster

❍ c. MaintainList

❍ d. DomainMaster

Question 10

Your company uses disk mirroring on all Windows NT Servers. You are asked to implement a new fault tolerance standard for the entire company network.

Required result:

- The new fault tolerant standard must be able to recover from a single drive failure.

Optional desired results:

- The new fault tolerant system should place less demand on the system memory and the CPU than disk mirroring.
- The new fault tolerant system should provide better read performance than disk mirroring.

Proposed solution:

- Implement disk striping with parity on all Windows NT Servers.

Which result does the proposed solution satisfy?

❍ a. Meets the required result and both optional desired results.

❍ b. Meets the required result and one of the optional desired results.

❍ c. Meets the required result and none of the optional desired results.

❍ d. Does not meet the required result.

Question 11

Over time your system seems to have become sluggish. To improve performance on your Windows NT Server, which of the following changes should you consider? [Check all correct answers]

- ❑ a. Use disk striping
- ❑ b. Install faster hard disks
- ❑ c. Install another disk controller
- ❑ d. Rearrange file to balance disk access
- ❑ e. Implement disk mirroring

Question 12

In a single master or multiple master domain model, where should all accounts be located? [Check all correct answers]

- ❑ a. Master domains
- ❑ b. Trusting domains
- ❑ c. Trusted domains
- ❑ d. Resource domains

Question 13

You have six hard drives. The first is your system drive. The other five are part of a fault tolerant implementation of disk striping with parity. You lose two of your striped drives. How can you recover?

- ❍ a. Replace the failed drives, then use your Emergency Repair Disk.
- ❍ b. Replace the failed drives, then restore the stripe set from backup.
- ❍ c. Replace the failed drives, then use the Windows NT Regenerate command from Disk Administrator.
- ❍ d. Replace the failed drives, then break and reset the set from Disk Administrator.

Question 14

If a trusting domain breaks a trust, what action must be performed to re-establish that trust relationship?

❍ a. Immediately re-establish the trust.

❍ b. Totally break the trust and then re-establish it.

❍ c. Use the Emergency Repair Disk.

❍ d. Do nothing. WINS will automatically repair the broken trust.

Question 15

When viewing the trust relationships from User Manager For Domains, you notice that for one of the domains, the same name appears in trusted and trusting text boxes. What does this mean?

❍ a. A one-way trust has been established.

❍ b. A two-way trust has been established.

❍ c. A master domain model has been established.

❍ d. A complete trust has been established.

Question 16

You are the manager of a nationwide WAN that uses TCP/IP as its primary protocol. Your users report that response time is sluggish, especially in the morning and late afternoon. At your Chicago site, you have a PDC installed with WINS and DHCP to support the WAN.

Required result:

- Increase WAN performance.

Optional desired results:

- Reduce WINS and DHCP overhead.
- Provide login fault tolerance for the corporate location.

Proposed solution:

- Install a BDC at each remote location. Install WINS and DHCP on each remote BDC as well.

Which results does the proposed solution satisfy?

❍ a. Meets the required result and both optional desired results.

❍ b. Meets the required result and one of the optional desired results.

❍ c. Meets the required result and none of the optional desired results.

❍ d. Does not meet the required result.

Question 17

You install a new network server and are concerned about security of sensitive data and performance for users who access it from the network. The server is equipped with 256 MB RAM and two Adaptec 2940 SCSI controllers with three 2 GB SCSI drives on each controller. All drives are formatted using the FAT file system.

Required result:

- Maximize access performance for both local and network applications.

Optional desired results:

- Provide ability to set object level security to sensitive data files.
- Provide for recovery in case of failure.

Proposed solution:

- Convert all drives to NTFS.
- Mirror the boot drive and create a stripe set over the four remaining drives.
- Move the paging file to the stripe set.

Which result does the proposed solution satisfy?

❍ a. Meets the required result and both optional desired results.

❍ b. Meets the required result and one of the optional desired results.

❍ c. Meets the required result and none of the optional desired results.

❍ d. Does not meet the required result.

Question 18

Which of the following selections, when checked, would create audit log events when any changes to the Directory database of the domain FAIL?

- ❍ a. User and Group Management/Failure
- ❍ b. User and Group Management/Success
- ❍ c. Security and Policy Changes/Failure
- ❍ d. Security and Policy Changes/Success

Question 19

Ms. Jackson, a user in the Corp domain, wishes to access information on the company server. The administrator shares the Data directory with share permissions for the Users group set to Full Control. The administrator sets NTFS permissions for Users to No Access, but sets Ms. Jackson's permissions specifically to Change. What is the effective permission for Ms. Jackson?

- ❍ a. Full Control
- ❍ b. Read Only
- ❍ c. No Access
- ❍ d. Change

Question 20

Suppose the following situation exists:

Your growing company is experiencing higher demand for storage resources on the server. There are four drives in your server computer. Two are mirrored and contain the system and boot files. The other two are mirrored and contain data files. Your company's current solution implements disk mirroring for ease of recovery owing to any failed drive, but company management feels that 100 percent disk overhead is excessive.

Required result:

- Provide for recovery of any single drive failure.

Optional desired results:

- Support maximum performance.
- Implement a fault tolerance strategy that uses disk space effectively.

Proposed solution:

- Add a fifth drive, implement disk striping with parity for the three data drives, and mirror the system and boot files.

Which result does the proposed solution satisfy?

❍ a. Meets the required result and both optional desired results.

❍ b. Meets the required result and one of the optional desired results.

❍ c. Meets the required result and none of the optional desired results.

❍ d. Does not meet the required result.

Question 21

Users complain that one server on your network responds very slowly. You suspect that one of the disk partitions is having problems. What object should you select from Performance Monitor to check your hunch?

❍ a. Logical disk

❍ b. Physical disk

❍ c. Memory

❍ d. Redirector

Question 22

What are your effective NTFS permissions if you have Read, Change, and No Access by virtue of various group memberships?

❍ a. Change

❍ b. Read

❍ c. Read, Change

❍ d. No Access

Question 23

Suppose the following situation exists:

Your WAN includes two domains: Chicago and New York. Users in Chicago seem to be fine but users in New York indicate that network browsing takes "forever." Additionally, general performance in New York is terrible in the morning when users log on.

Required result:

- Increase WAN performance for New York users.

Optional desired results:

- Reduce early morning New York logon overhead.
- Optimize TCP/IP service traffic with WINS and DHCP.

Proposed solution:

- Place a Chicago domain BDC in New York with DHCP installed.

Which result does the proposed solution satisfy?

❍ a. Meets the required result and both optional desired results.

❍ b. Meets the required result and one of the optional desired results.

❍ c. Meets the required result and none of the optional desired results.

❍ d. Does not meet the required result.

Question 24

You've just created a share on the DATA directory. You have not assigned permissions or made any changes to the defaults. What access does a user have to that share?

- ❍ a. Full Control
- ❍ b. Change
- ❍ c. Change and Full Access
- ❍ d. No Access

Question 25

Which of the following can be configured or restricted through Windows NT user policies? [Check all correct answers]

- ❑ a. Desktop color schemes
- ❑ b. Disable Registry editing
- ❑ c. Taskbar settings
- ❑ d. Network printer connections
- ❑ e. Display settings

Question 26

You have 300 Windows NT Workstation users accessing a Windows NT 4 member server. You also have a small Access database on that server that's accessed by several users.

Which option provides the best performance for this machine?

- ❍ a. Minimize Memory Used
- ❍ b. Balance
- ❍ c. Maximize Throughput For File Sharing
- ❍ d. Maximize Throughput For Network Applications

Question 27

There are two domains, Corp and Sales, where Sales trusts Corp. Both Corp and Sales have a PDC, BDC, member servers, and several Windows NT Workstations. You want to back up the PDC, BDC, member servers, and all Windows NT Workstations in both domains with a Backup Operators group.

Required result:

- Members of the Backup Operators group must be able to back up both domain controllers.

Optional desired results:

- Members of the Backup Operators group must be able to back up all member servers.
- Members of the Backup Operators group must be able to back up all workstations.

Proposed solution:

- Create a global group called "Backup Operators" in the Sales domain and add this new global group to the local "Backup Operators" group on all domain controllers, member servers, and workstations.

Which result does the proposed solution satisfy?

❍ a. Meets the required result and both optional desired results.

❍ b. Meets the required result and one of the optional desired results.

❍ c. Meets the required result and none of the optional desired results.

❍ d. Does not meet the required result.

Question 28

Ten members of the Sales group with laptops with Windows NT Workstation installed need remote access to Windows NT Server resources.

Required result:

- Only sales group members should be allowed to dial in remotely.

Optional desired results:

- Require password encryption.
- Require data encryption.

Proposed solution:

- Configure RAS and give only the Sales group access to remote dial-in services, create account policies where minimum password length is eight characters, and set up the RAS server to allow Any Authentication Including Clear Text.

Which result does the proposed solution satisfy?

❍ a. Meets the required result and both optional desired results.

❍ b. Meets the required result and one of the optional desired results.

❍ c. Meets the required result and none of the optional desired results.

❍ d. Does not meet the required result.

Question 29

You have one domain with two locations. One location is in Scotland with one member server and 40 clients. The second location is in Houston and has 100 clients with one PDC and no BDCs. The PDC in Houston also acts as a DHCP server as well as a WINS server. The two locations are connected via a 56 K link and users in Scotland complain that the time it takes to log on is too long.

Required result:

- The network response for Scotland logon should be the same as Houston.

Optional desired results:

- WINS traffic over the 56 K link must be minimized.
- DHCP traffic over the 56 K link must be minimized.
- Logon traffic over the 56 K link must be minimized.

Proposed solution:

- Install a DHCP server in Scotland and make the member server in Scotland a WINS proxy agent.

Which result does the proposed solution satisfy?

❍ a. Meets the required result and all of the optional desired results.

❍ b. Meets the required result and one of the optional desired results.

❍ c. Meets the required result and none of the optional desired results.

❍ d. Does not meet the required result.

Question 30

A single domain model would be appropriate in which of the following situations? [Check all correct answers]

❑ a. More than 25,000 users

❑ b. Split organizational structure

❑ c. Fewer than 10,000 users

❑ d. Inadequate network hardware

❑ e. The network can function as an organizational unit

Question 31

Payroll has just called and the printer has jammed at the exact instant your paycheck was printing. How can you reprint your check after clearing the paper jam?

❍ a. Choose Resume from the Printer menu

❍ b. Choose Restart from the Printer menu

❍ c. Choose Resume from the Documents menu

❍ d. Choose Restart from the Documents menu

Question 32

A user logs in to the Corp domain from a computer attached to the Sales domain. Which resources can this user access if the user's account also resides in the Sales domain?

❍ a. All folders in the Corp domain for which Corp\Domain user has access

❍ b. All folders in the Corp domain for which Sales\Domain user has access

❍ c. All folders in the Corp domain for which Corp\Guest user has access

❍ d. All folders in the Corp domain for which Sales\Guest user has access

Question 33

In a single master domain model of the Marketing trusts Corp, you log in to the Corp domain with a machine in the Marketing domain. What are your effective rights?

❍ a. Marketing\Domain Users

❍ b. Marketing\Domain Guests

❍ c. Corp\Domain Users

❍ d. Corp\Domain Guests

Question 34

All domains in your company trust the Gensing domain. What types of user accounts or groups can be added to a global group in the Gensing domain?

❍ a. Only user accounts from the Gensing domain

❍ b. User accounts from both the Gensing domain and from any trusting domain

❍ c. User accounts and other global groups from the Gensing domain

❍ d. User accounts and local groups from the Gensing domain and from any trusting domain

Question 35

You are the network administrator for National Herbal Products. To reduce network traffic, you have subnetted your network into two segments. You want to use WINS to resolve NetBIOS names to IP addresses on each of the segments. All workstations on each segment are WINS-enabled. Providing fault tolerance for the WINS database is a concern. What is the best way to configure WINS on your network to keep traffic between the segments to a minimum?

❍ a. Install a WINS server on one of the subnets. Configure a Windows NT Server computer on the other subnet as a WINS proxy agent.

❍ b. Install separate WINS servers on each of the subnets. Configure the WINS-enabled computers on each subnet to use the WINS server that resides on their subnet.

❍ c. Install WINS onto a computer that has an IP address on both subnets so that both subnets can access the same WINS database.

❍ d. Install separate WINS servers on each of the subnets. Configure the WINS servers to be push-pull partners to each other.

Question 36

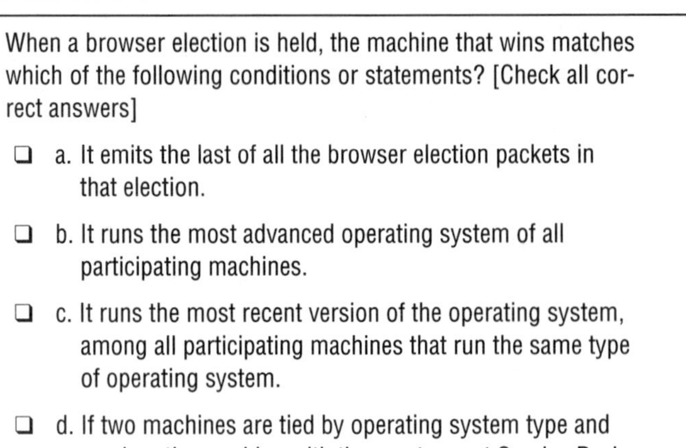

When a browser election is held, the machine that wins matches which of the following conditions or statements? [Check all correct answers]

- ❑ a. It emits the last of all the browser election packets in that election.
- ❑ b. It runs the most advanced operating system of all participating machines.
- ❑ c. It runs the most recent version of the operating system, among all participating machines that run the same type of operating system.
- ❑ d. If two machines are tied by operating system type and version, the machine with the most recent Service Pack installed wins.

Question 37

Which of the following statements best describes what's required to direct print output from a Windows NT Server to a Unix host, or to a networked print device that uses only TCP/IP for print jobs and related information?

❍ a. Install the DLC protocol through the Add button on the Protocol tab in the Network applet, and then configure a network printer in the Printers applet on the print server.

❍ b. Start the Remote Printer Service in the Services applet in Control Panel; configure the service with the printer's IP address, and then configure a network printer in the Printers applet on the print server.

❍ c. Add the LPR service from the Services tab in the Network applet in Control Panel; configure the service with the printer's IP address, and then configure a network printer in the Printers applet on the print server.

❍ d. Add the Microsoft TCP/IP Printing service from the Services tab in the Network applet in Control Panel. To add an LPR printer, use the Add New Printer application in the Printers applet. In the Printer Ports dialog box, click on LPR Port, and then click on New Port. In the Name Or Address Of Server Providing lpd field, enter the DNS name or the IP address of the host of the printer you are adding. In the Name Of Printer Or Print Queue On That Server field, type the name of the printer as it is known by the host.

Question 38

Your company has 500 users with 1 PDC and 3 BDCs at a single site. What domain model should be used?

❍ a. Single

❍ b. Single master

❍ c. Multiple master

❍ d. Complete trust

Question 39

You discover an application that crashes repeatedly. Microsoft Windows NT technical support wants you to capture a dump of system memory. What tool should you use to do this?

- ❍ a. Sysdiff
- ❍ b. Dr. Watson
- ❍ c. Crash Debug
- ❍ d. Server Manager

Question 40

When you install all of the eligible client-based administration tools on a Windows 95 or Windows 98 machine, which of the following extensions to My Computer and Explorer also apply? [Check all correct answers]

- ❑ a. Change security on Windows NT File System (NTFS) drives.
- ❑ b. Manage Windows NT printers.
- ❑ c. Manage Macintosh volumes and security on Windows NT Servers running Services for Macintosh.
- ❑ d. Manage NetWare gateway settings on Windows NT Servers running Gateway Service For NetWare (GSNW).
- ❑ e. Manage Windows NT Servers running File And Print Services For NetWare (FPNW).

Question 41

You are assigning rights and permissions to a local group on a PDC. What resources can access those rights and permissions through the same local group?

❍ a. Any BDC

❍ b. BDCs for that PDC

❍ c. BDCs for any PDC

❍ d. Any workstation in the domain

Question 42

Your management team has asked that mandatory user profiles be implemented to stop users from changing their desktop environments. How would you go about implementing mandatory profiles?

❍ a. Change NTUSER.DAT to NTUSER.MAN

❍ b. Change NTCONFIG.POL to NTCONFIG.MAN

❍ c. Change CONFIG.POL to CONFIG.MAN

❍ d. Change USER.DAT to USER.MAN

Question 43

The Sales Reps need RAS access to the network for sales target materials. They must be able to access your network using Dial-Up Networking.

Required results:

- The Sales Reps must be able to access your network using RAS.
- All data transmitted between your RAS server and client computers must be encrypted.

Optional desired results:

- All passwords transmitted between your RAS server and client computers must be encrypted.
- Inbound telephone numbers must be authenticated before allowing anyone to connect to the RAS server.

Proposed solution:

- Set the minimum password length to eight characters in the Account Policy dialog box for the domain, grant all Sales Reps dial-up access to the RAS server, configure the RAS server for Require Microsoft Encrypted Authentication, and configure callback security on the RAS server to use the Set By Caller option.

Which result does the proposed solution satisfy?

❍ a. Meets the required results and both optional desired results.

❍ b. Meets the required results and one of the optional desired results.

❍ c. Meets the required results and none of the optional desired results.

❍ d. Does not meet the required results.

Question 44

Your boss is confused about global groups. Global groups are properly described by which of the following? [Check all correct answers]

- ❑ a. Global groups are defined in a domain's SAM.
- ❑ b. Global groups can contain domain user accounts.
- ❑ c. Windows NT Server provides standard global groups.
- ❑ d. Global groups can contain local groups.
- ❑ e. Global groups can be used anywhere in a domain to assign permissions.

Question 45

You have been asked to share a printer that is attached to a Windows NT Server. What group memberships permit such a share to be defined? [Check all correct answers]

- ❑ a. Account Operators
- ❑ b. Server Operators
- ❑ c. Administrators
- ❑ d. Printer Operators
- ❑ e. Backup Operators

Question 46

Which file systems on Windows NT 4 work with disk mirroring? [Check all correct answers]

- ❑ a. FAT
- ❑ b. CDFS
- ❑ c. NTFS
- ❑ d. HPFS

Question 47

You have four hard disks and are using Windows NT Server 4. The first drive contains the system and boot partitions. The remaining three drives are set up as a stripe set with parity and contain user files and data. The first disk fails. What steps must be taken after the failure?

❍ a. Install a new drive, reinstall Windows NT Server, and use Windows NT Backup to restore the system Registry.

❍ b. Install a new drive, reinstall Windows NT Server, and use the Emergency Repair Disk to restore the system Registry.

❍ c. Install a new drive, reinstall Windows NT Server, and use the User Manager tools to restore the system Registry.

❍ d. Install a new drive, then regenerate the failed drive from Disk Administrator.

Question 48

You have recently made several changes to Windows NT Server 4. You reboot your machine and the blue system stop screen appears. What should be your first course of action?

❍ a. Use the Emergency Repair Disk to repair the system configuration.

❍ b. Use the Windows NT Server boot disk and then perform a repair using the Emergency Repair Disk.

❍ c. Select the Last Known Good Configuration from the startup screen by pressing the spacebar.

❍ d. Select the Last Known Good Configuration from the startup screen by pressing the Enter key.

❍ e. Reinstall Windows NT Server.

Question 49

You have several file and print servers installed in the National Herbal Products domain. You add another domain to your network and would like to move some of the current file and print servers to the new domain. What must you do to accomplish this? [Check all correct answers]

- ❑ a. Move each server from the current domain to a temporary workgroup.
- ❑ b. Reinstall Windows NT because servers cannot be moved between domains.
- ❑ c. Join the new domain.
- ❑ d. Join a second domain; servers can be members of up to five domains.

Question 50

Without the RIP protocol, how must router tables be maintained?

- ❍ a. Automatically
- ❍ b. Manually
- ❍ c. Using OSPF
- ❍ d. Dynamically, at startup

Question 51

Following startup of the DHCP service, which tool can you use to administer DHCP?

- ❍ a. Server Manager
- ❍ b. User Manager For Domains
- ❍ c. DHCP Manager
- ❍ d. DHCP Administrator

Question 52

Which services does Internet Information Server (IIS 3) support? [Check all correct answers]

❑ a. WWW

❑ b. Archie

❑ c. FTP

❑ d. Gopher

Question 53

Which of the following statements is false?

❍ a. Gateway Service For NetWare transfers file and directory information and user and group account information from a NetWare server to a Windows NT domain controller.

❍ b. Gateway Service For NetWare enables Windows NT Servers to access NetWare file and print resources.

❍ c. The passwords from the NetWare server can be migrated across to Windows NT by selecting the Migrate Passwords checkbox.

❍ d. RIP packets are transmitted every 60 seconds.

Question 54

Pete is trying to verify that logon requests are reaching the server with the correct user names because several users are not getting validated correctly. How can he verify that a particular user name is being transmitted to the logon server?

❍ a. Have each user attempt to log on locally at the console.

❍ b. Ask Pete to watch them enter their names and passwords.

❍ c. Run Network Monitor on the logon server.

❍ d. This is not possible.

Question 55

A network has a large number of Windows NT Workstations and Windows 98 clients. Select any techniques that could help reduce network traffic. [Check all correct answers]

- ❑ a. Reduce the number of protocols used.
- ❑ b. Turn off File And Print Sharing.
- ❑ c. Add network cards to the servers on the network.
- ❑ d. Install SNMP.

Question 56

Your system has experienced a STOP error and a memory.dmp file was created. Which tool can be used to examine the contents of this file?

- ❍ a. Debug
- ❍ b. Dr. Watson
- ❍ c. Dumpexam
- ❍ d. Windows NT Diagnostics

Question 57

Which of the following methods explains how you can create or manage local groups on member servers or Windows NT Workstations within a domain from a domain controller?

- ❍ a. Using Server Manager, highlight the target machine, and then pick New Local Group from the Users menu.
- ❍ b. Using Server Manager, highlight the target machine, pick Properties from the computer menu, and then click on the Groups button.
- ❍ c. Using User Manager For Domains, choose Select Domain from the Users menu. Then, enter the UNC name for the target computer in the Domain text box in the Select Domain window. From there, you can create or manage local groups on the target machine.
- ❍ d. Using User Manager For Domains, select Manage Member Server or Manage Domain Workstation from the Options menu and select the target machine from the domain computer name display that results. After you select the target machine, you can create or manage local groups on the target machine.

Question 58

By default, which of the following properties apply to the Guest account in a Windows NT domain? [Check all correct answers]

- ❑ a. User Must Change Password At Next Logon is unchecked.
- ❑ b. User Cannot Change Password is checked.
- ❑ c. Password Never Expires is unchecked.
- ❑ d. Account Disabled is checked.
- ❑ e. Account Locked Out is grayed out (in other words, inaccessible).

Question 59

To monitor a server's memory behavior, which of the following Performance Monitor counters should you observe? [Check all correct answers]

- ❑ a. Memory:Available Bytes
- ❑ b. Memory:Pages/sec
- ❑ c. Processor:%Processor Time
- ❑ d. Processor:Interrupts/sec
- ❑ e. LogicalDisk:Avg. Disk Queue Length (for the drive where the paging file resides)
- ❑ f. PhysicalDisk:Avg. Disk Queue Length (for the drive where the paging file resides)

Question 60

On a network with a large number of Windows 98 and Windows NT clients, you decide you must reduce the amount of network traffic to help ease occasional congestion problems. Which of the following techniques should you employ to achieve this goal? [Check all correct answers]

- ❑ a. Upgrade all systems to Windows NT.
- ❑ b. Reduce the number of network protocols in use.
- ❑ c. Increase the number of NICs in each network server.
- ❑ d. Remove file and print sharing from all client machines.
- ❑ e. Subdivide the network so separate groups operate on independent cable segments.

Answer Key #2

1. d
2. b
3. b
4. d
5. a, b, e
6. a, c
7. b
8. b
9. a
10. b
11. a, b, c, d
12. a, c
13. b
14. b
15. b
16. b
17. b
18. a
19. c
20. b
21. a
22. d
23. b
24. a
25. a, b, e
26. c
27. d
28. c
29. d
30. c, e
31. d
32. c
33. c
34. a
35. d
36. a, b, c
37. d
38. a
39. b
40. a, b, e
41. b
42. a
43. d
44. a, b, c, e
45. b, c, d
46. a, c
47. a
48. c
49. a, c
50. b
51. c
52. a, c, d
53. c
54. c
55. a, b
56. c
57. c
58. a, b, d, e
59. a, b, e
60. b, c, d, e

Question 1

The correct answer is d. The only group that can take ownership of files is the Administrators group. Once an Administrator takes ownership, the Administrators group becomes the owner. By default, the creator of a file or directory is its owner. None of the other roles mentioned has the right to take ownership. Therefore, answers a, b, c, and e are all incorrect.

Question 2

The correct answer is b. Interactive users are those users logging on locally to a computer; they have the default right to log on locally. Creator/Owners are the owners of objects they create, but do not have the right to log on locally. Therefore, answer a is incorrect. Network users are users who log on over the network, not locally. Therefore, answer c is incorrect. It doesn't make sense for the Everyone group to have the right to log on locally; therefore, answer d is also incorrect.

Question 3

The correct answer is b. In trust relationships, users are in one domain and resources are in another. Relate this to a parent and child. The parent has the car and the child wants it. The parent must trust the child in order for the child to use the car. The parent is trusting and the child is trusted. The user, therefore, is the child, and the resource, held by the parent, is the car. The trust arrow points from the resource to the user. Answer b is correct because the parent, or Gensing, trusts its Accounting, Marketing, and Sales domain children. Answer a is incorrect because it does no good for the child to trust the parent to get a resource; it must be the other way around. The two one-way trusts mentioned in answer c will work, but creating the additional trusts just creates more maintenance work and might give users in the Gensing domain access to resources in the other three domains that they don't wish to share. Therefore, answer c is not the best answer. Answer d is incorrect because without trusts, users in one domain cannot access resources in another domain.

Question 4

The correct answer is d. The Shares button shows you a list of all shares; when you select any particular share, it displays a list of connected users, time, and if the share is in use or not. The In Use window shows the computer's open shared resources, but not the number of users; therefore, answer a is incorrect. Answer b opens the Properties dialog box, but leaves you one mouse click short and is also incorrect. The Replication window manages directory replication, not shares. Therefore, answer c is also incorrect. The Alerts window permits registration to receive administrative alerts, but says nothing about shares; therefore, answer e is also incorrect.

Question 5

The correct answers are a, b, and e. The NetLogon service provides logon validation for a domain, pass-through authentication when accessing resources in other domains, and synchronization of the SAM database between the PDC and all BDCs. Because this service provides neither server management nor resource share management, answers c and d are incorrect.

Question 6

The correct answers are a and c. Winnt\System32\repl\import\scripts and the Netlogon share are actually the same location (but the Netlogon share is read only). Answer b is incorrect because it names the export directory (which you might use for export purposes, but is not where Windows NT looks for this file). Answer d is incorrect because there is no default users share in Windows NT.

Question 7

The correct answer is b. Stabilize indicates whether files in an export directory wait a specified time after changes have been made before being exported. Answer a is incorrect because Lock prevents any files from being exported while the lock remains in place. Because answer b is correct, answer c must be wrong. Answer d does not apply to the dialog boxes and attributes for the Directory Replication service, so it is also incorrect.

Question 8

The correct answer is b. The single domain model is not recommended in a WAN; however, the solution does satisfy the required results. Central account administration occurs at the PDC in Chicago, satisfying the first optional desired result. To manage access to resources, you would have to implement a single master domain model, not a single domain. Therefore, the required result and one of the optional desired results are met.

Question 9

The correct answer is a. MaintainServerList specifies whether the server will maintain a browse list (if set to Yes, it does maintain a list; if set to No, it will not maintain a list. MaintainServerList is the only valid Registry key in this set of options, so answers b, c, and d are all incorrect.

Question 10

The correct answer is b. Disk striping with parity, or RAID 5, is capable of sustaining a single drive loss in the array; therefore, the required result is satisfied. Although RAID 5 provides better read performance due to concurrent reads, it places a higher CPU and memory demand on the system, thereby satisfying only one of the optional desired results.

Question 11

The correct answers are a, b, c, and d. There are several ways to improve performance on a Windows NT Server: Use disk striping instead of disk mirroring; install faster hard disks; install an additional disk controller; or rearrange files to balance disk access. Of the available answers, the only one that slows a system is disk mirroring, because data must be simultaneously written to multiple disks. Therefore, e is the only incorrect answer.

Question 12

The correct answers are a and c. Accounts are centralized in the master domains. Resources trust users; thus, the master domains would also be the trusted domains. The trusting and resource domains are where resources, not accounts, reside. Therefore, answers b and d are incorrect.

Question 13

The correct answer is b. RAID 5, or disk striping with parity, can survive a single disk failure. However, when two drives fail, we hope you have a backup! To recover from two drive failures, you must replace the failed drives, then restore from backup. Answer a is incorrect because an ERD cannot recover a stripe set with parity from a drive failure. Answer c works only if a single drive fails, but not when two fail. Answer d is incorrect because this describes a fix for a mirrored or duplexed set, not for a stripe set with parity.

Question 14

The correct answer is b. Because passwords are reassigned and then unknown after the trust has been established, the trust has to be totally broken and then re-established if it has been broken from one of the participating domains. You cannot immediately re-establish the trust because an existing trust must be broken first; this makes answer a incorrect. The ERD can't help repair trust relationships. Therefore, answer c is incorrect. Doing nothing won't fix this problem, so answer d is also incorrect.

Question 15

The correct answer is b. In reality, a two-way trust is two one-way trusts. That is why the name appears twice, which makes b the correct answer. In a one-way trust, the domain name appears only once, which makes answer a incorrect. Even in a master domain model, you still have trusts. Just because it is a master domain model doesn't automatically make the name appear multiple times, so answer c is incorrect. In a complete trust model, you would indeed see the name twice. However, you would see each domain name twice, not just for one domain; therefore, answer d is incorrect.

Question 16

The correct answer is b. Because you have offloaded logon authentication to the remote sites with a BDC and added WINS and DHCP servers to the remote sites, you have effectively reduced WAN traffic, satisfying the required result. Although adding WINS and DHCP servers to those BDCs will indeed reduce WINS and DHCP WAN overhead, this solution does not deliver login fault tolerance at the corporate location. Therefore, only one of the optional desired results is met.

Question 17

The correct answer is b. Creating a stripe set and moving the paging file to the stripe set maximizes local and network access performance, satisfying the required result. NTFS supports object level security, which satisfies the first optional desired result. But because the proposed solution did not specify a stripe set with parity (RAID 5), but rather a plain stripe set, no fault tolerance is delivered.

Question 18

The correct answer is a. User and Group Management/Failure is where the directory database is handled for auditing purposes, and because failure events are selected. Answer b is incorrect because it audits success rather than failure. Security and policy changes have nothing to do with the Directory database, making answers c and d incorrect.

Question 19

The correct answer is c. Effective permissions are simple to remember. Share permissions plus NTFS permissions take the most restrictive permission. NTFS takes only the least restrictive permission. In both instances, if No Access exists for any user or group, No Access permission wins. Because the Users group has No Access, Ms. Jackson has No Access. Because only answer c is correct, answers a, b, and d are all incorrect.

Question 20

The correct answer is b. Mirroring the system and boot drives provides fault tolerance for the system files. A stripe set with parity provides fault tolerance for the data files; thus, the required result is met. Performance is slightly slower than a stripe set without parity (not fault tolerant) and disk duplexing (fault tolerant); thus, a stripe set with parity does not provide the best performance. The first optional result is not met. A stripe set with parity does effectively utilize disk space, which delivers the second optional result.

Question 21

The correct answer is a. Partitions relate to logical, not physical, disks. Answer b is incorrect because it checks only entire drives, not partitions.

Answer c is incorrect because memory activity is not directly indicative of disk behavior. Answer d is incorrect because the redirector object has no direct relationship with disk partitions.

Question 22

The correct answer is d. The answer here is simple; for effective permissions, No Access always wins. Therefore, answers a, b, and c are all incorrect.

Question 23

The correct answer is b. A Chicago-based BDC in New York would improve WAN performance and reduce logon overhead. Therefore, the required result and only one of the optional desired results are met. DHCP access would be improved, but WINS is not addressed in the proposed solution.

Question 24

The correct answer is a. Any time a network share is created, Windows NT automatically assigns the Everyone group Full Control permissions to that share. Answers b, c, and d are all invalid answers, so they are all incorrect.

Question 25

The correct answers are a, b, and e. The policy editor allows you to configure desktop color schemes, display setting options, and to disable programs such as Registry editing tools. You cannot, however, restrict Taskbar settings or printer connections in Windows NT user policies. Therefore, answers c and d are incorrect.

Question 26

The correct answer is c. Maximize Throughput For File Sharing is best for file and printer sharing for large groups of users (which Microsoft defines as more than 64 users). The level of database usage is quite low, and Access doesn't really qualify as a network application. Minimize Memory Used is for 10 users and under, and does not apply to these circumstances; therefore, answer a is incorrect. Balance is for up to 64 users, and doesn't apply, either; therefore, answer b is incorrect. Maximize Throughput For Network

Applications is used to maximize working set access to memory for networked applications such as SQL Server; therefore, answer d is incorrect. For more information, visit this control in the Services tab in the Network applet in Control Panel, select the Server Service, view properties, and then read the associated Help files.

Question 27

The correct answer is d. Creating a global group in the Sales domain would serve no purpose. It must be created in the Corp domain.

Question 28

The correct answer is c. Configuring RAS and granting dial-in access for Sales satisifies only the required result. However, neither password nor data encryption are addressed in the proposed solution; therefore, this solution fails to deliver either of the optional desired results.

Question 29

The correct answer is d. The poor network response during logins would be improved by adding a BDC for account authentication in Scotland. Adding a DCHP or WINS proxy doesn't help.

Question 30

The correct answers are c and e. Criteria for selecting a domain model include: number of accounts (up to 25,000 per domain according to Microsoft, but under 10,000 according to most outside Windows NT experts), geographic scope, and how users and resources will be defined. Advantages of a single domain model include centralized administration and ease of management. Thus, a single domain model would be appropriate for a small number of users, and a centralized (single unit) organizational structure. Answer a is incorrect because it requires a multiple master domain model. Answer b is incorrect because the single domain model works best for centralized organizations, not split ones. Answer d is incorrect because domain controllers tax network hardware, so using any domain model with inadequate hardware is asking for trouble.

Question 31

The correct answer is d. The Restart command from the Document menu will reprint the entire print job starting from the beginning, thus ensuring your check is printed. The Printer menu does not contain a Restart or Resume command. Therefore, answers a and b are incorrect. The Resume command from the Document menu will continue printing from the point at which the error occurred. However, because the printer may host a buffer where data is sent before it is printed, some portion of the print job could have been lost. Resuming printing in most cases will print an incomplete document. Therefore, answer c is incorrect.

Question 32

The correct answer is c. Because no trust relationship is mentioned, do not assume that one exists. Based on that realization, the only possible level of access is the Guest account in Corp. Answers a, b, and d all require access to the home domain for authentication; because this can't happen without a trust relationship, none of these scenarios is possible.

Question 33

The correct answer is c. Users are always in the trusted domain and resources are in the trusting domain. To log in to the Corp domain, it is assumed that you are a user in the Corp Domain. Your user account has been assigned rights in the domain. By default, Guests do not have rights, making answers b and d incorrect. Answers a and b are incorrect because they indicate you logged in to the Marketing domain, not the Corp domain.

Question 34

The correct answer is a. A global group can contain user accounts from the same domain in which the global group exists or user accounts from a trusted domain if the global group is from the trusting domain (this second method is not listed as an option in this question). Answer b is incorrect for the same reason. Global groups cannot contain other global groups, which makes answer c incorrect. Global groups cannot contain local groups either, which also makes answer d incorrect.

Question 35

The correct answer is d. Installing a WINS server on each subnet allows local name resolution, thus reducing network traffic. Making the WINS servers push-pull partners enables replication of each database to the other server at regular intervals, thus providing fault tolerance for the WINS database. Answer a is incorrect because WINS proxy does not provide fault tolerance. Answer b is incorrect because replication of the WINS database must occur for proper name resolution to occur. Answer c is incorrect because it doesn't reduce traffic and provides zero fault tolerance.

Question 36

Answers a, b, and c are correct. As stated in answer a, machines that participate in an election continue to send election packets until a machine that trumps them sends an election packet. Thus, the machine that sends the last of all the browser election packets in an election is the one that becomes the Master Browser. Indeed, as stated in answer b, only a machine that runs the most advanced operating system can win a browser election, in this order: Windows NT Server, Windows NT Workstation, Windows 98, Windows 95, Windows For Workgroups. Indeed, as stated in answer c, only a machine that runs the most recent version of the most advanced operating system can win a browser election. If two or more machines running the most advanced OS type and most recent version participate in an election, the one whose name appears first in Network Neighborhood or Server Manager (which is to say, whose name appears first when sorted in ascending ASCII collating sequence order) wins. Service Packs do not affect the outcome of a browser election (but please note that for domain controllers, all or none must run SP 4). Therefore, answer d is incorrect.

Question 37

Answer d is correct. To use the line printer daemon in a Windows NT environment, you must first add the Microsoft TCP/IP Printing service as described, and then configure an LPR port for the printer or print server to be accessed. DLC is not a TCP/IP-based protocol, and doesn't work with Unix hosts or with TCP/IP based-printing services. Therefore, answer a is incorrect. There is no Remote Printer Service in the Services applet, or elsewhere in Windows NT. Therefore, answer b is incorrect. There is no LPR Service available from the Services tab in the Network applet. Therefore, answer c is incorrect.

Question 38

The correct answer is a. Based on the number of users and domain controllers, you would use a single domain model. This puts all users and resources in a single domain with centralized account administration. Answer b requires another domain and another PDC. This is overkill for 500 users, which makes answer b incorrect. Answers c and d both require too many trust relationships for 500 users, so they are incorrect as well.

Question 39

The correct answer is b. If an application fails, Dr. Watson can capture a dump of system memory for later examination. Sysdiff is a utility used to handle differences between multiple installations of Windows NT. Therefore, answer a is incorrect. Crash Debug does not enable system memory dump; therefore, answer c is incorrect. Server Manager has no utility to perform memory dumps. Therefore, answer d is also incorrect.

Question 40

Answers a, b, and e are correct. When all the eligible client-based administration tools are added to a Windows 95 or Windows 98 machine, you can change security settings on NTFS drives, manage Windows NT printers, and manage Windows NT Servers running FPNW. Adding all the eligible client-based administration tools to a Windows 95 or Windows 98 machine confers no ability to manage Macintosh volumes and security on Windows NT Servers, nor does it confer the ability to manage GSNW settings on Windows NT Servers. Therefore, answers c and d are incorrect.

Question 41

The correct answer is b. A PDC and its BDCs share identical account databases (SAMs); however, such BDCs must belong to the same domain as the PDC. By extension, because both answers a and c fail to specify the domains to which their BDCs belong, both are incorrect. Only domain controllers can run User Manager For Domains by default, which makes answer d incorrect as well.

Question 42

The correct answer is a. The NTUSER.DAT file is where user profile information resides. To make a profile mandatory, meaning that users cannot change system settings persistently, rename NTUSER.DAT to NTUSER.MAN. That profile then becomes mandatory. Because the other answers fail to identify the correct file name, answers b, c, and d are all incorrect.

Question 43

The correct answer is d. The solution does not meet the required results. Microsoft Encryption will encrypt the passwords. Data, however, is not encrypted unless the Require Data Encryption checkbox is also selected. The proposed solution does not address the data encryption; therefore, the solution does not meet the required results.

Question 44

The correct answers are a, b, c, and e. The principle to remember here is AGLP—that is, accounts go in global groups, global groups go in local groups, and local groups are assigned permissions. Global groups can be created only on domain controllers; thus, they are defined in the domain SAM, which makes answer a correct. Global groups can contain only users from within their domains; therefore, answer b is correct. Windows NT provides standard global groups such as Domain Admins; therefore, answer c is correct. Global groups can be used anywhere in the domain, making answer e correct. Global groups cannot, however, contain local groups; it works only the other way around, so answer d is incorrect.

Question 45

The correct answers are b, c, and d. For Windows NT, there are three predefined groups permitted to share printers. Server Operators can share (and stop sharing) for all server resources, including printers. Therefore, answer b is correct. Administrators have full control over all domain operations, including sharing printers; therefore, answer c is correct. Printer Operators can manage printers in a domain, including sharing (or stop sharing) such printers. Therefore, answer d is also correct. Account Operators can manage user accounts, but not printers, which makes answer a incorrect. Backup Operators can back up and restore servers, but can't manage printers, which makes answer e incorrect as well.

Question 46

The correct answers are a and c. Both FAT and NTFS partitions can be mirrored in Windows NT 4. CDFS, or the Compact Disk File System, is for CD-ROMs and is not a writable file system. Therefore, answer b is incorrect. The High Performance File System (HPFS) is no longer supported in Windows NT 4, which makes answer d incorrect as well.

Question 47

The correct answer is a. The disk that failed was not using a fault tolerant strategy, such as disk mirroring or duplexing. Therefore, the only option is to replace that drive, reinstall Windows NT Server, and restore from a backup that includes the original Registry. Answer b is incorrect because the ERD does not restore the Registry fully, only certain hives. Answer c is incorrect because User Manager includes no tools for Registry backup or restoration. Answer d is incorrect because that approach works only on stripe sets with parity.

Question 48

The correct answer is c. Your first course of action is to select the Last Known Good Configuration from the startup screen by pressing the spacebar. This restores the last working machine configuration and allows you to try other configurations to fix the problem. The ERD and the Windows NT Server boot disk approach is not the first choice here, because these tools are designed primarily to repair boot disks and related files, not hardware problems, so answers a and b are both incorrect. Answer d is wrong because you press the spacebar, not the Enter key, to launch the LKGC. Reinstalling Windows NT Server is a fix of last resort, not first resort, which makes answer e incorrect as well.

Question 49

The correct answers are a and c. Unlike BDCs, file and print servers and member servers maintain their own account databases and SIDs. Hence, they can be moved between domains. They cannot, however, belong to multiple domains simultaneously. Windows NT does not require reinstallation for member servers to move between domains, so answer b is incorrect. Servers can belong to only one domain at a time, which makes answer d incorrect.

Question 50

The correct answer is b. RIP, or Routing Information Protocol, is a distance-vector based protocol used for routing in Windows NT. With the RIP protocol, tables are maintained automatically. Without RIP, such tables must be maintained manually. By extension, answer a is therefore incorrect. OSPF, the Open Shortest Path First protocol, is a distance-vector based algorithm that many routing protocols use, but it has nothing to do with how Windows NT maintains its router tables. Therefore, answer c is incorrect. Because manual table maintenance is required in the absence of RIP, answer d is also incorrect.

Question 51

The correct answer is c. DHCP dynamically allocates and maintains TCP/IP client configurations and address leases in a Windows NT network. DHCP Manager is used to administer the Dynamic Host Configuration Protocol (DHCP). Server Manager manages shares, connected users, alerts, and PDC/BDC promotions, demotions, and synchronization, but not DHCP; therefore, answer a is incorrect. User Manager For Domains is used to create and manage global and local groups and users, not DHCP. Therefore, answer b is also incorrect. There is no such application named DHCP Administrator, which makes answer d incorrect as well.

Question 52

The correct answers are a, c, and d. IIS supports the World Wide Web (WWW) service, File Transfer Protocol (FTP), and Gopher. Windows NT does not include support for Archie with IIS, which makes answer b incorrect.

Question 53

The correct answer is c because the NetWare Migration Tool does not include a Migrate Passwords checkbox. Windows NT will not import passwords during a migration, unless a separate script file is supplied by an administrator. GSNW includes the NetWare Migration Tool, which can transfer file, directory, user, and group information from NetWare to a Windows NT domain controller, so answer a, although true, is incorrect. GSNW does indeed permit the Windows NT Servers where it is installed to access NetWare file and print services (on behalf of other users), so answer b is also incorrect. Finally, RIP packets are indeed transmitted once per minute, so answer d is incorrect as well, if something of a nonsequitur.

Question 54

The correct answer is c. Network Monitor permits viewing of packets transmitted over a network. Running Network Monitor at the logon server allows packet information to be checked for user names. Logging on locally will not verify that the logon information is being transmitted correctly across the network, which makes answer a incorrect. Watching users enter account information is error prone and better done with Network Monitor, which makes answer b incorrect. Because answer c is correct, answer d must be incorrect.

Question 55

The correct answers are a and b. Reducing the number of protocols helps reduce unnecessary broadcasts and network traffic; therefore, answer a is correct. Removing the ability to create and use shares also reduces network traffic; therefore, answer b is correct. Adding additional network cards by themselves, without subnetting or other network division techniques, will not reduce network traffic. This makes answer c incorrect. SNMP adds to network traffic, but does not reduce it by itself, which makes answer d incorrect.

Question 56

Answer c is correct. Dumpexam is the tool to use to examine the contents of the memory.dmp file created by a STOP error. Debug is a tool used to troubleshoot the system startup environment. Therefore, answer a is incorrect. Dr. Watson is used to capture the state of a virtual machine's memory in the event of an application failure. It cannot be used to view the contents of dump files it creates or those created by the system for STOP errors. Therefore, answer b is incorrect. Windows NT Diagnostics is a utility used to examine the state and configuration of the operating system environment. Therefore, answer d is incorrect.

Question 57

Answer c is correct. Using the UNC name for the target machine is the key to accessing local group information through User Manager For Domains (which turns into a remote version of the User Manager utility on the target machine by extension). Server Manager does not have a Users menu (it's in User Manager For Domains). Therefore, answer a is incorrect. The Properties window in Server Manager does not include a Groups button. Therefore, answer b is incorrect. There is no Manage Member Server or Manage Domain Workstation entry in the Options menu in User Manager For Domains. Therefore, answer d is incorrect.

Question 58

Answers a, b, d, and e are correct. By definition, the Guest account is shared. Thus, users are not permitted to change passwords for this account, lest confusion set in. Therefore, answers a and b are correct. The Guest account is disabled by default. Therefore, answer d is correct. No account will be locked out unless a policy to enable account lockouts is enabled, and an illegal number of login attempts is made against specific settings for the Guest account. Because the account is disabled by default, this cannot occur, so it's absolutely predictable that the account lockout entry would be grayed out here. Therefore, answer e is correct. Because users cannot change the password for the Guest account, the password should not have an expiration date. This checkbox should therefore be checked, rather than unchecked. Therefore, answer c is incorrect.

Question 59

Answers a, b, and e are correct. Microsoft recommends that Memory:Available Bytes be at or over 4 MB at all times and notes that values of less than 1

MB almost always indicate memory shortages. Memory:Pages/sec shows the impact of paging on memory. Sudden increases over the baseline can also indicate memory shortages. The behavior of the partition (or partitions) where the paging file resides can be an important index of memory activity. Although Processor:%Processor Time is an excellent all-purpose counter, it's not strictly necessary to monitor CPU to understand memory behavior on a server. Therefore, answer c is incorrect. Although Processor:Interrupts/sec is an excellent all-purpose counter and can indicate potential device problems when sudden spikes over the baseline value appear, it's not strictly necessary to monitor interrupts per second to understand memory behavior on a server. Therefore, answer d is incorrect. PhysicalDisk counters aggregate counts for the entire physical hard disk where the paging file resides. This counter is useful only if the paging file resides on a single partition on that drive (and would be equally well represented by the preceding LogicalDisk counter). Therefore, answer f is incorrect. Remember that using both logical and physical disk counters requires enabling those counters using the **diskperf -y** command at the Windows NT command line, then rebooting the system (to turn off those counters, use **diskperf -n**).

Question 60

Answers b, c, d, and e are correct. By reducing the number of network protocols in use, you reduce the amount of overhead on the network by the amount associated with the protocol or protocols you eliminate (less the increased overhead for remaining protocols). This is especially useful if you can eliminate chatty protocols like NetBEUI. Therefore, answer b is correct. Increasing the number of NICs in a server may improve its ability to handle incoming network traffic and to respond more quickly to client requests. It won't reduce network traffic by itself, but when combined with subdivided networks, it can help quite a bit. Therefore, subject to this additional requirement (used in tandem with subdivision of existing networks), answer c is correct. By removing file and print sharing from client machines, you stop those clients from acting as sources for shared resources and eliminate their need to participate in browse service announcements. This can substantially reduce network traffic when large numbers of clients are involved. Therefore, answer d is correct. "Divide and conquer" refers to the approach in which large amounts of traffic or resources on a single segment are subdivided, then distributed across multiple segments to balance the load. This is a traditional technique for reducing network traffic on congested segments, especially when other techniques to reduce traffic have already been applied. Some of the other approaches in this question might be likened to reducing the number of cars on the road; this approach is like increasing the number of roads to accommodate more cars. Therefore, answer e is correct. Upgrading all clients to Windows NT will not directly affect network traffic. Therefore, answer a is incorrect.

Scenarios

Scenario 1

Suppose the following situation exists:

You're the system administrator for a large company. You must design a networking system that will support your company's online needs.

Required result:

- Ensure that all users and groups are centrally managed.

Optional desired results:

- Allow resources to be managed from within the department in which they are located.
- Support a user base expansion to at least 10,000 individuals.

Proposed solution:

- Deploy a single master domain model network based on Windows NT Server 4.

Which results does the proposed solution produce?

❍ a. The proposed solution produces the required result and produces both of the optional desired results.

❍ b. The proposed solution produces the required result and produces only one of the optional desired results.

❍ c. The proposed solution produces the required result but does not produce any of the optional desired results.

❍ d. The proposed solution does not produce the required result.

The correct answer is a. The proposed solution of a single master domain will provide for centralized control over users and groups, and allow resources to be managed on a departmental basis. In addition, a single domain can host up to 25,000 users theoretically, with a practical maximum of 10,000. Therefore, the proposed solution fulfills the required result and both of the optional desired results.

Scenario 2

Suppose the following situation exists:

You're the system administrator for a large company. You must design a networking system that will support your company's online needs.

Required result:

- Ensure that all users and groups are centrally managed.

Optional desired results:

- Allow resources to be managed from within the department in which they are located.
- Support a user base expansion to at least 10,000 individuals.

Proposed solution:

- Deploy a mesh domain model network based on Windows NT Server 4.

Which results does the proposed solution produce?

❍ a. The proposed solution produces the required result and produces both of the optional desired results.

❍ b. The proposed solution produces the required result and produces only one of the optional desired results.

❍ c. The proposed solution produces the required result but does not produce any of the optional desired results.

❍ d. The proposed solution does not produce the required result.

The correct answer is d. The proposed solution of a mesh domain model eliminates centralized control over users and groups. Even though it's possible to employ a mesh design so only a single domain hosts the user accounts, it does not prevent the proliferation of user accounts throughout the multidomain network. Furthermore, the typical structure of a mesh domain model has both users and resources in each domain. With a mesh domain model, resources can be managed by administrators from other domains. The model does support more than 10,000 users; however, the proposed solution does not fulfill the required result.

Scenario 3

Suppose the following situation exists:

A recent merger has brought another domain into your administrative responsibilities. XYZ Corp.'s domain is named xyzdomain. You must configure a trust relationship over a WAN link to connect this domain to your company's existing domain named HomeDomain.

Required result:

- Allow users from HomeDomain to use resources on xyzdomain.

Optional desired results:

- Prevent xyzdomain users from gaining access to HomeDomain resources.
- Enable HomeDomain administrators to manage resource access on xyzdomain.

Proposed solution:

- Establish a two-way trust between xyzdomain and HomeDomain.

Which results does the proposed solution produce?

❍ a. The proposed solution produces the required result and produces both of the optional desired results.

❍ b. The proposed solution produces the required result and produces only one of the optional desired results.

❍ c. The proposed solution produces the required result but does not produce any of the optional desired results.

❍ d. The proposed solution does not produce the required result.

The correct answer is b. The proposed solution of a two-way trust allows HomeDomain users access to xyzdomain resources and allows HomeDomain administrators to control access to xyzdomain resources. However, the solution does not prevent xyzdomain users from accessing HomeDomain resources. Therefore, the proposed solution fulfills the required result and only one of the optional desired results. The best solution for this situation would be a single trust between the two domains, so xyzdomain trusts HomeDomain.

Scenario 4

Suppose the following situation exists:

You're aware of the increased administration responsibilities caused by trust relationships. You must employ trust relationships to establish proper communications over your company's multiple domains and networks, but you want to keep the use of trust relationships to a minimum. You have four domains—D1, D2, D3, and D4.

Required result:

- Keep the number of trusts fewer than four.

Optional desired results:

- Ensure that all users reside on and are controlled from D1.
- Provide the ability to manage all resources from D2, D3, or D4.

Proposed solution:

- Create a single master domain model layout with one-way trusts in the form of D2 trusts D1, D3 trusts D1, and D4 trusts D1.

Which results does the proposed solution produce?

❍ a. The proposed solution produces the required result and produces both of the optional desired results.

❍ b. The proposed solution produces the required result and produces only one of the optional desired results.

❍ c. The proposed solution produces the required result but does not produce any of the optional desired results.

❍ d. The proposed solution does not produce the required result.

The correct answer is a. The proposed solution employs only three trusts; therefore, the maximum number of trusts remains fewer than four. Furthermore, a single master domain model implies that all users are stored in a single domain, D1, and resource domains trust the user domains D2, D3, and D4. Therefore, the proposed solution fulfills the required result and both of the optional desired results.

Scenario 5

Suppose the following situation exists:

You have a multiserver domain that hosts valuable data. You must protect this data from loss. Your network is managed by four administrators, and each of them has a unique administrator account. The administrators are members of the local Administrators group only on the server they are assigned to control.

Required result:

- Maintain a backup of all data on all servers.

Optional desired results:

- Store a week's worth of data on a single media type.
- Automate the backup process.

Proposed solution:

- Install a backup device on a single server with enough capacity to store a full backup and several days of incremental backups on the same media.
- Add your user account to the Backup Operators group on the server hosting the backup tape device.
- Configure the backup software to protect all data on all servers by performing a full backup every Friday and an incremental backup every other day.

Which results does the proposed solution produce?

❍ a. The proposed solution produces the required result and produces both of the optional desired results.

❍ b. The proposed solution produces the required result and produces only one of the optional desired results.

❍ c. The proposed solution produces the required result but does not produce any of the optional desired results.

❍ d. The proposed solution does not produce the required result.

The correct answer is d. The proposed solution fails due to problems with group membership. The way this network is configured, each administrator is only an administrator on a single server. This means the administrators are not members of the Domain Admins group. By placing your user account into the Backup Operators group, you're not actually adding any new capabilities to your user account. Administrators already have the user rights of backing up and restoring files. Both the Administrators group and the Backup Operators group are local groups. Therefore, they have an effect on resource access only for the server on which they exist. This means that you do not have access to the data on the other servers and cannot back them up. If your user account was a member of the Domain Admins group or a custom global group with the proper user rights created, then the remainder of the proposed solution would be sufficient for this situation.

Scenario 6

Suppose the following situation exists:

You want to delegate management responsibilities to several astute users.

Required result:

- Grant limited resource and server control to a few specific users.

Optional desired results:

- Grant the ability to change system time.
- Grant the ability to log on locally to servers.
- Grant the ability to shut down the system.
- Grant the ability to back up files and directories.

Proposed solution:

- Grant group membership to the selected users to the Backup Operators group.

Which results does the proposed solution produce?

❍ a. The proposed solution produces the required result and produces all of the optional desired results.

❍ b. The proposed solution produces the required result and produces only three of the optional desired results.

❍ c. The proposed solution produces the required result and produces only two of the optional desired results.

❍ d. The proposed solution does not produce the required result.

The correct answer is b. The proposed solution of granting membership to the Backup Operators group will grant the ability to log on locally, perform system shutdowns, and back up files. Therefore, the proposed solution fulfills the required result but only three of the optional desired results. The optimal solution for this scenario would be to grant membership to the Server Operators group.

Scenario 7

Suppose the following situation exists:

You want to delegate management responsibilities to several astute users.

Required result:

- Grant limited resource and server control to a few specific users.

Optional desired results:

- Grant the ability to change system time.
- Grant the ability to log on locally to servers.
- Grant the ability to shut down the system.
- Grant the ability to back up files and directories.

Proposed solution:

- Grant group membership to the selected users to the Account Operators group.

Which results does the proposed solution produce?

❍ a. The proposed solution produces the required result and produces all of the optional desired results.

❍ b. The proposed solution produces the required result and produces only three of the optional desired results.

❍ c. The proposed solution produces the required result and produces only two of the optional desired results.

❍ d. The proposed solution does not produce the required result.

The correct answer is c. The proposed solution of granting membership to the Account Operators group will grant the ability to log on locally and perform system shutdowns. Therefore, the proposed solution fulfills the required result and only two of the optional desired results. The optimal solution for this scenario would be to grant membership to the Server Operators group.

Scenario 8

Suppose the following situation exists:

Your network is spread across six buildings in a single office park. You have a single domain. Each building is connected with a high-speed microwave bridge, so communications can occur between buildings. The PDC and two BDCs reside in the main headquarters building. Every other building in the network has three BDCs within it. Overnight, the cleaning crew spills the mop bucket over the power supply of the PDC, which causes instant destruction of the entire computer.

Required result:

- Restore the domain to a fully functioning state.

Optional desired results:

- Retain the current system identity.
- Keep downtime to a minimum.

Proposed solution:

- Promote a BDC to a PDC.
- Restore the failed hardware, reinstall as a BDC, and then promote the server back to its original state as a PDC.

Which results does the proposed solution produce?

❍ a. The proposed solution produces the required result and produces both of the optional desired results.

❍ b. The proposed solution produces the required result and produces only one of the optional desired results.

❍ c. The proposed solution produces the required result but does not produce any of the optional desired results.

❍ d. The proposed solution does not produce the required result.

The correct answer is a. The proposed solution of promoting a BDC to a PDC while the original PDC is down, repairing the failed hardware, reinstalling as a BDC, and then promoting the server back to a PDC will return the domain to a fully functional state. These activities will retain all system identities, because all BDCs take on the SIDs of their PDCs. Plus, downtime is kept to a minimum. Therefore, the proposed solution fulfills the required result and both of the optional desired results. Another solution to this situation would involve repairing the PDC and then restoring its entire contents from backup. However, this solution would not return full domain functionality until the entire process was complete.

Scenario 9

Suppose the following situation exists:

Two networks have been folded into a single domain. One part of the domain is in New York at the company headquarters, and the other portion is in Los Angeles. A dedicated 56 Kbps leased line connects the two domain halves. The PDC and one BDC reside in New York, and three BDCs reside in L.A. The company manages small, incremental, financial transactions. This causes the bandwidth of the WAN link to be fully utilized nearly 24 hours a day. You've noticed that every few days or so, it seems that changes to the security settings on the system are not fully distributed across the entire domain; for example, passwords aren't being updated, and group memberships aren't being enabled.

Required result:

- Improve the domain controller synchronization.

Optional desired results:

- Guarantee that at least one BDC in each portion of the domain is up to date.
- Keep the level of synchronization traffic to a minimum.

Proposed solution:

- Set PulseConcurrency to 1.
- Set ReplicationGoverner to 50.

Which results does the proposed solution produce?

❍ a. The proposed solution produces the required result and produces both of the optional desired results.

❍ b. The proposed solution produces the required result and produces only one of the optional desired results.

❍ c. The proposed solution produces the required result but does not produce any of the optional desired results.

❍ d. The proposed solution does not produce the required result.

The correct answer is c. The proposed solution should improve the synchronization of domain controllers across the WAN link. There's no way to guarantee that at least one BDC in each portion of the domain is up to date, nor is there a real way to keep synchronization traffic to a minimum. Yes, it's possible to set the timeouts longer so synch packets are transmitted less, but when synchronization is required, bandwidth usage is not the most important concern—success of the communication is. Setting PulseConcurrency to 1 will restrict the PDC to updating a single BDC at a time. This should improve the odds of the synchronization process of the WAN link. Setting the ReplicationGoverner to 50 will reduce the size of the packet used to perform the synchronization. This will result in twice the amount of packets but will increase the chance that they will be delivered over the saturated WAN link. Therefore, the proposed solution fulfills only the required result.

Scenario 10

Suppose the following situation exists:

Your network is spread across six buildings in a single office park. You have a single domain. Each building is connected with a high-speed microwave bridge, so communications can occur between buildings. The PDC and two BDCs reside in the main headquarters building. Every other building in the network has three BDCs within it. Overnight, the cleaning crew spills the mop bucket over the power supply of the PDC, which causes instant destruction of the entire computer.

Required result:

- Allow users to continue to use the network and access resources still present on the network.

Optional desired results:

- Allow changes to the SAM database.
- Restore resources hosted on the original PDC so users can regain access.

Proposed solution:

- Add a new member server to the network.
- Restore the data files from a backup of the original PDC to the member server. Share these resources and grant access based on existing groups.
- Install all applications previously hosted by the original PDC. Configure these applications for network access based on existing groups.

(continued)

Scenario 10 *(continued)*

Which results does the proposed solution produce?

❍ a. The proposed solution produces the required result and produces both of the optional desired results.

❍ b. The proposed solution produces the required result and produces only one of the optional desired results.

❍ c. The proposed solution produces the required result but does not produce any of the optional desired results.

❍ d. The proposed solution does not produce the required result.

The correct answer is c. The proposed solution only grants users the ability to log on and continue to use existing resources. However, this is achieved through no action but is the default mechanism of a domain when the PDC fails and a BDC has not been promoted to a PDC. Adding a new member server to the network is not possible without a PDC present. Therefore, the proposed solution fulfills only the required result. To fully resolve this situation, you would have to promote a BDC to a PDC while the original system is repaired and restored to its original capacity.

Scenario 11

Suppose the following situation exists:

Your Windows NT Server-based domain includes several non-Microsoft servers, namely a Sun SparcStation, a NetWare server, and a Unix server. Each of these alternate servers offers file resources required by most of the network's users. You decide to map network drives on each client via a logon script so access is as simple for users as possible.

Required result:

- Enable users to gain access to the drive shares using a local drive letter.

Optional desired results:

- Keep administration to a minimum so accessing each client system individually is not required.
- Ensure that updates to the logon script can be made quickly and easily, and changes are distributed to clients automatically.

(continued)

Scenario 11 *(continued)*

Proposed solution:

- Employ the Replication service, export from the PDC, and import to all BDCs, using the typical or default configuration of the Replication service.
- Configure all user accounts to launch the nonmsdrivemap.bat script each time they log on.
- Place the nonmsdrivemap.bat script in the %SystemRoot%\System32\Repl\Export directory on the PDC.

Which results does the proposed solution produce?

❍ a. The proposed solution produces the required result and produces both of the optional desired results.

❍ b. The proposed solution produces the required result and produces only one of the optional desired results.

❍ c. The proposed solution produces the required result but does not produce any of the optional desired results.

❍ d. The proposed solution does not produce the required result.

The correct answer is d. The proposed solution does not enable the logon script to be accessed when users log on. The listed directory is incorrect; it should be %SystemRoot%\System32\Repl\Export\Scripts. This directory is where the NETLOGON share is mapped from and where all user accounts will attempt to locate and launch logon scripts from. Furthermore, the Replication service will only replicate data in subdirectories of the Export directory, not files in its root. Therefore, the proposed solution does not satisfy the required result. The optimal solution for this situation would be to place the logon script in the %SystemRoot%\System32\Repl\Export\Scripts directory, and then export to all domain controllers, including the PDC.

Scenario 12

Suppose the following situation exists:

A user complains that his custom desktop settings do no follow him around the network. Each time he logs in to a new system, he gets the default desktop layout.

Required result:

- Configure a profile to follow the user around the network.

Optional desired results:

- Allow the user to configure his own profile.
- Prevent other users from altering his profile.

Proposed solution:

- From a client system where the user has logged in to previously, copy the local profile to a network share.
- Change the configuration setting of the profile from Local to Roaming on the Profiles tab of the System applet.
- On the network share where the profile has been copied, change the NTUSER.DAT file to NTUSER.MAN.

Which results does the proposed solution produce?

❍ a. The proposed solution produces the required result and produces both of the optional desired results.

❍ b. The proposed solution produces the required result and produces only one of the optional desired results.

❍ c. The proposed solution produces the required result but does not produce any of the optional desired results.

❍ d. The proposed solution does not produce the required result.

The correct answer is b. The proposed solution creates a roaming profile for the user that cannot be changed by other users. However, it also cannot be changed by the intended user. Changing the NTUSER.DAT to NTUSER.MAN defines the profile as a mandatory profile, which does not retain custom settings made during a logon session. Therefore, the proposed solution fulfills the required result but only one of the optional desired results. The optimal solution for this situation would be to retain the NTUSER.DAT name and simply set the security controls to the intended user and administrators, and not to define the same profile path for any other user account.

Scenario 13

Suppose the following situation exists:

You've been instructed to restrict control of several functions on user desktops to improve network security. You decide to employ system policies to accomplish your tasks.

Required result:

- Prevent users from changing device drivers' settings.

Optional desired results:

- Define exactly what items appear in a user's Start menu.
- Prevent users from manually mapping network shares.

Proposed solution:

- Employ system policies. Create a default user policy that prevents access to the Control Panel and prevents mapping of shares.
- Create a logon script to automatically create all the network shares a typical user will require.
- View the root directories of each roaming profile to ensure that each NTUSER file has a .DAT extension.

Which results does the proposed solution produce?

❍ a. The proposed solution produces the required result and produces both of the optional desired results.

❍ b. The proposed solution produces the required result and produces only one of the optional desired results.

❍ c. The proposed solution produces the required result but does not produce any of the optional desired results.

❍ d. The proposed solution does not produce the required result.

The correct answer is b. The proposed solution will prevent access to device configuration utilities in the Control Panel and will prevent manual mappings of network shares. However, system policies are not used to define the contents of the Start menu (to be specific, they can prevent items such as Settings and Run from appearing in the Start menu, but they aren't fine-tuning tools for the Start menu). Therefore, the proposed solution fulfills the required result and only one of the optional desired results. To define the contents of users' Start menus, mandatory profiles must be enforced (that is, each NTUSER file must have a .MAN instead of a .DAT extension), and Start menu folder trees must be edited for each profile.

Scenario 14

Suppose the following situation exists:

Your network consists of the following systems:

- Servers:
    - *Windows NT Server 4*—1 PDC, 4 BDCs, 19 member servers
- Clients:
    - *Windows NT Workstation 4*—602
    - *Windows 98*—309
    - *Windows 95*—81

Users have the ability to share local resources with the network. You've noticed that your PDC is operating extremely poorly.

Required result:

- Improve the PDC's performance.

Optional desired results:

- Improve overall resource access.
- Improve authentication process performance.

Proposed solution:

- Set the MaintainServerList Registry entry on all domain controllers to No.
- Set the MaintainServerList Registry entry on all member servers to Yes.
- Set the IsDomainMaster Registry entry to True on one of the member servers.

Which results does the proposed solution produce?

❍ a. The proposed solution produces the required result and produces both of the optional desired results.

❍ b. The proposed solution produces the required result and produces only one of the optional desired results.

❍ c. The proposed solution produces the required result but does not produce any of the optional desired results.

❍ d. The proposed solution does not produce the required result.

The correct answer is a. The proposed solution will improve PDC performance, overall resource access, and authentication process performance. The issue in this situation is the extremely large browse list of resources due to the ability of clients to share resources. By default, the PDC in a network will serve as the Master Browser and up to three BDCs will serve as Backup Browsers. With the number of clients in this network, this places a severe burden on these domain controllers, preventing them from performing their primary functions as efficiently as possible. By disabling their participation in maintaining the browse list and placing this burden on nondomain controllers, all aspects of authentication are improved, and a client's ability to obtain a resource list and access said resources is improved. Therefore, the proposed solution fulfills the required result and both of the optional desired results.

Scenario 15

Suppose the following situation exists:

You need to impose fault tolerance on your Windows NT Server. You've just installed a second SCSI drive controller and connected four hard drives to it.

Required result:

- Create a fault-tolerant drive configuration.

Optional desired results:

- Enable file access auditing.
- Place no restrictions on the number of files in the root directory.

Proposed solution:

- Create a disk stripe set. Format the set with NTFS.

Which results does the proposed solution produce?

❍ a. The proposed solution produces the required result and produces both of the optional desired results.

❍ b. The proposed solution produces the required result and produces only one of the optional desired results.

❍ c. The proposed solution produces the required result but does not produce any of the optional desired results.

❍ d. The proposed solution does not produce the required result.

The correct answer is d. The proposed solution of a disk stripe set does not offer a fault-tolerant drive configuration. This configuration only offers performance improvements. Although the use of NTFS on the configuration allows for auditing and unlimited root directory files, the proposed solution does not fulfill the required result. An optimal solution for this situation would be to create a disk stripe set with parity.

Scenario 16

Suppose the following situation exists:

You need to protect the data on your Windows NT Server system by deploying a fault-tolerant drive configuration.

Required result:

- Protect data stored on the Windows NT Server system.

Optional desired results:

- Provide continuous access to data via protection from drive controller failure.
- Provide continuous access to data via protection from a single drive failure.

Proposed solution:

- Use the NTBACKUP tool native to Windows NT.
- Configure a full backup of the server to occur on Friday evenings. Be sure to select to back up the Registry.
- Configure an incremental backup to occur on every night except for Friday. Be sure to select to back up the Registry.
- Use the AT command with batch files to automate the launching of the backups.

Which results does the proposed solution produce?

❍ a. The proposed solution produces the required result and produces both of the optional desired results.

❍ b. The proposed solution produces the required result and produces only one of the optional desired results.

❍ c. The proposed solution produces the required result but does not produce any of the optional desired results.

❍ d. The proposed solution does not produce the required result.

The correct answer is c. The proposed solution of a regularly scheduled backup will provide protection for the data stored on the server. However, it will not provide continuous uninterrupted access to data if a drive or controller failure occurs. Therefore, the proposed solution fulfills only the required result. An optimal solution for this situation would require a duplex set.

Scenario 17

Suppose the following situation exists:

Your Windows NT Server is protected from device failure with a disk duplex of the system partition. For an unknown reason, the drive hosting the system partition fails. You attempt several reboots only to discover the drive will no longer power up. All drives on the system were formatted with NTFS.

Required result:

- Return the system to a functional state.

Optional desired results:

- Employ a reusable solution.
- Make no changes to the server other than restoring operation

Proposed solution:

- Remove the duplex destination drive from the damaged server. Place the drive into another computer of similar configuration.
- Boot the new system with a DOS floppy, and then employ FDISK to mark the first partition active.

Which results does the proposed solution produce?

❍ a. The proposed solution produces the required result and produces both of the optional desired results.

❍ b. The proposed solution produces the required result and produces only one of the optional desired results.

❍ c. The proposed solution produces the required result but does not produce any of the optional desired results.

❍ d. The proposed solution does not produce the required result.

The correct answer is c. The proposed solution will return the system to a functioning state; however, it will not be a reusable solution (because a new duplex set will not be created), nor will it retain the original state of the server (by making no unnecessary changes). Therefore, the proposed solution satisfies the required result but neither of the optional required results. An optimal solution for this situation would require a custom boot disk for the original server to boot to the duplex drive. When a replacement drive is available, install it and re-create a duplex set using the new drive as the destination of the duplex.

Scenario 18

Suppose the following situation exists:

You've configured a service (named NetMon4) to launch with the security context of the NetApp user account. The service in question is an in-house application that is often tweaked by the programmers. You want to be notified if the service begins to perform extraneous or dangerous operations.

Required result:

- Obtain data regarding the use of the NetApp account.

Optional desired results:

- Track the use of User Rights.
- Track the activation and termination of the NetMon4 service.

Proposed solution:

- Enable auditing. Select to audit both the Success and Failure of the following event types: Logon and Logoff, User of User Rights, and Process Tracking.

Which results does the proposed solution produce?

❍ a. The proposed solution produces the required result and produces both of the optional desired results.

❍ b. The proposed solution produces the required result and produces only one of the optional desired results.

❍ c. The proposed solution produces the required result but does not produce any of the optional desired results.

❍ d. The proposed solution does not produce the required result.

The correct answer is a. The proposed solution of using auditing will collect data about the NetApp user account's logon and logoffs, track the use of User Rights, and record process information about the service itself. Therefore, the proposed solution fulfills the required result and both of the optional desired results.

Scenario 19

Suppose the following situation exists:

Your network is the result of combining three legacy networks: the first was primarily NetWare-based and used IPX/SPX, the second was a Unix-based network, and the third was a Windows NT Advanced Server network that used NetBEUI. After combining the networks, establishing a Windows NT 4 Server-based domain, and adding 50 Windows 98 clients, you need to focus on improving performance.

Required result:

- Improve the performance of the network as a whole.

Optional desired results:

- Simplify administration.
- Grant clients access to resources on a broader range of servers.

Proposed solution:

- Reconfigure all clients and servers to use TCP/IP only.
- Install Microsoft TCP/IP Printing and Simple TCP/IP Services on a Windows NT Server system.
- Install GSNW and FPNW on a Windows NT Server system.
- Deploy IIS with Web and FTP services on a Windows NT Server system.
- Configure the existing clients to employ one or more of these new services.

Which results does the proposed solution produce?

❍ a. The proposed solution produces the required result and produces both of the optional desired results.

❍ b. The proposed solution produces the required result and produces only one of the optional desired results.

❍ c. The proposed solution produces the required result but does not produce any of the optional desired results.

❍ d. The proposed solution does not produce the required result.

The correct answer is b. The proposed solution improves network performance by removing all unnecessary protocols and configuring all systems to use TCP/IP. Because the solution retains TCP/IP and adds five new services, there's definitely an increase in administration overhead. The solution also offers multiple avenues for TCP/IP clients to gain access to services hosted on all of the servers in the network. This might not allow every client to access every type of resource, but it grants a very broad range of access for most clients. Therefore, the proposed solution fulfills the required result and only one of the optional desired results.

Scenario 20

Suppose the following situation exists:

You add a Windows NT Server system into a legacy NetWare network. The existing network hosts various versions of NetWare and several Macintosh clients.

Required result:

- Enable the Windows NT Server to participate in the network.

Optional desired results:

- Allow any Windows-based NetWare client to access resources on the Windows NT Server.
- Allow any Macintosh NetWare client to access resources on the Windows NT Server.

Proposed solution:

- Install NWLink on the Windows NT Server. Set it to AutoDetect Frame Type.

Which results does the proposed solution produce?

❍ a. The proposed solution produces the required result and produces both of the optional desired results.

❍ b. The proposed solution produces the required result and produces only one of the optional desired results.

❍ c. The proposed solution produces the required result but does not produce any of the optional desired results.

❍ d. The proposed solution does not produce the required result.

The correct answer is c. The proposed solution of using AutoDetect Frame Type will cause the Windows NT Server to use only the first detected IPX/SPX frame type. The Windows NT Server will be able to participate in the network, but only with those systems using the detected frame type. There's no guarantee that the detected frame type will be the same one used by all of the NetWare clients. Therefore, the proposed solution fulfills only the required result. An optimal solution for this scenario would be to use Manual Frame Type on the Windows NT Server and define all the frame types in use on the network.

Scenario 21

Suppose the following situation exists:

Security is the most important feature of your company's network. Recently, you've been asked to configure the network to accept dial-up connections for telecommuters.

Required result:

- Enforce security on telecommuter links.

Optional desired results:

- Distinguish between local and remote access.
- Log all attempts to connect over the RAS link.

Proposed solution:

- Deploy a RAS server.
- Configure auditing for Logon and Logoff.
- Create a second duplicate user account for all telecommuters. Grant only the second account dial-up access. Set the Callback option to Set By Caller.
- Audit all File and Object Access for the dial-up enabled user accounts.
- Configure the RAS server to use Microsoft Encrypted Authentication and to encrypt all data.

Which results does the proposed solution produce?

❍ a. The proposed solution produces the required result and produces both of the optional desired results.

❍ b. The proposed solution produces the required result and produces only one of the optional desired results.

(continued)

Scenario 21 *(continued)*

❍ c. The proposed solution produces the required result but does not produce any of the optional desired results.

❍ d. The proposed solution does not produce the required result.

The correct answer is d. The proposed solution does not establish secure telecommuter links, because setting the Callback option to Set By Caller defines the number option. Therefore, the proposed solution does not fulfill the required result. An optimal solution for this scenario would include setting Callback to a predefined number.

Scenario 22

Suppose the following situation exists:

You've subdivided your TCP/IP network into eight segments. Each segment is its own subnet. These subnets are connected by multihomed Windows NT Server systems.

Required result:

- Allow subnets to communicate with each other.

Optional desired results:

- Reduce DHCP and other broadcasts.
- Automate the process of maintaining the routing tables.

Proposed solution:

- Install RIP for IP.
- Allow IP forwarding.
- Configure the DHCP Relay Agent to forward all DHCP messages to the only DHCP server on the network.

Which results does the proposed solution produce?

❍ a. The proposed solution produces the required result and produces both of the optional desired results.

❍ b. The proposed solution produces the required result and produces only one of the optional desired results.

❍ c. The proposed solution produces the required result but does not produce any of the optional desired results.

❍ d. The proposed solution does not produce the required result.

The correct answer is a. The proposed solution allows the multiple subnets to communicate using the Windows NT Servers as routers by enabling IP Forwarding. The DHCP Relay agent reduces DHCP broadcasts, and RIP for IP automates the process of routing table maintenance. Other broadcasts are reduced or at least confined to their own subnet due to the standard operation of routers; Windows NT Server is acting as a router in this scenario. Therefore, the proposed solution fulfills the required result and both of the optional desired results.

Scenario 23

Suppose the following situation exists:

Your Windows NT Server network allows remote Windows NT Workstation clients to dial in. Your primary network is a routed network that is not quite complex enough to justify a DNS server, but it does change often. When RAS clients request resource access, response is very slow. You've determined that this response latency is not due to the RAS link bandwidth.

Required result:

- Improve resource access responsiveness.

Optional desired results:

- Fully automate the RAS improvement solution.
- Keep administration to a minimum.

Proposed solution:

- Create a HOSTS file.
- Place the HOSTS file in the NETLOGON share.
- Create a logon script that copies the HOSTS file from a domain controller to the client's system.
- Configure all dial-up users to launch the logon script when authenticated.

Which results does the proposed solution produce?

❍ a. The proposed solution produces the required result and produces both of the optional desired results.

❍ b. The proposed solution produces the required result and produces only one of the optional desired results.

(continued)

Scenario 23 *(continued)*

❍ c. The proposed solution produces the required result but does not produce any of the optional desired results.

❍ d. The proposed solution does not produce the required result.

The correct answer is b. The proposed solution will improve resource access responsiveness by improving name resolution via placing a HOSTS file on the client. Creating a logon script to copy the HOSTS file to the client simplifies administration and automates the distribution task. However, the HOSTS file will need to be manually updated often, because it cannot be updated automatically. Therefore, the proposed solution fulfills the required result but only one of the optional desired results.

Scenario 24

Suppose the following situation exists:

At the XYZ Corporation, the Research department produces 100+ page documents on a regular basis, yet they have all kinds of shorter documents they need to print during working hours. You've been asked to configure their print services so shorter jobs will not be impeded by the longer, book-length printouts. The Research group is the only group that should have access to the Research group's printers.

Required result:

- Set up print services so book-length jobs print during nonwork hours, from 11:00 P.M. through 5:00 A.M.

Optional desired results:

- Configure short jobs to print immediately.
- Block users who do not work in Research from using the Research group's printers.

Proposed solution:

- Create two logical printers for the network printer.
- Set up the first logical printer for short print jobs.
- Set up the second logical printer for long print jobs and allow the printer to operate only between the hours of 11:00 P.M. and 5:00 A.M.

(continued)

Scenario 24 *(continued)*

- Check permissions on the logical printers to make sure only members of the Research group have print access.
- Instruct users to print short print jobs to the first printer, and book-length print jobs to the second printer.

Which results does the proposed solution produce?

❍ a. The proposed solution produces the required result and produces both of the optional desired results.

❍ b. The proposed solution produces the required result and produces only one of the optional desired results.

❍ c. The proposed solution produces the required result but does not produce any of the optional desired results.

❍ d. The proposed solution does not produce the required result.

The correct answer is a. The proposed solution properly creates a multilogical-printer environment in which short print jobs are submitted to the printer immediately and longer jobs are printed after hours. In addition, the logical printers are secured against access outside of the Research group. Therefore, the proposed solution fulfills the required result and both of the optional desired results.

Scenario 25

Suppose the following situation exists:

You have a small network consisting of a Windows NT Server acting as a PDC with three Windows 98 clients. You want to provide Internet access to the clients by connecting the Windows NT Server system to an ISP.

Required result:

- Grant the clients Internet access.

(continued)

Scenario 25 *(continued)*

Optional desired results:

- Allow clients to be assigned Internet IP addresses on demand.
- Support encrypted data transmission and authentication.

Proposed solution:

- Use RAS to make a PPP connection to an ISP.
- Deploy a proxy server to grant clients Internet access but isolate them from direct external communications.
- Configure clients to use a private IP address and to communicate with the proxy server for all Internet communications.

Which results does the proposed solution produce?

❍ a. The proposed solution produces the required result and produces both of the optional desired results.

❍ b. The proposed solution produces the required result and produces only one of the optional desired results.

❍ c. The proposed solution produces the required result but does not produce any of the optional desired results.

❍ d. The proposed solution does not produce the required result.

The correct answer is b. The proposed solution grants all clients Internet access via a proxy server. Because PPP is used to connect to the ISP, encrypted authentication and data transfers are supported. The use of private IP addresses on clients, and the positioning of a proxy server between the clients and the Internet, prevents on-demand assignment of Internet IP addresses. Although this means one of the optional desired results is not fulfilled, the proposed solution is a more secure configuration. Therefore, the proposed solution fulfills the required result but only one of the optional desired results.

Scenario 26

Suppose the following situation exists:

On a Windows NT Server-based domain, you want to add several Macintosh clients. Your company policy states that all data files must reside on a server.

Required result:

- Allow Macintosh clients to communicate on your network.

Optional desired results:

- Provide a share for Macintosh clients to use for file storage.
- Audit network logons of Macintosh clients.

Proposed solution:

- Enable auditing for Logon and Logoff.
- Install the AppleTalk protocol.

Which results does the proposed solution produce?

❍ a. The proposed solution produces the required result and produces both of the optional desired results.

❍ b. The proposed solution produces the required result and produces only one of the optional desired results.

❍ c. The proposed solution produces the required result but does not produce any of the optional desired results.

❍ d. The proposed solution does not produce the required result.

The correct answer is d. The proposed solution does not enable Macintosh clients to communicate on the network. The Windows NT Services for Macintosh add-on must be installed first, with an NTFS partition present, and then AppleTalk can be installed. Therefore, the proposed solution does not fulfill the required result.

Scenario 27

Suppose the following situation exists:

You're the system administrator for a large company. You must design a networking system that will support your company's online needs.

Required result:

- Ensure that all users and groups are centrally managed.

Optional desired results:

- Allow resources to be managed from within the department in which they are located.
- Support a user base expansion to at least 40,000 individuals.

Proposed solution:

- Deploy a single domain network based on Windows NT Server 4.

Which results does the proposed solution produce?

❍ a. The proposed solution produces the required result and produces both of the optional desired results.

❍ b. The proposed solution produces the required result and produces only one of the optional desired results.

❍ c. The proposed solution produces the required result but does not produce any of the optional desired results.

❍ d. The proposed solution does not produce the required result.

The correct answer is c. The proposed solution of a single domain network will offer centralized control over users and groups; that's the benefit of a domain over a workgroup. However, it will not limit resource control to departments because any administrator can manipulate resources and a single domain cannot support 40,000 users. Therefore, the proposed solution fulfills the required result but does not fulfill either of the optional desired results.

Scenario 28

Suppose the following situation exists:

You have a multiserver domain that hosts valuable data. You must protect this data from loss. Your network is managed by four administrators, and each of them has a unique administrator account. The administrators are members of the local Administrators group only on the server they are assigned to control.

Required result:

- Maintain a backup of all data on all servers.

Optional desired results:

- Store a week's worth of data on a single media type.
- Automate the backup process.

Proposed solution:

- Install a backup device on a single server with enough capacity to store a full backup and several days of incremental backups on the same media.
- Create a user account called BackupOps and grant it membership in the Domain Admins group.
- Configure the backup software to protect all data on all servers by performing a full backup every Friday and an incremental backup every other day.

Which results does the proposed solution produce?

❍ a. The proposed solution produces the required result and produces both of the optional desired results.

❍ b. The proposed solution produces the required result and produces only one of the optional desired results.

❍ c. The proposed solution produces the required result but does not produce any of the optional desired results.

❍ d. The proposed solution does not produce the required result.

The correct answer is a. The proposed solution provides a means by which the backup software is automatically executed on a regular basis with sufficient privileges (via user rights) to back up all data on all drives. Therefore, the proposed solution fulfills the required result and both of the optional desired results.

Online Resources

Here's a collection of online resources that might help you to prepare for your Microsoft certification exam. Many of these Web sites include sample questions, study materials, and study tips for Windows NT Server in the Enterprise and other exams.

- **http://209.207.167.177** is the BrainDump Heaven site, on which you can find peer discussions on topics and issues.
- **http://home.nycap.rr.com/blaineman/mcselinks.html** is a personal page that contains links to MCSE-related sites.
- **http://imedoff.virtualave.net/mcse.htm** is a personal page that con tains links to MCSE-related sites.
- **http://leuthard.ch/mcse/** is the Checkpoint MCSE site, on which you can find free practice tests and links to MCSE-related sites.
- **http://stsware.com/microsts.htm** is the Self Test Software site that has practice tests for sale.
- **www.america.net/~dhack/mcse** is a personal MCSE page that con tains links to newsgroups and other resources.
- **www.axxa.com/certcorner/default.asp** is the Axxa Corporation page that contains a collection of study materials, reference sites, and MCSE information.

- **www.certificationinsider.com** is The Coriolis Group's Certification Insider Press site, on which you can find information about Exam Cram/Exam Prep books and other certification products, as well as free online sample tests.
- **www.certificationshack.com** is the Certification Shack site, on which you can find general MCSE information.
- **www.certify.com** is the Cyber Pass site. You can order MCSE practice tests from this site.
- **www.commandcentral.com** is the CommandCentral site, on which you can find free practice tests.
- **www.computingcentral.msn.com/topics/windowsnt/chat.asp** is the MSN, Computing Central, Windows NT chat forum where you can ask questions of peers and experts.
- **www.cramsession.com** is the CramSession site, on which you can find study guides, free practice questions via email and online, and general certification information.
- **www.cyber-1.com/mcse** is an MCSE study group site.
- **www.geocities.com/~mcse_mct** is a personal page that contains MCSE information and resource links.
- **www.goodground.com/index.htm** is the GoodGround site, on which you can find links and free online sample tests.
- **www.hardcoremcse.com** is the HardcoreMCSE site, which contains study aids and links, and sells practice exams.
- **www.inquiry.com** is the Inquiry.com site, on which you can find gen eral technology information.
- **www.internexis.com/mcp** is an MCSE chat and study site.
- **www.learnquick.com** is LearnQuick's site, which offers accelerated MCSE training and tons of MCSE resources.
- **www.matisse.net/files/glossary.html** contains a glossary of Internet terms that can be very helpful.

- **www.mattscasa.com/netindex.htm** is a personal site that contains free practice tests.
- **www.mcpmag.com** is the Microsoft Certified Professional online magazine.
- **www.mcseinfo.com** is the MCSEInfo.com site that includes study tips, review information, and links to MCSE-related sites.
- **www.mcsetutor.com** is the MCSETutor.com site that offers test dis cussions, book reviews, and links to free online tests.
- **www.network-info.com/Links/links.html** is the Network-Info.com site, on which you can find links to MCSE-related sites.
- **www.ptek.com/links.asp** is a personal page that contains many MCSE/ MCP-related links.
- **www.rad.com/networks/netterms.htm** is RAD University's general networking information and reference page. It's not MCSE specific.
- **www.saluki.com/mcp** is the MCP Online site that contains questions and topical discussions. This site is the host of an MCSE mailing list.
- **www.tekmetrics.com/cert** is the e-certifications site that contains in formation about non-Microsoft certifications.
- **www.testfree.com** is the TestFree site that offers free practice tests.

Glossary

AATP (Authorized Academic Training Program)—This program authorizes accredited academic institutions of higher learning to offer Microsoft Certified Professional testing and training. The institutions are also allowed to use the Microsoft Education course materials and Microsoft Certified Trainers.

account—See *user account.*

account policy—A setting that establishes how passwords on a domain or a workstation are used.

ACL (access control list)—The attribute of each object that defines which users and groups have what level of services for an object.

Administrator—The person responsible for the upkeep, management, and security of a network. Also, the Administrator is a built-in user in Windows NT that has full control of the system.

advanced user rights—The set of user rights that are not commonly associated with normal network use. These rights aid with software development and specialized process operation.

alias—An alternate name for an email address.

AppleTalk—Apple Computer's networking protocols and software.

architecture—A network's setup and how the network's components interconnect.

ASCII (American Standard Code For Information Interchange)—A way of coding that translates letters, numbers, and symbols into digital form.

ASP (Active Server Pages)—A type of HTML or other Web document-distribution system used by IIS version 3.

assessment exam—Similar to the certification exam, these tests give you the opportunity to answer questions similar to the questions appearing on the certification exams but, at your own pace. Assessment exams also utilize the same tools as certification exams, which allows you to familiarize yourself with the exam tools.

ATEC (Authorized Technical Education Center)—The location where you can take Microsoft Official Curriculum courses taught by Microsoft Certified Trainers.

auditing—In the Security log of a server or workstation, it is the method of tracking and recording the activities of various users.

Auto Frame Type Detection—A process in Windows NT that automatically detects the frame types for a network. This setting must be changed for NWLink (IPX/SPX).

AUTOEXEC.BAT—A DOS batch file that is launched when a computer is started or booted.

backup—A method of fault tolerance where computer data is saved on some type of external storage media.

Backup Browser—Computer on a Windows NT network that maintains a duplicate list of the network's resources and acts in a similar way within the Browser service as BDCs act within domain control.

backup operators—A designated group in Windows Windows NT that has the permission to log on to a domain and back up a particular server or workstation.

basevideo—A command-line parameter switch used on the BOOT.INI file. It forces Windows NT to boot using 16-color VGA video at 640×480. This setting appears by default on the ARC name line identified by "[VGA mode]".

BDC (Backup Domain Controller)—A backup server that protects the integrity and availability of the SAM database. BDCs are not able to make any changes or modifications, but they can use the database to authenticate users.

beta—A version of software released for general public testing. A beta is pre-final release and often contains unresolved issues, bugs, or undocumented features.

beta exam—A test exam given to participants at a Sylvan Prometric Testing Center before the development of the Microsoft Certified Professional certification exam. The final exam is based on the results of the beta exam.

BIOS (Basic Input/Output System)—A system that houses the buffers used to transfer information from a program to the hardware devices receiving the information.

blue screen—A screen that appears when a GPF occurs in Windows NT. This is a test display of the STOP message error. There are lots of details included on this screen, such as the location of the error, type of error, and whether or not a memory dump is created.

blueprint survey—A part of the development process of the Microsoft certification exam where data is gathered from qualified job function experts. This survey determines the importance, required competence, and weighting for each individual exam objective.

boot disk—A hard drive or floppy with bootstrap files on it that enable an operating system to launch.

boot menu—The text menu that appears immediately after the hardware test on a Windows NT machine. It lists all known operating systems present. The OS listed first is booted by default when the timeout period expires unless an alternate OS is manually selected.

BOOT.INI—One of the files placed on the system partition that contains the location of the system files for each OS installed on the machine. The locations are listed using ARC names.

BOOTP—Protocol used by diskless workstations to obtain boot data on IP-based networks; precursor to DHCP (which remains backward compatible with BOOTP to this day).

BOOTSECT.DOS—The file containing DOS boot sector data, which appears in the system partition only on a multiboot machine that numbers DOS, Windows, Windows 95, or some other near-DOS equivalent among the list of boot options in BOOT.INI.

bottleneck—The effect of trying to force too much information through a system with inadequate bandwidth, causing the system to slow significantly.

break mirror—The first step in repairing a mirrored set. This is accomplished in the Disk Administrator utility, using the Break Mirror option in the Fault Tolerance drop-down menu.

broadcast packets—The information packet sent from one user to all other users on a network.

browse list—The list of available computers and resources on a Windows NT network. This list is never viewed directly by the user; however, numerous applications pull data from this list to offer users a context-based selection of resources.

Browser service—A utility that maintains a list of network resources within a domain, and provides lists of these domains, servers, and resource objects to any Explorer-type interface that requests it (e.g., browse lists).

buffer settings—Controls the buffer size used by Network Monitor to store captured frames.

buffer space—In the Capture Trigger dialog box, it is the area used to set the accepted percentage levels for usage of system objects.

cache—A specified area of high-speed memory used to contain data that is going to be or recently has been accessed.

callback—A security feature in which a RAS connection is only established after the server has disconnected the inbound call and then called the user back.

capture—The process of recording data for later perusal. Network Monitor captures frames to be viewed for protocol-level inspection.

change permissions—In NTFS file systems, it is one of the standard access file permissions. It allows an object's access permissions to be altered.

Chart view—In Performance Monitor, it is the view that allows users to peruse realtime data in a line graph or histogram form.

checksums—The sum of a group of data. The sum is used to guarantee that data is transmitted without any errors.

command line—A DOS prompt that accepts DOS-based commands.

computer name—The name of a computer on a LAN that is specific to an individual workstation or server.

CONFIG.POL—In the NETLOGON share, this is the file where all policies are stored.

Control Panel—In Windows, this is the area where you modify system settings, such as fonts, screen color, SCSI hardware, and printers, among others.

CPU (central processing unit)—The "brains" of your computer. This is the area where all functions are performed.

CSNW (Client Service For NetWare)—Designed for Windows NT Workstations that require a direct link to NetWare servers, CSNW lets Windows NT machines link up to and browse NetWare resources alongside Microsoft Windows Network resources.

cut score—On the Microsoft Certified Professional exam, it is the lowest score a person can receive and still pass.

default—A factory-enabled setting placed in effect until a user specifies otherwise.

device driver—Software that gives Windows NT the ability to use hardware connected to the computer. This hardware includes modems, printers, mouse, monitor, even the computer itself.

DEVICE.LOG—A log file used by RAS to capture communications between software and a modem when attempting to establish a dial-up connection. This file is located in Winnt\System32\ras.

DHCP (Dynamic Host Configuration Protocol)—A service that enables the assignment of dynamic TCP/IP network addresses, based on a specified pool of available addresses.

Dial-Up Networking—A utility found in the RAS Phonebook|Programs|Accessories folder of the Start menu that controls the dial-out capabilities of RAS.

directory replication—A service designed to disseminate often-used and regularly updated data (such as user profiles, logon scripts, and system policies) to multiple computers to speed file access and improve reliability.

disaster recovery—A plan that determines how to reinstate computer operations if a disaster or catastrophe occurs.

Disk Administrator—An administration application in the Administrative Tools group that lets an administrator create and delete stripe sets and various disk partitions, change the assignment of drive letters, and display facts about a partition's size and setup.

disk duplexing—A fault tolerance method used by Windows NT that uses a duplicate physical and logical drive on a separate hard disk where the drive is connected to the system via a separate controller. If the original drive or controller fails, the system continues to operate using the duplexed drive.

disk mirroring—A fault tolerance method used by Windows NT that creates an exact duplicate of one physical and logical storage device on a separate physical storage device, both attached to the same controller.

disk partition—A portion of a hard disk that acts like a physically separate unit.

disk striping—A fault tolerance method used by Windows NT that stores data across multiple physical storage devices.

distribution files—The 80+ MB of files used to install Windows NT. These are located on the CD in the \i386 directory for the Intel platform, \mips for MIPS, \alpha for DEC Alpha, and \PPC for the Macintosh Power PC. This can also refer to the additional driver library stored in the \drvlib directory.

DLC (Data Link Control)—A protocol used to interoperate with IBM mainframes and provide connectivity to network-attached print devices.

DLLs (dynamic link libraries)—Small executable program routines or device drivers stored in separate files and loaded by the OS when called upon by a process or hardware device.

DMB (Domain Master Browser)—In Windows NT networks, a browser that communicates resource lists across subnets within the same domain.

DNS (Domain Name Service)—A system used to resolve host names into IP addresses.

domain—A group of computers and peripheral devices that share a common security database.

domain controller—A computer that authenticates domain logons as well as manages the Security Accounts Manager (SAM) database.

domain database—A database maintained by a PDC or BDC that stores three types of information: user accounts, computer accounts, and group accounts. Each user account requires 1 K, each computer account requires 5 K, and each group account requires 4 K.

domain guest—A group in which the members are given the minimal level of user access to all domain resources. The Guest account is automatically a member of this group.

domain model—A tool used by Microsoft to describe and define organizational schemes for networks. In theory, the domain model can scale up to handle any size network.

DOS (Disk Operating System)—The most common of all PC operating systems. It reaches back into the early 1980s to provide a primitive single-user OS.

drivers—Software that bonds a peripheral device to the operating system.

election packet—The electronic communication used by a browser (Master, Backup, or Potential) to initiate a new selection of a Master Browser when the current Master Browser is no longer accessible or when a new machine goes online.

encryption—The method of coding data so a person has to have a decoding key to decipher the information.

ERD (Emergency Repair Disk)—A miniature first aid kit for Windows NT. This single floppy contains all the files needed to repair system partition and many boot partition related problems.

Ethernet—The most widely used type of LAN, developed by Xerox.

Event log—An option in the Event Viewer in the Administrative Tools group that displays the events that have taken place on a particular computer.

Event Viewer—An application in Windows NT that displays log files and lets you modify them.

Everyone—A default group that lists each user within a domain as a member. This group cannot be deleted or renamed.

Exam Preparation Guides—Guides that provide information specific to Microsoft Certified Professional exams to help students prepare for the exam.

Exam Study Guide—Short for *Microsoft Certified Professional Program Exam Study Guide*, it contains information about more than one of the Microsoft Certified Professional exams.

FAT (File Allocation Table)—A table originally used by the DOS file system to keep information about the properties, location, and size of files being stored on a disk.

fault tolerance—The ability of a computer to work continuously, even when there is a system failure.

firewall—A barrier between two networks made of software and/or hardware that permits only authorized communication to pass.

FPNW (File And Print Services For NetWare)—A service that makes resources from a Windows NT Server available to NetWare clients, without requiring additional software or configuration changes.

FQDN (fully qualified domain name)—The complete site name of an Internet computer system.

FTP (File Transfer Protocol)—A protocol that transfers files to and from a local hard drive to an FTP server located elsewhere on another TCP/IP-based network (such as the Internet).

Full Control—In Windows NT Server, a permission that grants a person general permissions in addition to the authority to change permissions.

GDI (Graphics Device Interface)—Provides network applications with a system for presenting graphical information. The GDI works as a translator between an application's print request and a device driver interface (DDI) so a job is rendered accurately.

global groups—Groups that apply to all computers within a network. A global group needs to be defined only once for each domain. Global groups may only have users as members.

Gopher services—Provides text-only information over the Internet, most suited to large documents with little or no formatting or images.

GPF (general protection fault)—A severe error in the Windows 95 or Windows 3.x environment that causes the PC to crash or freeze.

graphics—Pictures and images created on a computer.

groups—Collections of users defined together with a common name and resource permissions.

GSNW (Gateway Service For NetWare)—A service that enables Windows NT Server to map a drive to a NetWare server and provides access to NetWare server resources for Windows NT Workstations (via a gateway).

GUI (graphical user interface)—A computer interface that uses graphics, windows, and a trackball or mouse as the method of interaction with the computer.

HAL (Hardware Abstraction Layer)—In the Windows NT operating system, it creates a bridge between the Windows NT operating system and a computer's CPU.

hard drive—Permanent storage area for data. It is also called the hard disk.

hardware—The physical components of a computer system.

HCL (Hardware Compatibility List)—A list that comes with Windows NT Server that tells you what hardware is compatible with the software. The most updated versions of this list can be found on the Microsoft Web site or on the TechNet CD.

hive—A section of the Windows NT Registry.

HOSTS file—A static list of FQDNs mapped to IP addresses.

HTML (Hypertext Markup Language)—Based on SGML, it is the markup language used to create Web pages.

HTTP (Hypertext Transfer Protocol)—This is the World Wide Web protocol that allows for the transfer of HTML documents over the Internet or intranets that respond to actions like a user clicking on hypertext links.

IDE (Integrated Device Electronics)—A type of storage device interface where the electronics required to operate the drive are stored on the drive itself, thus eliminating the need for a separate controller card.

IEEE (Institute Of Electrical And Electronic Engineers)—A group of technical professionals who sponsor technical conferences worldwide, publish over 25 percent of the world's technical papers, and contribute significantly to the establishment of technical standards.

IIS (Internet Information Server)—A Web server software by Microsoft. It is included and implemented with Windows NT Server.

instructor-led course—Usually held in a classroom setting, a course led by an instructor.

interdomain trusts—Another, more descriptive name for a trust. A trust is established between two domains connected only by electronic network pathways. Thus, any trust within Windows NT is an interdomain trust.

Internet—The collection of TCP/IP-based networks around the world.

intranet—An internal private network that uses the same protocols and standards as the Internet.

I/O error—A computer malfunction relating to the communication between one component and another. I/O errors usually relate to storage devices or modems.

IP address—Four sets of numbers separated by decimal points that represent the numeric address of a computer attached to a TCP/IP network, such as the Internet.

IPC (Interprocess Communications)—Within an operating system, it is the exchange of data between applications.

IPCONFIG—In the Windows NT version of TCP/IP, a command-line utility that displays IP configuration details.

IPX/SPX (Internetwork Packet Exchange/Sequenced Packet Exchange)—The name of Novell's NetWare protocol that was reinvented by Microsoft and implemented in Windows NT under the name NWLink. This protocol is fully compatible with Novell's version and, in many cases, is a better implementation than the original.

IRQ (Interrupt Request)—On a PC, it is a hardware interrupt.

ISA (Industry Standard Architecture)—An acronym that refers to the design of the 16-bit AT bus developed by IBM.

ISDN (Integrated Services Digital Network)—A dedicated form of digital communication that has a bandwidth of 128 Kbps.

ISO (International Organization for Standardization)—An association based in Paris that is responsible for setting international data communications standards.

job function expert—A person who knows just about everything about a particular job function and the software products/technologies related to that job. Typically, a job function expert is performing the job, has recently performed the job, or is training people to perform the job.

kernel—The essential part of an operating system that provides basic services.

Kernel Debugger—A feature that records the activity of Windows NT during boot up and when a STOP error occurs.

LAN (local area network)—A network confined to a single building or geographic area and comprised of servers, workstations, peripheral devices, a network operating system, and a communications link.

LAN Manager—A network operating system product developed by Microsoft that is deployed as a server application under OS/2.

Last Known Good Configuration—A recording made by Windows NT of all the Registry settings that existed the last time a user successfully logged in to a server.

LMHOSTS—The predecessor to WINS, it is a static list of NetBIOS names mapped to IP addresses.

local group—A group of users on a single domain that is set up and given privileges and rights to local resources on that domain. Local groups may contain users or global groups.

lockout—In Windows NT security, it is a feature used to prevent compromised accounts from being used.

logical partitions—The segments created when a physical hard drive is divided. Each segment can be used independently of the others, including belonging to separate volumes and hosting different file systems. Most logical partitions have a drive letter assigned to them and can be referred to by an ARC name.

logical printers—The software component used by Windows NT to direct print jobs from applications to a print server. A physical printer can be serviced by numerous logical printers.

logoff—The process by which a user quits using a computer system.

logon—The process by which a user gains access or signs onto a computer system.

logon scripts—Files that consist of a set of network commands that must be carried out in a particular order.

LPD (Line Printer Daemon)—Originally a Unix component, the LPD service receives documents from LPR clients and sends them to a printer. An LPD is essentially a print server.

LPR (Line Printer Remote)—A command-line utility provide by Windows NT used for directing and monitoring print jobs aimed for Unix host printers.

MAC (Media Access Control)—In the IEEE 802 network, it is the lowest of the two sublayers of the Data Link layer.

Master Browser—A tool used to maintain the main list of all available resources within a domain (including links to external domains).

master domain model—An organizational structure in which user management is centralized in a single domain, resource management is centralized into separate resource domains, and trusts are set up between the domains to provide user access to resources.

MBR (Master Boot Record)—A BIOS bootstrap routine used by low-level, hardware-based system code stored in Read-Only Memory (ROM) to initiate the boot sequence on a PC.

MCI (multiple-choice item)—An item within a series of items that is the answer to a question (single-response MCI) or one of the answers to a question (multiple-response MCI).

MCP (Microsoft Certified Professional)—An individual who has taken and passed at least one of the Microsoft certification exams.

MCSD (Microsoft Certified Solution Developer)—An individual with this certification has passed the four necessary exams and is qualified to create and develop business solutions using the Microsoft development tools, technologies, and platforms.

MCSE (Microsoft Certified Systems Engineer)—An individual with this certification has passed the six necessary exams and is an expert on Windows NT and the Microsoft BackOffice integrated family of server software. This individual can also plan, implement, maintain, and support information systems associated with these products.

MCT (Microsoft Certified Trainer)—An individual who is qualified by Microsoft to instruct Microsoft Education courses at sites authorized by Microsoft.

Microsoft certification exam—A test created by Microsoft to verify the mastery of a software product, technology, or computing topic.

Microsoft Certified Professional Certification Update—A newsletter for Microsoft Certified Professional candidates and Microsoft Certified Professionals.

Microsoft official curriculum—Microsoft education courses that support the certification exam process and are created by the Microsoft product groups.

Microsoft Roadmap To Education And Certification—An application based on Microsoft Windows that takes you through the process of determining your certification goals and planning how you can achieve them.

Microsoft Sales Fax Service—A service provided by Microsoft where you can obtain Exam Preparation Guides, fact sheets, and additional information about the Microsoft Certified Professional program.

Microsoft Solution Provider—An organization not directly related to Microsoft that provides integration, consulting, technical support, and other services related to Microsoft products.

Microsoft TechNet (Technical Information Network)—A service provided by Microsoft that provides helpful information via a monthly CD-ROM. TechNet is the primary source of technical information for people who support and/or educate end users, create automated solutions, or administer networks and/or databases.

mirror set—A pair of disks that have been duplicated using the Windows NT disk mirroring fault tolerance method.

Modems applet—An application you use to install and maintain a modem.

MOLI (Microsoft Online Institute)—An organization that offers training materials, online forums, user groups, and online classes.

motherboard—A term that refers to the main circuit board in a computer system.

MPR (Multiprotocol Router)—A device that converts various email formats.

MRI (multiple-rating item)—An item that gives you a task and a proposed solution. Every time a task is given, an alternate solution is provided, and the candidate must choose the answer that gives the best results produced by one solution.

MSDN (Microsoft Developer Network)—The official source for Software Development Kits (SDKs), Device Driver Kits (DDKs), operating systems, and programming information associated with creating applications for Microsoft Windows and Windows NT.

multicasts—Transmitting a message to several recipients simultaneously.

multichannel—Having more than a single inbound or outbound communications port, link, or connection.

Multilink PPP (MP)—The combining of the bandwidth of multiple physical links, which increases the total bandwidth that can be used for a RAS connection.

multiple master domain model—A domain model that has two or more master domains that trust each other via two-way trust relationships. The model also provides centralized administration of user accounts.

multitasking—The ability to run more than one computer application on a system at a time.

NDA (nondisclosure agreement)—A legal agreement that binds two parties to maintain secrecy regarding the subject of the agreement; an instrument commonly used by Microsoft to keep its vendors and partners quiet about software until it's commercially released.

NDIS (Network Driver Interface Specification)—A device driver specification developed by both Microsoft and 3Com that provides hardware and protocol independence for network drivers. NDIS is used by LAN Manager and Vines, and it is supported by several vendors of network cards.

net commands—The collection of DOS-based commands used to modify and operate a network. A net command is the leading executable "net" followed by parameters indicating the function to be performed.

NetBEUI (NetBIOS Extended User Interface)—A simple Network layer transport protocol that was developed to support NetBIOS networks.

NetBIOS (Network Basic Input/Output System)—Originally developed by IBM in the 1980s, this protocol provides the underlying communication mechanism for some basic Windows NT functions, such as browsing and interprocess communications between network servers.

NETLOGON—An administrative share that is created and used within domain controllers for authenticating users who are logging on to the enterprise domain.

netmask—When using static routing, it is one of the options presented in the command-line command **route**. It specifies the subnet mask value to be associated with the **route** entry.

Netstat—A utility that displays TCP/IP status and statistics.

NetWare—A popular network operating system from Novell.

Network Client Administrator—Located in the Start|Administrative Tools menu, it's used to create a boot disk or a set of startup disks for DOS workstations.

Network Monitor—A tool used for investigating network-related problems.

NIC (network interface card)—An adapter card used to connect a computer to a network.

non-seed router—A Macintosh term referring to an AppleTalk router (usually a software implementation) that is unable to distribute new network addresses to clients.

NTFS (New Technology File System)—A naming file system used in Windows NT.

NTLDR file—The executable program launched by the boot files that load the Windows NT kernel. The name is a shortened version of "NT Loader."

null modem cable—An RS-232 cable used to enable two computers within close proximity to communicate without a modem.

NWLink—Microsoft's "clean room" implementation of Novell's IPX/SPX protocol suite for NetWare networks.

ODI (Open Data-link Interface)—Developed by Novell, this is a device driver standard that lets you run several protocols on the same network adapter card.

operating system—A software program that controls the operations of a computer system.

OSI (Open Systems Interconnect)—A standard by the ISO that defines the framework required to implement seven-layer protocols within worldwide communications.

pagefile—The file used by the virtual memory manager to temporarily store segments or pages of memory to hard disk.

PAP (Password Authentication Protocol)—A clear-text authentication protocol.

parity—Redundant segments of data used to provide fault tolerance for stored information. Within Windows NT, this term is most commonly used when discussing stripe sets with parity. Parity is a disk storage configuration where additional data is written in separate drives in 64 K blocks so that in the event of a single drive failure, all data can be reconstructed.

partition—A portion of a hard disk or memory.

passwords—A word used by an individual to gain access to a particular system or application.

PDC (Primary Domain Controller)—The central storage and management server for the SAM database.

Performance Monitor—A graphical application that lets you set, graph, log, and report alerts. It is also referred to as PerfMon.

permissions—A setting configuration assigned to files and folders to determine who has access rights to the resources.

PGP (Pretty Good Privacy)—An encryption program that is not native to Windows NT.

Phonebook entry—A collection of settings used by RAS to establish a connection with a remote dial-up server. A phonebook entry contains details such as phone number, name, password, protocol settings, and encryption type.

physical disk—The hardware component that adds additional storage space. A physical disk must be partitioned and formatted with a file system before data can be stored on it.

PING—A TCP/IP command used to verify the existence and connect to remote hosts over a network.

policies—A set of specifications or limitations that delimit the environment of a user. Windows NT has three policies: account, user rights, and audit.

Potential Browser—A computer that can participate in the support of the list of resources for a domain. A Potential Browser is automatically elected to a position of Backup or Master browser by the Browser Service as needed.

Power Users—A user group found on Windows NT Workstation. Also, users who are well versed in the operation and modification of a computing system—users who push an operating system to its limits.

PPP (Point-To-Point Protocol)—An industry standard protocol used to establish network-protocol-supporting links over POTS lines using modems.

PPTP (Point-To-Point Tunneling Protocol)—Enables "tunneling" of IPX, NetBEUI, and TCP/IP inside PPP packets in such a way as to establish a secure link between a client and server over the Internet.

primary partition—A logical designation on a physical hard drive where the main files for an operating system can reside. In Windows NT, a physical disk might contain four primary partitions or three primary partitions and a single extended partition.

print device—The physical hardware device that produces printed output.

print driver—The software component that enables communication between the operating system and a physical printing device.

print jobs—A document or image sent from a client to a printer. A print job is typically in Windows EMF or the RAW language of the printer.

Print Operators—A default group that has full control over all printers within a domain.

print queues—The list of print jobs waiting to be sent to a printer for processing. The print queue can be viewed by opening the printer folder for any individual logical printer.

print server—The computer that hosts the spool file for a printer and is physically attached to the printer.

printer—Typically refers to the logical printer (software component) within the Windows NT environment as opposed to the physical printing device.

printer pool—A collection of identical printers that are served by a single, logical printer.

printing device—The hardware device that creates marks on paper in the pattern dictated by the driver software.

priorities—The method of designating the order or importance of a process to gain processing time.

process tracking—A type of Audit event that records process activities, such as handle duplication, indirect object access, and process termination.

protocol binding—The process Windows NT uses to link network components from various levels of a network architecture to enable communication between components.

protocols—In networking, this is a set of rules that define how information is transmitted over a network.

proxy server—A computer that intercepts network communications attempting to cross defined boundaries. A proxy server also performs the needed operations on behalf of originating clients. A proxy server allows dissimilar or restricted networks to communicate while isolating the identity of the client.

RAID (Redundant Array of Inexpensive Disks)—A standardized method used to categorize fault tolerance storage systems. Windows NT implements Level 0, Level 1, and Level 5 RAID through software.

RAS (Remote Access Service)—A Windows NT service that provides remote network communication for remote clients over telecommunication lines. RAS connections are different from standard, direct-network connections only in relation to speed.

RDISK—The second segment of an ARC name, used with the initial segment of MULTI, to indicate the ordinal number of the physical storage device.

Read access—The ability to view and open a file or document.

redirector—A software component that intercepts and guides I/O requests to the proper server.

Registry—The hierarchical database that serves as a repository for hardware, software, and OS configuration information.

replication—A service of Windows NT that automatically distributes files and directories from one server to multiple servers and workstations on a network.

Replicator group—The default group whose members have permissions to access the replication service and directories. This group is exclusively used by the Directory Replication service and the user account created for the service.

Resource Kit—Additional documentation and software utilities distributed by Microsoft to offer added information and instruction on the proper operation and modification of Microsoft products.

rights—Settings that define the ability of a user to access a computer or domain.

RIP (Routing Internet Protocol)—A router protocol that enables communication between routers on a network to facilitate the exchange of routing tables.

router—A device or a software implementation that enable interoperability and communication across networks.

SAM (Security Accounts Manager)—The security database of Windows NT that maintains a record of all users, groups, and permissions within a domain. The SAM is stored on the PDC and duplicated on the BDCs.

SAP (Service Advertising Protocol)—An IPX service that broadcasts services and addresses on a network.

SCSI (Small Computer System Interface)—A standard interface defined by ANSI that provides high-speed connections to devices such as hard drives, scanners, and printers.

security—A manner of protecting data by restricting access to authorized users.

seed router—A Macintosh term that refers to an AppleTalk router (usually a software implementation) that is able to distribute new network addresses to clients.

segment—A division of a network. Usually a single length of cable or a collection of cables and hosts that share a common element or purpose.

Server Manager—The Windows NT administration utility where computer accounts are managed.

Server Operators—The default group whose members can manage domain servers.

Service Pack—A patch or fix distributed by Microsoft after the final release of a product to repair errors, bugs, and security breaches.

Services applet—The Control Panel utility where services can be started and stopped, and their startup parameters modified.

SFM (Services For Macintosh)—The set of file system extensions and AppleTalk support modules that permit Macintosh clients to access files, printers, and other services on a Windows NT Server.

share-level permissions—The setting of user/group access on a network share. The permissions of a network share must be met by users before access to the object itself is granted.

shares—A network construct that enables remote users to access resources located throughout a network.

SID (Security ID)—A code assigned to users, groups, and computers by Windows NT to identify them. Even when the name of an object changes, Windows NT recognizes the object by its SID. Every SID is unique.

SLIP (Serial Line Internet Protocol)—An older industry standard for RAS communication links. SLIP is included with Windows NT only for establishing connections with Unix systems that do not support the newer PPP standard.

SMP (Symmetric Multiprocessing)—A processing scheme for multiprocessor systems where each CPU can execute any process.

SMS (Systems Management Server)—A Microsoft product used for high-end management and administration of an enterprise-level network.

SMTP (Simple Mail Transfer Protocol)—An Internet protocol used to distribute email from one mail server to another over a TCP/IP network.

SNA (Systems Network Architecture)—A communications interface used to establish a link with IBM mainframes and AS/400 hosts.

SNMP (Simple Network Management Protocol)—A protocol used to monitor remote hosts over TCP/IP network.

sockets—A Microsoft API used to establish an interface between programs and the transport protocol in use over a network link.

spooler—A software component of the print system that stores print jobs on a hard drive while they wait in the print queue.

SQL Server—A Microsoft product that supports a network-enabled relational database system.

stripe set—A hard disk construct where segments of data are written in sequence across multiple drives.

subnet—A portion or segment of a TCP/IP network.

swap file—Another name for the pagefile used by the Virtual Memory Manager to temporarily store pages of memory on a hard drive.

synchronization—The replication of the domain database between the PDC and one or more BDCs.

System log—The log viewed through Event Viewer where general system information and errors are recorded.

system policy—A setting configuration created through the System Policy Editor that restricts the work environment of users based on a computer, group, or user.

System Policy Editor—The administrative tool used to create and modify system policies for computers, groups, and users.

Take Ownership—The act of taking Full Control authority over an object.

tape drives—Devices used for backing up data that employs metal film cassettes for storage.

TAPI (Telephony Application Programming Interface)—An interface and API that defines how applications can interact with data/fax/voice devices and calls.

Task Manager—A utility where applications and processes can be viewed, stopped, and started. Task Manager also offers CPU and memory status information.

TCP/IP (Transmission Control Protocol/Internet Protocol)—The most widely used protocol in networking today because it is the most flexible of the transport protocols and is able to span wide areas.

Telnet—A terminal emulation utility used to interact with remote computers.

Token Ring—A network topology where computers are arranged in a ring and a token is used to pass the privilege of communicating over the network.

trusts—A link between two domains that enables pass-through authentication so users from one domain can access the resources of another. A trust is only a one-way relationship.

two-way trust—The establishment of two one-way trusts.

UDP (User Datagram Protocol)—A TCP/IP component that transmits data through a connectionless service but does not guarantee the delivery or sequencing of sent packets.

UNC (Universal Naming Convention)—A standardized naming method for networks taking the form of "\\servername\sharename."

Unix—An interactive time-sharing operating system developed in 1969 by a hacker to play games. This system developed into the most widely used industrial-strength computer in the world and ultimately supported the birth of the Internet.

UPS (uninterruptible power supply)—A semi-intelligent, rechargeable battery system that protects a computer from power failures and fluctuations.

user account—The collection of information stored by Windows NT about a specific network user, such as name, password, group memberships, access privileges, and user rights. User accounts are managed through the User Manager For Domains utility.

User Manager For Domains—The Windows NT Server administration utility controlling account management, group membership, and security policies for a domain.

user name—The human-friendly name of a user account. The user name is one of two items of data used to log on to Windows NT. Windows NT does not recognize an account by the user name, but rather by the SID.

user profiles—The collection of desktop and environmental settings that define the work area of a local computer.

user rights—Settings that define the ability of a user to access a computer or a domain.

users group—This is another term for "group."

VGA (Video Graphics Array)—A PC display standard of 640×480 pixels, 16 colors, and a 4:3 aspect ratio.

VMM (Virtual Memory Manager)—The executive service within Windows NT's kernel that manages physical and virtual (swap or pagefile) memory.

volume set—A disk construct comprised of one or more logical partitions formatted with a single file system.

WAN (wide area network)—A network that spans geographically distant segments. Often the distance of two miles or more is used to define a WAN; however, Microsoft equates any RAS connection as establishing a WAN.

Windows NT Workstation—A Microsoft OS product that is a client version of the Windows NT system. It is the same as Windows NT Server but without the ability to host multiple services and resources for a network.

WINS (Windows Internet Name Service)—A Windows network service used to resolve NetBIOS names to IP addresses.

workgroups—A collection of networked computers that participate in a peer-to-peer relationship.

World Wide Web—An information-distribution system hosted on TCP/IP networks. The Web supports text, graphics, and multimedia. The IIS component of Windows NT is a Web server (which can distribute Web documents).

Write permissions—This setting grants the ability to create or modify files and directories.

XCOPY—A command-line utility used to copy files and subdirectories while maintaining the directory tree structure.

Index

Bold page numbers indicate sample exam questions.

B

C

D

O

P

Q

R

S